INVESTIGATING FAMILIES

Investigating Families

MOTHERHOOD IN THE SHADOW OF CHILD PROTECTIVE SERVICES

KELLEY FONG

PRINCETON UNIVERSITY PRESS

PRINCETON & OXFORD

Published by Princeton University Press
41 William Street, Princeton, New Jersey 08540
99 Banbury Road, Oxford OX2 6JX

press.princeton.edu

All Rights Reserved

Library of Congress Cataloging-in-Publication Data

Names: Fong, Kelley, 1987– author.
Title: Investigating families : motherhood in the shadow of child protective services / Kelley Fong.
Description: Princeton : Princeton University Press, [2023] | Includes bibliographical references and index.
Identifiers: LCCN 2022060357 (print) | LCCN 2022060358 (ebook) | ISBN 9780691235714 (hardback ; alk. paper) | ISBN 9780691235738 (ebook)
Subjects: LCSH: Child welfare—United States. | Child abuse—United States—Prevention. | Children—Services for—United States. | BISAC: SOCIAL SCIENCE / Social Work | POLITICAL SCIENCE / Public Policy / Social Services & Welfare
Classification: LCC HV741 .F636 2023 (print) | LCC HV741 (ebook) | DDC 362.70973—dc23/eng/20230227
LC record available at https://lccn.loc.gov/2022060357
LC ebook record available at https://lccn.loc.gov/2022060358

British Library Cataloging-in-Publication Data is available

Editorial: Meagan Levinson & Erik Beranek
Production Editorial: Ali Parrington
Jacket Design: Karl Spurzem
Production: Erin Suydam
Publicity: Kate Hensley & Kathryn Stevens
Copyeditor: Elisabeth A. Graves

Jacket image: © Phoebe Shuman-Goodier

This book has been composed in Arno

Printed on acid-free paper. ∞

Printed in the United States of America

10 9 8 7 6 5 4 3 2 1

CONTENTS

Introduction   1

1 The Specter of the State   23

2 Making the Call   47

3 Fear and Surveillance in the Investigation   77

4 From Needs to Risks   107

5 Here to Help?   132

6 Devastation and Demobilization Beyond the Investigation   162

   Conclusion   194

                    Methodological Appendix 213
                      Acknowledgments 241
                          Notes 245
                       References 263
                         Index 277

INVESTIGATING FAMILIES

Introduction

IT BEGAN WITH A phone call.

After Jazmine Acosta's housing case manager placed the call, there was no turning back. A few hours later, a state investigator showed up at Jazmine's apartment, knocking on her door to question her and see her two-year-old son, Gabriel.

Jazmine, a Black and Puerto Rican woman with curly hair dyed blonde, had grown up going back and forth between relatives due to her mother's addiction. Now twenty-three, she and Gabriel lived in New Haven, Connecticut, in an apartment subsidized by the nonprofit organization whose case manager made the call. (All the names of research participants in this book are pseudonyms.) When the investigator came, money was tight. After Jazmine totaled her car the month before, her boss had taken her off the schedule and given her work hours to someone else with a car. She was scrambling to find an affordable apartment before her housing subsidy ended in a couple months. But she'd been getting by and feeling hopeful. She reflected that, as Gabriel's mother, "I have a motivation and I have somebody who loves me. I have somebody who depends on me."

The investigator's visit threatened to upend that. This stranger had the power to whisk Gabriel away in an instant, separating the toddler from his home and family. Jazmine wouldn't have to agree to this; the investigator and his colleagues at Child Protective Services (CPS) could decide unilaterally and get a court to sign off later. So when the investigator arrived, telling her he'd received a report alleging that Jazmine hit Gabriel while they met with her housing case manager, Jazmine was terrified. She thought about not letting the investigator in but figured that would only give him more reason to take her son. She decided she would do whatever he asked. "Everything now is on the line," she later said. During the visit, she recalled, "all I was thinking about was: Just answer this man's questions. If I tell this man everything now, he can see that I'm being honest and that I just want him to get the hell out."

In this spirit of openness, when the investigator sat on Jazmine's couch to inquire about the stressors in her life and any substances she used, she shared that marijuana helped her cope with stress, anxiety, and depression—"so I don't go to my dark place," she said. The investigator listened, then gently asked, "What can we do to help you?" He started explaining his interest in identifying a therapeutic program that would work for her, when Jazmine interjected.

"*This*"—she drew circles in the air with her pointer finger—"is not gonna make it any better. Imma let you know right now. It's not." She began to cry.

The investigator explained to Jazmine that he wanted to help her manage her stress so things didn't escalate to endanger Gabriel. She told me afterward that she appreciated his calm demeanor and respectful attitude. As the investigator wrapped up his questions that evening, he assured her he wouldn't be taking Gabriel with him. No one thought the toddler was in imminent danger—not Jazmine, or her new investigator, or the housing case manager who placed the call.

And yet, the investigator's visit amplified Jazmine's sense of anxiety and vulnerability. "Nobody likes CPS," she told me two days after that first meeting. "When somebody says that word, nobody says, 'Oh, yay, CPS.' No. Your stomach is dropping."[1] She compared the investigation to walking on a tightrope—a high-wire act with ruinous consequences for the tiniest misstep.

This tightrope walk happens every day, all over the country. Each year, state CPS agencies investigate the families of more than three million U.S. children following reports of suspected child abuse and neglect, defined broadly as things caregivers do (or don't do) that place children at risk of harm. One out of every three children in the United States—and fully *half* of all Black children—can expect to have a CPS investigator come knocking at some point during childhood.[2] Remarkably, U.S. families' engagement with the child welfare system is comparable in scale and concentration to the high levels of criminal legal system intervention in poor communities of color. As such, CPS is essential to our understanding of contemporary families, parenthood, poverty, and racial inequality. In this single agency, we see some of our country's deepest tensions: our inclination to treat structural problems as individual deficiencies, our ongoing racism and racial stratification despite purportedly "color-blind" policies, our failure to support mothers even as we valorize motherhood.

"Child abuse" evokes horrific images of children tortured and starved. We see these headlines, we hear about children who die from abuse or neglect—nearly two thousand each year, according to federal data—and it's human nature to want to do everything we can to rescue children from that fate.[3] So we've empowered people like Jazmine's housing case manager and investigator to act upon any suspicions of abuse. But as the investigator told Jazmine at his next visit, "I just see a mom who has a pretty significant trauma history, single parent, going through a lot, and could probably use some support." To me, he summed up her situation by saying, "There's a lot on her plate." Likewise, a training session for new CPS investigators in Connecticut began with the instructor reframing CPS work for the group: "Some of you came to CPS, filled the application out, interviewed, and said, 'I'm gonna stop all these people who are abusing kids.'" But, the instructor emphasized, that wasn't what the agency primarily dealt with: "We work in large part with parents who are challenged with caring for their children for one reason or another." Often, that reason is poverty and its associated stressors and hardships. As another mother reflected, after the agency visited, "I wasn't a *bad* mom, but I was a *stressed* mom."

These reflections are the starting point for this book. What does it mean that so many parents with a lot on their plate, stressed parents, parents facing challenges in caring for their children, find child abuse investigators at their doors? To find out, I spent years interviewing and spending time with more than one hundred mothers in Connecticut and Rhode Island and months shadowing some of the CPS investigators who knocked on their doors. I had the unique opportunity to accompany investigators as they visited families and then meet separately with the mothers under investigation as well as many of the frontline professionals who triggered CPS's investigation. To look beyond the investigative moment, I spoke with low-income mothers not presently under investigation, sometimes before CPS ever got involved, other times years afterward.

We know that mothers like Jazmine, raising children with limited socioeconomic resources, contend with precarious economic arrangements such as work, welfare, and housing.[4] In this research, I saw how they also confront another form of precarity, one borne of the very social policy called to respond to the challenges they face. As I learned, CPS is a first-line response to family adversity that renders motherhood itself precarious for already marginalized mothers. By precarity, I mean the recognition that you can readily lose something you have, that someone else can take something you cherish. The word originates from the Latin *precārius*, "held through the favor of another."[5] As Jazmine concluded, "Now it's up to them to see if my child is worthy or not to stay with me. . . . Now I have a complete stranger in my life, and they have to evaluate to see if I'm a fit parent." Even well before the investigator came by, she knew that her mothering could be called into question at any time. "When I was pregnant," she told me, "everybody would say, 'Oh, be careful what you do—somebody'll call CPS on you.'" Growing up in "the hood," she recalled, it seemed people had CPS "on speed dial." For mothers like Jazmine on the margins of society, motherhood is subject to the state's review, to be potentially (even if not actually) revoked. Moreover, it's an entity within the state's social welfare arm—supposedly the bulwark against insecurity—that generates this precarity.

This book examines the ramifications of responding to family adversity writ large through CPS. As in Jazmine's case, most investigations conclude with no findings of abuse or neglect, even by CPS's own standards.[6] As we will see, turning so readily to an agency fundamentally oriented around parental (especially maternal) wrongdoing organizes assistance around surveilling, assessing, and correcting mothers, which affects how mothers experience this "help." Although mothers may ultimately appreciate their investigators, as Jazmine did, investigations undermine their sense of security and shape how they marshal resources for their families. With CPS saturating poor neighborhoods, experiences of precarious motherhood extend even to mothers who haven't (yet) been drawn in. Through seemingly routine, low-level encounters, through often well-meaning people trying to help, governments perpetuate marginality and reinforce existing inequalities.

Who and What Draws Child Protective Services Attention

Ensuring children's basic needs are met should be a priority for every society. Jazmine recalled growing up with a mother in the throes of addiction. "My mom was always not a mom," she said. "She would leave us for a day, then it would be a week, and then, at one point, she just didn't come back." After the police arrived one day to find sixth-grader Jazmine and her brother home alone, unsure if or when their mother would return, Jazmine's grandmother took her in. This kind of childhood adversity can have long-lasting, negative effects on health and well-being.[7] Adults enmeshed in carceral and child welfare systems have often endured lifetimes of trauma and violence, beginning in childhood family environments.[8] When children are in unsafe situations, few would disagree that societies should intervene to make sure they are not subjected to ongoing harm.

The idea of vulnerable children in danger creates a noteworthy exception to cherished ideals of family privacy and autonomy—a "private realm of family life which the state cannot enter," in the words of the U.S. Supreme Court.[9] Under the *parens patriae* doctrine (literally, "parent of the country"), we authorize the state to intervene in private life to protect children and others unable to protect themselves. And intervene it does: On any given day, foster care rates for U.S. children, at 563 per 100,000, exceed imprisonment rates for U.S. adults, at 539 per 100,000.[10]

These aggregate statistics mask vast disparities in exposure to CPS. In affluent White communities, CPS is virtually absent, perhaps entering parents' awareness only when they see news reports about tragic things happening to other children. For others, the system is a common part of childhood and parenting. In Connecticut neighborhoods where over 20 percent of families live below the poverty line, one in three children will encounter CPS by their fifth birthday.[11] A recent California study found that children with births covered by public insurance—a proxy for low income—came to CPS's attention during childhood at over twice the rate of those privately insured at birth (38 percent compared with 18 percent).[12] The most recent data reveal that *one in eleven* Black children and *one in nine* Native American children will enter foster care during childhood.[13] As legal scholar Dorothy Roberts has compellingly articulated, this is a stark manifestation of historical and ongoing racial oppression, as well as a means through which this oppression persists.[14]

Amid this concentrated intervention in Black communities, Native American communities, and poor communities (including poor White communities), CPS investigates mothers in particular. Mothers are the primary caregivers for 80 percent of children subject to investigations, and among children deemed abused or neglected, CPS holds mothers responsible in 69 percent of cases.[15] State intervention with Black women through the child welfare system thus runs parallel to state intervention with Black men through the criminal legal system.

It might seem natural to attribute this unequal intervention simply to higher rates of child abuse or neglect among particular groups.[16] Research consistently finds poverty strongly associated with child maltreatment (measured in a variety of ways), as poverty often creates hardships and stress that make caregiving challenging.[17] Systemic racism differentially distributes the resources parents need along racial lines, and child-rearing responsibilities tend to fall on mothers. For mothers like Jazmine, meeting their children's needs is no simple matter in the face of material hardship, racism, exclusion, and adversity.

One view, then, sees CPS directly responding to the social problem of child maltreatment, an umbrella term encompassing physical and sexual abuse as well as neglect of a child's physical, medical, educational, or emotional needs. Yet child abuse and neglect are not objective, self-evident phenomena. Like crime, child maltreatment is socially constructed, which means that there is no discrete thing constituting "child maltreatment." Instead, societies decide what behaviors to classify as maltreatment, making moral judgments about what (and whom) they deem appropriate or inappropriate, right or wrong.

Categorizing brutal beatings and sexual abuse as child maltreatment seems relatively clear-cut. But beyond these extreme cases, it's less straightforward. The state declines to intervene in many things parents do every day that could conceivably endanger children. For instance, parents who allow their children to ride bicycles without helmets are arguably placing children at risk of harm, yet suggesting that CPS pursue such parents would surely provoke accusations of a nanny state. And although we can agree that parents shouldn't intentionally starve their children, who gets to decide whether parents' actions are intentional, and on what basis? Moreover, the same behavior may be perceived differently depending on context: Can you make the case that letting elementary-age children play outside unsupervised threatens their safety? How about if they live on a busy street or in a neighborhood with high levels of violence? Or if they have special needs?

As we see, drawing the child maltreatment line is far from a neutral, value-free determination. All kinds of behaviors can be cast—or not—as abuse or neglect, and what's considered standard or appropriate parenting has varied considerably over time and across societies. With the flexibility of the child maltreatment category, CPS intervention is a political tool that can expand (or contract) to bring more (or fewer, or different) families under its purview.

In my research, it soon became apparent that "suspected abuse or neglect" means all kinds of things in practice. Jazmine smacked her son a few times to discipline him. Sabrina's family was staying in a rodent-infested attic. Gina, recently widowed, turned to alcohol in her grief. Imelda's toddler daughter got out of the apartment and onto the street. Nikki's partner was hitting her. As we will see, much of what's shuttled to CPS today reflects family adversity in some form, from substance use to domestic violence to unmet mental health needs. The vast majority of CPS reports allege neglect rather than abuse, alleging parents' failure to provide adequate supervision, medical care, shelter, food, or clothing—"failures" often rooted in poverty and structural racism.[18] Thus, CPS is not just in the business of responding to child maltreatment, however defined. It's in the business of managing problems of poverty and marginality.[19]

The Turn to Child Protective Services

Our response to families like Jazmine's reflects specific historical and political understandings about what to do with caregivers—typically mothers—who may be struggling to meet children's needs. One possible response entails shoring up motherhood. Another involves destabilizing or challenging it. In turning to CPS to manage marginality, we've chosen destabilization.[20] After all, it was fairly easy to send an investigator out to Jazmine's apartment: Her housing case manager just picked up the phone. Meanwhile, it felt nearly impossible to get her what she needed to support herself and Gabriel. She and her housing case manager scoured job opportunities together, but the jobs she got had variable hours and didn't pay enough to live on. They looked for apartments but couldn't find anything within her budget. They strategized to juggle bills, with Jazmine paying what she could to the electric company to prevent a shutoff. When I first met Jazmine, after she'd lost all her hours at work, her monthly welfare check totaled just $487, a fraction of what it cost to raise a child in New Haven. With our limited public investments in children and families, U.S. children have for decades faced higher poverty rates than their peers in other, comparable nations.[21]

This arrangement wasn't inevitable.[22] In the Progressive era, reformers pressed for governmental cash assistance to support single mothers (envisioned as White widows) raising children at home, declaring that "the home should not be broken up for reasons of poverty."[23] With advocates, predominantly middle-class White women, interested in boosting families' economic security to support children at home, the 1935 Social Security Act funded welfare assistance rather than foster care. Notably, however, this welfare aid disproportionately excluded Black families and other families of color.[24] In the late 1960s, in response to this exclusion and dovetailing with the federal War on Poverty, Black women, alongside Puerto Rican and Native American organizers, led a national movement advocating for welfare rights for poor women of color. But the backlash came swiftly: As welfare began serving more Black families, the imagined welfare recipient shifted from a White widow to an unmarried Black mother. Racist and sexist stereotypes about Black "welfare queens" cheating the system made providing financial assistance to poor mothers politically unpopular.

Meanwhile, the issue of child abuse had burst onto the national scene. In 1962, pediatric radiologist Henry Kempe identified what he called "battered child syndrome," based on his observations of children with severe and nonaccidental physical injuries. The issue quickly took hold, drawing substantial media and political attention.[25] Within five years, all fifty states placed new laws on the books requiring certain professionals to report suspected child maltreatment to state authorities, and states formalized processes for responding to these reports.

By the early 1970s, then, Nixon-era backlash to antipoverty programs stood alongside popular support for a conception of child abuse as a pathological "syndrome" and an emerging governmental infrastructure to respond to child maltreatment reports. This was the situation facing Senator Walter Mondale as he sought to improve conditions for children. Advocates like Mondale, spearheading the Child Abuse Prevention and Treatment Act (CAPTA), explicitly separated child protection efforts from antipoverty work, viewing this approach as more politically palatable.[26] For instance, Mondale had recently sponsored legislation to provide universal subsidized childcare, only for President Nixon to veto it.

Passed in 1974, CAPTA allocated new federal funds for child protection, contingent on states operating CPS agencies to receive and respond to child abuse reports. Reports rose precipitously, from approximately 10,000 in 1967 to 800,000 annually within a decade and 2.1 million another decade later.[27] These reports extended well beyond the serious physical injuries documented by Kempe. Nevertheless, the framing of child abuse as a syndrome stuck, such that CAPTA organized the governmental response around parents' individual deficiencies. Increasingly, CPS intervened with Black families, in line with state authorities' long-standing tendency to blame social problems on the pathology and dysfunction of Black families, especially Black mothers.[28] Progressive-era advocates thinking of poor White families' needs had devised direct aid; when it came to poor Black families, social policy turned to accusations of abuse and neglect that could prompt family separation. In the 1970s, 1980s, and 1990s, foster care caseloads swelled, accelerated by the moral panic around "crack babies" that demonized poor, Black mothers.

In 1996, after promising to "end welfare as we know it," President Bill Clinton eliminated poor families' entitlement to cash assistance. In the decades since, the proportion of poor families receiving welfare has plummeted, the real value of benefits has declined, and recipients are subject to substantial monitoring under threat of sanctions.[29] This withdrawal of welfare support leaves us with the child welfare system as our means of responding to children in need. Initially, Title IV of the 1935 Social Security Act focused solely on enabling states "to furnish financial assistance . . . to needy dependent children" living at home.[30] Title IV has since become the primary federal funding source for foster care, and states allocate $2.6 billion in welfare funding to their child welfare systems each year.[31] Child welfare system expenditures total $33 billion annually, far exceeding spending on government assistance such as welfare benefits, at $6.7 billion, and the Housing Choice Voucher program, at $22 billion.[32] And the Children's Bureau, a federal agency with a lofty mission of "improv[ing] the overall health and well-being of our nation's children and families," took on issues such as infant mortality and child labor at its founding in 1912.[33] Today, its jurisdiction is limited to CPS. Though obstacles to child well-being could conjure a number of possible responses, the present policy and practice approach addresses such threats through CPS.

The Trajectory of a Child Protective Services Case

As a primary path we've forged to respond to children and families in need, CPS has become a central part of our social welfare state. Each state operates its own child welfare system, with a few states operating county-administered systems; federal legislation provides guidance and some funding. The contours of the child welfare system—which encompasses state CPS agencies as well as courts overseeing child protection cases and private organizations providing foster care and other services—are broadly consistent nationwide, though state policies vary somewhat: A state (or county) agency receives and investigates reports of suspected child maltreatment and then continues oversight in selected cases, sometimes removing children from home to place them in foster care. (See Figure 1.) I refer to these agencies as "CPS," though their specific names vary by locale; Connecticut has the Department of Children and Families, for instance, and New York City, the Administration for Children's Services.

Families come to CPS's attention through a diffuse array of third parties. Jazmine's case began not with an investigator stopping her on the street or identifying her from video surveillance but with her housing case manager calling the state's CPS hotline to file a report. Every state requires certain professionals,

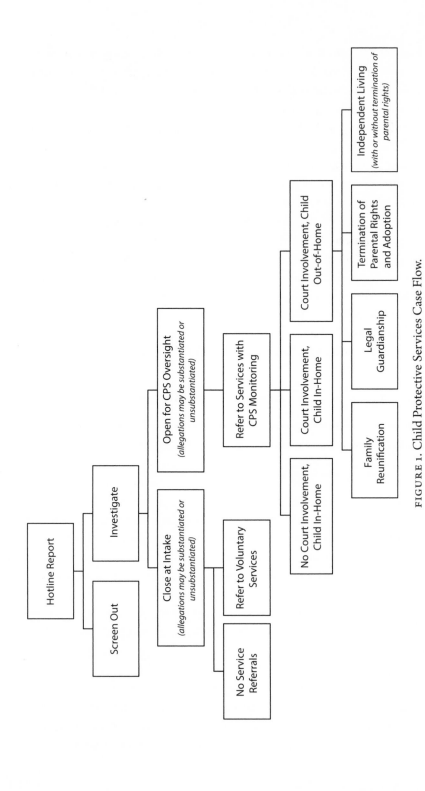

FIGURE 1. Child Protective Services Case Flow.

such as doctors, police officers, teachers, mental health clinicians, and childcare providers, to report suspected maltreatment. Most reports, approximately two-thirds, originate from these professionals mandated to report.[34] But anyone can file a report—friends, neighbors, relatives, and strangers—meaning that everyone a parent meets could, potentially, turn them in to CPS.

CPS screens incoming calls to decide whether to respond. So in Jazmine's case, hotline staff at the agency's central office in Hartford listened to her case manager recount the incident. Upon determining that the allegations fell within Connecticut's definitions of maltreatment, specified in civil statute, staff sent the case to the New Haven office to investigate. (Some CPS agencies, including Connecticut's, assign reports to different types of responses, but as I will discuss, this may be a distinction without much of a difference for families.) If hotline staff instead "screened out" the case, Jazmine wouldn't hear from CPS.

Jazmine's case, like other incoming reports, was assigned to a CPS staff member to investigate.[35] This investigator would visit Jazmine and her son at home multiple times during the investigation, interviewing household members and others involved with the family. Had Jazmine's case involved allegations of severe maltreatment constituting violations of criminal law, CPS might work alongside police investigators. In any event, the investigator could refer Jazmine to social services based on what he learned; he might also offer advice on things like alternative discipline techniques. Throughout the investigation—in Connecticut, approximately six weeks—the investigator would document his notes in the case record and discuss the case with his supervisor. If at any time they felt that Gabriel was unsafe at home, they could take custody of him on an emergency basis, until the local family court decided whether to return Gabriel home or keep him in foster care.

At the conclusion of the investigation, Jazmine's investigator and his supervisor would determine whether they had found sufficient evidence to substantiate (i.e., confirm) the allegations of abuse or neglect.[36] They would also decide whether to close Jazmine's case or keep it open for ongoing oversight. If the case closed, CPS would stop visiting unless another report came in; CPS could still make service referrals but would not monitor the family's participation.

In cases kept open after investigation, CPS may take custody of children or children may remain home. Either way, CPS devises a "service plan," directing family members to participate in services such as drug treatment and family therapy, usually through private providers that contract with the state to provide these services. The service plan is not restricted to services pertinent to the initial maltreatment allegations, and CPS can modify it at any time. A CPS caseworker visits regularly, usually at least monthly, to oversee parents' compliance with this plan.[37] Participation in services is voluntary only in the most technical sense. As CPS wants parents to address the agency's concerns, the agency escalates (or winds down) its involvement based on parents' compliance. In other words, to get children home or to keep children at home, parents must do what CPS says.

To get a court order requiring that parents participate in services or to take custody of children, CPS files a petition in family court. There, a judge determines whether the agency has shown sufficient evidence of child maltreatment, as defined by state statute. Judges can order children's removal from home (or continued placement out-of-home) as well as children's return home. In these civil child protection cases, judges have wide latitude—much more so than in criminal court—to impose all manner of additional conditions as they review case progress, from ordering parents to participate in a particular service to requiring that CPS visit the family more frequently.[38]

For children removed from home, CPS arranges for their placement with relative caregivers, with foster families, or in group care. These cases can stretch out for years, until courts ultimately order reunification with parents, adoption, or another permanent living arrangement. In some instances, courts—petitioned by CPS—permanently and involuntarily terminate parental rights, among the most substantial ways the government reshapes families.

Precarious Motherhood

Jazmine's home health aide job was supposed to be full-time, but in the month before CPS came by, she worked only intermittently as her client went in and out of the hospital. After losing that job, she cobbled together short-term hourly jobs in the months that followed. With the rise of these unstable, temporary labor arrangements offering few protections for workers, Pierre Bourdieu declared in 1998 that "precarity is everywhere today" (*précarité est aujourd'hui partout*).[39]

With respect to employment, scholars argue, not only has widespread precarity transformed the nature of work, but it has also engendered an affective experience of insecurity that shapes personal, familial, and social life more broadly.[40] This insecurity extends beyond those put out of a job. As

Bourdieu contends, "Through the fear it arouses," precarity conveys to all workers that "their work, their jobs, are in some way a privilege, a fragile, threatened privilege. . . . Objective insecurity gives rise to a generalized subjective insecurity."[41]

For Jazmine and others like her, precarity characterizes *motherhood* as well. Just as precarious workers cannot feel completely secure in employment, precarious mothers cannot feel completely secure as parents. State agents can take their children, and there isn't much they can do to stop it.[42]

Recognizing this precarity shifts our attention from family separation to the looming *threat* of separation. When people think of the child welfare system, it's typically the system's most extreme intervention that comes to mind: taking children. The titles of Dorothy Roberts's landmark books on the system— *Shattered Bonds, Torn Apart*—evince this emphasis. Ethnographic research by Jennifer Reich and Tina Lee has powerfully illuminated the perspectives of parents working to reunify with their children.[43] As in the realm of work, though, loss is only part of the story. Just under 6 percent of children subject to CPS investigations enter foster care in the period following the investigation.[44] Six percent isn't trivial; it represents hundreds of thousands of children. But foster care isn't the typical experience.

Instead, lower-level investigative contacts are increasingly the face of CPS. At the turn of the twenty-first century, approximately 300,000 children entered foster care annually. Two decades later, that number dropped to 250,000, a decline of 18 percent.[45] In some cities, such as New York, foster care populations shrank even more dramatically: The number of New York City children in foster care fell from 40,000 in the mid-1990s to 8,000 in 2019.[46] Yet foster care declines have not been met with a concomitant decline in investigations. In New York City, the number of investigations fluctuated between 50,000 and 60,000 during the same period. Nationwide, as Figure 2 shows, investigation rates have actually increased in recent decades.[47] In 1996, 3.6 percent of children experienced a CPS investigation. By 2019, this stood at 4.7 percent.[48]

All these investigations don't mean that millions of parents are abusing their children. Recall that child maltreatment is a subjective designation, one easily applied to manifestations of poverty, adversity, and racism. Even in CPS's own estimation, a substantial majority of investigations conclude with no findings of maltreatment: Over 80 percent of children subject to investigations are not deemed victims of abuse or neglect following CPS's investigation.[49] These cases aren't necessarily false reports; CPS might have insufficient evidence to

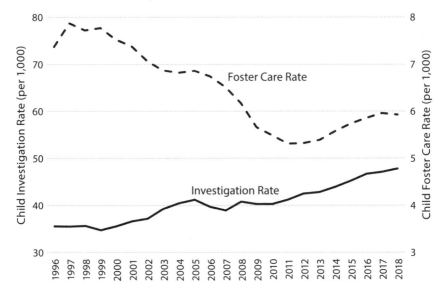

FIGURE 2. Rates of U.S. Children Subject to Child Protective Services Investigations and Foster Care, 1996–2018. Sources: Investigation rates come from the Administration for Children and Families' *Child Maltreatment* reports (e.g., HHS 2006b). Foster care rates come from Roehrkasse 2021.

confirm allegations or might determine that a situation does not rise to the level of maltreatment as defined in state statute. Nevertheless, the state is investigating a large and growing share of parents who—according to the investigating agency itself—do not pose a clear and present danger to their children.[50]

Yet even low-level contacts can have far-reaching effects. We see this in research on the consequences of policing: People who have been arrested—even if never convicted or incarcerated—are less likely to participate in political, labor market, educational, financial, and medical institutions; even those just stopped by police for questioning report lower levels of trust in the government.[51] In marginalized communities, especially Black communities, ubiquitous policing has reconfigured social relationships and heightened residents' experiences of exclusion and injustice.[52] Just as our understanding of the penal state would be incomplete if we overlooked policing and arrests to focus exclusively on incarceration, earlier-stage contacts are essential to our understanding of CPS. Examining what's happening in these initial encounters brings into focus the broader threats that investigative contacts represent.[53] Mothers may have what they cherish—the ability to raise their children—but this hold is tenuous and provisional.

The precarity that permeates motherhood on the margins isn't inevitable—it's actively cultivated and negotiated. As scholars have done with precarious work, we can trace the public policy logics and routine practices undergirding widespread insecurity. We can also examine people's reactions to this arrangement to understand how precarity shapes subjective experiences and social life.

A Threatening Institution

It might seem counterintuitive that an agency touting *protection* and *services* could generate widespread precarity. But this is neither accidental nor incidental; threatening parenthood, especially motherhood, is fundamental to CPS. The agency may aim to assist children and families, but it does so with the authority to separate families and with a focus on parental faults.

Those without much exposure to CPS may not think of it as a threatening institution. After all, the agency sends out social workers, not law enforcement officers. Jazmine's investigator didn't arrive with handcuffs or a gun but, rather, a neon accordion folder stuffed with brochures about safe sleep and child development. He wore not a uniform but a polo shirt with khakis and a lanyard around his neck. He wasn't looking to lock anyone up but, instead, to connect Jazmine to social services. From frontline staff up to leaders at the highest level, CPS envisions itself as supporting child and family well-being. "Strengthening families and preventing child abuse and neglect" stands atop the mission statement of the Children's Bureau, the federal entity overseeing state and county CPS agencies.[54] Connecticut's Department of Children and Families, likewise, identifies its mission as "partnering with communities and empowering families to raise resilient children who thrive."[55] To CPS, investigations are opportunities to provide guidance, information, and social service referrals so that family challenges do not escalate. With these aspirations, CPS weaves itself into the U.S. social safety net.

Indeed, the investigator saw himself as assisting, rather than punishing, Jazmine. In line with his training, he hoped to identify and build on her family's strengths. He wanted to do what he could to help her manage her stress and improve conditions for little Gabriel. Even before Jazmine met him, though, she knew she didn't want him in her life. As she understood, CPS social workers are not just friendly visitors, serving at the pleasure of parents.

Families rarely initiate CPS contact voluntarily, and CPS's involvement ends when the agency says it does. The agency can forcibly remove children at any time and petition the court to keep them and place them wherever it likes. Thus, no matter how helpful individual CPS staff may want to be, their assistance occurs under the perpetual threat of family separation.

Alongside its power to split families up, CPS is organized around remedying wrongdoing—specifically, the wrongdoing of individual parents. It is not simply a social service agency; its intervention requires an allegation of abuse or neglect. And legal definitions of child maltreatment, which are limited to the harm inflicted by *caregivers'* actions or inactions, overlook the corporations, the elected officials, and the broader social, political, and economic structures endangering children.[56] CPS has no answer to societal neglect, as when children go hungry because wages and food assistance benefits are insufficient to cover family meals. But CPS *can* tell parents what to do differently and send them to therapeutic programs focused on things like parenting and substance use. Fixing what's wrong with parents falls squarely within CPS's domain; meanwhile, the agency can do little to fix what's wrong with the conditions under which parents are raising children.[57]

These two aspects of the agency—its ability to forcibly separate families and its focus on parental faults—are immutable and inescapable. This doesn't mean that CPS never helps families or that its assistance is always disingenuous. But any help provided by CPS specifically hinges on precarity, on jeopardizing the parenting of (predominantly) marginalized mothers. As such, scholars and advocates are increasingly conceptualizing CPS as an institution of social control pursuing "family policing," rather than "child welfare."[58]

In providing "help" through scrutiny, blame, and coercive threats, CPS epitomizes our response to poverty and adversity more broadly.[59] In recent decades, the U.S. approach to managing poverty has become particularly disciplinary and paternalistic.[60] Accessing support, such as welfare assistance, requires subjecting oneself to surveillance, monitoring, and the risk of punishment. Such practices follow from a long history of government agents evaluating mothers seeking public aid.[61] What distinguishes CPS, then, is not that it scrutinizes marginalized mothers but that it puts their motherhood itself on the line in doing so. Here, mothers must meet government agents' standards not as a condition of receiving aid but as a condition of raising their children. CPS reveals a profoundly intimate side of our response to children and families in need.[62] Threatening parenting—and mothering in particular— has become central to governmental efforts to assuage family adversity.

At first glance, such threats might seem empty and thereby inconsequential. Most CPS encounters, all told, turn out to be relatively mundane. The agency's wide reach places many families under investigation whose children will *not* be removed, whose cases will promptly close. These cases make up the bulk of CPS investigators' work; in most child welfare scholarship, they are little more than data points added to a mounting total. For mothers, though, the experience can't be pushed aside so easily, precisely because CPS represents the agency poised to brand them bad mothers, to take what they treasure most. Her investigator may have wanted to help, but Jazmine was clear: The investigation wasn't making things better. This book analyzes the implications of passing so many families like Jazmine's through an agency that polices parenting and threatens family separation.

Studying Child Protective Services

To learn how CPS intervention unfolds and how mothers experience it, I conducted multimethod, multiperspective qualitative research in Rhode Island and Connecticut. The fieldwork offers complementary data rather than a cross-state comparison: The Connecticut research provides an in-depth account of the investigation, and the Rhode Island study extends the investigative moment to understand mothers' perceptions and experiences more broadly, before and after CPS's investigation. (The appendix provides additional information and reflections on the research.)

I did not previously have any personal experience with CPS, nor had I grown up or raised children in communities where CPS involvement was common. Thus, I first wanted to listen to parents likely to be exposed to CPS so I could learn from their perspectives. In 2015, I began interviewing low-income mothers in Providence, ultimately sitting down with eighty-three mothers. Typically, they invited me into their homes, where I began by asking them to tell me the story of their lives. I followed their lead from there, generally over the course of a couple hours, probing their experiences with systems such as schools, welfare, and health care. At the end, I raised the topic of CPS, though nearly two-thirds brought it up spontaneously. We talked about what they thought of the agency and any experiences they or others they knew had had with CPS. The extent of their involvement with CPS ranged widely, from those with no personal experience to those whose parental rights had been legally terminated.

Over the next several years, I reached out to mothers periodically to follow up. I interviewed most of the Rhode Island mothers at least twice, with some sitting down for four, five, or even more interviews. I spent additional time with some mothers, doing things like running errands together, accompanying them to court hearings and CPS meetings, and tagging along to doctors' visits. I also accessed the CPS records (or lack thereof) of over two-thirds of the Rhode Island mothers, with their permission. This follow-up enabled me to reflect with mothers on what I was learning and keep up with their lives and CPS cases. I met their new babies and visited them at new homes across the state and beyond. Some had kids removed and returned. One was shot and seriously injured outside her home. At least five, I learned, passed away.

The Rhode Island mothers' accounts of CPS investigations—especially their aversion to CPS intervention, even if CPS closed out their case—made me want to learn more about this experience. To connect with mothers during an investigation, I had to go through a CPS agency. As the appendix details, I ultimately went to Connecticut, conducting research in two field offices of the Connecticut Department of Children and Families from February to August 2018, following four months of weekly informal observations.

To understand multiple perspectives on the CPS investigation, I organized the research around focal cases. For each of thirty-seven investigations, I observed a CPS visit with the family—usually the first visit, when the investigator met the family and conducted an initial assessment—and briefly interviewed the investigator, typically on the drive back to the office. To see how mothers learned about the agency, I prioritized cases where mothers had no prior CPS history as parents. I interviewed twenty-seven of the mothers, almost all during the investigative period, and conducted follow-up interviews and/or additional observations with some of them. All but one of the mothers interviewed granted me access to their CPS records. I also interviewed thirty-eight local professionals required to report suspected maltreatment to CPS; most had reported one of the focal cases, and others were recruited separately.

When I wasn't doing the case-specific fieldwork, I spent time with investigators at the two offices: one covering the city of New Haven and the other covering twenty small towns in Connecticut's "Northeast Corner." In both places, CPS occupied two floors of a larger building—a towering box of an office building by the harbor in New Haven and a former nineteenth-century cotton mill in the Northeast Corner. At the public entrances, guarded by security staff with metal detector wands, visitors arrived to rooms set up for parents to spend time with children placed out-of-home. In the staff-only area, each division—investigations, ongoing cases, foster care and adoption, trainees, adolescent cases—had its own section of the office where frontline staff worked in cubicles, with supervisors and managers in offices nearby. Frontline staff spent their office time doing administrative work like typing up notes and making phone calls. Sitting beside them, I did the same, writing field notes and trying to schedule interviews. I shadowed investigators on visits with dozens of other families and chatted informally with them in the car and in the office. I also attended training sessions, staff meetings, and office celebrations. Finally, in both states, I reviewed relevant documents, including policies, practice guides, watchdog reports, and press.

The Connecticut and Rhode Island studies both include Latina, White, and Black mothers in similar proportions. Due to my study eligibility criteria, all Rhode Island mothers had incomes qualifying them for the Supplemental Nutrition Assistance Program (SNAP). Most Connecticut mothers had low incomes as well, consistent with what we know about poverty and CPS involvement. Still, I met mothers in a range of situations. Some were experiencing substantial adversity, cycling through homeless shelters, addiction treatment, mental health services, and jail; others were relatively stable. In Connecticut, a few of the Northeast Corner mothers owned homes.

Although this book does not focus on differences across the research locations, the sites reflect some of the demographic variation in the region. Two research sites, Providence and New Haven, are higher-poverty urban areas with substantial shares of Black and Latinx residents. The Northeast Corner, nicknamed the "Quiet Corner," consists of predominantly White small towns and rural areas with pockets of poverty—many former mill towns that supported Barack Obama and then Donald Trump.

Of course, no two states can stand in for the nation. Both Connecticut and Rhode Island are small, politically liberal states that have expanded Medicaid, offer relatively robust social services, and provide higher welfare benefits than most others. Thus, although the cost of living in these places is also relatively high, the study sites may represent a best-case scenario for low-income families. CPS report rates in Connecticut and Rhode Island are reasonably comparable to national rates, perhaps slightly higher.[63] The two states operate similar reporting and investigative processes, though some specific policies vary. (Most notably, since 2012 Connecticut has sent reports deemed lower-risk to a "family assessment" track intended to focus more on families' service needs; Rhode Island added a similar track in 2018, after most of my interviews there.) Foster care rates are similar to national rates in Connecticut and higher in Rhode Island.[64] In both states, as nationwide, children of color are disproportionately represented in the child welfare system, even as agencies intervene with many White families as well.

Consistent with national patterns, most cases in the Connecticut study closed after investigation, with maltreatment allegations unsubstantiated and children remaining home. And most of the Rhode Island mothers had never lost custody of their children. So although chapter 6 turns to mothers' experiences with child removal, this is not primarily a book about severe maltreatment or foster care. Instead, it is a book focused on the *threat* of foster care and child removal that low-income mothers navigate.

Additionally, though the research included some observations and conversations with other family members, I focus on mothers, typically the primary emphasis of CPS's investigation. This is not a book about children but, rather, about their caregivers, whose experiences with CPS matter for child well-being because nearly all children remain home after CPS investigates and even those removed usually return home. Fathers likely have different experiences, given the gendered nature of CPS intervention,[65] and many children are raised by extended family or community members whose perspectives on CPS might differ. My focus on mothers does not imply that these other actors are unimportant. But I begin with mothers as those whose behavior is most often subject to CPS investigation, whose situations are most often constructed as suspected maltreatment.

Overview of the Book

How do families like Jazmine's come to CPS's attention? What happens during the ensuing investigative encounters? And how does CPS intervention ultimately affect mothers, from those who haven't been investigated at all to those whose children CPS removes? This book takes readers through mothers' experiences with the agency, beginning outside of CPS intervention, through the report and investigation, and finally, deeper into the system. Although the chapters incorporate analysis and examples from both states, chapters 1 and 6 draw primarily on data from Rhode Island, while chapters 2–5 are based largely on the Connecticut research.

Beginning in Rhode Island, chapter 1 demonstrates how the specter, the possibility, of CPS renders mothering in the context of poverty and adversity precarious. Even self-identified "good mothers" worry about CPS, given their attachment to motherhood and what they have heard about the system. As I show, the prospect of CPS intervention shapes mothers' engagement with children, social relations, and social service providers in ways that can undermine the social and institutional connections that are so critical to child and family well-being.

Chapter 2 examines how so many marginalized families get shuttled to CPS. Reports to the agency typically center on family adversity in some form or perhaps a family straying from professionals' expectations. But CPS reports are not automatic or inevitable responses to these conditions. Shifting to Connecticut, the chapter traces the social production of CPS reports, showing how reports emerge because people see CPS as a tool to address social problems. Callers, usually frontline service professionals, rarely think that children are in grave danger but summon CPS hoping that the agency can rehabilitate and regulate families. Individual, organizational, and systemic racism and classism structure the reporting process to bring marginalized families in particular under investigation.

Calls to the CPS hotline launch a bureaucratic process organized around abuse and neglect. Like a machine programmed to respond a certain way, CPS's fundamental role and capacities structure how it proceeds and how mothers react, regardless of whether the agency finds evidence of maltreatment. The following three chapters trace how—even as the agency may aspire to partner with families to promote child well-being—the ensuing response organizes "help" around surveilling, evaluating, and correcting mothers, making motherhood precarious.

Chapter 3 takes us to CPS's arrival at the door—a terrifying moment for mothers, given CPS's power to separate their families. During investigations, CPS leans on its role spanning care and coercion to probe all aspects of mothers' personal lives. Chapter 4 examines how CPS uses the information it gathers to assess mothers. Attuned to how parents' past and present situations may predict future harms to children, CPS casts family needs as risks, shifting the most marginalized families deeper into the system. Social and economic precarity thus begets motherhood precarity.

And yet, CPS hopes to help families in need. Chapter 5 considers the assistance on offer. Many investigated mothers appreciate CPS's efforts to help them, but the agency's focus on parental wrongdoing makes it ill-suited to address families' chronic material needs, and any aid offered comes with the possibility of coercive intervention. Furthermore, even when mothers appreciate their investigators' assistance, investigations threaten mothers' privacy, their autonomy, and their very identity as mothers. As such, mothers come to distrust whoever they believe called CPS in the first place. In these ways, even as CPS may offer the promise of help, it ends up perpetuating marginality.

Mothers drawn more deeply into the child welfare system find the experience especially traumatizing. Here, precarity turns to loss and grief. Chapter 6 returns to Rhode Island to follow mothers as they lose custody of children, work toward reunification, go to court, and try to stave off the termination of their parental rights. Even with zealous advocacy, mothers' experiences with the system usually leave them feeling increasingly cynical and disempowered, reinforcing their marginal social status.

The book concludes by drawing out what these mothers' experiences mean for scholarship and public policy. I imagine few of us would want to leave Jazmine and Gabriel alone to fend for themselves. We want Gabriel to have a safe, healthy childhood. As it stands, we send state investigators into the home in pursuit of this goal, targeting motherhood itself. This means that in addition to navigating economic and social precarity, mothers on the margins of society must also reckon with their precarious motherhood. Ultimately, relying on an entity organized around parents' faults and imbued with coercive authority as our first-line response to family adversity has profound implications for mothers and, by extension, their families. Once we recognize this, we can ask whether protecting Gabriel requires destabilizing Jazmine's motherhood or how we could, instead, better support it. Reflecting on what the women I met shared with me highlights fundamental limitations of CPS as a response to family adversity. The present child welfare system undoubtedly helps some families, but the question is at what cost—and whether we can do better.

1

The Specter of the State

I MET CHRISTINA RAYFORD when she was behind the counter at McDonald's, ringing me up. She had just given birth to her first child, a son, two months prior and readily agreed to share her thoughts about social services. "I actually wanted to talk to someone," she said. "I was just asking my friend about agencies."[1]

On her day off, I went to visit her at a modest, two-story house in a quiet residential area, where she and her baby were staying with her mother. Christina, a young Black woman, had just woken up. She wrapped a short, bright pink hooded robe around her as we lounged on the living room couch. Cradling the baby, she told me about growing up in Providence. "I'm twenty-one, but I think I lived a life that is forty years old," she reflected. Her mother beat her as a child, she said, and she'd never met her father, who was serving a life sentence. Christina described a "rebellious" phase during her teen years, leading to time in a juvenile justice facility.

"Then I decided I needed to change my life around," she recalled. "That's exactly what I did. When I got out, I graduated high school, and then I went on to college. Then I ended up working two jobs just for myself. No help. Just me." She felt her rebellion didn't reflect her true self. "Who I am is, I'm a homebody. I like to stay in the house."

Later, when her stepfather arrived home, we moved up to her bedroom, where she'd set up a crib next to her bed. A mobile with little animals hung above the crib. Baby Anthony, with a full head of curly, dark hair, mostly napped while we talked. When he fussed, Christina gave him a pacifier and went to fix a bottle.

Christina had big plans. Sitting on her bed, she told me about her goal of starting a nonprofit to help "troubled teens" like her past self: a place that would take young people in and truly support them. She brought out note-books from her closet to share some of her brainstorming for her business plan. "That's my goal, to start that," she said. "I think about it every day." This was Christina's north star; she remained resolute in her vision and came back to it each time we met over the next several years.

Determined not to let her past define her, Christina loved inspirational stories, stories about people succeeding. She tried to incorporate advice from people like Suze Orman and Robin Roberts into her life. *The Blind Side*, a movie about a wealthy White woman taking in a homeless Black teenager, was one of Christina's favorites. "I was crying in that movie," she said. She saved a picture of the family from the movie to her phone, "'cause that is what you call a family. That's what I want. That's what you strive for. The mother is who I am. I'm the helper. I like to help. That's exactly what I want. I loved that movie so much."

Most of all, Christina loved being a mother. With Anthony's father in jail and strained relationships with her family, she felt she was raising the baby on her own. Christina relished every moment. For Anthony, she wrote on social media, she would conquer the world. Anthony motivated her to hold fast to her goals, even as money was tight with her limited income from McDonald's. "I want him to know his mom is a very independent, strong woman," she told me.

I asked her about various social services: welfare, food stamps, housing assistance. When I got to CPS, Christina was quick to say she couldn't stand the agency. In her view, CPS was "dangerous . . . just there to take your kid and not really help you." CPS had removed a friend's children, and someone had called to report her cousin. But Christina contended that she wasn't wor-ried about the agency coming into her life. She'd pushed it out of her mind, concluding, "If I don't think about it, it shouldn't come my way."

After two and a half hours, I wrapped up the interview. Thinking of Chris-tina's goal of helping others and seeing how she cared for her son, I mentioned offhand that she would make a great home visitor, meeting with expectant and new mothers to help them get things they needed, answer questions, and offer support.

Christina shook her head, saying she didn't do anything like that. Home visiting programs aim to serve low-income, young, single mothers like Chris-tina. These programs, which research links to improved parenting and child development, are central to contemporary efforts to support low-income children, receiving $400 million in federal funding each year.[2] But Christina, wary, described home visiting services as "CPS bait." She elaborated: "Like, before you gotta get the fish, you gotta put the bait on the thing? That's the bait on the thing. . . . Once they see something wrong with my baby, CPS is like 911. They're definitely gonna call." The hospital kept encouraging her to accept home visiting services. Christina assessed her options.

> I always think of the good and the bad. The good is they do help you. But the bad is, do I really wanna risk if they feel as though I'm not taking care of my baby according to their book? Do I wanna risk all that? 'Cause if you're not doing what their book says, then you're a bad parent.

So she decided to keep her distance. When she got calls asking her to participate, she declined: "No, no thank you, that's okay. I'll just take care of my kid by myself." Christina didn't live in constant fear of CPS; she maintained confidence in her mothering. Still, as she cared for her infant son, she felt she had to exercise vigilance to keep threats to her motherhood at bay.

Research on parents and the child welfare system has focused on parents' direct experiences with CPS, but as we see with Christina, CPS generates a sense of precarious motherhood that affects parenting well before the agency comes knocking.[3] Dorothy Roberts has argued that given the agency's concentrated intervention, CPS impacts entire groups.[4] That is, CPS is experienced by *communities*, not just individual families.

This chapter examines what this community experience of CPS looks and feels like for low-income mothers. Those I interviewed cherished their roles as mothers, affirming their parenting capacities even as they faced trying circumstances. Yet, in saturating mothers' social networks and communities, CPS fosters a diffuse sense of insecurity beyond its direct intervention with families. Even before the agency arrives, mothers recognize their vulnerability to CPS. What they've experienced as children, heard from family and friends, and seen on the news or social media breeds cynicism about the system, teaching mothers that the agency harms families as much as it might help them. So, like Christina, they do their best to ward off CPS, carefully managing interactions with children, social network ties, and service providers even if not (yet) drawn into the system. These rational responses may protect their families from unwanted state intrusion—no home visitor reported Christina to CPS. But nor did baby Anthony benefit from the assistance a home visiting service might have provided. By fostering a sense of constraint and distancing families from potential supports, the specter of CPS perpetuates marginality and social exclusion.

"Three Heads, Three Butts, Six Legs": Mothering in Poverty

Jazmine, whom we met in the introduction, started our interview by saying, "I never really had a family." Even after her uncle adopted her, she felt unwanted. "I had to do everything by myself," she recalled. Trying to defend herself, she started getting in fights, which landed her on probation. Doctors prescribed medications that left her feeling lifeless; she started smoking marijuana to cope. When Jazmine was sixteen, her uncle kicked her out and signed her out of school. She ended up in Job Corps and then went back to get her high school diploma through adult ed. She was almost done with school when she learned she was pregnant with a baby boy.

When we met, Jazmine had covered her scars from cutting with tattoos representing her healing and strength. Earnest and reflective, she described herself as "a loner" before she had Gabriel, now almost three. But becoming a mother opened up her world: "I want to take him everywhere. I want him to see the world even though I didn't see it. . . . I want him to grow up watching me be the parent I didn't have." Jazmine fixed breakfast for Gabriel each morning before he woke up: some combination of eggs, sausage, bacon, French toast, pancakes, and oatmeal. "I be tired, but I make it every morning," she said. When Tony, her boyfriend, watched Gabriel for an hour or two, Gabriel always asked for his mother. "He loves Mommy," Tony said. Jazmine took Gabriel to different parks when she was off work and used her benefits card to get tickets to the aquarium.

Motherhood, Jazmine reflected, had brought motivation and purpose to her life: "It just turned me into this person that I'm so proud of." Low-income mothers like Jazmine told me how profoundly motherhood had changed them. The mothering role meant everything, providing a sense of identity and pride. Their children were the center of their worlds; they aspired to provide a better life for their kids. "They're like my gas—they give me life," one, Yonersi, said. Another, Gloria, proclaimed, "If I could, I'd buy my kids the world." "My whole life's based around them," echoed Brooke. To the mothers I met, good parenting involved love, care, and sacrifice for children.[5] Child abuse and neglect, meanwhile, ran counter to the "good mother" identity to which mothers subscribed. As another mother, Isabela, explained, "What makes a good parent is being there for your child and taking care of them." She added, before I'd mentioned CPS, "A bad parent is someone who abuses their kids, neglects their kids, and who is not there for their kids."

Research finds that far from neglecting their children, mothers facing poverty and/or racism work to provide for their children and keep them safe from negative peer and neighborhood influences—no small feat given the constraints they face.[6] Parenting is challenging all around, especially so in the United States given paltry public supports for child-rearing, such as limited childcare assistance. But parenting in poverty means parenting under especially trying circumstances. Many parents are shut out of the labor market, and low-wage work doesn't provide enough to make ends meet. Due to systemic racism and discrimination, this disproportionately affects parents of color. When she worked full-time, with a high school equivalency degree and several certificates, Jazmine took home about $250 a week. She couldn't find an apartment affordable on that income; median rent in New Haven, at $1,200 monthly, exceeded her paycheck. Welfare and other benefits, like food assistance, don't provide nearly enough, and millions are left behind. Recall that Jazmine— living in Connecticut, a state more generous than most—received under $500 monthly from welfare when she didn't have income from work, leaving her well below the federal poverty line.

Privileged and marginalized families not only have different resources with which to raise their children but access different local institutions, including schools, community centers, and parks. Residential segregation concentrates poor families and families of color in neighborhoods subjected to persistent public and private disinvestment. In such environments, parents may be susceptible to—and may have limited resources to manage—significant daily stresses, which can exacerbate challenges related to substance use, violence, and mental health.

The mothers I met recognized the challenges of mothering amid inadequate social and societal support. As Jazmine put it, "I try to be the best parent that I can be, but sometimes it just gets hard." In addition to the everyday trials of motherhood—difficulties potty training, her lasagna not turning out quite right—Jazmine's job had cut her hours, just as she was trying to move and save up for a car. Vera, a Haitian mother, laid out the situation:

> I feel like if you're a single mom right now . . . the state is not giving you no child support. You're trying to get your school done. The state don't wanna give you no day care, because there's a time limit. Now, your time is off. Now, you don't have no job. You don't have no day care. How we supposed to better [our] life for our kids if we don't have a way of getting there? . . . You gotta have a lot of strength to keep going in this state.

Decades of social science research documents how weak welfare and labor market supports leave families without sufficient resources.[7] Parents get caught in, rather than caught by, the social safety net, generating substantial stress. So, somehow, mothers must make it work, finding inventive ways to meet their families' needs.[8]

Many low-income families face challenges beyond limited material resources. As sociologist Matthew Desmond has written, poverty is not solely an experience of financial hardship but often involves a "linked ecology of social maladies and broken institutions."[9] The mothers I interviewed described high exposure to adverse and traumatic experiences, dating from early childhood. Though such experiences were not universal, many mothers shared accounts of childhood exposure to violence, placement in foster care or other institutional settings, and difficulties in school. As they aged into adolescence and adulthood, they faced adversities such as homelessness, domestic violence, sexual abuse, addiction, incarceration, and physical and mental health challenges. Often, multiple adverse experiences compounded, subjecting them to substantial hardship.

Mothers in especially difficult situations sometimes recognized how in those circumstances, without support, they could not adequately care for their children. Michelle, a White mother, recalled her drinking and cocaine use years before, after her father passed. "I remember [my son] in a dirty diaper, laying next to me. It was like, really dirty." Depressed, she couldn't bring herself to change it, calling herself a "horrible mother" to her son at that time. Desiree, a Dominican and Puerto Rican mother, felt immense guilt about the conditions to which she'd subjected her two young daughters when she was actively using. "I used to leave them alone in crack houses just so I could go and get my fix. . . . I would leave them anywhere. I would leave them on the street, street corners." If Desiree came into $20, she purchased heroin first, to keep from getting sick, before getting diapers and formula for her daughters. Her daughters' father wasn't much help. Still, facing extraordinary adversity, motherhood remained resonant. "No matter how bad the situation is," she said, "your child is always going to need you." Several years removed from her active use, she felt that her two daughters should hate her. Instead, she said, they loved her more than ever. During the interview, Desiree's older daughter, now six, came in to show us a drawing from her notebook. "I Love You, Mom," it said, surrounded by hearts.

"As much as these kids have gotten on my nerves these last two hours, I can't picture myself without them," Desiree, relaxed on her living room sofa, shared. "This is me now. This is my package deal. I have three heads. Three butts. Six legs. You know? This is me."

"Things Happen": Precarity amid Confidence

The gulf in experiences of motherhood—between those parenting under conditions of poverty, racism, or other forms of oppression and their more privileged counterparts—extends beyond the resources mothers have. Motherhood on the margins is also defined by a recognition of what can be taken.[10] As sociologist Patricia Hill Collins argues, centering the experiences of women of color brings issues of maternal power to the forefront—specifically, the power to keep one's children.[11]

Seven months into her first pregnancy, Simone awoke in the middle of the night with bad abdominal pain. When she arrived at the hospital, staff rushed her in for an emergency C-section. After nine days in the hospital and three blood transfusions due to a serious pregnancy complication, Simone was reunited with her newborn baby girl, born at two pounds.

I'd first talked with Simone during her pregnancy, sitting in the front parlor of the duplex where she lived with her aunt. A quiet, contemplative young Black woman with long bangs framing her face, she described her childhood as "a normal life," growing up with her mom and siblings on the south side of Providence; she didn't mention any traumatic or adverse experiences. She made the honor roll every year, graduated from high school, and then went on to college. Simone started classes toward a medical assistance degree, until juggling her coursework with the multiple jobs she took to pay the bills became too much. When we met, she was working at a call center, earning $10 an hour.

In the neonatal intensive care unit, her newborn lay in an incubator, monitored for vital signs. When we met again at the hospital, I raised the topic of CPS. Simone shared:

> I'm scared of CPS, honestly. I'm not gonna lie. I'm so scared of them. I've never been involved with anything with them or anything, but it just scares me to even think about that. It's just like, oh my God, I would never wanna have my daughter be involved with that or into any of that. Even for a house visit or anything, I'll be so scared.

Simone had never had a run-in with CPS—not as a child or as a parent. She wasn't using substances or experiencing domestic violence; she had a place to stay with the baby after the hospital discharged them. But even without personal experience, just two weeks into new motherhood, Simone articulated a profound fear of CPS coming into her life. Simone's fear wasn't all-consuming;

she reasoned that if kids were taken care of, CPS should have no reason to come out. Still, the possibility lingered in the back of Simone's mind as she engaged with hospital and social service staff.

Like Simone, mothers, particularly those without open CPS cases, didn't usually frame CPS fears as structuring their lives, asserting that they didn't worry about CPS. Still, they recognized their vulnerability to CPS intervention. As anyone at all could call CPS, even exemplary motherhood couldn't fully safeguard against reports. Others could misjudge things—how mothers interacted with their children, for instance—in ways that might lead to a report.

Mothers facing adverse situations such as homelessness, domestic violence, substance use, and mental health needs felt vulnerable to CPS because they understood that such challenges could draw CPS attention. One January, I spoke with Brittni and her boyfriend, Pete, both White. Brittni's two toddlers from a previous relationship snuggled with her as we talked. She and Pete opened up right away about living in their car before entering a local family shelter a few weeks prior. They'd come to Rhode Island from another state to live with Pete's uncle, but when the uncle kicked them out, they had nowhere to go. Brittni didn't tell her parents about the situation; they already judged her for her young, single motherhood, and she didn't want to disappoint them further.

So for six months, they told me, they stayed in the car with the kids and all their things. They went to the park, spent time at the library, and tried to scrape together money from odd jobs for an occasional motel stay to shower and do laundry. As autumn became winter, they took turns staying up and turning on the car for heat. They recalled their greatest fear during that time: CPS coming to take the children. Brittni said that it was just "common knowledge" that police, CPS, and passers-by would frame their situation as child neglect. "You gotta figure, there's no place to prepare food, there's no running water, there's no place to shower, so it's not a good environment whatsoever to raise a child in." Still, they emphasized their devoted care for the children.

> PETE: We don't neglect the kids. I'd do anything for these kids. You'd think they'd be able to see it.
> BRITTNI: There are days where we wouldn't eat just so they could. Stuff like that. We've always put them forward, but that's not how CPS sees it.

Even as Brittni and Pete affirmed their commitment to their children, they felt vulnerable to CPS, recognizing that others would see their adversity as requiring CPS intervention.

CPS's substantial presence in mothers' social networks and communities also makes the agency's intervention feel like a real possibility. Many low-income mothers remember seeing the agency intervene with their own parents, and CPS saturates low-income neighborhoods and neighborhoods of color. I asked mothers what proportion of families they knew, or families in the area, they thought had had CPS involvement. Of the sixty Rhode Island mothers offering an estimate, thirty said at least half, with many guessing well over that.[12] "Everybody, 90 percent of people, they have CPS in their life or they got CPS in the house," remarked Selena, a Dominican mother. Not all mothers perceived such high levels of CPS involvement, but even new mothers, with no prior CPS experience, were acutely aware of the agency. "Everybody knows about it—it's common," said Odalys, a Latina mother whose firstborn was just three months old.

When CPS has scrutinized so many friends, relatives, and neighbors, even self-assured good mothers know that they can get caught up. Simone had a friend whose landlord called CPS after a disagreement; she'd seen women on social media threatening to call CPS on one another. Vera commented, "I know people who does things right and, like I said, it's that one little thing you could do in front of the wrong person who's judgmental." Donna, a White mother, recalled a friend recently reported to CPS because her child wasn't wearing a jacket in the cold, even though the child kept taking the jacket off. "Things happen," she said. "Like, if you were walking down the street and you had a couple of kids and you were swearing . . . someone calls the state on you." With *allegations* of maltreatment sufficient to draw CPS attention, mothers could simultaneously express confidence in their parenting while recognizing their vulnerability to CPS.

Beyond their social networks, mothers' own experiences inform their CPS concerns. Even when they have not (yet) encountered CPS themselves, marginalized mothers find their parenting scrutinized from all directions. Judgmental comments—a visiting nurse's admonishment about a baby's too-tight T-shirt or health care providers lecturing about the perils of juice—sting, conveying mothers' diminished parental autonomy. When others challenge their motherhood, it's not much of a stretch to think that CPS could get involved. Experiences of others judging or blaming them stayed with mothers, teaching them that even as they felt confident about their parenting, others might not see it that way. When White mother Colleen's newborn twins weren't gaining weight, for instance, she recalled the doctor making her feel as though she was doing something wrong, as though she wasn't providing for them. "I don't like when people make me feel like an inadequate mother, 'cause I'm not," Colleen said. "I do everything for my kids." Yajaira, a Dominican and Puerto Rican mother, recalled doctors questioning her about her residential instability. Yajaira explained, "There's ways to speak to people, but they tend to speak to you in such a way where they make you insecure about yourself."

Parenting in public, too, mothers face critiques and interventions from strangers. A couple years after we met, Christina recalled a recent doctor's visit when Anthony misbehaved. She swatted his hand to discipline him. Staff reprimanded her, interjecting with something a parent might say to a young child, in Christina's recollection: "We don't do that. You use your words." This affront to her parenting upset Christina. "I'm like, excuse you? . . . Please stay in your lane. This is my son." Some mothers recalled instances where passers-by jumped in to pass judgment on their parenting—hurtful experiences for mothers trying their best. Laura, a Latina mother, explained why a recent incident like this upset her so much: "I treasure my kids. They're like, honest to God, my life. . . . I just love being a mom. You know what I mean? I'm about to cry."

With gendered expectations for parents, mothers feel others' judgmental gaze directed specifically at them. As Amy, a Puerto Rican mother, said, "The whole society thinks that you need to be a perfect mom" while not holding fathers to the same standards. Amy worried about scrutiny from social services: "It's just the extra pressure of, oh my God, the house looks a mess, are they gonna call CPS on me? Are they going to judge me?" When Native American mother Yvonne's teenage daughter started skipping school and staying out, Yvonne was frustrated that court officials instructed her to attend every hearing while saying nothing of the sort to her daughter's father, also the child's legal guardian: "I have to do it, but he didn't have to. He wouldn't get in trouble. I feel like if I didn't do it, I'd get in trouble. . . . I just didn't want them to look at me as if, 'Oh, she's a parent who just don't care.'" Yvonne saw authorities holding her, as a mother, to different expectations.

Scrutiny of mothers is also racialized. Black mothers in particular must contend with stereotypes of the "bad" Black mother who neglects her children.[13] Fran, a Black mother with two sons, fourteen and eleven, spoke with me a couple weeks after police assaulted her older son outside her window. As Fran explained, her son was just riding his bike but supposedly fit the description of a break-in suspect. She and her husband rushed outside to see seven or eight police officers holding down her son. Her son, terrified, was resisting; one of the officers punched him. "I'm saying, 'Don't hurt my son. Don't hurt my son.' I'm going crazy. They're trying to choke him. They're trying to mace him. It was terrible. Right here in my parking lot." The police told Fran that her son had broken into someone's house.

"Oh, really?" Fran replied. "I'm not raising my son like that."

"Well, evidently you are," Fran recalled the officer telling her.

Fran, reflecting on this exchange, found the officer's retort infuriating: "I'm a damn good parent. I'm a damn good parent. . . . How dare you tell me that evidently I am raising my son like that when you don't even know me? You don't know my life. You don't know anything about me."

These presumptions about her parenting compounded the trauma Fran and her family experienced that night. Low-income Black mothers like Fran know that just as their children are subject to racialized criminalization, they are subject to racialized scrutiny of their parenting.[14] In this context, even self-identified "good mothers" see CPS as a realistic possibility.

Most directly, mothers understand themselves as vulnerable to CPS because those in their lives—schools, exes, relatives, and others—sometimes explicitly threaten to call. Christina's day care raised CPS as a possibility if she was late picking up her son. Carmen, a Latina mother, was having trouble getting her son to school on time, as they had to take the public bus. She met with school staff who wanted to know why her son had so many tardies. "They said, 'Oh, if [it's not addressed], we'll have to have somebody come over to your house and see what's going on.' I knew it was those people [CPS]." The school's comment hurt Carmen. Even the mere suggestion of neglect, she said, wasn't right—"because you try to do the best for your kids and try to work."

Absent any personal encounters with CPS, low-income mothers recognize their vulnerability to the agency based on their own parenting experiences and the experiences of their social networks. This sense of precarity is most acute among mothers facing greater adversity and those in social networks more highly exposed to CPS. Still, even low-income mothers not in particularly adverse situations—perhaps especially low-income Black mothers—understand CPS intervention as a risk.[15]

"CPS, It's Always a Bad Thing"

The mothers I met knew of children subject to abuse and neglect; some were once those children themselves, poignantly wishing others had provided sufficient protection from harm. Thus, mothers generally supported CPS's child protection aims, recognizing the need for state intervention in some instances. Yet they weren't sure that CPS could meet that need. In line with other research on marginalized communities' perspectives on police and CPS, mothers expressed ambivalence about CPS operations and practice.[16] Often, they didn't see the agency living up to its child protection ideals.

Reflecting on her childhood experience with CPS and what she'd seen and heard, Jazmine didn't think highly of the agency: "In the hood, CPS is not a good thing," she said. "To me, it never was good. It never helped me in any way." Like Jazmine, the mothers I met were quite cynical about CPS even before encountering the agency as parents. Their childhood experiences, the experiences of their social network ties, and media coverage taught them that CPS didn't meet its professed goals of protecting children and supporting families.

Mothers' attachment to their children made the prospect of CPS intervention especially ominous. Given their love for their children and the salience of the motherhood role, they saw calling CPS as the most hurtful weapon someone could wield—worse than calling the police or threatening their housing or welfare benefits. As Jazmine put it, "When you say CPS, that's the worst thing that you could possibly do." The prospect of losing their children was heart-wrenching. "Those are my babies. Those are of me," Bethany, a White mother, explained. Beyond the heartbreak of separation, Bethany didn't know what kind of care her children would receive in state custody. "Are they going to treat him or her like I would treat them?" she wondered. "Are they going to make her feel like she's not wanted?"

Like Bethany, mothers were skeptical about CPS's capacity to care for the children in its custody. They didn't see CPS as a system that helped children and families but, rather, as a system that failed children and families. "When I hear the word *CPS*, it's always a bad thing. It's never anything good," said Roberta, a Black mother.

CPS has a negative reputation across the board. Almost no one thinks that the system works well. Politicians, the media, and advocacy groups consistently highlight the agency's failures: children harmed under the agency's supervision, children growing up in foster care. Every CPS agency nationwide consistently fails to meet federal benchmarks for children's safety, permanency, and well-being outcomes.[17] In marginalized communities, these failures are not just news stories. Community experiences with CPS shape collective knowledge about the harm the agency inflicts.

In this way, CPS parallels the police. In the policing context, scholars have conceptualized Black communities as overpoliced yet underprotected.[18] Similarly, mothers repeatedly emphasized that CPS intervened in the wrong families. As Aaliyah, a Black mother, said, "There's a lot of kids out here that need to be taken from their parents." She thought about stories she'd seen on television and social media. "You got these people where their house been so goddamn nasty," with dead animals. "That's some of the people you have to go after and really investigate." Instead, Aaliyah said, "they always go after somebody that [made] a little mistake."

To Aaliyah and others, CPS ignored children in serious danger while scrutinizing other families over minor issues. Often, the mothers I interviewed empathized with the CPS-involved parents they knew, even if they didn't have CPS experience themselves.[19] As mothers saw it, even as CPS missed instances of serious maltreatment, the agency didn't recognize all that low-income parents and parents of color did to care for their kids. Jazmine explained:

> Because we are the minority and we're in the hood, we're struggling, we sit here and we have to do what we have to do for our child to make sure that our child eats, that our child sleeps, that our child has clothes, that our child has water, that our child has lights, that our child has paper, pens, a backpack, shoes.

But, she continued, based on what she'd seen growing up, CPS ignored these herculean efforts to provide for children's needs, jumping on parents' deficiencies:

> They just see: Oh, if you don't got a job, you can't support your child. Oh, you don't got a house, you can't support your child. Oh, you on welfare, you can't support your child. . . . They don't see us as hardworking parents trying to make it out somewhere because we don't have the resources, we don't have the funds to get where we want to be.

As Jazmine saw it, CPS judged and blamed parents for the challenges they faced, even as parents found creative ways to make do. In this view, the agency didn't so much protect children as police poor parents.

To mothers, CPS wasn't a helping agency. Sometimes, they recognized that individual caseworkers might care about families. And when discussing their perceptions of CPS, a few mothers pointed to the services the agency could provide. For instance, Lizette, a Latina mother, recalled CPS "harassing" neighbors and friends for years over things like marijuana and unstable housing. But she'd also "seen them do a lot of good for people," such as helping with school clothes and beds, so Lizette recognized the "up and down" with CPS.

Despite these benefits, mothers didn't want to turn to CPS for help, as Grace, a recently widowed Liberian mother, explained. After Grace's husband passed, her teenage daughter started acting out and shared thoughts of self-harm with a friend. Grace knew that parents could reach out to CPS about difficulties involving their children, but she didn't want to involve them. As she explained:

> When you call CPS, they're not coming to say, "Oh, sorry. You got no money? Okay, we'll get you that money for you to do this." No. When you contact CPS, first, they are in your house now. They coming to see what you're doing to the kid. They're coming to see what is the problem. . . . *CPS looking for the fault from you.* What is it that you're doing to this child, that they cannot stay in the house? What is it you're doing to this child that they're going through this? (emphasis added)

As Grace articulated, inviting CPS in to address children's challenges means turning the lens back on parents, given the agency's focus on abuse and neglect. In her words, they look for the fault. Grace told me about a friend's sister-in-law who did everything for her three children. The sister-in-law called CPS out of desperation when her teenage son kept running away. CPS placed him in foster care, where, as Grace put it, he met "some bad kids" and took up stealing. One day, he stole a car with friends; in the ensuing police chase, the car crashed, killing him on the spot.

Grace remembered how the church congregation fell silent at the funeral as the child's uncle spoke for nearly an hour. "CPS is not a good organization. They just come and mess up your family, mess up your children," she recalled the uncle saying. "Look around. Look around. You see any CPS person here now?" CPS was in the family's home "every second," but not a single CPS representative had shown up that day. Grace had no experience with CPS herself but concluded, "You gotta be careful how you deal with [them]." Bringing the agency into a family could have tragic consequences.

Not all mothers had such sharp understandings of CPS and its impacts. In particular, White mothers, even if lower-income, may be relatively insulated from CPS if not facing substantial adversity. Alicia, a White mother with a preschool-age daughter, worked at a day care for $11 an hour and lived with her husband, a truck driver, in New Haven. She hadn't encountered CPS as a child and didn't know anyone with CPS experience. Her social networks were middle class: Alicia's sister, a nurse, lived in a large house with her husband, a manager; Alicia's cousin had a "beautiful house" and worked in the finance industry. Before her own investigation, Alicia didn't know much about CPS, suggesting, "I just figured CPS helped families that are in need." Because she had always loved kids, she'd thought about becoming a CPS worker when she was younger, as she'd learned in school that CPS tried to help children. Mothers like Alicia, less exposed to CPS, shared vaguely positive perceptions of the agency or just repeated news headlines about its shortcomings. Others, steeped in social and community networks where CPS was pervasive, understood CPS as an entity that could not be trusted, one to avoid at all costs.

Withdrawal and Constraint

As this chapter has demonstrated, the threat of CPS hangs over marginalized mothers, who find themselves vulnerable to a system that jeopardizes their mothering. To protect against this insecurity, mothers strategically navigate social and institutional relationships. In the shadow of CPS, even seemingly benign interactions pose dilemmas—think of Christina concluding that home visiting services weren't worth the risk. Even for mothers never reported to CPS, the *possibility* of reports creates trade-offs that foster a sense of constraint and make it risky to disclose difficulties to people who might help. Most mothers I interviewed about this issue (sixty-seven of eighty-three Rhode Island mothers), across racial and ethnic groups, with and without CPS experience, described proactive strategies they pursued to protect themselves from CPS reports.[20] This strategizing parallels marginalized groups' efforts to avoid other enforcement authorities, such as police and immigration enforcement.[21] Ultimately, mothers' risk-averse approach—a rational response to CPS vulnerability—perpetuates marginality by reinforcing a sense of constraint and distancing families from assistance.

Even those not (yet) investigated by CPS and not in the most marginal social positions described parenting in the shadow of the state. Christina proactively declined home visiting services despite never having been reported to CPS; likewise, Simone, the mother with the premature newborn, had no personal experience with CPS but worried that leaving the hospital, even briefly, could prompt allegations of abandonment from hospital staff. Mothers like Christina and Simone parent not only with an eye to what is best for their children but also attuned to how they can shield their families from coercive state intervention. This caution extends into various spheres of social life, shaping how mothers approach interactions with children, social networks, and social service providers.

As any member of the public could call CPS, several mothers described a self-conscious, performative approach to public interactions with their children to keep others from jumping to conclusions. For example, White mother Genevieve initially asserted that she didn't worry about CPS. But "on second thought," she suggested, her two-year-old daughter, Adana, was a "drama queen." Genevieve recalled a couple recent instances when Adana physically resisted Genevieve's efforts to buckle her into the stroller. "If you had been driving by, you probably would have thought I was beating her," she said. "Something like that maybe I would be worried about—somebody just driving by and thinking they see something that's not going on." Genevieve tried to guard against potential misunderstandings:

> I'll be like, "Come on Adana, put your arm through. Come on Adana, can you please bend your arm? Don't make Mommy have to—you're gonna end up hurting yourself, please bend your arm. I don't wanna have to pull your arm and hurt you." I say stuff like that to her so people don't think that I'm beating her in the stroller or something. Or I'll be like, "Adana, stop screaming. Look it, you're embarrassing Mommy. These people think Mommy's hurting you, can you stop?"

Aware that others might draw conclusions, Genevieve sought to portray herself as engaged in normal, not abusive, parenting behaviors.

Mothers also know that their disciplinary tactics can come under scrutiny. Sociologist Patricia Fernández-Kelly, drawing on fieldwork in Baltimore, shows how poor Black parents seek to protect their children from negative peer influences; children, in turn, assert their autonomy by reporting parents' discipline to authorities.[22] Mothers thus find themselves in a bind: they must manage their children to promote children's well-being and avoid criminalization themselves, but doing so may invite CPS intervention. Crystal, a Black mother staying in a shelter, recognized this dilemma. She recalled the shelter telling residents that they could not discipline their children beyond time-outs, which she felt was "crazy."

> As far as popping them, verbally . . . yelling at them, hitting them—any form of that nature, they call CPS. . . . That's just like saying, okay, I can let them jump all over your furniture and jump off the walls . . . and I can't say nothing because if I say something, then you guys are going to call CPS.

Such restrictions on parental autonomy—restrictions not placed on affluent mothers in spacious, privately owned homes—made Crystal feel caught in a no-win situation:

> So it's just like, okay, I'm just gonna sit here and let 'em do whatever they want. Then soon as you let your kids do whatever they want, then that's when you wanna have meetings, like: You need to control your kids. You need to do this with your children. You need to do that with your children. *What should [the shelter] do instead?*
> [*pause*] Um—mind their business and let people raise their kids the way that they raise their kids. I'm not saying let the parent just go in the room and just beat all on their children, but if discipline is in order, discipline in order.
> *Respect the parents.*
> Exactly. You're in a shelter. We know not to abuse our kids. But at the same time, I don't let my kid disrespect me neither.

As Crystal saw it, *not* disciplining her kids would invite scrutiny by authorities. But disciplining them could prompt a CPS report, even if this discipline did not rise to the level of abuse.

Aware that onlookers might be watching them with their children, mothers exercised caution. Gillian, a Black mother, felt that parents needed to discipline children if children acted up. But she advised, "Don't do it in front of somebody that looks kinda fishy or something." Several mothers felt that these constraints on parenting impeded positive child development. "You're not allowed to discipline them no more, and then they wonder why the kids are the way they are," mused Roxanne, a Latina mother. A study of West Indian immigrants' child-rearing, too, found that teenagers "did not think that [CPS] was protecting them or looking out for them"; instead, youth "echoed the parents' concerns that [CPS] came between parents and children and was responsible for high rates of delinquency."[23] As we see, constrained parenting does not imply heinous abuse curbed by social norms and legal structures. Instead, CPS concerns make everyday parenting—already challenging given limited supports—more difficult and stressful.

With social relations a pathway to CPS, mothers recognized their social networks as another risk to navigate. Friends, partners, relatives, and neighbors can be important sources of material and emotional support for low-income mothers; researchers find that social support reduces the risk of child maltreatment.[24] Yet, ironically, because social ties can file CPS reports, mothers saw truncated social networks as protective against state scrutiny. Almost universally, mothers had heard about others calling CPS out of anger, jealousy, or revenge, teaching them that personal disagreements could lead to unwanted state intrusion.

Crystal acknowledged that anyone could be reported to CPS but felt that her limited social network alleviated her concerns:

> To me, it's all about the way that you live and the people that you hang out with. If you keep to yourself, mind your business, and do what you have to do for you and your kids, there's no worries. But if you hangin' out with Tom, Dick, and Harry, doing all of this and this and this with everybody . . . then that gives them means of people getting in your business, knowing what you doing, having a reason to—oh, if she asks you to borrow $5 one day and you tell her no, "Oh, I'm calling CPS because you don't do this, this, this." See? It's stuff like that, see? I keep my circle small. I only deal with the few people that I only deal with. Other than that—you can never hear nobody say, "Well, Crystal did this, and she did this."

As Crystal explained it, limiting her relationships prevented the conflicts that could lead to a vengeful call and ensured that others did not have information about her personal life that could be used against her. Pruning her network helped Crystal feel that there were "no worries" about CPS reports. "I feel like if I stay by myself, I'll have no problems," Christina echoed. Acquaintances, so-called weak ties, promote positive mental health and daily flourishing, connect people to new resources and opportunities, and facilitate community organization.[25] Yet, as mothers explained, they also introduce risks, potentially channeling families to CPS.

This notion of expansive social networks as risky with respect to CPS encourages a risk-averse approach to social relationships. Yajaira had grown up in Providence and was living in public housing when we met. She told me that only a couple of her family members knew where she lived, explaining:

> I feel like distancing myself from them avoids . . . confrontation, avoids a lot of miscommunication. If I could avoid it, perfect. I would avoid it. I don't need to surround myself around people that are always upset or feel the need to wanna call CPS on you over anything. I keep away.

In contrast to the rich exchange and support networks of low-income Black mothers that have sustained generations,[26] Yajaira preferred to keep her kinship ties at arm's length. Certainly, CPS is one of multiple reasons low-income mothers say they "stay to themselves"—such assertions help them feel safe and protect them from emotionally and financially draining relationships.[27] The prospect of CPS involvement constitutes yet another risk of engaging with and trusting others. Mothers invoked this risk to justify their restricted social networks.

Beyond interactions with children or with social networks, encounters with professionals are especially perilous for mothers trying to keep CPS at a distance. Although anyone can call CPS—from strangers to close friends and relatives—most reports come from educational, health care, and other professionals legally required to report suspected child maltreatment. To navigate these interactions, mothers described declining voluntary services, concealing adverse experiences, or, alternatively, making themselves visible to systems. These responses are reasonable from the perspective of mothers who love their children above all, but they also exacerbate family marginality and undermine service systems' child well-being goals.

Mothers worried about the ramifications of disclosing challenges such as homelessness, housing instability, difficulties meeting children's material needs, parenting practices and stressors, substance use, and domestic violence. Being forthcoming about one's needs is fraught when doing so can lead to a CPS report. Desiree outlined this catch-22. After her welfare benefits were cut off, she had no formal income for months. Reaching out to welfare and sharing the severe deprivation she was experiencing might have opened up opportunities for assistance but could also invite a CPS report:

> I feel like if let's say I tell welfare, "Hey, this mess is going on, and I can barely afford to keep my kids." "You can't afford to keep your kids? You know we're gonna have to call the city on you. We're gonna have to call CPS." I'm damned if I do. I'm damned if I don't call them. . . . I don't eat so that my kids can eat, but I'm scared to ask for any help these days, because I'm scared that it's gonna work against me.

Desiree put it plainly: "I have to lie." She understood that this made securing assistance difficult but opted to downplay her hardship to protect against CPS reports, worried that service providers would view her situation as neglect.

Similarly, Susan, a White mother, had one of her five children in her custody when we first met. Two years later, after CPS removed that child, Susan acknowledged that she was selling pills and selling her methadone while caring for her son. "I was still probably in active addiction," she added. "I tried to make it seem like I wasn't, I guess . . . so nobody would take my son. I felt like . . . if I asked for help, I would be judged by it, and they would take him, so I kept it to myself." For Susan and others, fears of CPS intervention impeded help-seeking. Mothers told me about declining voluntary services and staying away from psychiatric hospitals. Such decisions distance families from assistance, but mothers had to weigh the perceived benefits of support against the possibility of CPS reports.

Questioning from health care, education, and social service providers also creates anxiety and inhibits honest conversations about families' situations. Today, recognizing that social and family contexts shape health and education, doctors don't just ask about children's medical conditions and teachers don't only focus on schooling. This holistic approach can be stressful when mothers understand service providers as a conduit to CPS. Colleen said that parents "definitely" had to be careful when talking with "anyone who works for an agency . . . like Head Start, the doctors." As she explained, offhand comments about substance use, stress, or food insecurity could be misconstrued: "Some people, you say something to them, they'll take it out of context. They'll call CPS on you." When her visiting nurse asked questions, Colleen felt anxious. She and a friend who helped her with childcare commented:

> COLLEEN: It makes you *nervous* sometimes, when they come, especially if you know you're struggling or something, and you don't want them to know, because it makes you nervous that they could do something like ruin your life, even though you're doing the best you can.
> FRIEND: The doctor asks you questions, makes you nervous. When I took [Colleen's newborn son, a twin] to get weighed that day, they were asking me all kinds of questions, like, I don't know! Do they sleep in the same bed?

For Colleen, opening up about vulnerabilities carried risks, as providers were positioned to "ruin your life." Although service providers might ask questions to provide mothers with information and support, mothers like Colleen understood these inquiries as opportunities to be turned in for wrongdoing.

As chapter 2 will detail, disclosing these kinds of challenges *can* lead to CPS reports. In response, mothers described a strategy of providing only minimal information, noting that they were careful to watch their words around professionals. "I answer the question, but I really don't answer it," said Aaliyah. As another mother, Ruby, put it, "I tell them what I want them to know." Even as they asserted that they had nothing to hide, mothers weren't always clear whether authorities would find their situations objectionable, so they hesitated to speak openly in front of professionals.

Mothers' strategizing may protect against state scrutiny, but their disengagement also hinders the development of trusting relationships with service providers and cuts families off from critical sources of support. For instance, with waiting lists for housing assistance years long, going through the homeless shelter system could be the only way to secure subsidized housing promptly in Providence. Yet, in explaining why they chose not to enter homeless shelters during times of need, several mothers spontaneously pointed to shelters' practices of calling CPS. Brittni and Pete, the couple who stayed in their car, first mentioned CPS to me in passing, when they recounted their experience trying to obtain cash assistance and food stamps. As they shared, the local welfare office asked for proof of residency, but they had come to Rhode Island from out of state and didn't want to reveal their living situation. "I didn't tell [welfare] we were living in the car, because if they find out, they have to tell CPS, and CPS will come and take the kids away," Brittni explained. In this context, Brittni felt that she had to choose between alleviating material hardship and keeping her family together. She opted for the latter. Ideally, Brittni and Pete suggested, welfare would respond by offering housing assistance. But realistically, the couple felt certain that disclosing their situation would lead to CPS involvement, so they received no cash assistance or food stamps for six months. As we see, CPS fears generate strategic responses from parents trying to care for their children, but such responses can also impede this care.

CPS concerns entered into mothers' awareness in relatively small moments—they might feel anxious about disclosing their housing instability to doctors, for instance—but also as they weighed major life decisions. Bethany described how her newborn tested negative for substances at birth, but the hospital notified CPS because of Bethany's prior CPS involvement. She outlined the options she saw for herself if she had another child:

> The only way around it, I think, is to move to another state. . . . It makes me think, "What am I gonna do if I get pregnant and I wanna have a baby? Where am I gonna go? Can I go over to Fall River [Massachusetts] and have the baby?" But I'm on methadone, and I'm gonna have to tell them I'm from Rhode Island, and I'm scheming on different ways of where I can go to have a baby just so I can have a baby come home. That's not right.

I've heard about that, where people wonder if they could go to other states. Other states to have babies, I've seen them where they do national searches. I don't think they do a state-to-state unless they have a reason to believe that you're from another state. I was thinking, if I could get away with actually making them believe I'm from Mass or Maryland or wherever and maybe not even mention Rhode Island, they might not even do a search.

Like several other mothers I met, Bethany contemplated going to another state to give birth, a possibility inhibiting consistency in health care services and making mothers in recovery feel like fugitives on the run.[28] CPS loomed as Bethany thought about her future and the opportunities available for her family.

Strategizing around CPS did not always involve retreat from social service systems. Aware of professionals' expectations and power, mothers sometimes felt compelled to make themselves visible to systems. For those wanted by police, sociologist Alice Goffman writes, "following the rules (e.g., appearing in court, showing up to probation meetings, or turning oneself in when accused) may hasten one's removal to prison."[29] In contrast, low-income mothers sometimes saw engaging with service systems as a way of conveying fit motherhood to professionals. Being known to systems helped mothers feel confident that they could keep CPS away. As Cassandra, a White mother, asserted, "The only reason CPS will come in for [mental health] is if you don't do anything about it."

Although mothers' strategic visibility promoted social service participation, this participation fostered a sense of constraint when undertaken with an awareness of CPS. Gloria, a Black mother, described how she sought immediate medical care for her son even for minor concerns. During our evening interview, she said, "I'm so bad with it that if he started to cry with his throat right now, I would take him right now. When I go, it's not an infection yet, so I gotta go back when it's an infection, but I don't wait." Her cousin had waited to take a child to the hospital after an injury, leading to a CPS report. "From that, you coughing, let's go. I don't take no chances. I don't want them to feel like I'm neglecting my kids." Gloria oriented her response around how she felt authorities would see the situation. Despite her own serious health challenges—just climbing the stairs to her apartment left her out of breath, so she mostly stayed home—she wanted doctors to see that she was responding promptly, even if she didn't feel her son needed formal health care: "I make sure they have it on record that I came ASAP." This extreme caution ensures that children receive medical attention but also strains health care resources and undermines parenting autonomy. Even when mothers access social and health care services, then, their participation may be reluctant; what looks like engagement may instead be superficial compliance. The prospect of CPS reporting frames service systems as adversaries poised to turn mothers in, rather than as partners working with mothers around shared goals of supporting children.

Mothers want to engage with doctors, schools, and other services, but in ways that do not expose them to CPS intervention. Because discipline can be misconstrued as abuse, poverty can constitute neglect, and anyone at all can make a report, low-income mothers parent with an eye to protecting their families from unwanted state intrusion. They strategize not so much to shove severe abuse underground but to keep adverse experiences in the shadows. Although this withdrawal and constraint may protect against the CPS reports mothers fear, it ultimately reinforces marginalized mothers' limited autonomy and obscures children's needs from the systems tasked with supporting them.

Previous scholarship documents how low-income mothers orient their parenting around child protection: protecting children from neighborhood violence, negative peer influences, and criminalization by authorities, for instance.[30] We see in this chapter how this protective parenting also encompasses attending to potential intrusion by the state's own child protection efforts—additional labor taken on by marginalized mothers. Beyond affirmatively providing for their children, these mothers also work to protect themselves and their families from state authorities that threaten mothers' ability to raise their children in the first place.[31] As an institutional presence in poor communities, the child welfare system fosters a diffuse sense of precarity. It hangs over parenting like a large cloud—mothers wonder if or when the rain will hit and how they can take shelter.

This awareness of CPS isn't all-consuming. Like affluent mothers, low-income mothers take pride in their mothering, enjoying school events, Christmas surprises, and trips to the zoo. Yet, unlike their more well-off counterparts, low-income mothers face adverse experiences that render them particularly vulnerable to CPS intervention, they see the agency visiting other families for minor issues and misunderstandings, and they routinely find their parenting subject to scrutiny. From what mothers have seen and heard, CPS doesn't do right by children and families. With its power to remove children, the agency also threatens what they cherish most, so mothers see CPS as something to avoid at all costs. Even as they affirm their confidence in their motherhood, the prospect of catching a CPS case constitutes a risk that mothers—especially those highly exposed to CPS and those facing substantial adversity—attach to interactions with children, social networks, and service systems. In response to this insecurity, mothers strategically navigate these relationships in ways that may minimize CPS risks but may also distance their families from critical resources.

The reach of the child welfare system thus extends beyond direct interactions to penetrate spaces where the system is not currently or physically present. As an idea, a possibility, the system inserts itself into everyday life to undermine familial, social, and institutional relationships. These adaptive responses thwart help-seeking and social solidarity among poor families, including those without prior system contact.

Apprehension around CPS is so pervasive in part because of the system's fuzzy boundaries. With doctors, teachers, and even friends and family conduits to CPS, mothers can't necessarily identify who might turn them in. Nor can they predict what may draw suspicion, given subjective, vague criteria for reports. The specter of CPS becomes an expansive and gendered experience of social control. While Black men in high-poverty neighborhoods learn to evade the police and the people and places that might ensnare them, low-income women with children must be wary of those who might report them to CPS. Trip wires, all around, are easily triggered by those with whom low-income mothers come into contact, as the next chapter will demonstrate.

2

Making the Call

Note: Chapter includes references to attempted suicide.

JENNIFER, A MID-FORTIES Puerto Rican mother of two in New Haven, had had a traumatic summer. Jennifer's adult daughter had found Jennifer's younger daughter, twelve-year-old Faith, unconscious, hanging in her closet after attempting suicide. Jennifer, shaken by the incident, put her energy into supporting Faith. "That's my job, to get her better," Jennifer asserted. They completed an intake appointment at a local mental health service provider after Faith left the hospital. But in the ensuing weeks, Marla, the White clinician who conducted the intake, saw that Faith was not receiving the mental health care services her office had recommended.

That same summer, Jazmine—the Black and Puerto Rican mother of two-year-old Gabriel introduced earlier—met with her housing case manager, a White woman named Cate, in Jazmine's apartment. As they filled out job applications on Cate's laptop, Gabriel threw a plastic bucket at Cate. Jazmine took Gabriel into his bedroom and smacked him on the hand a few times. Cate heard loud slaps and Gabriel screaming at Jazmine to stop. Jazmine told me that she didn't like putting her hands on him, but upon hearing the bucket hit Cate, she wanted him to understand that his behavior was inappropriate.

How should we understand these situations? The United States responds to families like Jazmine's and Jennifer's through a lens of *child maltreatment*: Both Marla and Cate phoned Child Protective Services. But this framing is not inevitable. This chapter examines how CPS enters so many marginalized families' lives to directly challenge mothers' parenting. As we'll see, CPS reporting doesn't follow directly from whatever we might call maltreatment. Instead, it's a *social* process.

CPS investigators arrive at families' doorsteps because people like Marla and Cate send them there. The agency doesn't patrol the streets looking for families to investigate but, instead, deputizes other professionals and community members to report suspected abuse and neglect. Research rarely considers the perspective of these critical actors, who, in their discretionary reporting decisions, determine the scope of state intervention into family life. Parents reported to CPS are often facing some form of adversity and/or doing things that may be detrimental to child well-being. Yet, as this chapter shows, beyond families' specific situations, the aspirations, constraints, and resources of those in a position to file reports construct CPS as an appropriate—even desirable—response. In particular, CPS's dual role as helper and disciplinarian appeals to professionals who see rehabilitating parents as a way to improve conditions for children. Trainings, policies, and laws also encourage expansive reporting. The broad category of "maltreatment" means that nebulous concerns about children can reasonably be transferred to CPS and labeled suspected abuse or neglect. Notably, this widespread reporting does not fall evenly on families. Individual, organizational, and systemic racism and classism bring marginalized families disproportionately under investigation for child maltreatment. Help for families facing adversity, especially marginalized families, comes in the form of an agency that threatens motherhood.

Allegations

All CPS investigations begin with allegations: someone alleging that a caregiver is (or may be) subjecting a child to harm or the imminent risk thereof. Staff working the CPS hotline determine whether what's being reported falls within definitions of maltreatment, as identified in state statute. If so, CPS "screens in" the report and dispatches an investigator. Official statistics show that most reports allege neglect and some allege abuse, but these categories don't tell us much about the specific incidents and situations that CPS investigates. State policies define maltreatment broadly; for instance, Connecticut defines physical neglect as, in part, permitting a child "to live under conditions, circumstances or associations injurious to [their] well-being"[1]—an umbrella under which many behaviors and situations could conceivably fall.

I reviewed and discussed hundreds of CPS reports over the course of my research. The allegations in these reports vary considerably, so no single descriptor can cover all of them. What unites them is hotline staff deciding the allegations constitute child abuse or neglect. But by and large, reports to CPS

involve *adversity*, encompassing manifestations of poverty, trauma, and marginality. Sometimes, families face acute challenges, such as material hardship,
domestic violence, substance use, or mental illness. Challenges may also be
more diffuse, such as high stress impacting parents' interactions with children.
Other times, adversity involves families deemed challenging—parents deviating from expectations about how they should interact with systems or what
they should do. This, too, constitutes a form of marginality. Attending to the
adversity embedded in CPS reports helps us see how the "maltreatment" label
isn't self-evident, even if callers and hotline staff can reasonably make the case
for it.

First, because neglect definitions encompass inadequate provision of shelter, food, and clothing, some CPS reports allege material deficiencies, typically
housing needs. In many states, lack of housing, food, or clothing due to poverty alone does not constitute neglect,[2] but CPS callers often cannot (or, more
cynically, opt not to) make that distinction. Christina, introduced in chapter 1,
was reported several times one summer for housing conditions. First, staff at
a housing program evicting Christina reported that she had smoked marijuana
in the apartment, likely with her son at home; that the apartment "was a mess,"
with dirty diapers and rotten food throughout; and that the utilities might
not be on at the place where she was now staying. A few weeks later, a social
service provider reported Christina sharing that she had slept in her car with
her son the previous night and would do so until a shelter bed opened up. The
third time, a different social service provider called CPS making similar allegations; two months had passed, and Christina was still calling emergency help
lines seeking shelter for herself and her son. Rhode Island CPS deemed these
allegations "unfounded," closing the case each time after investigating. In these
cases, the connection to poverty—and the inadequate social safety net, more
than inadequate parenting—is clear.

Second, a large portion of CPS reports involve allegations of domestic violence, parental substance misuse, and/or parental mental health needs. Such
adverse experiences were common in the reports I saw and heard about; a
recent California study likewise found that CPS documented at least one of
these conditions in 59 percent of investigated neglect reports reviewed.[3]
Though such conditions do not automatically threaten child safety, they can
become allegations of neglect through the lens of "inadequate supervision."
For example, a report came in stating that Selena, in Providence, locked herself
in the bathroom with her baby, "made a concoction of over the counter meds,"
and said that she wanted to kill herself and the baby, according to CPS records.

Was Selena putting her baby in danger? Potentially, yes. Parents' mental health needs or substance use may inhibit them from providing adequate care for children, and exposure to domestic violence can traumatize children. Still, framing such situations as maltreatment is a choice; people may disagree about whether CPS should get involved. In Selena's case, a family member got into the bathroom, took the baby from her, and took her to the hospital. Her family told the hospital that they wanted help for Selena, rather than CPS involvement. Instead, the hospital notified CPS.

A third category of CPS reports calls out parents' management of their children, citing corporal punishment or unsupervised children. Allegations of "physical abuse" often involve parents disciplining their children, under considerable stress—recall Jazmine smacking Gabriel upon hearing that he hit her case manager. Regarding inadequate supervision, Marsha, a Black mother in Providence, recounted a recent report. Her five-year-old son, Xavier, liked to play with other children in the field behind her apartment complex. "I used to call for his name, and he's like, 'Mommy, I'm in the field.' I said, 'All right.'" A neighbor told CPS that he saw Xavier outside every day, from early in the morning until sunset, sometimes without shirt or shoes. According to the report, Xavier told neighbors that he was hungry because he had no food at home. Marsha instructed Xavier not to do this anymore: "I told him, 'You might see people eating popsicles or snacks. At the end of the month, Xavier, we only get so much food stamps. . . . You have food, but you might not have snacks and stuff, like the things you want.'" Child-rearing styles are socially and culturally specific; in other contexts, Marsha's and Jazmine's approaches might not raise concerns. (In fact, unstructured outdoor play with peers, common in decades past, promotes children's mental health.[4] And although research links corporal punishment to negative child outcomes, most U.S. parents of toddlers spank their children.[5]) But in an environment where such behaviors—closely intertwined with stress and limited food assistance—are condemned, they prompt CPS calls.

Finally, some reports involve families deviating from systems' expectations. This includes reports of educational or medical neglect, alleging children not going to school or the doctor. Other reports reflect educational, medical, or mental health personnel at odds with parents over what children need. These disagreements can have high stakes—children not receiving (what professionals see as) urgent medical or mental health care. Parents, meanwhile, may be resisting professionals' recommendations, may be implementing them in other ways professionals are not aware of, or may just be overwhelmed with the trials of parenting under difficult circumstances. In Jennifer's case, a service provider believed that Faith needed multiple therapy sessions each week. "That's their recommendation. *Their recommendation,*" Jennifer emphasized. Of course, conflicts between families and systems are not limited to low-income families; the few reports I observed involving more affluent families generally fell in this category. Yet privileged families have more resources to meet systems' expectations or, where they disagree, to marshal "experts" to make their case. For instance, Jennifer could not accommodate the recommended service given her work schedule; she was frustrated to receive no transportation assistance. "Where are you helping me?" she asked rhetorically. "Because I am a working mother. I am a *single* working mother." Viewed another way, Jennifer's supposed noncompliance reflected social service systems' failure to meet her family's needs.

Understanding reported situations as adversity doesn't ignore potential harms to children; a whole research literature documents long-lasting impacts of children's adverse experiences.[6] When mothers shared their life histories, many recounted difficult, traumatic experiences as children—from observing repeated, severe domestic violence to navigating parents' addiction—that stayed with them. I refer to "adversity" to focus on the specific issues at hand without attributing (or denying) blame. Like all people, parents reported to CPS make choices; sometimes, they do things that jeopardize their children's safety. Still, reports almost never involve parents willfully inflicting harm on children.[7] And their actions are informed and constrained by social conditions like poverty that make it more difficult to meet children's needs, as chapter 1 described.

Moreover, allegations range in severity. Some reports pose more serious concerns, whereas others involve relatively minor issues, accidents, or misunderstandings. Not all reported families are in dire straits; recall, again, how CPS investigates more than half of Black children and most investigations are summarily dismissed.[8] In the next few chapters, reading allegations made against parents, you might be surprised to read about families *not* in absolute crisis situations. This is the nature of CPS investigations today, perhaps especially among families reported for the first time. With CPS heralded as a means of preventing child maltreatment, a first-line response to adversity, the hope is that CPS can intervene early to keep situations from escalating.

Situations that could constitute maltreatment don't automatically flow to CPS. Many experiences children later identify as maltreatment are never reported to authorities.[9] For CPS to get involved, someone must affirmatively decide to call in. Thus, to understand how CPS ends up knocking on so many families' doors, we must consider not only the situations of families themselves but the perspectives and goals of those in a position to report them.

Reports from Professional Contacts

Families' situations coalesce into formal allegations of child maltreatment because CPS is a tool that solves problems for people in a position to file reports. About two-thirds of reports come from education, law enforcement, social services, medical, mental health, and childcare professionals, legally mandated to report suspected maltreatment. Personal relations, such as parents, other relatives, friends, and neighbors, contribute about half of the remaining cases, with the rest originating from anonymous, other, or unknown sources.[10] Professional and personal contacts alike use CPS as a means of compensating for their own limitations, easing their burdens, and exercising power. Families marginalized by race and/or class disproportionately come to CPS's attention not only because they experience high levels of adversity but also because racism and classism structure the reporting process.

After Jennifer and Faith completed the intake appointment with Marla, Marla wasn't initially too worried. Marla recalled her conversation with Faith, a soft-spoken preteen with light brown skin and black hair in tight curls: "I asked her, 'When you woke up in the hospital and you realized that you were still alive, how did you feel?' She said, 'Disappointed.' She felt like she had failed." Still, Jennifer assured Marla that she would not leave Faith alone, and Faith confirmed that she would ask for help if she needed it, so Marla felt that Faith was safe. Marla recommended individual therapy, psychiatric services, and family therapy.

But as the weeks wore on, Marla grew increasingly concerned about Faith's unmet mental health needs after hearing that Jennifer had not returned calls from the referred service provider and was "resistant" to the referral. "That's when I was feeling uneasy." Marla wrestled with what to do. She didn't want to see Faith removed—"The very worst thing for this kid right now would be to take her away from her family," she said—and she "didn't want to throw CPS at" Jennifer. Marla explained:

> I think that it was just out of my hands and it needed some supervision that, from provider to provider, can get lost. I can make a referral, but if I don't follow up on that referral, who's responsible? We don't know who's responsible. I think that's something that we try to do in mental health, and because I'm seeing so many families, things get lost and they fall through the

cracks. I'm pretty diligent about it, but I notice how much effort it takes to remember those kids and to follow up on them. I have a running list all the time of, "Don't forget to do these things," because when you refer, you're feeling like it's off your plate. . . . When she didn't [follow up on referrals], it was time to say, "Okay. I can't continue to monitor and continue to supervise what she does or doesn't do with services. It's gotta go to the big guys."

As a helping professional, Marla wanted to make sure that Faith received recommended services. But in addition to her work doing intake assessments, she carried a full caseload of twenty to twenty-five families. "It's a lot. There's a lot of heavy cases that come through [this place]." Given her workload, she did not have the bandwidth to continue following up with Jennifer to ensure that Faith received mental health services. So she turned it over to "the big guys."

Faith wasn't just a number to Marla, another case—she was a child Marla wanted to help. So Marla's legal mandate to report was not top of mind. Sitting in her office, overflowing with children's toys, books, and games, Marla said that she would have reported even without the legal requirement, as she worried something terrible would happen.[11] "Honestly, this case was really difficult for me to sit with. I don't know if you can tell by the way that I'm talking about it, but I had dreams about this kid, that she successfully completed suicide," Marla said. "She's been on my mind a lot."

Like Marla, reporting professionals, almost to a person, said that they would have reported their most recent report absent the legal mandate, often expressing no hesitation as they said they "absolutely" or "definitely" would have reported. "I don't think of it, 'Oh, my God. I'm a mandated reporter. I have to do it.' I don't think like that. I think: This mom needs help. This baby needs to stay safe," a maternity ward nurse said. As a school social worker put it, "I need to be able to sleep at night."

Frontline workers such as police and counselors are not unfeeling bureaucrats who apply rules robotically. Instead, research finds that moral commitments drive them, such that they bend the rules if needed to act in line with their normative sensibilities.[12] Consistent with this idea, reporting professionals invoked ethical justifications for reporting when describing specific cases. "I think the moral piece of making a decision, at least for me, would outweigh the legal," offered a day care director. Many reports come from therapeutic personnel at hospitals and schools, who aligned calling CPS with their professional ethic. A new hospital social worker completing his master's degree in social work commented that after going through "the whole social work ethics and values and everything that's drilled into your head over and over and over again . . . I hope I would report it [without the legal mandate]. Otherwise, I think I missed it. I think I missed the point of this program."

Conceptions of children as innocent, voiceless, and vulnerable undergirded reporting professionals' beliefs about the need to call CPS. As a social service provider remarked, "These kids are so little. They can't talk for themselves, and so they need somebody to do it for them. Even if I wasn't a mandated reporter, I would still use the [CPS hotline] just for that reason." These professionals framed invoking CPS as part of a shared responsibility for child well-being. An assistant principal described the sense of duty she felt for the students in her care: "This might sound cliché, but it's truly how I feel. These nine hundred kids, whether they're a pain or not, are my responsibility. . . . When I go home and I say, 'my kid,' they're like, 'Which ones?' I'm like, 'Not my biological ones. My other ones.'" Just as Marla worried about Faith, reporting professionals didn't want anything bad to happen to the children they met. Feeling that they had to do something, they saw CPS as an appealing option.

Seeking Rehabilitation

Marla did not want CPS to separate Jennifer and Faith. Nor did Cate believe that Gabriel was in serious danger, necessitating his removal from Jazmine's care. "I want her to realize that we're not trying to have your child taken away from you," Cate told me. Almost all the reporting professionals I interviewed concurred.[13] Reporting professionals generally summoned CPS to address diffuse concerns about families, rather than to rescue children in immediate danger. Beyond child removal, CPS reporting offered something else to them: an outlet for their rehabilitative aspirations. They called on CPS to support and discipline parents—goals that were not separate or contradictory but one and the same. Think of Jennifer's case: Marla's desire for Jennifer to follow up with recommended mental health treatment for Faith after Faith's suicide attempt reflected an effort to assist, but also control, Jennifer's family. Reporting professionals hoped that CPS reports would convey the gravity of the situation to parents, remind parents of their responsibilities to their children, and pressure them to take up recommended services. In this framing, the implicit threat wielded by CPS—court intervention and even child removal—became a means of helping families.

Cate knew that Jazmine's time in the transitional housing program was rapidly coming to an end and Jazmine would need a way to cover the rent on her own. For two years, Cate had visited Jazmine weekly, recognizing that Jazmine struggled with maintaining employment and paying her portion of the rent on her limited income. Cate worried about how Jazmine's mental health and "anger issues"—Jazmine had gotten into physical fights, Cate relayed—were affecting Gabriel, an active toddler who had taken to grabbing and hitting the family's pet cat. Cate hoped that CPS could connect Jazmine with parenting classes and perhaps even housing. Whenever waiting lists for housing vouchers opened, Cate's program helped clients apply, "but so does everyone else in the state of Connecticut. She's never been picked, but hopefully the CPS worker can help intervene with Mom and get her onto Section 8 as well."

Nearly all reporting professionals I interviewed cited goals of support in notifying CPS. Recognizing challenges families were facing, they felt that CPS would know better how to help. As a maternity ward nurse explained, "They know more about what's in the community than I do right now. . . . I don't know what's available." An elementary school principal said, "What I have found in the Northeast Corner . . . [is] there aren't enough resources to be had in this area, where CPS might have access or know more of that information than what our [school] family resource center can give." Maternity wards and schools are supposed to serve children and families, but when staff couldn't provide the resources they felt families needed, they hoped that CPS could assess family needs holistically and connect families with services.

Relatedly, reporting professionals often wanted CPS to educate parents regarding "appropriate" behavior. In their view, parents were not intentionally trying to hurt their children; they just did not know any better. For example, a police officer hoped that CPS could help parents understand that domestic violence "is not normal" and "is wrong." A clinician providing services at a middle school called CPS with concerns about a student, including possible exposure to sexual activity. She described what she felt the family needed:

> There are basic needs issues. I'm hoping that they can get the family some outside services, if nothing else. Because the goal is never to take the child away. . . . Unless they see something I don't, which I would respect that if they did, I don't think this is a kid that's in imminent danger, necessarily. I just think they need some more education. I think they could use some parenting skills, knowing what's appropriate, what's not appropriate.

This clinician recognized that the family's poverty presented challenges; she didn't feel that family separation was warranted. Instead, she hoped that CPS could connect the family to additional services and teach the parents about "appropriate" behavior.

These aspirations to help were wrapped up in paternalism—beliefs that parents needed guidance from professionals to do what was best for their children. And reporting professionals understood "help" to involve discipline and monitoring in addition to resource provision. As Marla said of Jennifer's case, "I felt like CPS needed to get involved in order to just supervise so that Mom was accountable to somebody." A hospital social worker, reporting a mother who accidentally overdosed, explained what she wanted from CPS: "Oversight. Someone checking in that's not family to see how they're doing and just making sure that they are going to counseling and they're getting the supports that they need."

A frontline workforce composed predominantly of women may present CPS, in contrast to police, as a kinder, gentler way to guide families. Still, reporting professionals often viewed the "teeth" CPS could bare as useful in encouraging parents' service participation. Jazmine had not taken up the mental health and other referrals Cate had made, so Cate hoped that CPS's involvement might nudge Jazmine to get the support Cate believed she needed. "I hope this is a push in the right direction. Sometimes, a lot of times, our clients need a little fire underneath their feet to actually start doing things," Cate said. "A lot of people are afraid of CPS, so a lot of times they're like, 'I don't wanna piss off CPS, because it won't be pretty.'" Likewise, a middle school principal acknowledged that she could recommend social services to parents. But she added, "I can't tell a parent they have to do that. . . . I think [with CPS] parents kind of realize, 'Oh, I need to do this.' It's kind of that thumb that CPS has over parents." Reporting professionals saw CPS's authority over families as an effective tool in disciplining families. So reporting professionals' purportedly benevolent aims also reflect their conviction that they know what families need and that an enforcement agency can pressure families to behave in ways deemed appropriate. In this light, CPS's rehabilitative aims alongside its coercive power make it a useful place to turn.

Summoning the All-Purpose Agency

Public administration scholar Michael Lipsky referred to frontline workers like Cate and Marla as "street-level bureaucrats" who, in their discretionary decision-making, essentially make public policy. In his foundational book, Lipsky identified the central dilemma facing bureaucrats such as teachers, social workers, and police officers: they often pursue these positions wanting to improve people's lives, but amid limited resources, conflicting demands, and clients' complex needs, "the very nature of this work prevents them from coming even close to the ideal conception of their jobs."[14]

Lipsky outlined several ways street-level bureaucrats manage this gulf between their aspirations to help people and the reality of their jobs. For instance, they might ration limited services or reframe their work or clientele. CPS reporting offers another way out of the street-level bureaucrat's dilemma: Frontline workers can pass families off to CPS, feeling reassured that someone else will look into the situation and respond accordingly.[15] To reporting professionals, CPS can compensate for whatever they lack or are unable to do, offering time, resources, attention, expertise, knowledge, and coercive authority. Because CPS offers a range of possible interventions—repeated home visits, needs assessments, short-term case management, service referrals, and even legal intervention—it becomes a sort of all-purpose agency that many types of professionals can call upon.

In this sense, CPS reporting is less about sounding the alarm about children in danger and more about solving problems for overwhelmed frontline bureaucrats. Sometimes, these problems are immediate, as when police encounter a toddler found alone on the street and police, on patrol duty, cannot babysit. But usually, CPS addresses a more diffuse problem: the disconnect Lipsky identified between reporting professionals' desire to meaningfully improve people's lives and their inability to do so given limited time and resources.

CPS seemed to offer something to everyone. A police officer called the hotline expecting "somebody else who is more qualified in dealing with the child aspect of it." Meanwhile, others extremely knowledgeable about child development also found reasons to turn to CPS. To a clinician working with young children, CPS offered a whole-family assessment she believed was essential: "Because we can't just only focus on the child." A hospital social worker on the pediatric inpatient unit said that they didn't have much time with families, as children might only stay a couple days. "We need [CPS] to take it from there," she said, getting "eyes on the kid" and assessing the need for additional services.

A staff member at a women's services center helped connect women with community resources when they arrived facing a crisis such as domestic violence. In this role, she might seem well positioned to provide the service referrals many reporting professionals sought from CPS. Yet this staff member readily turned to CPS. "This is the tool that we have," she explained.

Have to do what?

In some ways, have to impact the safety of the kids in an immediate way. . . . I do help moms get counseling for their kids often, and obviously get a lot of supports for themselves, but I don't ever go to homes. All my work is office-based. I don't get to see what's happening. I only know what they're reporting, and often, that's not the whole story. I used to do a lot of in-home work, so I know that being in the home, you see a lot of different things, and you can really assess the situation more fully. That's where I think CPS has some leverage, is being able to go to the home and see, okay, here's the difficult relationship between the parents. That's one thing to work on, but also you have an infestation. Let's get you pest control services. Let's make sure you have somewhere safe. Make sure your kids both have beds. Those sorts of things that don't always come out here sometimes might be a place for CPS to intervene.

As she pointed out, CPS did home visits, an activity beyond the scope of her job. She recognized that beyond the specific incident bringing women to her office, things like infestations also affect family well-being. In her view, CPS could support families in ways she, without this fuller understanding of family situations, could not.

Alongside boundaries in their professional roles, reporting professionals' limited resources also made CPS an appealing option—recall Marla passing Jennifer off to CPS to follow up on mental health treatment for Jennifer's daughter. A longtime state trooper in the Northeast Corner, Thomas, clocked out to talk with me in his patrol car, the dispatch radio frequently puncturing our conversation. He described the area he covered: "There's no money up here. . . . For the most part, people are living check to check, if that." After years on the night shift, he said, "My idea of success is seeing kids play on a playground without needles, without drunks flopping down" or big fights. But, he pointed out, the region had limited social service availability. With only six beds in the psychiatric unit of the local hospital, troopers had to figure out how to respond to people facing mental health crises, all while dealing with neighbor complaints, working with people with special needs, and performing other tasks. As Thomas reflected, "I had a mother ask me if I was trained to deal with children with a specific type of autism. No, I'm not. . . . It's frustrating, because they want more and more from us, and there's less and less of us." He recalled the most recent case he had reported. Neighbors called the police about a father yelling, throwing things, and slapping his wife—"a fight for resources,

because he's an alcoholic." Thomas said that the young children were screaming, trying to get their father to stop, and he arrived to find the mother bruised.
Regardless of departmental reporting guidelines, Thomas felt strongly about
calling CPS. He explained that, serving on a local review board, "I see the aftermath on these kids. . . . I want to be able to give them the services that they
need, so . . . the next generation of cops or troopers will not have to arrest little
Mikey because all he's seen is Dad abuse Mom."

Thomas felt that someone needed to talk with the parents and connect
them with counseling. He explained how he saw the division of labor:

> [CPS has] the ability to focus on just this portion of the whole thing. If they
> can focus on this, I can focus on that. I can't focus on the needs of the
> children and be able to have resources dedicated to here. Like I said, we
> don't have enough resources here. We have to mix and match and patch-
> work everything. . . . If they can focus on that part, that's great, 'cause I don't
> have—and I know it's gonna come out wrong—I don't have the time.

Thomas shifted tasks related to children's needs to CPS so that he could attend
to the many other requirements of his job.

Similarly, a middle school teacher recalled a recent situation where staff
suspected substance use after seeing a parent acting erratically in the school
pickup line. She felt that this was a clear CPS report, legal mandate aside: "I
would want [CPS] to establish with the adult that you don't operate a moving
vehicle in an altered state of mind . . . [and] that they cannot be the care provider for their child when they're in an altered state of mind." When I asked
whether the school could impart this to the parent, the teacher replied that
this was beyond their capacity:

> I don't know how you could give the school one more responsibility. I don't
> know where you would squeeze it in. The whole child comes to school, and
> we have to service the whole child. We don't have anything to say about the
> kids when the bell rings at 2:44 and they leave. There's a lot of hours after
> 2:44. We already have workshops on Internet safety. We have workshops
> on, 'You're a new middle school student, here's what you have to deal
> with.' . . . Now we're gonna give substance abuse lessons? I don't know
> where you can fit that in.

This teacher worked at a school in a relatively affluent, predominantly White
community. Even still, she felt that school staff had enough to manage already
and could not take this on. To compensate for their bounded roles and limited

resources, she and other reporting professionals turned to CPS to address their concerns about children and families.

Examples cutting against this general trend show how reporting professionals' own limitations construct CPS as the safe and desirable option. A clinician working with families in an intensive in-home parenting support program said that she did not rush to pick up the phone and report: "You want to make sure it's necessary." Whereas others might report physical discipline, she said, "that's the work. . . . This is the opportunity. That's why I'm involved . . . [to] help [the mother] become aware of this stuff and help her grow." A clinician in a different intensive in-home program focused on children's behavioral needs also saw reporting as "a last resort." Because she regularly visited families at home, she could respond quickly herself if a situation escalated. And, she pointed out, CPS would usually "just put in place or confirm everything that we're already doing." These clinicians were in the home multiple times each week meeting with parents and seeing children; they worked with families already participating in highly intensive services. In instances where CPS does not offer much more than reporting professionals do, professionals see little need to involve the agency except in instances of severe harm. But this is the exception. In most cases, reporting professionals feel limited in what they can do to assist families and assess children's safety, so they summon CPS to respond to family adversity.

Better Safe than Sorry

CPS's broad reach also stems from social and policy structures that encourage widespread reporting. Systems are organized around eliminating "false negatives" (unreported maltreatment) rather than "false positives" (reported nonmaltreatment). Reporting professionals, attuned to the potential dangers of not reporting, framed calling CPS as the safe and harmless option.[16] "It's better to err on the cautious side. I don't want to take any chances," said a marriage and family therapist. "Usually it's, you see something, you say something. . . . You don't want to be timid about it," echoed a firefighter and EMT. Professionals encountering families in short-term, crisis-driven contacts, such as police officers and emergency room staff, saw reporting as a particularly easy decision with few or no drawbacks. When I asked a hospital social worker whether she saw any downsides to reporting, for example, she replied: "No. It doesn't scare me to call. Sometimes we have to be the voice of a child who doesn't have one. I would feel horrible if a child gets hurt and I could've called." Even as such events are nearly impossible to predict without the benefit of hind-sight, the specter of the tragedy that could have been averted had someone sounded the alarm looms large.

Reporting professionals often felt that they had insufficient information about the situations they reported. With so much unknown, they turned to CPS to assess. For example, a domestic violence victim advocate described her approach:

> Even though this time the child was in his bed sleeping, but in reality, how do you know if he was sleeping? Maybe he was under his bed scared because he heard Mom and Dad fighting, or okay, he really was sleeping this time, but two weeks ago he watched Dad throw Mom against the wall. You just don't know, and I'd rather be cautious and make that good faith report . . . than find out that I didn't make it and something happened.

This advocate recognized that there was much she did not know about family dynamics, so rather than responding to the specific situation confronting her, she imagined the worst-case scenario and acted accordingly. (Cate, too, said she told Jazmine that hearing her smack Gabriel "makes me concerned what you're doing when I'm not around.") Reporting professionals invoked CPS not only in situations of perceived harm but also in situations of uncertainty about harm.

CPS specifically encourages this inclination to report when plagued by unknowns and "what if" questions. One August morning, I went to a local child-care center with Annie, a White CPS trainer. We crowded around a small table, sitting on brightly colored, toddler-sized plastic chairs as Annie informed the staff about their responsibility as mandated reporters. She had just started her PowerPoint slides when a young woman tentatively interjected to ask about cases "kinda on the line." She mentioned that she was a mom herself, "so if anyone ever called CPS on me for doing something. . . ." She trailed off, clarify-ing, "I take really good care of my kids." The group laughed. She wondered whether CPS would go in and take the children even if the parents were "good parents" who just needed help.

Annie validated her question, acknowledging that people often worry about whether calling CPS will make things worse rather than better. She told the group that they could fall back on two things when they had doubts about reporting. First, she said, they might ask themselves, if they did not report and something bad happened, "How's that helping that child and how's that gonna feel for me?" Second, she said, mandated reporters are not the investigators;

they do not need all the answers about what happened or what constitutes maltreatment. In bold, italicized, and underlined, the training slide emphasized: "CERTAINTY OR PROBABLE CAUSE IS NOT REQUIRED" to report. Annie explained to the group that the hotline will not accept reports that do not meet statutory definitions of abuse or neglect. "And that's it. Nothing bad happens." She assured the group that "no harm is going to come" from erring on the side of caution by calling—except that they might have to wait on hold for a while. Mandated reporter trainings and guides around the country likewise advise reporting at the slightest suspicion of maltreatment.[17]

In interviews, reporting professionals echoed this notion of reporting in all instances to let CPS decide. Consistent with her training, Cate did not check Gabriel for bruises or weigh the "reasonableness" of Jazmine's discipline, key indicators for determining physical abuse in Connecticut, before calling CPS. As a police officer noted, "If you think about CPS, then just call them . . . [to] be on the safe side and then let them rule it out." A home care nurse said, "I've always called, and they can always say no. . . . I just feel like it's safer that way." In this view, even an inkling of suspicion about possible maltreatment, a nagging feeling or question, is enough to report.

Even putting reporting professionals' personal proclivities aside, every guardrail is erected in one direction. In an informal conversation, the social work director at a local hospital explained that they took reporting seriously, which is why CPS received so many reports from them. The director explained that social workers must call the hotline even if they disagree with the medical staff's decision to report; they cannot override the team of doctors and nurses. At the same time, social workers *can* override the team if they feel that a CPS report is needed. Thus, any staff member's concerns about maltreatment trigger a report, but objections to reporting cannot stop a report. Taking reporting seriously means supporting any inclinations to report the staff might have.

Organizational hierarchies operate in much the same way. Frontline professionals described bringing cases they were unsure merited CPS reports to their supervisors, who, in turn, directed them to report. As a therapist explained: "Oftentimes, I'll go in to my supervisor. . . . There are times where I'm iffy. I'm like, 'I don't know. It could go either way.' She always just tells me, 'Just report to be safe. Don't not report, because we'd rather overreport than underreport. It won't hurt anyone if you report.'" Patrol officers said that supervisors, reviewing their police reports, sometimes instructed them to go back and file a CPS report. One officer recalled a recent incident where, he said, they could "prove" that the woman had falsely reported domestic violence, yet he was told to call CPS. "The kid was not harmed. The kid wasn't even present. . . . But I don't get to argue with the supervisor."

Meanwhile, with less firsthand knowledge of the situation, supervisors may find it difficult to discourage reporting. And, by law, they cannot prevent a CPS report from being made.[18] A middle school principal who frequently consulted with her staff about reporting said:

> One of my jokes with the teachers are that, "If ever I tell you that you can't make a report, that's when you need to hit me across the head with a two-by-four and tell me I need to retire," because I will never, ever tell a staff member that they shouldn't make a report.

Even if she disagreed about the need to report, she said she would still encourage her staff to call, "for me to be able to sleep at night," adding, "I'm not gonna risk my certification and my livelihood by telling someone they can't call."

As this principal's comments suggest, even as reporting professionals identified motivations for reporting beyond mandates when discussing specific cases, some also acknowledged licensure or legal liability concerns. A labor and delivery social worker said, "I don't ever want my name in the *New Haven Register* . . . that some child had an injury or died because I overlooked something, so [reporting is] what clears my mind of feeling that." These responsibilities, too, only go one way. Mandated reporters are immune from prosecution for reports they make in good faith—they face no professional or legal consequences for erroneous reports—but can be prosecuted for failing to report.[19] Connecticut's mandated reporter training makes this clear, also highlighting statutes that outlaw interference with reports and retaliation against employees who report.

Mandated reporters are rarely arrested for failing to report, but when this happens, typically following an egregious case, it can draw substantial public attention. Toward the end of my fieldwork, school administrators in Montville, a small town in southeastern Connecticut, were arrested when they did not report a substitute teacher who egged students on in a classroom "fight club."[20] The charges were ultimately dropped, but this story and a couple other high-profile "failure to report" cases made headlines across the state that fall, with administrators' names and pictures published in the local news. Reporting professionals I spoke with after the news broke often referenced the story. "Lately, because of some of the circumstances that happened at Montville . . . we err more on the side of caution now," said a patrol supervisor at a police department. Hotline reports rose precipitously in the months following the arrests.[21]

Failure to report can prompt follow-up from CPS even if there are no legal charges. In one case I studied, an elementary school student at an after-school program casually mentioned her mother swatting her with a hairbrush that morning. When the school principal learned of this comment a month later, she notified CPS, which investigated and promptly closed the case but flagged it as a possible instance of failure to report. A CPS manager told me that she had discussed several such cases with an agency attorney in the past month. They were not trying to prosecute, she said. Still, they typically contacted the people responsible for reporting to remind them of their responsibility and recommend additional training.

Thus, legal and policy guidance points in the same direction as reporting professionals' moral inclinations: when in doubt, report. When CPS and reporting organizations construct "erring on the safe side" to mean reporting without hesitation in situations of uncertainty, it's no wonder that individual frontline bureaucrats are quick to pick up the phone, expanding CPS's reach. And yet, as the next section will discuss, this isn't necessarily the case all around.

Unequal Reporting

Arguably the foremost feature of CPS is its stark disproportionality. It is a system that routinely intervenes with Black, Native American, and poor families, yet has virtually no contact with affluent White families. "Spend a day at dependency court in any major city and you will see the unmistakable color of the child welfare system," writes Dorothy Roberts.[22] Many low-income White families are swept up as well. Notably, families' vastly divergent exposure to CPS begins well before cases arrive in court; the bulk of inequality emerges at the point of reporting. In federal fiscal year 2014, Black children experienced CPS reports at a rate nearly twice that of White children. That year, Black children made up 14.8 percent of the U.S. child population but a substantially larger share of children subject to CPS reports (21.4 percent), nearly as high as their representation among children in foster care (24 percent).[23] Native American children and native-born Latinx children, too, disproportionately encounter CPS.[24]

As detailed at the start of this chapter, CPS reports typically involve manifestations of poverty and adversity—conditions especially prevalent among families marginalized by race/ethnicity and/or socioeconomic status. In addition to differentially exposing families to adversity, racism, classism, sexism, and their intersections also affect which families come to CPS's attention. This does not necessitate individual reporters motivated by animus—reporting Black families because they dislike Black people, for instance. Rather, as reporting is highly discretionary, it's no surprise that it reflects the racism present more broadly in society. Racism and other dimensions of oppression shape how reporting professionals interpret what they see and structure organizational resources and routines in ways that channel marginalized families in particular to CPS.

Jennifer recalled her experience with medical and mental health providers in the aftermath of Faith's suicide attempt. She only saw White professionals, except for a single Asian doctor. "I don't think there was another minority around." As a Puerto Rican mother earning over $60,000 annually, Jennifer felt that the White medical and mental health staff judged her based on stereotypes. "Caucasian people have systematically always pointed fingers," she reflected. "I think that they put minorities in a box and they treat them all the same." Jennifer's adult daughter put it bluntly, describing the "White savior complex" of the mental health care organization that called CPS: "White people are gonna swoop in and fix the poor minority folks because they need the help, 'cause they haven't figured it out themselves."

Jennifer's experience is not anomalous. Racist treatment of people of color in health care, education, law enforcement, and other systems that frequently report to CPS is well documented.[25] Lizette, a Latina mother living in a predominantly White area, said that she often saw other children playing outside in her apartment complex without parental supervision—the same thing that prompted her CPS report after a neighbor called the police. "I almost question: Is it a race thing?" Lizette wondered. "If I called the police on them, would they have the same experience as I? . . . I question, was it a thing of a young minority parent, is she capable, versus if it was a White family."

This kind of biased decision-making is difficult to prove.[26] When I raised the topic of racial inequality with reporting professionals, they identified it as a problem but stopped short of acknowledging their own contributions. For example, a hospital social worker, Emma, said that racially disproportionate reporting was a frequent topic of discussion, one she was particularly attuned to as a Hispanic woman. She emphasized the need to make "blind" decisions, saying that it "shouldn't matter" if a mother is rich and from a wealthy area.[27] Emma suggested that private pediatricians might drive disproportionality more, as she saw them hesitating to call CPS on White families that her team, "seeing it with neutral eyes," decided to report.

Could Emma and her team truly have "neutral eyes"? Local CPS staff themselves identified the hospital where Emma worked as racist and subjective in its reporting decisions. They saw this hospital declining to report White families for issues routinely called in for Black families. Given the system's stark racial disproportionality, Connecticut's training encourages mandated reporters to consider how their biases may drive racially disparate reports. Nevertheless, CPS cautions reporters not to dismiss their lingering suspicions or "gut feelings." Annie, in the mandated reporter training, told the childcare center staff to pay attention to "that little inkling you get" that something is not quite right: "Just trust your professional instinct on this stuff."

But the instincts of reporting professionals—often viewing families through middle-class, White lenses—likely raise suspicions about some families more than others. Meredith, the White director of a childcare center in a predominantly White town, explained how she thought about borderline cases:

> I think you always have red flags with families to begin with. Families walk through the door, you get to know them pretty quickly. . . . It's just like you or I, when we pick friends, we're like, "I really like her, but I'm not really sure about her." I think you have those red flags that automatically fit with that pit in your stomach. I think that would help you make a phone call quicker if you already had that red flag.
>
> . . . *What are the types of things—those cues, those signals—that put your antenna up a little bit more?*
>
> Not to stereotype, but your quick, first red flag would be a lower-income family. Where they live has a lot to do with it too—how the children come in. Everybody uses reusable clothes or hand-me-downs or recycled clothes, things like that. But if they've been recycled four or five times and now the child's wearing them, if they look a little different or maybe they're too large or not large enough, so you have those that send that pit in your stomach.

Like everyone, reporting professionals develop snap judgments about people based on race, ethnicity, class, and other characteristics; any notion of "neutral eyes" is impossible. A recent study of teachers, for instance, finds that they hold pro-White and anti-Black racial biases at similar levels to nonteachers.[28] Professionals are middle class and predominantly White—in majority Black and Latinx New Haven, nearly three-quarters of public school educators are White—so they likely identify with middle-class White parents.[29] These parents are the kinds of people professionals might be friends with, which means that they may get the benefit of the doubt. A reading specialist at a predominantly White elementary school recalled checking in with the school nurse after she saw marks on a child's arm. "The nurse is very close with the family, knows he has a lot of brothers and they roughhouse and stuff. She's like, 'No, I know this family. He's okay.'"

Meanwhile, signs of material hardship, such as worn and ill-fitting clothing, create a sense of unease about parenting. This bias—that parenting in poverty is poor parenting—is not unique to Meredith or even to reporting professionals. But reporting professionals' classist and racist judgments are consequential because they prime professionals to funnel marginalized families to CPS as a means of "rehabilitation" while giving their more privileged counterparts a pass.

Reporting professionals rarely acknowledged the role of race/ethnicity or socioeconomic status in their thinking as directly as Meredith. But racism (and classism) manifests in individual decision-making and interpersonal interactions well beyond treating otherwise similar families differently based on race (or class). As Dorothy Roberts argues, we do not need proof of prejudice among CPS decision makers such as reporting professionals to conclude that racism drives disparities in CPS reports.[30]

Intersections of race, ethnicity, class, gender, nativity, disability status, language, and more infuse what we understand as "appropriate" parenting. Jazmine, for instance, recognized racial overtones to her CPS report, suggesting that it was no surprise that Cate, a White woman, was exercising power over her, a Black and Puerto Rican woman, by calling CPS. Jazmine reflected, "I'm a struggling mom, and then I have this White privileged woman . . . thinking that me smacking my child for hitting her is a bad thing." Cate, in her interview, drew on her own upbringing in describing her perspective on physical discipline:

> She is allowed to reprimand her child, but she could do it in a different way instead of physical. I grew up never being physically reprimanded, so it is possible. I know culturally she grew up probably—but she has to also think, she also never lived with her mother. That might be a good example of, "Hey, yeah, you might've been reprimanded by your mother, but you also didn't grow up with her because your mom lost custody of you."

Child-rearing norms are not universal but, rather, vary across cultural contexts; endorsement of spanking varies by race and class.[31] Gabriel had started to fight and hit more, and Jazmine wanted to make sure that these behaviors did not continue, especially around authority figures. "Don't put your hands on her—that's what I was trying to get across," Jazmine said. Jazmine's perspective echoes research finding that Black parents use physical discipline to protect children and teach them how to survive in a racist society.[32] Cate, meanwhile, saw Jazmine's behavior as potential abuse. And because Jazmine was removed from her mother's care as a child, Cate felt justified that her approach was the right one.

Like Cate, when explaining situations they reported, professionals used their own (middle-class) perspectives and experiences to extrapolate what other parents could and should reasonably do for children. In one case, an elementary school assistant principal, Amaryllis, alerted CPS after a mother named Graciela did not respond to the school's calls to pick up her daughter with strep throat. Amaryllis felt that this was neglectful, as the child was miserable. "I think differently, I guess, as a parent . . . I would leave and come get my kid." With a laugh, she acknowledged, "I understand you're working. I work too."

But Amaryllis had the job flexibility and security to drop everything to pick up a sick child. Graciela was in the middle of her shift at Wendy's when the school called. Although Graciela initially answered the call, she could not be on her phone at work, so she hung up and had to wait until her break to return the call. By that time, CPS had already been notified.

Amaryllis understood that it was a "catch-22" with Graciela's job but felt that Graciela needed to put her children first. (As Amaryllis told it, when Graciela initially picked up the phone at work, she said that she would not be coming to pick up her daughter.) Amaryllis and her staff had never met Graciela. Graciela had not attended parent conferences, which Amaryllis attributed to Graciela's ethnic background: "I think it's a cultural thing. I believe they're Dominican." Both were Latina women who spoke fluent Spanish; Amaryllis focused on their differences, making judgments based on Graciela's nationality and immigrant status. Amaryllis surmised that Graciela likely had limited education and therefore might not understand things like strep throat and involvement with the school.

> She's just focusing on working and she's not really involved with the educational aspect because, I guess, she feels they just go to school . . . then they come home, and then she deals with them. . . . I don't think she understands the severity of the situation. To be honest, I don't know how the school system is in the Dominican Republic. Probably not very good. I'm not sure what their health regulations are.

Even imagining this broader context, Amaryllis called CPS. She was emphatic that Graciela did not intend to neglect her daughter, but Amaryllis inferred from Graciela's identity as a Dominican immigrant that Graciela did not know how to respond appropriately to the school's requests. Amaryllis wanted to involve CPS to teach Graciela a lesson, to discipline her: "She needs to understand that if we call you and we're telling you something, you need to do it."

As discussed earlier, reporting professionals like Amaryllis often saw CPS as a tool to educate wayward parents. Ideas about parents needing correction are highly racialized and classed, resting on erroneous perceptions of marginalized identities as linked to ignorance. A White police officer whose district covered a predominantly Black and Latinx neighborhood articulated this connection:

> The area especially that we live in—that we work in, rather, that all these other people live in—it's obviously, you can see the area is a lot poorer, less sophisticated. People think *ignorant* is a bad word, but it's actually a very accurate word. It doesn't mean that you're stupid. It just means you don't know any better, and you weren't taught, for whatever reason. You grew up in a home, or it's systemic, and it's just, "Well, this is the way we were raised. This is the way we were raised." Obviously it falls under a whole socioeconomic umbrella. Some people just have no business being parents, or they're young and they can't even take care of themselves. Now they're in charge of another kid, and they're kids themselves. The thought process doesn't compute that, "No, this isn't okay to do this." Sometimes I call just for the simple fact that I'd really like CPS to maybe step in and say, "Hey, you need to go to a class or something on basic parenting," anything, like, "Maybe you need counseling."

This officer began by acknowledging a clear boundary between himself and those he polices. He works there; they live there. Drawing on tropes of a self-fulfilling "culture of poverty," he portrayed neighborhood residents as lacking sophistication and parenting skills. This framing suggests paternalistic goals of enlightenment as a response to racial and socioeconomic inequity. Serving a poor Black and Latinx neighborhood, in this view, means identifying parents' deficits and calling on CPS to teach them how to behave.

Persistent stereotypes of Black mothers in particular make it easy to assume the worst from their everyday parenting travails and to attribute the adversity their children face to abuse or neglect, overlooking the hardships of racism, sexism, and, oftentimes, poverty. As Patricia Hill Collins argues, powerful "controlling images" such as the "'bad' Black mother" cast Black mothers as unfit, shirking their responsibilities to their children and failing to adhere to traditional motherhood ideals.[33] This insidious imagery makes certain presumptions about Black mothers especially accessible.

For instance, one case involved a two-year-old who got out of the house and ended up on a street with heavy traffic. Makayla, the child's mother, had arranged for her stepfather to babysit while she ran errands. When the stepfather fell asleep, the toddler got out. The responding officer, Justine—like Makayla, a Black woman—recognized that many of her colleagues had different backgrounds from those they policed. "Not a lot of people are from here," she said. Still, with only a single, brief interaction to draw on, Justine invoked widely available racialized, gendered, and classed tropes as she evaluated Makayla's parenting. To Justine, the incident defied expectations of total maternal responsibility and aligned with the controlling image of the "neglectful" Black mother: "[The stepfather] worked a double, and it wasn't really his responsibility to watch the kid. It was hers. And she does this a lot. She just leaves the kid and acts like her parents are her free day care." Justine saw Makayla's use of family networks as an automatic CPS call, alleging neglect by Makayla: "I think the mom was irresponsible, and then she spilled over her responsibilities onto somebody else and then they became responsible. . . . I do think that the mother was very young and very immature and that she should have some accountability." Justine said that she wanted "help" for Makayla. By help, she meant discipline from an authority figure: "She needs to hear it from somebody who's not on either side that she's not doing a good job."

These perceptions on the part of individual reporting professionals play an important role in CPS reporting. But teachers, police officers, and others do not work alone. They work at schools, police departments, and other "street-level bureaucracies" whose clientele, policies, practices, and resources shape which families are reported to CPS. Even if teachers treated all children within a school equally, different approaches *across* schools produce disproportionality in a context of segregation. Reporting thus has an organizational dimension that subjects families unequally to CPS.

Most directly, families are differentially exposed to people who might call CPS. Unlike their affluent counterparts, many poor families have visiting nurses or caseworkers coming through and observing home conditions and family life. For families living in apartment buildings, neighbors may overhear altercations and call the police, whereas spacious homes and yards afford other families more privacy. Parenting on the bus or the street is on display in ways it is not in private cars. Pervasive policing in poor communities of color puts residents in frequent contact with a main conduit to CPS. Sociologist Frank Edwards links police intervention with CPS reporting, finding that in counties where police make more arrests, they also file more CPS reports, even after accounting for characteristics such as the county's child poverty rate and racial composition. Edwards concludes that "the social and spatial organization of policing plays a central role in selecting children and families for scrutiny by child protection agencies."[34]

Moreover, even for entities such as schools and hospitals that all families encounter, practices differ across reporting organizations. Mandated reporters are subject to the same legal requirements, but organizations interpret these mandates in different ways. Some have strict, formal policies about reporting in certain situations, while others leave it to individual discretion.[35] Only some hospitals conduct drug tests of all new mothers or require families to meet with hospital social workers before newborns can be discharged. Only some school districts automatically file CPS reports after a certain number of absences. Only some police departments require officers to call CPS when they respond to a domestic violence incident with children present. CPS reporting is routine and top-of-mind as a response in some organizations but not others.

CPS staff recognized that some families are more likely than others to come to CPS's attention by virtue of which organizations serve them. And this variation is not random, meaning that unequal reporting does not require discrimination by individual reporting professionals. For example, Joe, a White investigator, felt that New Haven police did not necessarily treat White families differently, recalling a CPS report when the young child of two White emergency room doctors got out of the house in the middle of the night. Meanwhile, he said, "I have a buddy, White as can be, living in North Haven. The same thing happened. That wasn't even discussed. It seems to be more of a cultural thing with the police department itself."

It is no coincidence that the multiethnic, higher-poverty city of New Haven reported families in this situation to CPS while its adjacent suburb did not. In North Haven, 84 percent of residents are non-Hispanic White, and the median household income is well over twice that of New Haven. Residential segregation separates public services such as schools and police districts as well. For instance, 83 percent of New Haven public school students are Black and/or Hispanic, and only 12 percent are White. Next door, in North Haven, three-quarters of students are White, with Black and Hispanic students combining to make up just 15 percent of the student body.[36] Private providers of services such as mental health care, too, serve families with financial resources, while public providers work primarily with lower-income families.

This segregation makes organizational reporting practices effective engines of inequality. Systemic racism and classism means that organizations serving marginalized families tend to take a different approach than those serving privileged families. These distinctions are rooted in the same stereotypes discussed earlier. For example, anthropologist and legal scholar Khiara Bridges argues that we subject pregnant people receiving Medicaid, but not those privately insured, to a battery of personal questions because we attribute poverty to moral failings.[37] Regarding CPS reporting, organizations construct CPS as a natural and appropriate response for poor families and families of color based on stereotypes that they need monitoring and threats of punishment to ensure they are doing right by their children.[38]

Organizations frequented by affluent, White families, meanwhile, more readily turn to alternatives. Contrast Amaryllis, the elementary school assistant principal, with Meredith, the childcare center director. The student body at Amaryllis's school was over 80 percent Hispanic and under 5 percent White, with three-quarters of students eligible for free and reduced-price lunch; Meredith's center, meanwhile, served many children of faculty and graduate students at a local university. Whereas Amaryllis readily notified CPS when Graciela did not respond immediately to her call, Meredith talked about the lengths to which she would go before deciding that an incident rose to the level of calling CPS. Recently, for instance, a child had arrived with a lunch bag and coat smelling of marijuana. Meredith did not want to accuse the parents of smoking around the child, as the child could have been at a relative's house or just their things could have been exposed to marijuana. She said that if it became a recurring issue, she would talk with the parents about local substance use resources available. Meredith said that she might ultimately have to bring up CPS but would give parents a chance to resolve it first: "With me, letting families know ahead of time, 'Look, this is a reportable incident. Let's find a way to solve this issue,' helps a lot." Believing that the parents she worked with could adjust their behavior without involving a coercive entity, Meredith marshaled multiple alternative responses before activating CPS.

Invoking these kinds of alternatives to CPS reporting is more feasible for some organizations than others. Beyond systemic stereotypes, institutional racism and classism affect CPS reporting through inequitable resource distribution as well. As sociologist Victor Ray explains, organizations like those reporting to CPS "consolidate resources along racial lines." Given underinvestment in communities of color and poor communities, CPS becomes an enticing resource for organizations serving these families, especially when "combined with diffuse cultural schemas" such as anti-Blackness.[39] With school funding tethered to local property taxes, for example, schools serving affluent, White areas have the resources to address issues that might prompt CPS reports elsewhere—by following up with parents or making referrals to social services, for instance. Or recall Marla, juggling intakes with a full caseload at a major provider of mental health services for low-income families of color. A private therapist might have had time to follow up with Jennifer to ensure that Faith received recommended services. Organizations in marginalized communities, often acutely underresourced, may find handing families off to CPS an especially appealing option.

Reports from Personal Contacts

At least one in six CPS reports originates from a personal tie, such as a friend, relative, acquaintance, or neighbor. Here, too, CPS is a useful resource for these contacts to call upon, not just a self-evident response to parental behavior. The social contexts of people calling CPS in a personal capacity—their interpersonal conflicts or their own needs—cast alerting CPS as a reasonable response.

In contexts where CPS is omnipresent and thus front-of-mind as a weapon to wield in interpersonal conflicts, family adversity can become recast as reportable maltreatment when social relations rupture. The mothers I met widely acknowledged this phenomenon of people calling CPS as a means of revenge or out of spite. In interviews, they recounted numerous examples of reports they understood as vindictive. CPS staff, too, recognized spiteful calling as a widespread practice. Social ties might call CPS not upon learning new information about children's conditions but when relationships turned sour. Tatiana, a Black mother in New Haven, was reported by her boyfriend shortly after they broke up. "He called because he was mad, not at the fact 'cause I needed them," Tatiana said. CPS's assessment, too, concluded that Tatiana's boyfriend was emotional about not seeing his son: "Father reported that he made this report because he was mad at mother." Several mothers acknowledged calling CPS themselves when upset with another parent. Helen, a White mother in Providence, recalled reporting a friend who pawned her sons' PlayStations to buy drugs. When asked whether something in particular had happened before her call, Helen replied:

Well, she kicked me out of her house. . . . It was all over shampoo. She told me to go stay in the shelter. . . . She used my shampoo. And she woulda had a fit if I'd used the rest of her shampoo. So I had said something, and she threw the empty bottle at me. And when I was leaving the house, she was leaving the house with the [PlayStations]. So I was like, "Oh, all right." So I told [my husband], I said, "We're calling." He's like, "You shouldn't do that." I said, "Yeah, I shouldn't, but . . . she's sending me to a freaking shelter and I'm pregnant."

As Helen's example indicates, the fractured relationships precipitating reports were often borne of economic desperation. Arguments centered on issues such as stealing money, failing to repay borrowed money, using another's benefits card, and jeopardizing another's housing. With the agency highly salient in these mothers' social worlds, as described in chapter 1, CPS reporting became a readily available tool for those seeking to enact revenge or lodge grievances in contexts of scarcity.

Needs within parents' social networks also channel families to CPS. Relatives may require financial support for caregiving, prompting a CPS report. For example, Joyce, a Latina mother in New Haven, left her children in the care of their father. The father, seeking to transfer the children's benefits—from SNAP and the Special Supplemental Nutrition Program for Women, Infants, and Children (WIC)—to his name so that he could purchase food, called CPS. Bethany said that she twice arranged for her children to stay informally with her mother-in-law: once when she went to a detoxification program and again when she spent seventy-five days in jail. Both times, Bethany said, her mother-in-law called CPS so that she could receive state benefits to care for the children. A more well-off family would not need these benefits. But poor families find themselves caught: accessing state assistance requires formalizing informal care arrangements, often by summoning the child welfare system.[40] And for those without the means to hire private attorneys, CPS can be a resource to secure child custody as well.

At times, mothers themselves reached out to CPS, reflecting their own strategizing in contexts of adversity. A few recalled times when they desperately needed help. Years before I met her in Providence, Colleen was homeless with her boyfriend: "We had nowhere to go. Like, nowhere. And I was using drugs, and he was too." As CPS records affirmed, they called the CPS hotline to put their one-year-old and two-year-old into a voluntary foster placement. "I just didn't know what else to do. I had no family support. No one in my family was helping me. I was on the street . . . all cracked out." Mothers like Colleen called CPS as a last resort.

Others described inviting CPS into their lives as a strategy to protect themselves against more intensive child welfare system involvement. I spoke with Vanessa, a Puerto Rican mother in Providence, throughout her first pregnancy. Due to her marijuana use, she anxiously anticipated a report when the baby was born. Vanessa proactively notified CPS as her due date approached, worried that the baby would be taken. According to CPS's summary, Vanessa told the hotline that she wanted "to be honest and work with CPS versus anybody thinking she was not being cooperative or looking for help." Indeed, CPS looked favorably on Vanessa's decision. In its assessment, CPS listed Vanessa "call[ing the] hotline herself looking for services" as a "family strength." CPS referred Vanessa to voluntary services and closed her case. Colleen, Vanessa, and other mothers in similar situations came to CPS's attention not because they identified their actions as maltreatment but in a social context that framed reporting as the option that would best meet their needs.

CPS investigates millions of families—disproportionately poor families, Black families, and Native American families—each year, raising the question of how these families come into contact with this system in the first place. The simple answer is that people suspect maltreatment. But what does this actually entail? Digging deeper, a specific person connected with a family must identify CPS as the option they want to turn to in a given circumstance. In this way, CPS reports are socially produced.

The pathway from adverse family conditions to CPS is anything but automatic. (Indeed, upon investigating, CPS doesn't typically find evidence of maltreatment, consistent with reporting professionals' belief that the children they report are usually not in grave danger.) Those filing reports—usually professionals encountering families, but sometimes families' personal ties— do not evaluate parents' behaviors in a vacuum. Rather, they consider their options in a specific social context.[41] In some contexts, people opt not to call CPS to address parents' adversity or noncompliance. Such environments may be the norm for affluent White families; frontline professionals may implicitly trust them to care for their children without CPS intervention or may have more resources to respond without involving CPS. In other contexts, meanwhile, professionals see CPS as a way to get help, especially the kind of help— involving discipline and oversight—they believe marginalized families need. With the limited social safety net leaving them few alternatives, professionals turn to CPS as a preferable or at least acceptable response to marginalized families' situations. In a bind, they want to do *something*. If they can make allegations meeting state definitions of maltreatment, placing the call means that a social worker will go out and visit the family. A board member of the School Social Work Association of America and former director of student services in Broward County, Florida, the country's sixth-largest school district, explained to a journalist why teachers might call CPS about dirty children: "We do that so the child can get the attention and some intervention can happen. Whether it's abuse or neglect or poverty, it is still a child in need."[42]

Of course, whether the state response is looking for abuse or neglect or poverty affects everything about what happens next. CPS reports of marginalized families proliferate because people see adversity—children in need—and pin their hopes on CPS as a readily accessible response. In so doing, they essentially construct maltreatment, passing off family adversity to an agency organized around parental (especially maternal) inadequacy. As the following chapters demonstrate, calling CPS sets in motion a particular state response, one that produces a precarious motherhood for marginalized mothers. After all, CPS doesn't just send out any social worker but, rather, one tasked with assessing parents and empowered to separate families.

3

Fear and Surveillance
in the Investigation

ASHLEY KOVALSKY AND HER HUSBAND, high school sweethearts, had recently purchased their first home, a two-story house on a windy, narrow road abutting a forested area in the Northeast Corner. Ashley, a White woman with long, blonde hair, had adorned her new home with framed photos and decorative pillows bearing messages about family and love; her seven-year-old son's room had a *Cars* theme. The couple's relationship had been tumultuous lately, strained by stressors such as the trauma of Ashley's husband's military service and their son, Caleb, acting out in school.

One day, after leaving her childcare job, Ashley picked Caleb up from school. She planned to stop and get groceries on the way home when she received a call: A CPS investigator was at her house. Could she head right home to meet with him? Ashley immediately phoned her mother. "Now that CPS is on the way to the house, they're gonna take him. What am I going to do?" she recalled asking, her heart racing. "Just like that, in the pit of your stomach, like, oh my gosh. He's my world."

A social worker at Caleb's school had called CPS after Caleb mentioned his father hitting him on the head recently; school staff also felt that Ashley and her husband weren't partnering with them to address Caleb's behavioral outbursts. Still, the school social worker didn't think that Caleb was in danger. Likewise, driving over, the White investigator, Vance, told me that he expected the case would be "a nothing burger," attributing the report to the school's struggles to manage Caleb's behavior. Indeed, Vance closed the case after conducting his investigation. He didn't see any safety concerns; Caleb told Vance that his father swatted him on the back of the head after Caleb kept throwing a bouncy ball, but it wasn't hard and it didn't hurt. Vance, upon wrapping up the case, called it "pretty straightforward."

Tracing the ramifications of deploying CPS to investigate families like Ashley's—facing challenges or viewed as challenging—this chapter and the next two show how precarious motherhood takes shape in the CPS investigation. In this chapter, we see how CPS reports trigger a terrifying investigative process that opens up families' intimate lives to state authorities. Reporting professionals like Caleb's school social worker generally didn't anticipate child removal, as described in chapter 2. CPS investigators, it turns out, felt similarly, expressing ambivalence about whether many of the reports they received needed a CPS response. Recall that most cases close after investigation with no confirmed findings of maltreatment.[1] But given CPS's immense power to separate families, mothers like Ashley were apprehensive, their custody of their children hanging in the balance. "You just kind of think of the worst outcome," Ashley later told me.

In line with practice guidelines, Vance visited Ashley's home three times, interviewing each parent and Caleb separately. As Caleb zipped around the house and eagerly showed Vance a sand volcano he'd made, Ashley tried to make sure Vance had all the information he needed to understand the situation. But Vance didn't only ask about what Caleb said at school. During his visits, Vance learned about the couple swearing at each other during loud arguments; he learned about Ashley's husband's mental health diagnoses and his marijuana use. Vance used the parents' birth dates to check their CPS and criminal history. He contacted Caleb's school and pediatrician to see whether they had concerns. And he logged all of this in a lengthy narrative report in the CPS database. The school's report thus subjected Ashley's family to substantial state surveillance.

This surveillance is extensive in two ways. It is wide-reaching, encompassing many families like Ashley's where CPS does not believe that children are in danger. It also delves deeply into intimate family life, gathering highly personal information across numerous domains and from multiple systems. Compared with the analogous stage in policing—stops or perhaps arrests—CPS investigations are much more informationally invasive.[2]

CPS's specific role and focus make this expansive surveillance possible. The agency's emphasis on child safety encourages far-reaching information-gathering, with staff trained to leave no stone unturned to protect against all possible (parental) threats, however remote. CPS's position at the intersection of care and control, too, justifies and enables its surveillance. Though typically conceptualized as a tool of punishment, surveillance can have multivalent goals and outcomes.[3] Espousing aims of assistance, CPS frames its inquiries as opportunities to assess family needs holistically so the agency can offer appropriate social services. Simultaneously, its ever-present coercive power induces parents' cooperation with CPS's requests, pressuring parents—even those not deemed threats to their children's safety—to disclose personal information. And there's a labor dimension to CPS's surveillance, carried out by street-level bureaucrats.[4] Concerned about liability should something tragic occur, managers and supervisors hold investigators accountable for collecting comprehensive information in every case. These high work expectations encourage investigators to cultivate parents' acquiescence to ease their workloads.

CPS's arrival marks a perilous moment for mothers, one where they must directly contend with the state's power to take their children. Invoking an entity organized around child maltreatment, fusing care and coercion, provides state authorities with extensive capacity to compile information about (predominantly) marginalized families, even when evidence of wrongdoing is scant. Mothers' intimate lives become subject to state scrutiny.

"An Immediate Hit in My Gut": When CPS Arrives

When Deborah McLean saw a strange car drive up her gravel driveway one February afternoon, she trudged outside in an oversized sweatshirt to see what the visitors wanted. Deborah assumed that they were census workers coming again to follow up.

"Can I help you?" Deborah bent down to peer in the passenger-side window.

"Are you Deborah? I'm Sarah Forrester, from CPS. We got a referral."

Deborah paused. "About what?" She would later recall that moment as "an immediate hit in my gut. . . . My brain just started racing and then froze at the same time."

Sarah, one of the office's most experienced investigators, thought for a moment about how best to put it. "About—what happened at the hospital." Deborah had just returned the day before from five days in the intensive care unit, following an accidental fentanyl overdose, according to the hospital. A social worker there was worried about Deborah's children, twelve-year-old Mia and nine-year-old Paul; with the suicide of their father the prior year, they'd been through a lot. "What I've always been taught is, when in doubt, just call," this social worker said. "There was just this knot in my stomach. . . . Just, something wasn't right, so I just reported it." She hoped that CPS could check in with the McLeans to ensure they had the support they needed.

Sarah asked Deborah if we could talk for a few minutes. We followed Deborah up to the house. "I would have preferred to have another day to relax," Deborah suggested as we walked up onto the wooden porch.

"Well—," Sarah started.

"I understand." Deborah cut in to say that she knew all about this, as she had been a foster parent for relatives. "I know how it goes." She led us past a large couch and armchairs to a wooden, picnic-style table. The open oven, along with the wood-burning stove, warmed the space. When Deborah felt a draft, she went to cover the back window with a comforter that hung from the wall.

Until Sarah's visit that day, CPS hadn't come knocking for Deborah, a forty-year-old White mother with bushy brown hair. A devoted yogi, Deborah described herself as "crunchy." Her modest home, up on a hill surrounded by woods, housed cats and iguanas along with Deborah and her children. She chalked up recent chest and stomach pain to the high stress she'd felt since her husband's suicide. But in the small town where she lived, Deborah found a strong support network; everyone seemed to know everyone else. She made do on her husband's death benefits, SNAP benefits, and odd jobs such as baby-sitting, while working on a teaching credential part-time.

CPS wasn't an unknown entity, though. When she was a young adult, her younger siblings were in and out of foster care amid her father's alcohol addiction. So Deborah, recalling her siblings' experiences—"forever in, back, forth, back, forth," being molested in placement—knew that the system didn't live up to its ideals of care and benevolence. "When you're raised in that mentality of, social workers come to cause trouble, not to help, that's a tough thing to shake," she later told me.

We spent the next couple hours at the kitchen table while Sarah did her assessment. Sarah asked what had brought Deborah to the hospital. Deborah shared that she was helping a friend clean up after the friend's boyfriend overdosed. Seeing a white powder on the dresser, Deborah touched it, curious, then sniffed and tasted it. She didn't remember anything else after that. Later, doctors informed her she'd had a heart attack. While Deborah was hospitalized, her children stayed nearby, with Deborah's mother.

During Sarah's visit, Deborah later said, she tried to project "calm on the outside," even as thoughts she knew were irrational occupied her mind. The experience upset her. When I asked what made it so upsetting, she didn't equivocate: "It's the fear. It's the fear."

Mothers rarely articulated this fear explicitly to investigators, but it came through in interviews time and time again. Understandably, mothers were terrified at the prospect of CPS taking their children. "They're my everything," Deborah said of Mia and Paul. CPS's power to separate families was front-of-mind for mothers as they imagined this worst-case scenario. Another mother, Sherea, recalled CPS visiting the hospital after she gave birth: "I was panicking, like, 'Oh, they're going to take my baby.' . . . I was trying to stay calm. I wanted to cry." A mother named Imelda said, "I couldn't speak. The only thing that crossed my mind was that they were going to take them away."

Even as mothers asserted that they had done nothing wrong, their relative powerlessness and sense of uncertainty in the face of CPS fostered anxiety. As Deborah explained:

> You see things happen to other families. You know that you're powerless against people coming in your home and, for lack of a better term, screwing with the custody of your kids. . . . I wanna be like, "Dude, why is anybody gonna screw with us?" Then I look at real life and say, "But it happens, so who knows?" It's scary. . . . I can rationalize the way things go all I want, but . . . I might as well be nineteen in the projects with four kids, worried about them being taken, because that's the power it wields.

Deborah felt confident about her parenting but knew that it wasn't up to her, as CPS had "ultimate power at the end of the day. . . . It's somebody else that gets to make that decision." She summarized her mentality. "Always fear. Everything always ends up fear-based because it's fear of the unknown." Mothers identified as good mothers but couldn't be sure what CPS would do or whether CPS would recognize their care for their children. Could they trust that this stranger had their family's best interests at heart? What if investigators understood the situation but were overruled by the CPS supervisor, someone they'd never met?

Deborah's fear heightened when Sarah mentioned the positive opioid test. "My stomach dropped. I literally felt panicky," Deborah recalled later. "That scared me so bad." She knew that it would be on her to prove she wasn't misusing opioids, so she thought—and talked—fast. Deborah hurried to marshal all the evidence she could, phoning her mother to vouch for her and presenting the hospital's discharge papers, which didn't recommend follow-up treatment for substance use. "I'm floored," she kept saying, adding that she hadn't heard anything of the sort from the hospital.

Sarah, later, agreed that it was "odd" that the hospital staff hadn't made a referral for treatment if they were concerned about Deborah's substance use. After that first visit, Sarah anticipated that the case would close—she wasn't concerned about the children's safety—and, indeed, it did. Deborah felt reassured by Sarah's reaction; she believed Sarah understood. Still, Deborah said, "that underlying fear" persisted. "Is she just being nice right now, to tell me what I wanna hear, kind of a thing? It's always fear-based. Everything comes down to being scared."

"Everybody Calls CPS"

Sandra Peralta, too, felt frightened upon receiving a letter at her door from CPS—"because, I thought, that's where children are taken care of [*donde cuidan los niños*]." CPS had removed a friend's children, devastating her friend, and Sandra worried that the same could happen to her.

Petite and slim, with long, straight, dark hair, Sandra looked younger than her twenty-six years. Several years prior, she'd come from the Dominican Republic to New Haven. She worked full-time answering customer service calls and lived with her husband, their five-year-old son, Henry, and their one-year-old daughter. For Sandra, becoming a mother had changed her life. "My children are everything to me," she beamed. "What little I have is for my children."

Henry saw a clinician named Polly at his childcare center each week for behavior management support. One day, Polly noticed swelling above his lip, which Henry said happened when he fell off his scooter, riding without parental supervision. The childcare center had had other concerns about the family, some of which Polly acknowledged were "questionable": an arm injury from the scooter the prior year that kept Henry out of childcare for a few weeks; a bruise on Sandra's face once, perhaps suggestive of domestic violence; and Henry viewing pornography on his father's phone. After Henry told Polly that his parents weren't watching him when he fell, Polly said, "I felt like this was the time to get some support in for the family. I figured CPS can provide that for them or whatever it is that they're lacking or need support in, so I put a report." Polly knew that both parents worked; she was looking into additional services for them and hoped that CPS could help with that.

Recall from the previous chapter how reporting professionals like Polly often wanted CPS to intervene in ways they felt unable to. In doing so, they brought CPS to families' doorsteps, fostering anxiety and fear. Meanwhile, Dawn, the assigned investigator, felt frustrated by the childcare center's call. She questioned why Polly had turned first to CPS:

> I would think that the reporter who's been working with this child would know the parents a little bit better in order to get a better take on them. . . . Why don't you just call the parents and ask them what happened? There's such a lack of communication between the schools, the providers, and the parents. Everybody calls CPS or the police. It could have all been worked [out] if they had just talked to the parents.

Still, Dawn had to go through the full investigative process, assessing the family over multiple home visits. After clarifying what happened with the scooter— Henry's father was outside while Henry played by a cousin's house down the street, with another adult nearby—Dawn spoke individually with each parent and with Henry.

During Dawn's visit, Henry started taking things out of the freezer, screaming and kicking when his parents said no; eventually, he settled down with a popsicle to watch a video. Sandra found managing his behavior overwhelming. Henry was "a handful," she said. "It's like he wants to destroy the whole world." He sometimes punched or threw things at the walls. When he acted out, Sandra told Dawn, she put him in the bedroom and closed the door because it was too much. Sometimes, the stress brought her to tears. She wanted help. During the investigation, Dawn made a referral to an in-home service, offered some advice, and shared a list of local summer programs. Even leaving the first visit, Dawn knew that the case would "definitely be unsubstantiated" and nothing would change that: "You could definitely tell this is a very active boy." The case closed. Mothers like Sandra feared family separation, but CPS investigators like Dawn did not usually anticipate child removal or even ongoing CPS involvement.

This isn't always the case—sometimes investigators do think that children are unsafe at home. Alex, a White mother, tested positive for OxyContin at delivery after receiving Narcan for an overdose at eight months pregnant. Upon receiving the report, CPS was already looking toward removal. Staff rolled their eyes at Alex's explanation for the overdose, relayed by hospital staff: that she just had "a big bowl of stupid" that day. The investigator, Pat, also White, went to the hospital to meet with Alex. Pat calmly asked questions about Alex's history of heroin use and her mental health diagnoses. After Pat explained that they would convene a meeting to plan for the baby's safety,

Alex's mother looked for reassurance that CPS wouldn't take the baby, but Pat didn't offer it. In speaking with Alex, Pat maintained a distant demeanor; she didn't present herself as a support to the family (as Dawn had in Sandra's case) and at times grew exasperated when she felt that Alex wasn't giving her straight answers. After speaking with the family and observing their interactions, Pat and her supervisor thought that Alex's boyfriend and parents would enable Alex's substance use, potentially endangering the newborn. Pat also had concerns about whether Alex was adequately treating her complex mental health needs. Three days later, at the meeting Pat mentioned, CPS took custody of Alex's baby girl and placed her with Alex's boyfriend's mother.

Most CPS investigations don't end this way; investigators might do only a couple removals a year.[5] CPS received a lot of "fluffy stuff," in the words of an investigations supervisor—reports frontline staff felt didn't require CPS investigation. "Half the things that get called in, I wouldn't call in," an experienced investigator declared.[6] The previous chapter described reporting professionals' eagerness to pass things off to CPS. Investigators, meanwhile, believed that many reports, like Sandra's, could have been averted with a little more follow-up from those making reports. In the case of Graciela, the mother from chapter 2 who did not pick up her daughter with strep throat, the investigator, Dan, felt that the school could have continued trying to contact her. After all, he texted Graciela upon receiving the report and she responded right away. "Sometimes, with better communication with the schools, I think that these things could be avoided," Dan said. "There's gotta be a better way than to get CPS involved." Investigators recognized that people sometimes used CPS for their own purposes, as when social contacts reported out of spite or when schools "had it out" for families for whatever reason.

In Rhode Island, too, a CPS administrator I met echoed reporting professionals in saying, "It takes a village." But she used the proverb to shift responsibility back to these professionals, asking why they called CPS rather than reaching out to families. "Why be punitive?" She offered an example: a child late for school every day who mentioned her mother sleeping late. The report, in this administrator's view, became "a witch hunt" for a "litany of things." The mother worked nights, and although school staff could have contacted her to work out a plan, they left it to CPS, terrifying the family in the process. The administrator scanned the stack of reports on her desk and readily found another: a clinician reporting an adolescent's noncompliance with treatment and suggesting that CPS intervention could ensure cooperation. Again, as stated in chapter 2, such situations are not necessarily harmless to children. But in the administrator's view, the clinician's report reflected a service need, one other providers should take on. "We get these kinds of reports every day," she sighed.

In Connecticut, hotline calls come into a statewide central office, where staff screen them for allegations meeting statutory definitions of abuse or neglect. Many calls—over 40 percent nationwide—do get "screened out," with hotline staff taking notes and declining to pass them on to investigators.[7] For instance, I sat with a hotline worker as she took a call from a therapist reporting a father who locked his child outside in the cold after an argument; the therapist wanted to "send a message" to the father so things wouldn't escalate. The hotline worker screened out the call, telling me that this might not be the best form of discipline, but the family could address the issue in therapy. In another case, a father reported his child's mother, sharing a number of concerns, such as the child sleeping on the couch. The hotline worker understood that poverty played a role in the conditions the father reported and that the father, desperate to visit his child, was grasping at the options he saw.

Still, hotline staff face pressure to pass reports along to field offices as expeditiously as possible. Like the reporting organizations from chapter 2, hotlines are organized around avoiding inappropriately screened-out reports, rather than the reverse. And given limited hotline staffing, the unit aims to minimize call wait times. Callers sometimes waited an hour or more on hold. In response, the Connecticut hotline instituted technology to monitor frontline staff, allocating a certain number of minutes for staff to take each call and additional time to write it up. Staff had to manually extend these windows to get more time before the next call was patched through. A large screen displayed to all how long each staffer had been on the phone as well as the current hold time. "It's like Big Brother," lamented a hotline worker who said that, cognizant of the callers on hold, she often ate lunch while taking calls. With the click of a button, hotline staff could transfer reports to physically distant field offices to deal with; they wouldn't hear from investigators about the outcomes of these calls. In uncertain situations, then, hotline staff may find it easier to refer reports to investigators, rather than spend additional time on the phone questioning callers to ensure that a case merits investigation.

In response to the reports they received, investigators often found themselves stuck. They couldn't wave a magic wand to make families behave as professionals wanted, so they felt frustrated when they didn't see any levers the agency could pull to resolve the situation. (And as chapter 5 will discuss, CPS can't meaningfully address family needs such as housing, employment, and childcare.) One day, Dan was telling another investigator about his case involving a six-year-old with diabetes not adhering to his diet. The second investigator, Joe, shook his head and said, "Some of the stuff we get is just ridiculous," adding, "I know I'm supposed to be a miracle worker, but sometimes there's nothing we can do. We're not the morality police." Joe turned to me to emphasize this again, enunciating each word: "Put that in your report, Kelley. CPS. Is. Not. The. Morality. Police."

Even when investigators understood decisions to report, they didn't necessarily believe that reports needed a *child protection–specific* response—that is, one only CPS could deliver, oriented around identifying candidates for legal intervention. For example, a case came in after a Black mother, Tameka, was hospitalized following a suicide attempt; at the hospital, Tameka mentioned that her five-year-old son had not had pediatric care since he was two or three weeks old. The child was elsewhere when Tameka attempted suicide, and Tameka was open to mental health services and pediatric care, so, her investigator Heather mused, what was needed?

> Just telling her, "Oh, he needs to go for an appointment. You need to find a primary care pediatrician." To provide her with a list. But I think they called CPS to do those things. To do those case management things, which is where sometimes we lose the—it's not necessarily abuse or neglect.

Heather wasn't sure whether Tameka should have been reported; she thought that it was a "perfect" case for CPS to refer to another agency for case management services.

But other entities could do this same work. Bill, a veteran investigator, lamented all the calls from service providers for "very minor issues"—reports that CPS would just shuttle right back to them. Although callers could address the issues by educating families or making referrals themselves, he said, "They don't do that. They just pick up the phone and call us." I conveyed what I'd heard from reporting professionals: their belief that families would take CPS's recommendations more seriously. Bill countered:

> But sometimes now it makes it worse, because now you get the family on the defensive. They get an unnecessary CPS case. . . . Do the therapy, your job, educate, before you get to the next level and call us. Because once you call us, it's a whole different ball game. . . . We come in and we delve into

everything. Intrusive. For someone that doesn't need to go through that? Retraumatizing the kids by asking all the questions of the kids? Calling medical, calling educational [providers].

Frontline investigators had to investigate the reports that came across their desks. Often, they felt ambivalent about the need for their involvement, suggesting that the situations they encountered didn't need a response oriented around child maltreatment. Nevertheless, as CPS investigators, that was the response they delivered.

"We Literally Ask Everything"

As Bill's comments indicate, even when investigators know from the outset that cases do not need a child protection–specific intervention, they "delve into everything." CPS's surveillance is not only wide, reaching many families, but also deep, collecting extensive information from each of these families. Reports give the state license to go in; this justification for entry is a blank check of sorts, with no limits as to what CPS can inquire about. Although states vary in the specific activities and time frames required in investigations, national practice guidelines recommend visiting the home multiple times, collecting information from other systems and databases, and interviewing household members about an array of topics beyond the initial allegations. Such practices are common nationwide.[8]

Jazmine called her boyfriend, Tony, frantic, after learning that her housing case manager would be calling CPS. "They're gonna take my child," she insisted. She knew firsthand what could happen when CPS got involved, as she'd been in the system as a child herself. All her memories of CPS, all the accumulated, collective trauma of state scrutiny, overcame her. "I'm packing my stuff and I'm leaving. They're not gonna find me." Tony convinced her to go over to his place. That evening, when Fred, the investigator, finally called, Jazmine's stomach dropped. "Every bad thought was just going through. Every bad thought just was popping up as we got closer and closer." The uncertainty, combined with her relative powerlessness, terrified her. She traced her sense of precarity to her broader experiences of marginalization:

I'm not scared because I don't know how to not hit my child. I'm scared because nobody listens to me, because nobody takes my word for anything. . . . I don't know what's gonna happen. I don't know if I'm gonna have a dick for a caseworker. . . . You just don't know.

She had a lifetime of experiences—with her family and then in foster care—where her input, her desires, didn't seem to matter to those making decisions about her. And as a Black and Puerto Rican woman, Jazmine surmised that her housing case manager's perspective would hold sway: "She's a straight White woman, so they have that White privilege where their word will go over my word. It doesn't matter what I say. They're always gonna take her word."

Fred prepared to visit Jazmine by looking her up in the state CPS database. Seeing that she had CPS involvement as a child, he reviewed what he could before heading out to her home. Typically, investigators visited three times during the forty-five-day investigation or weekly for children under one and twice each week for newborns deemed "high-risk."

Fred parked in the small lot behind the three-story brick building where Jazmine lived. A tall, White investigator in his late thirties, Fred had been working investigations for the past year or so, after years working with families whose cases CPS opened after investigating. We waited in the muggy stairwell until Jazmine returned home, flanked by Gabriel as well as Tony and his mother.

"Fred Iverson. CPS. How you doing." Fred didn't smile as he introduced himself. Beforehand, Fred told me that he tended to start stern before "mellowing out." But he was careful not to accuse Jazmine of anything, explaining that he had received a report and had to do his job by coming to figure out what was going on. Jazmine opened the door to a living room furnished with two brown leather couches around a glass-top coffee table. "This is a nice place you have here," Fred said, as Gabriel scampered around, babbling, and Tony and his mother started folding the laundry on one of the couches to make room for everyone to sit down.

After Fred summarized the report's allegations, Jazmine, keen to share her perspective and be up front with Fred, reenacted the scene that afternoon. She mimed grabbing Gabriel's arm to show Fred how, once she heard Gabriel hit her case manager, she brought Gabriel to his room and slammed the door. "And I *smacked* him." She slapped her own hand, hard. "I said, 'You do not hit, you do not do that.'" Fred asked how many times she'd slapped Gabriel and how she typically disciplined him. Then, Fred went to Gabriel's room.

"My name's Mr. Fred," he said to Gabriel, squatting down to eye level on the Teenage Mutant Ninja Turtles rug and asking Jazmine to lift Gabriel's shirt so Fred could see his torso and arms. Fred noticed a small bruise on Gabriel's cheek, which Tony's mother explained came from Gabriel slipping and hitting the concrete when playing with toy cars outside.

Within the first several minutes of his arrival, Fred had checked out what was reported. He felt confident that Jazmine wasn't physically abusing Gabriel and the allegations would be unsubstantiated. But Fred spent nearly two more hours with Jazmine that evening, collecting the information required for his assessment. "I'm gonna apologize off the rip—at CPS we literally ask everything," he warned her.

This included questions about adults in households where children spent time—in Jazmine's case, Tony's and his mother's birth dates and the mother's maiden name. Later, back at the office, Fred would check everyone's CPS history, criminal records, protective orders, sex offender status, and pending criminal or motor vehicle cases. Investigators also had to contact nonresident parents. Fred asked about Gabriel's father—his involvement in Gabriel's life, how Jazmine met him—and learned that they weren't in touch. Still, Fred had to try to reach out. In his summary of the investigation, Fred wrote that he "made efforts to locate and engage [Gabriel's father] without success."

And in addition to his questions about the physical abuse allegations, Fred probed an array of other topics: employment, income, criminal legal system involvement, domestic violence, mental health, substance use. "Even though we may have one issue, it's a comprehensive evaluation," an investigator explained in a local news report. "We touch on everything when we assess a family."[9] Simply by virtue of being reported to CPS, mothers were questioned about deeply personal experiences, such as unfaithful partners, family relationships, and childhood traumas.

Fred asked whether anyone used marijuana. "I do," Jazmine, sitting on the arm of the couch, volunteered, adding that she was trying to stop. More questions followed: how often she smoked, whether she did anything other than smoking, what the marijuana did for her. Sighing, Jazmine said it calmed her down.

"Okay." Fred spoke softly, letting her continue. Tony's mother jumped in to add that Jazmine had depression and anxiety. Keeping his voice low, Fred asked whether Jazmine had ever talked to anyone about that.

Jazmine's voice quivered as she told Fred, struggling to get the words out, that weed was all she had to help her get by.

"So it relaxes you, you think," Fred reflected back.

"I don't do it just to do it," Jazmine clarified through tears. Tony reached out to rub her back. "It keeps me sane."

Though Fred couldn't endorse the marijuana as a state employee—Connecticut had not yet legalized recreational marijuana use—he empathized. "I *understand* it. I understand the anxiety of feeling like you have a lot of things on your plate . . . and just doing that helps relax you." Jazmine nodded.

Investigators assessed families' "protective" factors—capabilities and re-sources that could protect against maltreatment—as well as "risk" factors. So Fred asked about Jazmine's social supports and about what made her proud as a mom. With this last question, Jazmine looked down without answering, put-ting her fingers in her eyes to try to stop the tears.

Back at the office, with Jazmine's permission, Fred contacted Gabriel's pe-diatrician and dentist to ensure that he was up-to-date with medical appoint-ments. When families had children in childcare or school, investigators reached out to see whether schools had any concerns, such as about atten-dance. In this way, CPS's surveillance is interinstitutional, reaching beyond the home to collate information across systems.[10] Where applicable, CPS investi-gators obtained police reports and other documents and coordinated with professionals such as home visitors and mental health providers.

Sometimes, investigators also gathered information through online sleuthing, usually without families' knowledge. Occasionally, investigators looked up parents on Facebook before even meeting them.[11] And public records could help investigators locate parents, as when one investigator used a pending motor vehicle charge to identify a mother's address after CPS and other records yielded incorrect addresses. Sarah, who investigated Deb-orah's case, told a group of new caseworkers that Internet searches had helped her find many parents. "I usually go to 'Connecticut Voters' and I can find out dates of birth on everyone, if you ever need a date of birth. You can find them by address, which is really scary," she advised. "You can find all kinds of stuff."[12]

Fred met with Jazmine at her home three more times during the investiga-tion and wrote up his findings to enter into the statewide CPS database. In Connecticut, this documentation, including narratives that typically run five thousand to ten thousand words, remains in the database for at least five years and indefinitely in the case of substantiated reports. As the next chapter will discuss, investigations already in the system shape the trajectory of future re-ports that come in, elevating formal and informal risk assessments. And just as Fred began his investigation by reviewing Jazmine's childhood history with CPS, if little Gabriel grows up and catches a case as a father, investigators may peruse what Jazmine shared with Fred, even decades later. CPS's surveillance thus not only extends broadly and deeply into families but endures well be-yond the investigatory period, even intergenerationally.

Justifying Surveillance

Surveillance for Safety

How does CPS understand the purpose of its extensive and intensive surveillance, even in cases where investigators do not believe that children are in imminent danger? First, CPS's orientation around child safety justifies and organizes agency practice, including surveillance. When I began my fieldwork, it surprised me how little CPS staff referred explicitly to parents abusing or neglecting their children. Instead, they invoked the rhetoric of *safety*. Investigators completed "safety assessments" and wrote up "safety plans" to mitigate any "safety factors" identified. They talked about their work as ensuring children's safety, over promoting family welfare or even responding to maltreatment. "I'll certainly work with you, but it's my job to make sure your kids are safe," an investigator told the local news.[13] A trainer underscored this point on the first day of training for new investigators: "Our number one role here is child safety." (Of course, left unstated is CPS's relatively narrow conception of child safety as safety from caregivers, rather than from the wounds of poverty or racism. This child safety discourse also enables a sort of sleight of hand: Investigators need not emphasize parents abusing or neglecting their children—if children are unsafe, CPS must act.)

With this emphasis on safety, the agency focused on the most extreme possibilities, those that might seriously endanger children. Guarding against these threats, the logic went, required extensive surveillance, well beyond investigating the specific allegation reported. For example, Annie, training new investigators, said that it was important to collect information about parents' cars because parents sometimes took off with their children during visits. This possibility, however remote (after all, only cases where CPS took custody of children would have visits), justified surreptitious information-gathering: "When you pull into the driveway, jot down the make, model, and license plate," Annie advised. An attendee pushed back: What if it wasn't their car? Annie suggested saying something like, "I parked behind that white Altima— is that yours, or am I blocking your neighbor?" I did not observe any instances where CPS having this information protected children from harm; still, on multiple occasions I saw investigators write down details on cars parked in parents' driveways, without parents' knowledge.

For the agency, instances when child protection safety nets had failed underscored the need for more surveillance. In a professional development session presenting lessons learned from recent infant fatalities, a facilitator noted that in some of the cases reviewed, mothers' partners turned out to be "dangerous people," on the state child abuse/neglect registry: "We need to know that. We need to know criminal histories." A few people with such histories connected to tragic cases justified a widespread surveillance of intimate relationships, in which CPS obtained the names and birth dates of mothers' romantic partners no matter the allegation. Think of Tony, asked for personal information despite not even being present when Jazmine smacked Gabriel. Closing out the professional development session, another facilitator said that she hoped the discussion had inspired reflection among staff. "If that can increase your ability to do a more comprehensive assessment, we're happy." To CPS, effectively safeguarding children equated to extensive information-gathering.

Like many other states, Connecticut operates a "differential response" system, in which the agency designates incoming reports as either traditional investigations or, in cases deemed lower-risk, "family assessments." In theory, family assessments focus on engaging families and offering voluntary services, rather than on determining whether abuse or neglect occurred. But in practice, staff approached family assessments just as they did investigations.[14] Investigators asked the same questions and made identical requests of families; they could not always remember which track a case was on. Administrators emphasized that child safety should remain investigators' top priority no matter the designation. "We don't put safety out the window when we go out on [family assessment] cases," an investigations manager leading a training session advised.

As such, all cases in Connecticut received the full surveillance treatment, in part due to the agency's orientation around safety. In training sessions, trainers repeatedly urged investigators to take family assessments as seriously as traditional investigations. Explaining why investigators should question families the same way, one trainer said that the allegations of maltreatment "stay there until we prove the children are safe. . . . You're still looking at those allegations, still determining if they're accurate, still figuring out safety." At the end of the day, he added, "your job is to make sure those kids are safe."

Surveillance for Prevention

Scholars and practitioners suggest that even if investigators recognize right away that children are safe, CPS reports indicate "risk" of maltreatment.[15] As such, investigations present opportunities to prevent future maltreatment by intervening early and proactively referring families to services. CPS is often criticized for being reactive to maltreatment, so goals of prevention have gained traction in recent years, becoming central to CPS agencies' work. In this perspective, CPS gathers information to assess family needs holistically and intervene accordingly.

For example, because maltreatment allegations often involve a complex interplay of social factors, investigators probed widely to understand the root of the reported concerns. "Educational neglect is never just educational neglect," I frequently heard. Getting a report, a trainer explained, is "like an onion peeling"—investigators had to uncover each layer to get to the issues underlying the maltreatment allegation. For instance, investigators suggested, children might be missing school due to domestic violence, afraid something might happen to their mother. So staff wanted to learn about many dimensions of families' lives to contextualize and better address the maltreatment allegations they received.

CPS staff also understood broad information-gathering as a way to address families' needs beyond the initial allegations—for instance, by offering guidance and social service referrals. Dawn wasn't just investigating Sandra's son's scooter accident, the incident precipitating the report; she wanted to help Sandra manage her son's challenging behavior. As the logic went, if investigators learned of frequent absences after reaching out to children's schools, they could work with parents to address barriers to attendance.

In a training session for new investigators, the trainer, Deshawn, highlighted a perk of investigations work: While families deemed high-risk filled other workers' caseloads, "in investigations, 50 percent of cases go right into the garbage," he said lightly, miming tossing something into a trash can. This didn't mean that when they returned to their offices to two new cases, "Deshawn said, throw this first one in the garbage." The group laughed. Instead, Deshawn told investigators to "get all the information we need" and try to help families to the extent possible. Because most investigations close, he reasoned, "we need to be bringing something to the table." Deshawn urged investigators to ask themselves: "How can I leave the family in a better position than when I came?"

For example, at every visit with a family with an infant under twelve months—sometimes twice weekly—investigators had to talk with caregivers about safe sleep and observe where infants slept. With the dangers of "co-sleeping" drawing attention, promoting safe sleep was a major public health initiative in both Connecticut and Rhode Island. Investigators spoke with parents at length about their infants' sleep setups and requested to see children's bedrooms, even when initial reports did not make co-sleeping allegations. Chanell, a Black investigator, drove me to visit Tatiana, a Black mother whose boyfriend had called CPS after they separated. When we arrived, Chanell cooed over Tatiana's four-month-old, a big baby. "I'm from down south—we *love* healthy babies!" she enthused. Chanell went over safe sleep guidelines with Tatiana during the visit. Afterward, Chanell acknowledged that families not reported to CPS likely co-slept as well. "Let's just be real about it. Are we going to everybody's houses doing it [education and observations]? No." Still, she wanted to convey to Tatiana that co-sleeping could be fatal. "It's shocking to have that happen. . . . You're like, whoa. Bells start ringing. I really wanna be all over this . . . [and] educate her." For Chanell, questioning and inspecting the baby's sleeping arrangements was not merely a policy requirement but an opportunity to prevent future harm.

Investigators invoked goals of assistance in explaining their requests to families as well. As one investigator told a mother at the start of the visit, CPS gets involved for one thing but looks at everything "to understand the barriers and see what we can do to help." CPS framed these wide-ranging assessments as a way of obtaining a fuller picture of families' situations. Even in cases deemed "low-risk," staff conducted holistic assessments aiming to help families prevent future maltreatment. Most discussions of surveillance focus on surveillance in service of control and punishment; here, we see how invoking surveillance as a form of care also justifies expansive information-gathering.

Surveillance to Avoid Liability

As soon as CPS receives a call, the family becomes "known to the system," and the agency becomes responsible for whatever happens next. All eyes turn to CPS when children die or become severely injured due to maltreatment and the press picks up the case: What did CPS know? What should CPS have known? There are headlines; there are hearings.[16] Watchdogs write reports about what went wrong. Frontline staff and high-level administrators can lose their jobs. The possibility of this kind of public scrutiny permeates investigative casework to undergird comprehensive family surveillance.

Quality casework is difficult to measure, so investigators' work is reviewed for its compliance with policy and practice requirements. In my observations, supervisors pored over the materials investigators submitted and sent investigators back to get missing information. In regular "quality assurance" reviews of randomly selected investigative cases, reviewers had a long checklist of items to verify: Did the investigator meet with the child separately and alone? Did the investigator complete criminal background checks of all adults in the household? Did the investigator visit the family as frequently as required by policy?

I sat with Alison, an investigator, as she discussed a newly assigned case with her supervisor, Mark: a newborn with a positive toxicology screen. That morning, another supervisor reviewing the report had concluded that it was "ridiculous." The manager agreed that it was "stupid" and did not need to be reported, as the mother had a medical marijuana card and had smoked three times during her pregnancy. Still, Mark rattled off a litany of instructions for Alison: consider a referral to a service program, ask about the marijuana dispensary, get a drug screen, assess the baby's sleeping area, assess for intimate partner violence, assess for mental health, get household members' CPS and criminal history, visit once or twice weekly. It was a baby, Mark said, so they didn't want to get in trouble. Then, probably remembering I was there, he clarified, "I mean, of course, we care about kids' safety."

"Nice reframe," Alison replied.

"CYA," said Mark with a shrug.

Investigators cannot foresee which children will be severely harmed (or even die) after investigations close—none of us could. But they are on the hook if they miss something that turns out to be pivotal. So covering themselves means looking into everything they might be held accountable for, in all cases, and documenting their efforts. At an investigative staff meeting, the manager mentioned a co-sleeping fatality on an investigation recently closed. She recognized the investigator, Bill, for completing an "excellent" investigation. "Just great, with everything there." This was the mark of a laudable investigation: far-reaching information gathered and documented. The group applauded, relieved to know that the unit had done everything it could and, at least this time, would escape censure. The manager reminded them that they never knew when their work would be reviewed or audited.

CPS is also held responsible for verifying the information it collects, encouraging the agency to gather information from parents as well as their professional and personal contacts. In Rhode Island, a hospital called CPS about a newborn baby boy. Baby Tobi, as he became known, was discharged to his parents under a "safety plan," whereby his mother would not care for him alone given her severe mental health needs. Tobi's father worked but told the caseworker that he knew people who could help and provided the name and address of Tobi's day care. Three months later, an ambulance rushed Baby Tobi to the pediatric intensive care unit in cardiac arrest, with broken arms, a broken leg, a fractured skull, twelve fractured ribs, and human bite marks. Doctors removed Baby Tobi from life support after five months.

The horrified response from advocates, legislators, and journalists swiftly focused on the inadequacy of CPS's response to Baby Tobi's family. An oversight review revealed that the day care did not exist; the address given corresponded to a vacant building, a fact repeated in legislative hearings as evidence of CPS's unconscionable failures. And the supportive social connections the father referenced "were never identified nor vetted."[17] The implications, summarized in a watchdog report, were clear: CPS must take the time to verify all information provided by parents; doing so in Baby Tobi's case could have saved his life.

The Toll on Investigators

Although their stress paled in comparison to that experienced by mothers, investigators also found investigations taxing. Completing the visits, interviews, collateral contacts, consultations, and referrals on each and every case within the investigative period, as well as documenting these efforts, is no small task. A 2017 report revealed that in Rhode Island, eighteen of twenty-two investigators had caseloads above national best practice standards of eight to ten investigative case assignments per month; eleven had more than twenty active cases.[18] In Connecticut, too, time studies conducted the year before my fieldwork found that investigators could not feasibly complete assigned investigations within the forty-hour work week. Investigators often received two or three new cases per week. With the time study estimating nineteen to twenty-four hours of work for each case, investigators often worked after hours. "To meet all the requirements, it just happens that way," one told me.

When another investigator, Kerri, described the barrage of emails, phone calls, and requests she fielded, I asked whether she participated in the time study. Ironically, Kerri said, she did not have time. And, she pointed out, how could the time study take into account her doing three things at once? I sat in the passenger seat as she drove to a meeting, while on the phone with a colleague problem-solving on a case, while texting her supervisor about a different case at red lights. "To do this job right," an investigator said, "you have to be on twenty-four hours a day.... It's just too much."

But investigators had to get the work done; as described in the previous section, they would be responsible if assessments were not sufficiently thorough and tragedy ensued.[19] At a Rhode Island state legislative hearing following Baby Tobi's death, the chairwoman of the House Oversight Committee pressed the agency's commissioner about why Tobi's caseworker had not been terminated, saying that it was "preposterous" the person was still employed at the agency. She raised her voice in disbelief: "How bad does the behavior have to be to terminate? . . . Someone is to blame." The state's Child Advocate knew that investigative staff had high caseloads. But she, too, underscored individual workers' responsibilities, stating plainly, "Regardless of caseload, you need to do the work. If you can't, talk to your supervisor or the union. . . . You stay late or write it at home."

Along with the high workload, the possibility of uncertain and volatile situations amplified investigators' anxiety. Investigations work had high stakes. As a trainer told new investigators, "When you leave that first visit and walk away, you're saying that kid's safe, because you left." And investigators sometimes articulated the personal risks and fears associated with their work. One investigator described walking alone up back staircases to visit families and said that he often thought about how no one would find him if something happened. Investigators knew CPS staff assaulted on the job, and some had received detailed death threats against themselves and their families. One pointed out that although CPS and police work with similar populations, police work in pairs, while CPS staff go alone: "It's just you if a situation arises."

Investigators' lack of control over their schedules also made their work stressful.[20] A training session warned new investigators to rip up their calendars. Responding to a case could spiral into an all-day outing. After a report came in one morning, I accompanied an investigator named Natasha to a local school. We spent the rest of the day back and forth between the school and the family's home across town—waiting for the Swahili interpreter; waiting for the police; interviewing the child, her seven siblings, and her mother, one at a time. "This is how a case turns into eight hours," Natasha sighed. Even that was optimistic; she rescheduled her afternoon visits and consulted via phone with her supervisor and manager well into the evening. She had just a bag of Cheetos for lunch. We arrived back at the office around 9:00 p.m. to meet an on-call supervisor who would drive the child to a foster home, where Natasha picked her up early the next morning to take her to school.

"It ends when it ends," a local news story quoted one investigator as saying. "It's child safety, so you can't just say, 'OK, well I'm going home now.'" Another investigator told the journalist, "My family comes to realize that there are nights when I call up and say 'I'm not going to be home until 2 in the morning.'

And I have younger kids, so that can take its toll."[21] The job infringed on investigators' own family responsibilities. As we headed out to visits in the late afternoon or early evening, investigators often made frantic phone calls to their relatives or spouses to rearrange school pickups or try to cobble together childcare. "I'm running around making sure other kids are safe," said one investigator. "Meanwhile, mine. . . ."

In this context, investigative staff welcomed opportunities to move things off their plates; they did not need or want to police parents for minor infractions if they could hand off the case. On one case, Vance and I drove forty-five minutes to an address in the eastern region of the state. (Especially in the Northeast Corner, investigators spent a lot of time driving.) No one was home. Vance called the phone number he had and learned that the mother had been staying at a shelter in the Northeast Corner before heading to Rhode Island several days before to care for her father, who had cancer. Vance probed her plans. She said that she hoped to stay in Connecticut because her benefits and service providers were there but she would probably be in Rhode Island a few weeks while looking for a place in Connecticut. As soon as Vance hung up, he raised his arms above his head in a victory pose: "Yes! That gets me off the hook." He could have made the case that the mother was still a Connecticut resident. But he planned to call Rhode Island to do a quick well-being check. Passing off the case eliminated most of what he had to do. "That's why I'm like, 'Oh, are you going to stay in Rhode Island? Because I really think that's a *good idea*. . . .'" Managers tried to protect their staff by sending reports back to the hotline to screen out, to other field offices, or to other states. Still, there was only so much they could do. They had a responsibility to investigate reports meeting certain criteria, and agency policy dictated the information they needed to collect from families.

Cultivating "Voluntary" Disclosures

CPS investigations are not criminal investigations, so parents encountering CPS do not have the constitutional protections afforded to criminal suspects. For instance, they are not entitled to an attorney during CPS questioning. Nevertheless, parents do technically have the right to refuse entry to CPS and decline to answer investigators' questions. As a trainer told new staff, "If they say no, they say no." So CPS staff must gather information from parents without using physical or legal force. In my observations, I generally saw mothers comply with investigators' requests. Investigators exercised a soft power, leaning on mothers' fears and uncertainty to encourage them to open up their private lives to the state.

At times, mothers bristled at CPS's surveillance, asking the investigator (or wondering with me, in the interview later) why certain information, such as information about other household or family members, was necessary. And they weren't always fully forthcoming with investigators. But overall, mothers believed that answering investigators' questions could help CPS understand the situation in context. As Sandra put it, "I have nothing to hide. I feel that everything [Dawn] asked was to understand the case more fully, to see what is happening."

Despite their supposed rights in the investigation, mothers knew that they couldn't just turn investigators away without consequence. Jazmine answered Fred's questions and allowed him to observe Gabriel's body and bedroom because otherwise Jazmine thought that Gabriel "would be gone." That fear, that sense of precarity, hung over the entire interaction. Mothers ascertained—correctly—that silence communicated wrongdoing, that refusing made it look like they had something to hide. CPS's requests put mothers in a bind: to counter the allegations of maltreatment, they had to open up. Deborah, too, said that she never considered denying Sarah entry into her home:

> No, because I know what could happen. She could sit right at the bottom of that driveway . . . until the police officer comes back. They can get ahold of a judge. They can get orders. . . . They can sit right there until they have cause to take your children. . . . I'm going to cooperate with you because, at the end of the day, you're not going to take my kids.

Even though it was her first CPS report, Deborah knew that CPS could call on backup.[22] Rather than escalate the situation, Deborah put aside her afternoon for Sarah. When I asked mothers what advice they would give to other mothers being investigated, they generally recommended acquiescing to CPS's surveillance: "be honest," "let them do what they have to do," "cooperate with them." With CPS's power to remove children, mothers typically opted for the path of least resistance.

Mothers are not imagining the importance of cooperation. As Jennifer Reich finds, CPS rewards parents' acquiescence.[23] Per Connecticut policy, investigators give parents a brochure that outlines their rights and states that anything they say can be used against them in court. (Connecticut is the exception; in other states, CPS need not provide this information.[24]) But in communicating parents' rights, CPS also lays out the consequences of non-compliance, underscoring the agency's power to intervene legally and remove children. Although parents are not required to speak with CPS, the brochure warns:

> Please be advised that choosing not to communicate with a CPS employee may have serious consequences, which may include CPS filing a petition to remove your child from your home. It is, therefore, in your best interests to either speak with the CPS employee or immediately seek the advice of an attorney.

Investigators sometimes voiced these warnings to parents when going over the brochure, saying things like, "If you don't [let CPS in], it turns into a bigger deal than it needs to be." In part, these comments reflected efforts to be transparent. For instance, a trainer presented statements for new staff to mark as appropriate or inappropriate. In response to the statement "Explain to client that continuing to refuse may lead to legal action," the trainer emphatically told the group that this was "very appropriate" as "you're being honest, saying this is how it works." She added that sometimes using a nonthreatening tone to inform parents that legal petitions can prolong their involvement with CPS for at least a year encourages compliance.

As this trainer suggested, CPS explicitly invokes its power to convey to parents that cooperation will make things easier for everyone. Near the start of the visit, a mother named Sherea asked what the worst-case scenario for her would be. The investigator didn't hesitate: "The worst in this case is that you don't cooperate with me and then I have to get the court involved." When another mother, April, questioned the need for a drug test, her investigator acknowledged that she didn't necessarily have grounds to mandate it. "But"—she paused—"I get it, but it looks like you have something to hide if you say no." Parents' rights with CPS are thus illusory, as exercising these rights can adversely affect their cases.

Investigators recognized benefits, for children but also for themselves, of parents' apprehension. They sometimes tried to assuage parents' fears—for instance, telling parents that if no other concerns emerged, the case would go no further. When going over Henry's recent injury with Sandra, Dawn reassured Sandra that she knew these things happened. "Boys ride scooters and get hurt." But investigators usually stopped short of fully assuring parents that nothing would come from the investigation. This was partly because the case could take a turn, and they didn't want to make promises they couldn't keep.

But they also knew that some fear on the part of parents could induce parents to accede to CPS's requests.

Sometimes, investigators sought compliance in service of child safety. In Tatiana's case, when Chanell asked whether the baby slept in his own crib, Tatiana apologized, saying that she needed to build it.

Chanell's bubbly demeanor evaporated. She gave Tatiana a stern look. "You know he can't co-sleep."

"I'll build it today," Tatiana quickly assured her, adding that he had outgrown his bassinet. Chanell, normally energized and fast-talking, slowed down to tell Tatiana that it gets scary, referring to a recent co-sleeping death. After Tatiana again promised that she would build the crib that night, Chanell said that she would return the next morning to see the crib.

On the drive back, Chanell explained why she felt comfortable leaving Tatiana until the morning rather than returning that night to check. In part, she pointed to the fear and uncertainty Tatiana's lack of CPS history likely engendered. "With that, you're really scared. You're gonna be like, 'I don't know. CPS might come over here, and I don't have this crib together, and they gonna take my baby.' She doesn't know. You can use that kind of leverage."

Indeed, for Tatiana, the experience was "scary" and "nerve-racking," as she wasn't sure what Chanell would ask or do. Tatiana readily answered Chanell's questions, recognizing her authority: "I know how to be cooperative, because, I mean, she does have the power to take your kids." Tatiana stayed up until two in the morning building the crib. "I was tired, but I knew if I went to sleep and woke up and she saw it wasn't done, I would get in more trouble, so I stayed up and I did it."

Chanell knew that she could not remove Tatiana's baby due to co-sleeping: "I don't have the authority to do that." But she didn't make that clear to Tatiana. The worry in the back of Tatiana's mind, that just maybe Chanell would take her child—"For me, [that's] enough to know, yeah, she doesn't wanna push that line," Chanell said. Chanell saw Tatiana's fear as productive, facilitating compliance with her request and, ultimately, ensuring that the baby had a safer place to sleep.

Parents' compliance also made things easier for investigators, who did not want to create more work for themselves given their high workloads. If parents declined to meet with CPS, investigators had to continue attempting visits and meet with supervisors and managers regarding the case. I accompanied Bonnie, a White investigator, one summer evening as she visited Alicia, a White mother living with her boyfriend and four-year-old daughter in a tucked-away corner of New Haven. The report alleged marijuana use around the child, but Bonnie understood that the report was made vindictively, following an argument with neighbors. Alicia and her boyfriend met us in the driveway, eager to launch into the story of what had happened. They vehemently denied using marijuana. "You can test me all you want," Alicia offered. Later, Bonnie said that she did want them to do a drug test and evaluation, just to rule it out. Alicia's boyfriend wasn't sure about taking time off work; he worked eleven-hour shifts each day. Alicia, who worked full-time herself, told him to "just do it."

Reflecting on the visit in the car afterward, Bonnie was surprised by Alicia's willingness to do the drug test:

> Normally [with vindictive reports] I would get the pushback, but I would say at least 75 percent of the time we can get them to come around and be like, this will, believe it or not, make your life easier if you just do it versus not do it. In this case, if I have a crystal ball, I would probably see that we're still gonna close the case, even if they refused it, but it's so much more helpful that they agreed to do it, 'cause then I could just do a couple visits . . . close it out. *Tell me what's more helpful about it. . . . What would your life or case be like if they didn't?*
> I would have to keep bringing it up every time I talk to them, keep asking them to do it.

Bonnie didn't need to see a negative drug test to close the case.[25] But Alicia and her boyfriend agreeing to miss work to do the test and evaluation made Bonnie's job easier; it was one fewer thing she had to ask of them in subsequent visits.

CPS relies on parents cooperating voluntarily. Though the agency rarely wields explicit force, it uses mothers' fears, uncertainty, and relative powerlessness to encourage compliance. Thus, the disjuncture between mothers' fears of child removal and CPS's expectation of closed cases is not necessarily miscommunication. This mismatch enables CPS to secure cooperation from the wide array of families it investigates.

Resistance and Its Limits

Parents can negotiate and push back on CPS's requests—but only to a point. One afternoon, Alison went to investigate a report alleging home conditions unsuitable for young children. The apartment building was unlocked, so we walked right up to the second-floor unit. Alison knocked. Marlena, a mother of Middle Eastern descent with dark, curly hair pulled up high, opened the door just wide enough to speak with Alison. From the hallway, we smelled a pungent odor—perhaps rotten food or cat urine—and saw Marlena's two-year-old toddling around her legs. Alison introduced herself and asked whether she could come in and speak with Marlena. No, Marlena said firmly, she was not okay with that, because she did not know what this was about. Marlena listened to Alison summarize the report's allegations but didn't move to open the door or invite her in. Marlena asked if Alison could come another day, but Alison, looking apologetic, said that she needed to talk to everyone and see the children within twenty-four hours. (Per policy, she just had to *attempt* a visit within this time frame, which she was presently doing.) Marlena, starting to sound exasperated, said that she would call out of work that day so Alison could return later that afternoon.

"Hopefully she cleans up—that'll make my life easier," Alison murmured as we headed out; she wanted a straightforward case she could close. Having seen the child and peeked into the apartment, Alison felt comfortable leaving. So Alison was willing to negotiate; she didn't threaten to escalate the situation when Marlena declined. Still, Alison pressed Marlena to meet that day, just a couple hours later—a time frame that interfered with Marlena's work schedule but helped Alison with her assessment: "I was coming back in a small enough window where, if there were [major] concerns, they would not have time to fix that up."

In Deborah's case, Sarah mentioned early in the visit that she wanted to speak with Deborah's children, Mia and Paul. Deborah replied that she was not comfortable with that, as she didn't want to stress them out. She knew that this was her legal right. Sarah let that pass. Later, Sarah returned to the possibility of speaking with the children. Here, too, Deborah was quick to decline, insisting that she was "very protective" of them and wanted their therapist to be involved. Sarah again moved on.

Sarah stepped out to call her supervisor, who told Sarah to ask again. Sarah was reluctant. "I didn't like having to push back at her about talking to the kids," she said afterward. Aware that Mia and Paul had been through a lot, Sarah respected Deborah's decision. "There's that constant give-and-take . . . respecting family wishes and, at the same time, doing my job."

When Sarah returned, she broached the topic once more—"This is the not fun part," she said—adding that her supervisor wanted her to speak with the children. Deborah wondered aloud, "What happens if I say no? I hate to put you in the middle, but I kinda want to bluff it." Sarah didn't answer.

Deborah called the children's therapist, who encouraged her to go ahead. Sarah assured Deborah that her questions would be broad—how are you doing, who lives with you, anything that worries you—and Deborah could be in the room, just perhaps not in the children's line of sight. Deborah said that they had professionals in their life and that, if not for the opioid test, CPS would not have been called. "You're right," Sarah affirmed, noting that she was "getting pushback" but understood where Deborah was coming from. "I get it."

Deborah said that she could feel her rising anxiety in her chest. Sarah told her to breathe. In the end, Sarah spoke with Paul first and then Mia. Despite Deborah's hesitation and her efforts to exercise her rights, CPS interviewed them that day without using force or issuing an explicit ultimatum. Sarah empathized with Deborah's concerns, framed the request as coming from above, and stayed silent regarding what could happen if Deborah continued to decline.

Investigators' unspoken threats are not always empty; parents' noncompliance can have serious consequences. In a case assigned to Ria, a Black investigator, hospital and school staff reported Kory, a Black mother who lived with her husband and daughter and seemed to have severe mental health needs, including hallucinations. At the hospital, Kory declined to speak with Ria, saying that she wanted an attorney present. Ria affirmed Kory's rights. But, Ria cautioned, she was concerned about Kory being home alone with her daughter. "I don't know anything about you. . . . I have no clue what's going on with you," Ria said. To convince Ria otherwise, Kory would have to acquiesce to CPS's surveillance. Because she did not, her case escalated. Two months later, Ria was preparing a petition to the court alleging neglect of Kory's daughter. With Kory refusing requests to meet and telling Ria's supervisor that she did not want CPS coming to the house, "it's concerning," Ria said—they had "no idea" what was going on.

So parents' rights to privacy from state intrusion went only so far. Shutting CPS out could lead to legal intervention and child removal—off the table for mothers whose children were the center of their lives. CPS staff knew that family separation was highly improbable in most cases, yet this possibility loomed large for mothers, inspiring acute fear and enabling CPS's surveillance.

Sociologist Issa Kohler-Hausmann describes the high volume of misdemeanor cases stemming from "stop and frisk" policing—cases that rarely lead to formal sanctions—as a sort of "control without conviction."[26] In a similar vein, CPS engages in surveillance without substantiation. In its investigations, CPS gathers extensive information about families' personal lives through home observations, interviews within and beyond the household, and records checks. Interfering with family privacy may be justified when vulnerable people, such as children, are in danger. In reality, though, investigations do not usually involve safety concerns investigators deem serious. Most investigated families will see their cases close, but not before CPS has done a wide-ranging assessment.

Turning so readily to CPS to respond to family adversity thus feeds an immense surveillance system, one that reaches into the home and extends across multiple institutions.[27] In compiling all this information, CPS cites goals of intervening early to prevent future maltreatment. And we want to think that gathering a little more information can keep children from meeting awful ends. This line of thinking, though, justifies essentially boundless probing into families' personal lives. The realities of investigators' work—its inherent uncertainty and its accountability structures—further enshrine and expand CPS's surveillance.

Ultimately, all this surveillance is enabled by CPS's power. Beholden to seemingly endless policy and practice requirements, investigators, individually, may not feel that they have much power. Yet, as they are representatives of the state, authorized to take children, their power over the families they visit is undeniable. This dynamic means that the surveillance system can exploit parents' sense of precarity—their fear and stress about the prospect of losing their children. CPS may not intend to remove children, but the agency's arrival triggers intense emotions for mothers accustomed to systems batting them around. In theory, parents can resist CPS's intrusion. But in practice, when they are facing an investigator with an opaque power to take what they cherish most, parents' rights to privacy are illusory.[28]

Thus, CPS's dual embrace of care and coercion is particularly pernicious. The agency's therapeutic aims expand and justify state scrutiny well beyond parents who are endangering their children. Simultaneously, its coercive capacity pressures parents to acquiesce to this surveillance despite parents' nominal right to refuse. Although parents might welcome a holistic assessment of their needs to aid in connecting with available resources, from an agency authorized to remove children, such inquiries can be terrifying. These experiences of acute anxiety, diminished privacy, and constrained compliance make CPS investigations a critical site of state power even if CPS never explicitly exercises its authority—that is, even if cases close after investigation.

Surveillance is not just information-gathering for its own sake; it is a means to an end. Armed with the information investigators have compiled, CPS assesses families to determine whether and how to stay involved with them after the investigation. As sociologist David Lyon has written, surveillance is a process of social sorting: collecting personal information to categorize people in ways consequential for social inclusion or exclusion.[29] The next chapter examines how CPS draws on the information gathered during investigations to identify families where children are "at risk."

4

From Needs to Risks

SITTING ON HER living room couch, while two-year-old Gabriel played in his bedroom, Jazmine acknowledged that she was going through a lot. "Honestly, my stress level right now—like, this apartment, that my lovely caseworker got for me, failed inspection three times. Three times!" The apartment's lead levels were too high, she calmly explained to her CPS investigator, Fred. "So now I have to move." She wanted to stay in the New Haven area to be near her support network, but her housing case manager was suggesting apartments in other parts of the state, where rents were lower. Her rapid rehousing program was ending, meaning she would soon be responsible for the rent in full. Recall that without a car, she'd lost work hours at her home health aide job; she hoped to buy a car but couldn't afford one without logging more hours at work. She tried to stay busy so as not to dwell on traumatic experiences from her childhood. Though she had a strained relationship with her mother and brother, she leaned on her boyfriend and his mother for support and had found mentors in community organizations.

As Jazmine told Fred, marijuana helped her manage her stress and anxiety—"the only thing that can balance my lows," she called it—and she made sure to smoke when Gabriel wasn't around. When Fred replied by raising the possibility of therapy, Jazmine's frustration mounted, as she felt it wouldn't help. She told him how she'd cycled through a dozen mental health clinicians and sixteen different medications as an adolescent, none of which she'd found useful. "Let me do what I do so I can cope!" she exclaimed. "If you don't let me do that, then I go crazy—I do all this other stuff!"

Fred finished up the battery of questions and forms he had for Jazmine, her boyfriend Tony, and Tony's mother and then told Jazmine that he would call her later to set up their next meeting. During the six-week investigation, he and his supervisor would decide whether to substantiate (i.e., confirm) the allegations of abuse, whether to seek legal custody of Gabriel, and whether to keep the case open for ongoing CPS oversight. The first two decisions were straightforward: Fred swiftly concluded that Jazmine hadn't abused Gabriel by hitting him on the hand and that Gabriel could safely stay home with her.

But Fred had lingering concerns about what might happen to Gabriel going forward. As we drove back to the office that evening, he shared his take on the situation:

> This is a young mom who clearly has a history of trauma. She's been through quite a bit in her life. . . . She has that history, she's a single parent, she's not employed right now. There's all of the risk factors that you might expect to see, especially for a case of possible physical abuse, because it's a stressful situation and you could see how someone might be more likely to go a little too far with the discipline. . . . There wasn't that immediate sort of removal risk there, but I was sort of saying in the visit, there's factors there, there's a bunch of things going on.

Fred was worried about Gabriel, not because Jazmine was an uncaring or malicious mother but because the past and present circumstances of her life—her childhood trauma, her single parenthood, her unemployment—constituted "risk factors" that might portend future maltreatment if things continued as before.

If Fred decided to close the case, he could refer the family to social services available in the community, but the agency wouldn't continue visiting absent a new report. Alternatively, keeping the case open, the outcome for approximately one in five investigations in Connecticut, would dispatch a new CPS caseworker to visit regularly and monitor Jazmine's participation in substance use and parenting services. Fred had to make this decision without knowing for sure what would happen in the future either way. He'd gathered copious information, as we've seen, but he didn't have a crystal ball. Nevertheless, his assessment could have high stakes—for Jazmine, for Gabriel, and even for Fred's career if he made the wrong call. Ultimately, he and his supervisor reasoned that although Jazmine hadn't abused her son, everything else she had going on made the situation risky. They decided that CPS should stay in her life.

In interpreting Jazmine's situation through the lens of risk, Fred echoed broader CPS guidance. This perspective—"concerned with bringing possible future undesired events into calculations in the present [and] making their avoidance the central object of decision-making processes," in the words of social theorist Nikolas Rose—pervades governmental efforts to manage poverty.[1] In particular, risk has become an orienting framework in child welfare in recent decades.[2] It dominates scholarship and training in the field. A guide for CPS caseworkers from the federal government states that the investigation's "primary purpose is to assess the safety of the child and the risk of future maltreatment."[3] Alongside investigators' informal judgments, CPS agencies across the country use formal, quantified risk instruments to inform decision-making; in Connecticut, for instance, investigators answer a series of checkbox-style questions whose responses are summed to produce a "risk score" for each case.[4]

This chapter examines how investigators like Fred read risk to evaluate mothers under investigation. I focus primarily on investigators' informal assessments, which in Connecticut drive investigative decision-making.[5] As we see in Fred's take on Jazmine, investigators look beyond what's reported. This means that two cases that come in for similar reasons can sharply diverge. CPS doesn't evaluate families based on the precipitating event in isolation. Instead, the agency takes a holistic, future-oriented approach, looking at families' broader social background and context to try to predict what will happen.[6] (That said, presenting allegations certainly matter; cases like Alex's from the prior chapter, in which investigators confirm allegations they find concerning, are highly unlikely to close, no matter what.) CPS investigations aren't criminal cases—they aren't even before a court at this stage—so there's no concept of due process, and CPS can consider whatever information it likes in its assessment. Investigative staff have considerable discretion to determine what constitutes "risk." In their assessments, I saw investigators attend to parents' previous history with CPS, their material and social resources, and the extent to which parents seemed to understand the situation in line with CPS's interpretation—characteristics they understand to indicate something about children's future risk of maltreatment.

Because poverty and adversity strongly predict child maltreatment, perhaps it's unsurprising that ideas of risk largely correspond to the challenges families face. By zeroing in on parents' prior CPS encounters, their resources, and their ability to conform to the agency's expectations, investigators end up recasting family needs as individual, maternal risks.[7] Connecticut's formal risk instrument, too, reads like a checklist of family needs: number of children, age of the youngest child, primary caregiver with a mental health or substance use problem, any children medically fragile or developmentally disabled, unsafe housing, and so on. This is by design; the instrument consists of "items that have a demonstrated relationship with actual case outcomes," as training materials state.

This interpretation of risk may seem sensible, a pragmatic way to make decisions in highly uncertain situations. We can understand why Fred would want to make the best guess he could by connecting what he'd learned about Jazmine to patterns from research and other cases he'd investigated. Jazmine's socioeconomic insecurity and her high stress might indeed expose Gabriel to harm down the line, and Fred wanted to intervene before Gabriel got hurt. Fred figured that by keeping the case open, CPS could set Jazmine up with treatment to process her traumas and address her anxiety. As he told her, parents rarely hurt their children intentionally. But, he said, overwhelmed by the stressors in their lives, they could "lose it." So he explained that his job was to put her in the best position to lower that risk.

To do this job, he prolonged CPS's watch over Jazmine, even though he knew that she hadn't harmed her son. In responding to Jazmine's situation through CPS—an entity organized around harms parents inflict on children and empowered to separate families—a stressed mother became a risky mother; a risky mother became an especially precarious mother. Because parents face different challenges and expectations along lines of race, class, and gender, notions of risk end up deepening and stratifying precarious motherhood.[8] Ultimately, sending families facing adversity to CPS obscures the structural inequities that create so much adversity in the first place, instead framing those facing the greatest challenges as dangers to their children who require state oversight (rather than, as chapter 5 will explore, material support). Precarity, then, begets precarity.

Prior System Contact

"We know history is the best predictor of the future," an administrator instructed staff in a professional development session. For CPS staff trying to judge the likelihood of future maltreatment, a family's previous run-ins with the agency carried considerable weight. Just one prior report of neglect, substantiated or not, added two points to a family's score on the formal risk instrument; a case previously opened for CPS monitoring added one more. (A total of five points would elevate the risk level from "low" to "moderate.") Beyond the formal instrument, staff are highly attuned to CPS history from the moment a call comes in. Understandably, they want to learn from prior agency contacts. Hotline workers search the database for prior reports and summarize case history when they send a case to field office staff. Upon receiving reports, the first thing investigators and their supervisors do is review case history. This history, or lack thereof, shapes how investigators assess risk.

Allegations of her boyfriend's domestic violence brought Nikki, a Black mother, her first visit from CPS. Joe, the White investigator assigned to the case, had a booming voice and a straight-shooting approach, honed from years of investigations experience in New Haven. He didn't anticipate substantiating the allegations. "I don't like substantiating on victims, especially when she has no history with us," he declared. But he added, "Let's say we have three prior investigations, all for domestic violence, all with him. Then . . . at a certain point, you have to be able to keep your kids safe." Fred, investigating Jazmine, said that with families reported for the first time, "there's a little more leniency to say, 'All right, maybe this was a one-off incident.'" But, he explained, if the family is reported again, especially within a short period of time, CPS might look to keep the case open. Of course, the absence of prior reports does not imply a "one-off incident." In Joe's hypothetical, for example, we can imagine families where ongoing domestic violence has yet to come to CPS's attention because neighbors are not close enough to overhear or because responding police officers decline to notify CPS.

In the case of Deborah, the mother from chapter 3 who accidentally over-dosed, her investigator, Sarah, pointed to Deborah's lack of prior CPS reports as a reason she anticipated closing the case. Referring to Deborah's husband's suicide the prior year, Sarah explained that Deborah "clearly handled a very traumatic event appropriately, because we've never had any contact with this family before. I couldn't even imagine being in her shoes, living through the death of her significant other and then having to parent through all of that."

For Sarah, that no one called CPS in the aftermath of the suicide implied that Deborah responded appropriately to the situation. This is certainly possible. It's also possible that the medical, educational, and other systems Deborah encountered as a White mother gave her the benefit of the doubt or mobilized support for her outside of CPS. And a prior CPS report doesn't necessarily indicate an inappropriate response to trauma. As chapter 2 discussed, reports can come in for any number of reasons, including when callers believe that families need help; even reports resulting in no findings of maltreatment remain in the CPS database for at least five years, elevating perceptions of risk in any future reports that might come in.

As we see, case history isn't an objective accounting of families' situations.[9] Sarah Brayne, a sociologist studying quantified risk assessments in the Los Angeles

Police Department, writes that evaluating risk based on prior system contact "obscur[es] the role of enforcement in shaping risk scores," because police proactively intervene with residents in marginalized areas to a much greater degree.[10] Likewise, inequities in CPS reporting accumulate to institutionalize perceptions of risk. Although investigators tried to look beyond the number of prior CPS contacts to understand the qualitative nature of these reports, CPS history served as a useful shorthand, a highly salient lens through which investigators viewed families. Existing inequities thus compound to send families on diverging paths through CPS.

Material Resources

CPS also looks at families' current circumstances to gauge risk. For the purpose of prediction, this practice makes some sense; extensive research finds that child maltreatment is less likely among families with greater material and social resources.[11] At the same time, we know that these resources are distributed and interpreted along racial, class, and gender lines. Legal scholar Kimberlé Crenshaw, writing about women experiencing domestic violence, describes how the "multilayered and routinized forms of domination that often converge" in women's lives "hinder[] their ability to create alternatives" to the situations drawing the attention of service providers such as domestic violence shelters and CPS.[12] Limited resources absolutely make it challenging for parents to meet their children's needs, just as, in Crenshaw's articulation, women facing intersecting race, class, gender, and other oppressions often do confront additional obstacles. In the context of these real inequities, channeling families through CPS distorts their needs into risks and presumes that such risks should be remedied through supervision and sanctions.

In my observations, CPS staff tried to distinguish conditions of poverty from neglect. "This is definitely a poverty issue," one investigator said of a mother reported for housing instability and poor housing conditions. "Mom is doing everything possible." And staff emphasized that disheveled homes, so long as they did not threaten children's safety, should not be CPS concerns.[13] Alison, an investigator reflecting on her visit with Marlena, said that the condition of the carpets—stained with large, dark splotches, "almost like matted down with food and mud and stuff"—concerned her, especially as Marlena had toddlers at home. But Alison recognized the family's limited financial resources. "They don't even have the financial means to get beds," she said. "It could use a scrub-down, . . . but is that a CPS concern?" She closed the case.

Yet conditions of poverty nevertheless elevate CPS's perceptions of risk. The quantified risk instrument directs investigators to add one point to the risk score if CPS deems the family's current housing physically unsafe and two points if the family is homeless or about to be evicted. One more point is given if the primary caregiver "provides physical care inconsistent with child needs," as in the case of "persistent rat or roach infestations" or "inadequate or inoperative plumbing or heating." Even if CPS does not define homelessness itself as neglect, these items may well predict future maltreatment, perhaps by increasing stress. However, such situations nearly always result from poverty and are highly racialized, with Black and Latinx families especially likely to face homelessness, eviction, and poor housing conditions.[14] Shuttling families with inadequate housing to CPS pushes those in need deeper into an agency oriented around risk and maltreatment. (And as the next chapter discusses, CPS is ill-equipped to ameliorate the housing conditions that place children at risk, given its focus on maltreatment.)

Poverty also makes it more difficult to mitigate risks CPS may identify. Before Joe headed over to Nikki's home to investigate the allegations of neglect via exposure to domestic violence, he checked police records. He saw that Nikki had called the police twice in recent months—according to the police reports, once when her boyfriend, Cyrus, slammed her into a wall and another time when he turned on the gas stove and threatened to burn the house down.

We arrived to find several people sitting out front on the stoop of the triple-decker where Nikki lived. "Ms. Jackson?" Joe introduced himself and asked if we could talk in the house.

Nikki sighed. "Somebody called y'all?"

"Yep. We don't just drive around looking at people's houses," Joe smiled. "We're busy enough." Nikki led us around to the back door, where we entered through the kitchen to a large dining table.

Nikki sat quietly as Joe referenced the domestic violence incidents that had brought him there. Joe asked about her relationship with Cyrus. Nikki leaned back in her chair slightly, her arms crossed, replying that it was all right. As the visit continued, she opened up more. Things had been "rocky" with Cyrus, she knew, and she wasn't sure about the relationship's future. Nikki's eleven-year-old daughter told Joe she'd seen Cyrus drag and hit Nikki on multiple occasions; Joe later wrote in his report that Nikki's daughter said she "doesn't feel safe when [Cyrus] is at the home."

After hearing this, Joe was frank with Nikki: "I'm concerned. Okay? I'm concerned." Joe told her that Cyrus couldn't stay in the home with her children and asked her to sign a "safety plan" to that effect.

Nikki took in what Joe was saying. She assured Joe that she was already taking steps to get herself and her two kids out of the situation. "I was actually trying to move from here," she said, adding that she just had to find something she could afford. She made ends meet with her disability benefits, child sup-' port, and SNAP. After losing her housing voucher, Nikki was facing eviction when we visited.

Joe and Nikki talked through potential options. Cyrus could not go elsewhere, because he was on electronic monitoring for parole. Nikki's kids didn't want to stay with Nikki's mother, with whom Nikki had a strained relationship. Joe stepped out to call his supervisor, telling her he felt "stuck" and didn't know what to do. "I dunno how to resolve this," Joe muttered under his breath after they hung up.

Nikki agreed to have her kids stay with a neighbor that night, but this wasn't a sustainable solution. Joe didn't want to punish Nikki for experiencing domestic violence, but Nikki had limited options to address Joe's concerns and get CPS out of her life.[15] She couldn't pay for a motel room while she figured out next steps; she didn't have better-off relatives she could call on to assist.

In the end, Joe dealt with the risk himself. The next day, Joe spoke with Cyrus's parole officer about getting Cyrus out of the home—not by finding him another place but by re-incarcerating him. Joe told Cyrus's parole officer about the police coming by for domestic violence. Within the week, Cyrus was locked up again for this parole violation, leaving Nikki frustrated and upset with Joe.

Nikki's case shows how ideas of risk intersect with racialized poverty and racialized criminalization. With Nikki lacking the financial resources to ameliorate the risks CPS identified, CPS pursued a carceral approach, made possible by the mass supervision of Black people, especially poor Black men. With Cyrus out of the home, Joe could close Nikki's case. Families without sufficient resources to allay CPS's concerns to the agency's liking were subject to the tools CPS had on offer, whether criminalization, therapeutic intervention, or ongoing CPS monitoring.

Social Resources

While investigators sometimes hesitated to attribute risk based on (lack of) material resources—they did not want to explicitly punish parents for their poverty—there was no such ambiguity when it came to social resources. CPS staff were highly attuned to parents' social support, frequently and explicitly

evaluating risk based on the nature and strength of parents' social relationships. Take the cases of Norma Rivera and Sherea Williams. Both gave birth
within the same week, in the same network of hospitals. Both came to CPS's
attention shortly after delivery, following positive marijuana tests; both said
that they smoked to reduce nausea, to keep food down during difficult preg-
nancies.[16] Both received SNAP benefits, were working before giving birth, and
anticipated taking some time off to care for their newborns.

Norma perched on the couch in her hospital room, occasionally turning to
sip her Dunkin Donuts iced coffee as she talked with Ria, a Black investigator.
I sensed some nervousness in Norma's voice, especially early on, but she
seemed to keep talking animatedly as a way to get past it, smiling and laughing
with Ria as she shared stories about her family. A Puerto Rican woman in her
late thirties, Norma lived with her husband of many years and her two older
children, twelve and sixteen, in an area of the city she deemed "not so good."
Norma had become addicted to prescription pills a few years prior, so for the
past two years, she had gone to a methadone clinic. Thus, her newborn's toxicology screen had come up positive for methadone in addition to marijuana.

When Ria asked about Norma's "supports," Norma gushed that she was
"really tight" with her siblings. Throughout the visit, she referenced other close
family relationships: with her nieces and nephews, some of whom came to the
hospital to see the baby during our visit, and her husband's family, who lived
nearby and visited regularly with Norma and her children. Norma was disappointed that the baby's grandparents couldn't join her, her husband, and her
other children in the delivery room due to hospital limits.

Ria was very taken with the family, especially after meeting Norma's older
children. "Some families make my life easier," she sighed right after we stepped
out of the room. Norma's commitment to her children and her willingness to
participate in recommended programs impressed Ria. But Norma's social support networks, too, figured heavily into Ria's assessment:

> She has a lot of support systems, which I think is very positive. . . . She
> seems to have a very healthy relationship with her husband as well as her
> kids. The fact that all the family members were there, I feel like it's the big,
> happy, supportive family. . . . If she gets a little stressed, I feel like she has
> the support.

Norma's strong social connections—with her husband and extended
family—reassured Ria. And Ria suggested, "They don't seem to have a lot of
stressors, which kind of minimizes her usage as well." Ria reasoned that Norma

might indeed have smoked marijuana solely to address her nausea, meaning that she might not continue using going forward.

To weigh the risk to Norma's newborn, Ria considered the facts of the allegations in context. Norma's close-knit and supportive family and the absence of other "stressors"—such as economic or relationship instability—bolstered Ria's confidence in Norma's parenting. She knew that she would need to hear from Norma's methadone clinic and have Norma do a substance use evaluation. But she enthused, "Right now it seems as if she's doing a great job. I anticipate her to do an even better job given all the support and how happy she is with her family as a whole."

A week earlier, I'd driven over to the hospital with Gail, another Black investigator. Sherea's baby, her first child, was born early that Friday morning and would be discharged Sunday, so Gail canceled her afternoon meetings and rearranged her Friday evening to ensure that CPS could approve a plan for discharge. We arrived to Sherea up and about in a loose hospital gown, holding her hours-old newborn to her chest and rocking him. Sherea, a twenty-nine-year-old Black woman with her hair in long, thin braids, placed the baby down in the pram to sit across from us. Like Norma, she seemed a little apprehensive about Gail coming by—later telling me she felt "nervous and scared" to talk to Gail—but she tried to project an easygoing demeanor, presenting herself as open to Gail's suggestions. As Ria had done with Norma, Gail inquired about Sherea's supports.

"I don't really have no one as a resource," Sherea replied.

"Your sisters are not your resources?"

Sherea said that it was "complicated." By way of explanation, she told Gail that she had several sisters in the city, yet was staying with a friend, leaving Gail to read between the lines.

Sherea's mother had passed away. Gail asked about Sherea's father. "If you needed help, he wouldn't be able to help you?" Sherea shook her head.

The baby's father lived down south, and Sherea was contemplating moving down to join him. She'd lived there for about a year, until she and the father "bumped heads" and Sherea took a bus back to Connecticut a few months prior. Since then, she'd been staying with her friend Tyshonda, the only person who accompanied her in the delivery room.

When we stopped by Tyshonda's place—Gail had to check out where the baby would be discharged to—she wasn't home, but her boyfriend grudgingly let us in. Gail asked where Sherea's room was. Tyshonda's boyfriend, unsure, motioned to one of the rooms and then the pullout couch. Sherea didn't seem to have her own space in the apartment. But he assured Gail that Sherea always had a place to sleep.

After Gail finished up that evening, she deemed Sherea "cooperative" and "engaging"; indeed, Sherea readily participated in a substance use screening and evaluation. But Gail worried about Sherea's lack of social support, which in Sherea's case meant a lack of material support too. Gail was "nervous" for Sherea; one argument between Sherea and Tyshonda, Gail fretted, could leave Sherea and her newborn homeless. Gail also felt uneasy about the baby's father living out of state. She wanted to feel out the father's commitment to support-ing Sherea and the baby if they moved down south:

> If he says, "Yeah, even though we're not gonna be in a relationship, I'm gonna make sure that she has a place to stay, that the baby has all he needs and all that stuff," then that would give me some peace of mind. . . . If he doesn't say that, then I will definitely be able to keep the case open, if she decides to go down.

When I caught up with Gail the following week, she said that the baby's father was supportive, putting her "at ease."

And yet, CPS kept Sherea's case open—as the supervisor's note explained, "for future monitoring, and to ensure that Ms. Williams secures stable housing and cooperate[s] with treatment recommendation[s]." Tests found marijuana still in her system, so CPS wanted to monitor her marijuana levels. And Tyshonda was moving, so Sherea needed to find housing, reflecting the inter-section of economic and social needs. No one at CPS would call Sherea's hous-ing insecurity maltreatment. But in turning to CPS to assist her—isolated, on the verge of homelessness with a newborn—concerns about the *risk* Sherea posed predominated. In this framework, her needs became risks and thus rea-sons to continue monitoring her, deepening her sense of precarious mother-hood. When her case didn't close, Sherea felt that CPS was calling her a bad parent, "because when you hear that name, that's what you think." She didn't know what CPS would do. Sherea thought of an older sister whose kids CPS sent to stay with their grandmother. "That's what I'm afraid [of]. I don't want [that] to happen," she said. "I don't want nobody to take him."

Meanwhile, CPS closed Norma's case. It's difficult to say for sure that Nor-ma's social support alone made the difference. Still, with Norma married and identifying numerous close and supportive relationships, Ria wasn't particu-larly worried about Norma's children, describing Norma's family in glow-ing terms.

As with material resources, social resources make it easier to allay CPS's concerns. For example, after a mother named Elena picked up her young son from day care one day, she hit another car and drove off, her son in the back seat. The police pulled her over; she drove away again. When the police caught up with her, Elena failed the field sobriety test. Adam, the investigator assigned to the case, headed over the next day. Waiting on the porch for Elena to come to the door, Adam told me that he might have to ask Elena to leave the home.

Elena told us she'd made a "horrible mistake" and wanted help for her alcohol use. Adam planned to refer her for a substance use evaluation, which would recommend treatment. Until then, he said, they would put a "safety plan" in place, specifying that Elena would not be alone with her son. Elena didn't push back on this. Fortunately, her husband's work shift ended around the same time her son got out of day care; her husband's mother lived with them as well and was usually home.

As we see, CPS relies on families' private safety nets to mitigate its concerns. In an informal conversation with me, a Rhode Island administrator explained the importance of social support for child well-being. She recalled her own experience parenting a difficult baby and the toll this took, "normal feelings." What kept her baby safe, she said, was that she had supports—her husband, her relatives—who could step in when she felt as though she was going to lose it and needed to step away. Likewise, CPS staff reasoned that parents' drinking or marijuana use posed less of a concern when another adult was home to care for the children. These presumptions make sense; families' social resources, like financial resources, do support child well-being.

But is it *just* for CPS to evaluate families this way? Even as marginalized people provide one another with vital support in the face of brutal societal disinvestment, the strains of poverty, racism, and trauma erode social support and undermine trust in personal relationships.[17] Conflict-ridden social relationships are not specific to the poor. But living in desperation and deprivation places especially heavy burdens on such relationships and raises the stakes of transgressions.[18]

Families without material resources can sometimes compensate with social resources—Elena's family was poor, for instance—and vice versa. But families with neither get cast as risky, shifting the burden of responsibility for structural inequities back to parents. In one case involving a newborn with a positive toxicology screen, I asked the investigator what else she thought the family needed. Just "family supports," she responded, "and we can't develop a family." As the saying goes, it takes a village to raise a child. But paltry public supports and safety nets leave families to their private—and unequal—enclaves to raise children. If these enclaves lack sufficient resources to pitch in and offer support, the alternative for parents facing adversity is CPS, an agency focused on their risky behavior.

Gendered Responsibility and Risk

A risk framework is somewhat agnostic as to who or what is creating the risky environment. Instead, it foregrounds whether children are sufficiently protected from harm. In this view, if children are "at risk," CPS must intervene with their caregivers, even if their caregivers are not the primary source of risk. This seemingly evenhanded mandate makes notions of risk deeply gendered, due to cultural and institutional presumptions that caregiving is first and foremost a maternal responsibility.[19] When hotline workers in Connecticut create new cases in the CPS database, for instance, they put each case under a single name—almost always the mother's name, regardless of whom the report accuses of abuse or neglect. This name shows up all over caseworkers' computer screens; it's how they label their manila case folders. So staff referred to the "Nikki Jackson" case even though the case centered on domestic violence perpetrated by Cyrus, her boyfriend. I rarely saw cases under men's names. Even in the eight Connecticut focal cases involving married parents, only one was under the father's name.

When the behavior of fathers or others threatens child well-being, CPS still focuses its attention on mothers as primary caregivers of children. For example, Cassandra and Rob, whom I first met in Providence, were trying to co-parent their two-year-old daughter. At the handoff, they argued about the visits; Cassandra said Rob ran to his car, put their daughter on his lap, and put the car in drive. Cassandra tried to stop the car. "It turned out to be this whole thing—he was kicking the crap out of me." The police arrested Rob for domestic violence. Cassandra lived in Massachusetts at the time, so Massachusetts CPS investigated, but Rob, in Rhode Island, declined to respond. Nevertheless, Massachusetts CPS kept the case open for four months, visiting Cassandra regularly at home. "Oh my God, CPS's all up in my butt," Cassandra recalled. "I was so mad, though, because that was all due to Rob. He didn't have to deal with it. He lives in Rhode Island. Mass CPS couldn't touch him. All they could do was make sure that [our daughter], who was a resident of Mass, was okay in Mass," she said. "Technically, that whole thing, even though he endangered her by taking her in the front seat of the car, it was all an act against me." CPS's focus on the child's living conditions meant that the agency zeroed in on Cassandra rather than Rob as the object of monitoring and intervention; she, not Rob, had to deal with a visitor scrutinizing her parenting. Cassandra called it "a pain in the ass," as "everything you do has to be graded and judged." CPS visiting put her motherhood on shaky ground. After a previous case closed, she'd felt a sense of pride. But when the agency returned following the incident with Rob, she said, "it felt like my pride was being questioned."

CPS also holds mothers responsible for the shortcomings of men in their lives, policing their intimate relationships.[20] For example, CPS and courts cite mothers' "failure to protect" children from domestic violence. This is not to suggest that children should be around people likely to harm them but, rather, to highlight how CPS focuses on the actions of mothers more than fathers or mothers' partners. We see this in the case of Gina, a White mother seeing a man named Nathan whose domestic violence and substance use had led CPS to remove his other children. At the final investigative visit, the CPS investigator asked Gina to confirm that Nathan was "out of the picture," not in a caretaking role with the kids. A month later, with the case opened for ongoing services, the CPS caseworker stopped by to find Nathan at Gina's home. "I was told I have to choose to either keep my kids or keep Nathan," Gina texted me. The next day, CPS had Gina sign a "safety plan" stating that she would not allow Nathan in her home and would not allow him to have contact with her children. "If I violate that order, then they're gonna take my boys," she told me. At no point in the case did CPS instruct Nathan about appropriate behavior around the children—it was Gina's case. Focused on Gina's children and Gina's responsibility to protect them, CPS was poised to punish her for their relationship. CPS put the choice to her—her partner or her children—and made it clear that there was only one correct answer.[21]

CPS expects mothers to place the maternal role first and foremost and organize their lives around this devotion. Sociologist Sharon Hays documented the power of what she called an intensive mothering ideology, the notion that mothers should incur substantial financial, emotional, and time costs to devote themselves to child-rearing.[22] CPS assesses the risk mothers pose based on this ideal, even as mothers may face numerous barriers to achieving it (and may instead be mothering under an ideal of collective mothering, through kin and fictive kin networks).[23] Take the case of Joyce, a Latina mother. CPS had just completed an investigation of Joyce's family when her boyfriend, the father of her children, visited the CPS office seeking help. Joyce had left the home, and he wanted to get the SNAP and WIC benefits in his name so he could provide for the kids. The CPS case had closed, so staff told him to call the hotline if he had concerns. When he did, Sheila, the Black assigned investigator, was surprised that the situation was accepted for investigation. Nevertheless, poverty placed Joyce's family back on CPS's radar.

Sheila arranged to meet with Joyce at the CPS office. Sheila was frustrated because Joyce wasn't calling her looking for her kids; instead, Sheila had to be persistent in reaching out to Joyce. To Sheila, this suggested Joyce's lack of interest in her kids, whom she hadn't seen in several days. "Like, where's your mindset? I would be on the phone. . . ."

We met in a conference room. Joyce seemed tired. Her dark hair up in a bun, she rested her head in her hands. During the meeting, Sheila, calm and measured, asked about what happened, trying to get a sense of the timeline of events and how Joyce wanted to move forward.

Afterward, Sheila went to debrief with her supervisor, Bryan. Sheila said that she hoped to set up a visit so Joyce could see the kids. "But she wasn't like, I want them. Any mom would've been like, I want my kids with me, I'm ready." Sheila told Bryan that Joyce hadn't answered whether she even wanted her kids.

Bryan chuckled. "A nonanswer is an answer, right?"

Sheila shrugged. "I was like, whatever, lady. Your kids are good. They gonna stay with Dad. And you don't seem to be invested at all."

Sheila was right that Joyce was preoccupied. Joyce and her boyfriend had been arguing. "We have so much going on that we haven't really been getting along," she shared. Things had been stressful; they were facing eviction. A social services program had assured Joyce that it would cover her rent while she waited for cash assistance. But the program abruptly stopped its payments, later saying that Joyce had been denied. "Now that puts us in the hole for $1,700." The landlord's patience thinned. "Everything kinda falled up on us."

Sheila just listened. Joyce said that their combined incomes could cover rent but that the gas had recently been cut off. She paused and added that she was looking for a job, as well.

"That's a lot," reflected Sheila.

Joyce's stress bubbled over. "Like, what am I gonna do. I have no help from nobody, no family, no nothing." Her boyfriend tended to shut down when the pressure became too much. Joyce also became overwhelmed and needed to take some time for herself. She was staying with an aunt and occasionally sleeping in her car.

Sheila asked whether Joyce wanted her children with her. "However it's gonna go, either/or, I have to be prepared," Joyce replied. "With or without, I'm still a mother, you know what I mean? The job doesn't finish." Joyce knew that her boyfriend would take good care of the kids and recognized their attachment to him. So in hedging, perhaps she was looking out for their well-being.

But Sheila wanted to see Joyce willing to stop at nothing to be with her kids. As Sheila put it afterward:

> That desire of concern of where her kids are, that her kids need to be with her, that wasn't there. I feel when you talk to a parent, especially Mom, and you're asking them, "What do you want?" you're gonna say, "I want my kids with me" or "I need to see them. I need to talk to them."

We see in Sheila's comments how gendered this phenomenon is—it's mothers CPS expects to display this unflinching commitment to being with their children. Meanwhile, the resources mothers have constrain (or enable) their ability to meet CPS's expectations. Marginalized mothers recognize the power of intensive mothering in the eyes of authorities, crafting their narratives and labor accordingly to align with this ideology.[24] Those who cannot or do not—those open to spending some time away from their children, like Joyce—raise concerns.

Sheila anticipated closing Joyce's case because the children were with their father. But, she said, it was "concerning" that Joyce "just gets up and leaves when she wants to" when she got frustrated and overwhelmed. Sheila did not interpret this as a sign of Joyce's social support—that Joyce's boyfriend could step in when she needed some time away. Social resources could only pitch in to a certain point; CPS wanted to see mothers directing children's day-to-day lives.

As Joyce's case suggests, the notion of social support mitigating maltreatment risk is highly gendered. In assessing the extent to which social resources can protect children from maltreatment, CPS favors biological and legally recognized relationships in ways that reflect racialized gender and family norms. Fred, for instance, worried about Jazmine's lack of social support. After he asked whom Jazmine called when she felt stressed, she shook her head and looked down. Fred asked why she was shaking her head. She paused.

"You keep it in yourself?" Fred supplied. She didn't answer.

Jazmine's boyfriend of two years, Tony, and his mother helped out, watching her son, Gabriel, while Jazmine worked, for instance. But later, with me, Fred questioned the longevity of these supports:

> The thing with boyfriends is that boyfriends come and go, and so it's nice that they've been together for a little while, but he isn't the biological father. It's great if they're there now, but we can't always assume that they're going to always be around and be supports to her.

Fred acknowledged that Tony's mother seemed like a good resource for Jazmine but pointed out that the connection still ran through Tony. "It sounds like she just doesn't have any supports, and even if there are stable family members, her relationship is strained with them," he concluded. Jazmine described her mother as a "crazy drug addict" and said that Gabriel's father hadn't seen Gabriel since birth.

Yet these blood and biological parenting relationships are the ones the state can most easily recognize. In Sherea's case, too, Gail pushed to see commitment from the baby's father and held out hope that Sherea's father and sisters could provide support, despite their strained relationships. Gail worried that Tyshonda could kick Sherea out at any time. But Sherea's housing situation wasn't necessarily any more fragile than if she were living with a sibling. Sherea considered Tyshonda like family—they'd grown up together, with Sherea's mother considering Tyshonda a daughter and vice versa. This notion of biological relationships as most durable and supportive is deeply racialized. In particular, with the forcible separation of Black families during slavery and beyond, fictive kin relationships are central to Black family and social life.[25]

As we see, ideas about who is or will be responsible for child well-being shape how CPS understands and attributes risk in families. Mothers in particular become the focus of CPS's intervention, scrutinized for the "risk" they may pose. CPS takes mothers' familial and social connections into account as well—but the agency privileges some relationships over others, and none can supplant mothers' individual responsibility for their children's well-being.

Insight

To CPS, the appropriate, "low-risk" mother demonstrates what staff call "insight," perhaps the most amorphous factor investigators invoke in their evaluations. Investigations rarely focus on identifying "intent," as might be the case in criminal investigations; CPS staff know that parents under investigation almost never intend to harm their children. Instead, CPS assesses "insight," or the extent to which parents see the situation as CPS does and respond accordingly.[26] When discussing cases, CPS staff repeatedly talked about whether parents "got it" or were "minimizing." From CPS's perspective, parents who share the agency's view of the situation—and specifically, the harms to which they may have subjected their children—are more likely to do what CPS wants, reducing future risk to their children.

Thus, when staff believed that parents lacked insight, they brandished their coercive tools to try to impart the seriousness to parents. One case involved a Puerto Rican mother named Rosie reported after she and her girlfriend got into a physical altercation while her girlfriend was holding their infant daughter. Bridget, the White investigator, felt that it was a more significant domestic violence incident than CPS typically saw. Afterward Bridget said, "I feel like she downplayed it a lot. . . . I don't think she was able to own her part in it. There was a lot of blame." Although Bridget planned to close the case—she didn't think that the family needed ongoing CPS oversight—she was clear that "this needs to be substantiated for sure, no doubt." Substantiation wouldn't change the resources or service referrals CPS could offer the family; however, believing that Rosie minimized her role in the incident, Bridget wanted to send a message:

> I think sometimes being substantiated for neglecting your own child . . . will kind of be like, 'Oh shoot.' . . . As it stands right now, I don't think she gets it. I don't think she gets her role in this, and I think if I can substantiate and kind of show her that she is just as responsible for this as [her girlfriend] was. . . .

In other cases, CPS convened formal meetings that explicitly threatened child removal in order to put parents on notice. Of course, such threats and substantiations are not just for show. Even if they do not lead to family separation, they are stressful for families and, as described above, remain on parents' CPS records indefinitely, impacting any additional reports that come in.

To convey insight, mothers must show that they share CPS's concerns, that they take responsibility for their predicaments, and that they want to remedy the concerns in the way CPS recommends.[27] Yet the ill-defined nature of insight creates opportunities for biases or misreadings on CPS's part to take hold. And those with greater needs may be preoccupied with other concerns that constrain their ability to respond in ways CPS deems appropriate—recall Joyce, overwhelmed.

Imelda, a Puerto Rican mother displaced by Hurricane Maria, arrived in Connecticut a few months after the hurricane hit. She and her four children lived with her friend Erica, along with Erica's three children, Erica's sister, Imelda's girlfriend, and the girlfriend's son—twelve people in Erica's three-bedroom apartment. Erica, also displaced by the hurricane, was watching Imelda's children one day when Imelda's three-year-old let herself out of the apartment. A neighbor several doors down found the child, toddling around, her socks soaked from the rain, unable to say her name or where she lived. The neighbor called the police, which notified CPS. After knocking on doors on the street looking for the child's caretakers, the police arrested and held Erica for risk of injury to a child. Distraught, Erica told Imelda that she wanted Imelda and her children to leave that day.

The two investigators assigned to the case were exasperated at the women's seeming lack of alarm about the toddler outside on a busy street.[28] "We were all concerned, but they weren't," one investigator, Heather, said. "Everybody was upset about [Erica] being arrested, but nobody is upset that this three-year-old was walking on the street by herself. It was like, no remorse." To Heather, this spoke "volumes" in terms of "the risk level, taking the preventative measures . . . to recognize that, 'Whoa, this could have been bad,' and making sure that it doesn't happen again." She wrote in her report that Imelda, who said that Erica did nothing wrong, did not appear "to grasp the seriousness of the situation."

When I interviewed Imelda a few weeks later, at her kitchen table, she recalled her greatest fear from that day: that Erica would stay locked up or that she might end up in jail too.

> It broke my heart to see [Erica] in that condition. She has always looked after my children, since Puerto Rico. . . . I didn't know what to do, because she is my daughter, you know? And she is my friend, like my sister, so I felt I was between a rock and a hard place [*entre la espada y la pared*].

So Heather wasn't necessarily misreading Imelda's preoccupation. But in context, we can see Imelda's concerns linked to her children's well-being. Imelda and her children relied on Erica for housing and social support. That night, Imelda wept as she held her daughter close and reached out to everyone she knew for help. She called relatives in Puerto Rico and sold her laptop to raise Erica's $1,500 bail.

Imelda understood that her daughter had been in danger the day she got out of the house. As she expressed to me: "She doesn't know the neighborhoods or anything, so she wasn't safe. I thank God and the person who saw her, because if someone else had grabbed her, an imprudent person—there have been several cases of people who steal children." Heather's own report stated that Imelda "was nervous and asked about her child" upon returning home. After the police brought Imelda's daughter home, Heather wrote, Imelda "held her tight and began to cry." But Imelda's pleas for Erica not to be arrested conveyed, to Heather, a lack of insight.

Two other cases in the study also involved toddlers found alone outside. When we visited Lizette, she wiped her tears, sniffing. "It could've been so much worse—thank God." She told Lauren, her investigator, that she knew something awful could have happened—a thought that had kept her up at night since the incident. "God forbid, I'm not gonna experience that again." Lizette added that she was "very lucky." Afterward, Lauren deemed Lizette "appropriate." Lauren felt that it was "an isolated incident" and a clear-cut case to close.

Imelda's investigator, Heather, worked a few months later with Makayla, a Black mother whose two-year-old was found on her busy residential street. "The circumstances are very similar," Heather said, comparing Makayla's case with Imelda's. But Heather wasn't particularly worried about Makayla.

> In [Imelda's] case . . . nobody appeared concerned that this child had been outside on a busy street. They were just kind of like, "Oh, it happened, don't arrest anybody." Where [Makayla], at least, is concerned, like, "I know what could have happened." She wanted [her stepfather, who was supposed to be babysitting] arrested. She wasn't saying, "Don't arrest him." You know, she moved out of the house right then and there. . . . She got in a fight with her mom over this. I think in this case, at least, the mom kind of recognized the seriousness in the situation. . . . They were at least aware of the dangers or at least vocalized that.

The awareness Heather perceived alleviated her concerns because she believed that it signaled Makayla's approach going forward: "Hopefully, she'll take precautions to make sure it doesn't happen again."[29] When mothers articulated feelings of remorse and distress at the potential harms to which they had subjected their children, investigators felt more confident that they would take steps to prevent future incidents.

Beyond saying that they felt badly, mothers conveying remorse through their emotional expressions reassured investigators—think of Lizette's tearful laments. One morning, the snow fell heavily and quickly in an early April storm. When I drove to the Northeast Corner office that morning through the eastern portion of the state, the state road hadn't yet been treated or plowed. A call came into the office: an EMT reporting a five-year-old in a car accident, without a car seat as required by law. "It could've been, went off the road and hit a tree—that's what I felt like this morning," said Mallory, the White investigator assigned to the case. After calling the hospital, Mallory turned to the investigators nearby. "Multiple jaw fractures," she said, enunciating each word slowly and clearly for effect. The other investigators winced. "*Significant* dental trauma."

"'Cause she wasn't in a fucking seat," another investigator retorted.

Mallory was more sympathetic. "They probably feel so bad."

Another investigator shook her head regretfully. "You're gonna have to sub [substantiate] on this mama. Oh, shoot."

In the parking lot, Mallory and I brushed six inches of snow off the car before heading to the hospital, forty-five minutes away. She ordered a breakfast sandwich from the Dunkin Donuts drive-through to eat for lunch as she drove. We arrived at the child's hospital room, where she lay sedated, covered with a thin white blanket, her eyes barely open. Her face looked swollen, with a couple long scratches and some dried blood on her lip. Two large stuffed animals lay at her feet. Her mother, Danielle, and stepfather, Kevin, sat beside her.

Danielle's face was red, like she had been crying. A Latina mother of three, Danielle worked full-time at a rehab facility. She and Kevin looked shaken by the accident, like they were still processing what had happened. Danielle usually drove a minivan but had taken Kevin's truck that day because of the weather.

Mallory acknowledged that it was a rough drive that morning. "I get it." She assured them that "obviously this is a true accident," but she had to come out after a report. Mallory breezed through her questions, figuring she could press more in subsequent visits.

At one point, Mallory mentioned hearing something from the police about broken glass, perhaps from a picture frame in the car. Hearing this, Danielle and Kevin inhaled sharply. "Ohhhh," Danielle's eyes widened. Kevin stretched out, taking the information in. They explained that a picture frame in the pocket behind the front seat must have hit the child. Danielle's face crumpled. She buried her head in her hands.

To Mallory, this was a "clear-cut" low-risk case. If Danielle had tried to lie about the car seat, or if Mallory had had concerns about Danielle driving under the influence, Mallory might have felt differently. But she reasoned, "They were crying. They were red-eyed, remorseful." The booster seat might have been in Danielle's minivan. "Because of the weather, they thought it was safer [to switch cars], and now look what happened."

Still, driving back to the office, Mallory anticipated having to substantiate the allegations, noting that Danielle had broken a law, even if unknowingly. Mallory recited the neglect definition: Did Danielle do something to place her child in conditions or circumstances injurious to her well-being? "Bottom line, yeah, but that'd be a tough one. I'll do it if . . . that's the decision, but it's like, geez, obviously she's remorseful."

When we returned, other investigators fixated on Danielle's emotional presentation. Another investigator approached as we parked. Mallory rolled down the window, and they exchanged sympathetic looks. The other investigator asked how the parents were. "Crying?"

"Oh yeah," replied Mallory. "Bright red eyes."

Back in the office, Adam's first question was, "Parents were remorseful, apologetic?" He then asked whether they signed all of CPS's forms. Adam nodded, like that was what he needed to know to understand the case.

After speaking with Mallory, Mallory's supervisor discussed the case with the unit manager. The supervisor called it a "clear-cut sub if we want it," but the manager agreed that the parents had experienced punishment enough, so the staff on the case decided not to substantiate the allegations. Danielle never explicitly told Mallory that she felt awful about what had happened. Instead, Mallory read remorse in Danielle's emotional expressions, so CPS staff felt that Danielle did not need more reprimanding, in the form of a substantiation, to correct her behavior.

But parents' emotions are not always self-evident or easy to read. One mother, Charlene, was very polite and deferential to the Connecticut and Massachusetts investigators jointly assessing her in the hospital after she gave birth. She answered their questions quietly, without crying or getting upset. Charlene told them she knew that her choices—using marijuana and prescription opiates during pregnancy—were not great for the baby, but Sarah, the Connecticut investigator, replied that she was getting the feeling that there was "no sense of seriousness" about how Charlene's decisions affected the baby. "They just don't have any recognition of the impact that that's going to have," Sarah later said. I didn't hear Charlene justify her substance use or deny its impact. To me, when the investigators stepped out, Charlene portrayed her stone-faced demeanor as an effort to keep her composure and "not be an emotional wreck." Three days later, CPS placed Charlene's newborn in foster care, drawing heavily on Charlene's seeming lack of insight. As we see, CPS infers risk based on how mothers present themselves, with severe consequences for mothers who fail to comport with the agency's unstated expectations.

As Jennifer Reich has shown, tides turn when parents defer to CPS, when they are willing to partner with CPS and adjacent professionals.[30] Still, this doesn't mean that CPS requires mothers to passively submit. Take the case of Jennifer, introduced in chapter 2, whose daughter Faith had attempted suicide. Natasha, the Black investigator assigned to Jennifer's case, scribbled a note on the report printout she brought to visit Jennifer: "moment does not comply → legal consult," meaning a meeting with legal staff about the possibility of court intervention. Afterward, Natasha explained that she and her supervisor found the case concerning because "the hospital, who are the professionals, recommended an [intensive outpatient program], which Mom did not follow through with." Jennifer, meanwhile, said that the recommended program didn't fit with her work schedule and she wasn't going to drop everything for it. "I need to continue to secure my job," she told me. "I need to feed my kids. I need to house my kids." If professionals truly believed that Faith needed that specific program, Jennifer said, they should have helped her alleviate transportation and other barriers.

Jennifer had found a psychologist herself, a woman of color, for Faith, which she felt would suffice. But Natasha wasn't sure whether a weekly session fit the hospital's recommendation; she didn't think that Jennifer understood the need for a higher level of care. So the day after that first visit, Natasha didn't know how the case would go, saying that it was "50/50" and would hinge on how strongly CPS's mental health specialist felt about the intensive program and whether Jennifer continued to decline. "If Mom refuses, then it will be negligence on her part per se, because she's not following through with the medical recommendations that her daughter needs," Natasha reasoned.

In the end, CPS approved Jennifer's chosen psychologist, adjusting its assessment of her insight when the agency's mental health specialist met the psychologist and deemed Jennifer's response appropriate. "Risk" was not fixed but negotiable.[31] Nevertheless, CPS had the final say; had the specialist decided otherwise, Jennifer would have been considered neglectful. CPS framed Jennifer as potentially endangering her daughter, when Jennifer said that she needed help making the program work with her schedule. In the eyes of the agency, her needs became risks.

It's human instinct to want to jump in when we think that something bad might happen to a child. For CPS investigators, this goes beyond a moral intuition—it's their job. They don't want to ignore concerns they see, even if these concerns go beyond the initial allegation and reflect adverse social conditions rather than intentional parental cruelty. They hope that they can use the information they have to make better decisions. The child welfare system is often critiqued for responding to child maltreatment after the fact, for not doing enough to prevent maltreatment in the first place. As the previous chapter noted, CPS comes under fire when children "known to the system" die. So evaluating cases based on a measure of future risk makes both emotional and practical sense for CPS staff.

Moreover, the backgrounds and resources of individual parents, as well as what parents communicate to investigators, may indeed indicate something about children's future circumstances. When CPS staff invoke prior agency encounters, material conditions, social relationships, and perceptions of "insight" to assess risk, these may be pragmatic assessments about what is likely to happen. Perfect prediction is of course impossible. In my observations, though, investigators' expectations—based on their initial reads of the situation and their experience with similar cases—often did come to pass.[32]

But that CPS's assessments may often be *correct* does not necessarily make them *right* or *just*. Using information about the past and present to make a guess about the future stands in tension with broadly held ideals that people shouldn't be punished for things beyond their control or things they haven't even done yet. Specifically, the ability to present oneself as a "low-risk," appropriate parent is bound up in access to resources and gendered ideas of motherhood, both of which are racialized. This means that CPS rewards—or put another way, penalizes—parenting in racialized, classed, and gendered ways, amplifying precarious motherhood for the most marginalized mothers.

Through this focus on risk, inequality in CPS persists.[33] As we saw with CPS reporting in chapter 2, inequality does not require explicit discrimination based on race or other characteristics, the focus of scholarship and public discourse on the topic. Certainly, CPS staff are not immune to anti-Black stereotypes; making discretionary assessments in a context of persistent racism, they may indeed view Black parents as inherently more suspect and hold them to different standards.[34] Yet even supposedly race-neutral "risk factors," from CPS history to social support, are anything but. As we've seen, CPS draws on conceptions of risk that build in inequity and injustice behind the scenes, obscured from view.

With high levels of child poverty and limited public supports for families, U.S. children do not always have what they need and deserve. Turning to CPS to respond to children in such situations both frames the problem and circumscribes the proposed solution. An agency organized around harms inflicted by parents will, unsurprisingly, locate the problem in specific caregivers, especially mothers, essentially repackaging societal injustices as individual liabilities. Rather than systemic racism or extreme poverty, parents themselves—their insufficient support networks or lack of insight—become the chief threats to their children. The point is not that risk assessments are inaccurate or biased, though they certainly can be.[35] Even perfectly predictive assessments would not change what CPS is designed to do: zero in on risks posed by caregivers to continue monitoring those deemed highest risk.

Then, processing family adversity through CPS posits state oversight as the solution to families' needs, the way to mitigate the risks children face. When we see CPS's role as assisting families and preventing maltreatment, it seems reasonable—even desirable—to identify the most marginalized families for ongoing intervention. Because risks are essentially family needs, distributing CPS oversight based on risk is, in this view, simply responding efficiently in line with these needs. Jazmine might not end up endangering Gabriel, but what's the harm in continuing to check in with her to provide supportive services? Chapter 5 turns to this question.

5

Here to Help?

APRIL WATSON HAD HIGH hopes for her son Michael's new school. After learning about his prior school's poor performance and hearing about incidents that made her concerned for his safety, April had started exploring other options. After months of April pressing and waiting, Michael had a spot at another school that supposedly offered "so many more advantages."

But the new school wasn't working out. In April's words, ten-year-old Michael, a slim boy with big eyes and a bigger grin, was an entertainer and a class clown. In class, he was restless and easily distracted. April was frequently called up to the school, which couldn't manage his behavior and had started suspending Michael. Because he hadn't had these issues before, April, a Black mother, wondered about the role of racism. At Michael's previous school, predominantly Black, "most of the staff was minority," she noted. Maybe at this new school, April suggested, Michael's teacher "came in contact with a crazy Black mother who told him off, and he was, 'You know what? I ain't fixin' to mess with these Black kids no more like that.'" She sensed that the school was labeling Michael, putting him in the "bad pile."

One Tuesday, April picked Michael up at school and learned that school staff had called CPS. As the school told it, a school social worker asked a group of students where they would go if they could go anywhere in the world. Michael suggested Colorado, because marijuana was legal there and he could smoke as much as he wanted, adding that his father let him smoke. The social worker shared this exchange with the principal, who mentioned other recent incidents that raised concerns about Michael's marijuana use, such as classmates mentioning Michael having a bag of marijuana. In its report, the school noted that "both parents have been challenging to engage regarding Michael's progress and status."

Heather, a perky White investigator, stopped by the next day. I joined Heather to sit with April on the front porch of the apartment April shared with her mother, her brother, and Michael. April had grown up in the area and offered a cheery hello to everyone who walked by. Her hair, dyed burgundy and wound in tight curls, brushed her shoulders, and she had a presence difficult to miss. Like a stage actress, she spoke loudly and gestured expressively, moving her entire body as she talked and laughed. April was quick to crack jokes with Heather but recognized Heather's power. "Don't write that down!" she rushed to say after her quips. When Michael offered his account of what happened, he mentioned telling a classmate that his mom wouldn't let him smoke. April interjected to add, "Mom would kill him." Heather chuckled.

"Oh, don't put kill on the record!" April crowed.

"I'm not putting kill on the record," Heather assured her with a smile.

April knew that she hadn't done anything wrong; the school had accused Michael of having marijuana before but hadn't found anything on him when the staff searched. Still, when we spoke the day after Heather's visit, April described the "automatic panic and worry" she associated with CPS. "You see CPS, you see, clank, clank." Laughing, she mimed being handcuffed. She knew that the agency could blow things out of proportion. "All night long, barely being able to sleep," April said. "Did I say something wrong? What did I say? Oh, God. I am thirty-one, and it made me nervous. It made me wanna throw up all night long."

From the start, Heather wasn't particularly concerned, recognizing the "headbutting" between April and the school as well as Michael's penchant for saying things he knew would get him attention. "I just think a lot of these schools in New Haven are very quick to call in," Heather told me. Heather recommended strategies for working with the school as well as grief counseling services, mentioning a specific counselor April could ask for when she called: "She's awesome and great with kids." Before closing April's case, Heather also referred her to another agency that found and paid for a summer camp for Michael. Afterward, April gave Heather high marks: "I was blessed to get Heather. She seemed like she was very open-minded. She was totally doing her job."

April's case represents a best-case scenario; her worst fears didn't come to pass. Did summoning CPS help April's family? In one view, yes—April appreciated Heather's assistance. "They did plug me into some good resources," she reflected after her case closed. Michael loved the summer camp, and April was looking forward to meeting with a therapist she hoped would help Michael.

But even the most compassionate investigators cannot overcome what the agency represents and can do. April was adamant that she didn't want to be investigated again. CPS couldn't provide the financial support she needed to move into her own place. And the resources the agency offered came with other baggage, reinforcing her sense of precarity. For instance, April found CPS's surveillance "nerve-racking": "Now, I have eyes looking at me, and those eyes are—What the hell are you doing? What are you doing at home? Are you doing enough?" Even after her case officially closed, she remained apprehensive:

> Even though I say this went so wonderful, well, I also say random stuff happens. I don't know how that paperwork works. I don't know what system that now is in. I don't know how their databases work. I don't know how it works. After that, I walk down the street, get in an accident, now they're bringing up that time when my kid got—I have no idea.

April appreciated Heather's assistance but recognized that it came at a cost.[1] She couldn't just wash her hands of the experience; she now had a lasting, formal record with CPS.

The experience also left April even more frustrated with Michael's school. Given her active engagement with the school, it hurt that the principal called her "challenging." Rather than informing her about social work services available at the school, the school turned first to CPS. "You ain't even trying to handle the issue," she said. "I think that's where, most of the time, people get the lines blurred of, we wanna blame CPS, but that's not the person that did it. They just doing they job. This was the school." The experience confirmed to April that she couldn't trust the school—it wasn't looking to support Michael's needs but, rather, to target and blame her family. After the report, she planned to find another school for Michael.

This chapter interrogates the notion that CPS helps—or at least does no harm—during the investigation. CPS conducts investigations not just to identify safety concerns but to try to assist. Recall Deshawn, the CPS trainer from chapter 3 who wanted investigators to be "bringing something to the table," especially for the majority of families whose cases would close. Indeed, CPS connects families with social services. In Connecticut, investigators can make formal referrals to therapeutic programs, whether or not the agency keeps the case open. Some cases are eligible for a referral to a community agency offering case management services, with a small amount of discretionary funds available. Beyond referrals, investigators do what they can to help, finding a stroller for a family that needs one or offering advice about navigating various systems. Especially in cases that close after investigation, mothers often appreciate the assistance the agency provides, as April did.

Yet, as this chapter argues, this help cannot reach its full potential coming from CPS. Providing assistance through an entity organized around deficient parenting circumscribes and colors the support it can offer. CPS is ill-equipped to address families' chronic material needs, and tethering services to the threat of family separation discourages mothers from eagerly embracing them. For mothers, CPS intervention also undermines their broader sense of security, threatening their motherhood identity, their privacy, and their autonomy even when cases close and children remain home. Furthermore, with investigations reflecting accusations of improper parenting, CPS reports can prompt disengagement from those who notified CPS, often the very systems tasked with stabilizing and supporting families facing adversity. Turning to CPS to support families in need thus creates new forms of precarity—precarious motherhood—while not necessarily resolving, and perhaps even exacerbating, the broader socioeconomic insecurity families face.

What CPS Offers

CPS doesn't bill itself as a police force but, instead, as a service provider—an entity aiming to *help* families in need. Recall the mission of the Connecticut Department of Children and Families: "partnering with communities and empowering families to raise resilient children who thrive." When I asked mothers in Connecticut what their experience had taught them, many indeed said they learned that CPS was there to help.[2] This was the most common response I heard from mothers whose cases closed, whose investigations did not ultimately lead to the family separation they feared.

Tameka, reported following a suicide attempt, found the investigation "very scary," as she associated CPS with child removal. "I think thoughts at that point. I'm waking up and he's not there, or me being on record as a bad mom. I was really scared that it was gonna be just another traumatic experience that I had to go through." But the investigation showed Tameka a different side of CPS. Heather, also Tameka's investigator, struck a friendly, empathetic tone and identified service referrals for her. "I felt very happy that they were willing to help and do what they can," Tameka concluded.

Heather planned to refer Tameka to case management services and ensure that she was receiving mental health care. When I asked Heather what else she thought could benefit the family, her response was immediate: "I wish we had housing for people." Tameka, unable to afford an apartment, was staying with her mother, an environment Tameka said led her to overdose. Heather worried about Tameka returning to her mother's: "I think that if they had their own space, that they'd be off to a better start because then you're not putting her in that environment with that trigger, essentially."

But CPS couldn't get Tameka into an apartment. Instead, the agency's version of help came in the form of monitoring. Heather felt reassured that the referred programs would provide "accountability" and put "eyes on her even after [CPS closes]. If they suspect any or see any abuse or neglect . . . they're mandated reporters too." And CPS oversight, with its looming threat of family separation, would continue if Tameka did not comply with the agency's recommended services. "If she just decides, I'm not going to [the program] and I'm not gonna take the meds, we probably would keep the case open," Heather said. As we see, CPS can be a conduit to social services, but the assistance on offer from CPS is relatively narrow—and it comes with strings attached.

Narrow Capacities for Help

Sabrina, a Black mother in her late forties, cherished her fourteen- and thirteen-year-old daughters and her eleven-year-old son above all. "We're a team," she affirmed earnestly. "That's my team. That's my *team*. That's my team. Anything I could do for them, I would do my best to try. I would do anything, because they deserve it." Sundays were family day. Sometimes, they would check out local thrift stores. "We have a ball," she beamed, excitedly showing me the like-new white Sperry Top-Sider sneakers they'd just scored for $3 at Goodwill. Or they'd go to the Ikea in New Haven, overlooking the water. "We have the 99-cent breakfast, and we sit and look out the window."

But things had been rough in recent years. As Sabrina put it, she was "pretty much trying to survive." She had divorced her husband several years prior; shortly afterward, she was diagnosed with breast cancer and left her bus driving job. For the better part of a year, she and her children had stayed in the attic of a relative's house, sleeping on two mattresses on the floor of a windowless room. She kept the place free of clutter but couldn't do much about the stained carpets and cracked walls. Rodents and roaches roamed. The mice nibbled at the children's school clothes. Sabrina kept her silverware in the refrigerator. "I don't leave nothing out, not a spoon, not a fork. Nothing, because they're overtaking." She showed me pictures of the mice they'd trapped.

Sabrina just felt drained. She reflected, "Sometimes when I talk, I say to myself, 'I wish this was just a story and not true,' but it's so true. It's so true." She wanted to move, but her limited income from disability benefits wasn't enough, and she hadn't received any child support from her ex-husband. The eviction on her record, too, made it difficult to find a landlord to accept her. Once, with high hopes, she'd wired money for a place she'd found on Craigslist, only to find it a scam.

The housing stress had taken a toll on Sabrina's health. As she explained, "[I] pretty much push my health back to the side, because I feel like a roof over my head and somewhere stable and safe and clean for me and my children was my number one priority." In August, when Sabrina went to restart her cancer treatments, the doctor asked what was going on, as she'd missed appointments. "I just pretty much broke down," Sabrina recalled. With Sabrina amenable to seeing if CPS could help, the hospital made the call.

Ria, the assigned investigator, reviewed the hospital's report. "What do they want us to do, get rid of the roaches? What am I supposed to really do?" she asked, exasperated, on the drive over. "I don't see the kids being neglected." Although Ria did not think that it should have been reported—the situation reflected poverty, not maltreatment—she understood why the hospital called it in: "Primarily, I think, because they wanted to see what CPS can do to help the family."

Sabrina had just one wish for CPS: "Get me and my kids out of here. Nothing else would matter." But when they met, Ria explained that CPS didn't have housing. Ria tried to brainstorm other options. Sabrina had already applied for public housing assistance, so Ria called a couple landlords she knew. She knew that Sabrina's family needed help, and she wanted to help them, recognizing the family's close bond and Sabrina's sincerity. "If she gets the housing, I'll be happy as if it was my housing," Ria declared. Still, Ria sighed, "There's nothing we can do." CPS could not provide ongoing rental assistance, so Sabrina resigned herself to autumn in the attic. Ria closed the case, deeming the home environment safe.

CPS casts itself as a service provider or at least a gateway to supportive social services. Recall from chapter 2 how this promise of assistance appeals to reporting professionals in ways that expand CPS reporting. By and large, CPS's help comes in the form of therapeutic services. Investigators readily referred families to myriad programs aimed at fixing families' mindsets and behaviors: substance use treatment, intensive in-home parenting support, family therapy, domestic violence counseling, services for children's behavioral health needs, and more. With all these programs—part of the frenzy around "evidence-based" therapeutic interventions—I could barely keep track of the different acronyms.

The agency could occasionally provide limited, short-term material assistance. Investigators offered items such as bus passes, furniture, clothing, and strollers to families on their caseloads, soliciting donations from their own homes and communities. Sometimes, CPS funded a hotel stay when a family urgently needed a few nights' shelter before a planned move. The agency could also pay security deposits for families with incomes sufficient to maintain the rent. If Sabrina found an apartment she could afford, Ria knew that CPS could cover move-in costs: "I've paid up to the first month's, two months dedicated for my clients. Even gotten beds for the kids." Investigators also provided information and guidance when they could. For parents unsure where to turn or what to do, talking with someone knowledgeable about state and nonprofit resources could be quite helpful.

Though greatly appreciated by families, these efforts are just stopgap measures. CPS is not equipped to meet families' persistent, longer-term challenges. Organized around addressing parents' abusive and neglectful behaviors, the agency lacks the recourse and resources to address families' ongoing housing, employment, transportation, childcare, and other poverty-related needs, especially if these needs do not directly and imminently threaten children's safety. Reporting professionals may hope that CPS can move families up a housing waiting list, for instance, but CPS has no such sway in investigations that close. Ria reflected on the hospital reporting Sabrina's housing conditions:

> I think the entire community think CPS can save them all and provide housing and fix their financial problem. I think that's the misconception of people in the community. I'm not sure why, but I feel as if they cannot service the family, they feel like we will be the backup plan.

But CPS staff couldn't solve all the challenges facing families. "We're the child welfare *agency*, not the child welfare *system*," administrators often reiterated. As they emphasized, other entities—education, health care, welfare, housing, and more—had to play their part in child and family welfare too. After all, CPS is set up as a foster care agency, not a cash assistance or public housing agency. The unique tool CPS brings to the table is child removal. One investigator remarked that she tells parents in need of housing, "We can find housing for little people, not for big people." Little people housing, she clarified, laughing, is "called foster care." (I heard versions of this from other investigators as well.)

The relative ease with which CPS can get families into therapy, compared with subsidized housing, reflects the limited assistance available more broadly. Mothers sometimes appreciated the agency's referrals to voluntary case management services; April, for instance, deemed the service "fantastic." But such programs also find themselves hampered by an inadequate social safety net, unable to provide meaningful, long-term material support. In Sabrina's case, Ria knew that a case management referral wouldn't get the family out of the attic: "They could help them in the same respect when it comes to funding for a security deposit and stuff like that, but it cannot pay their rent for them."

In another case, Chanell explained the program to Tatiana, a mother separating from her infant's father, whom she relied on to provide informal childcare while she worked. When Chanell told Tatiana that the program could help with whatever she needed help with, Tatiana looked up hopefully. "Do they help with childcare?"

"They can help you *locate* childcare," Chanell clarified.

Tatiana's face fell—she didn't need that. Later, Chanell agreed: "What's she gonna use case management services for?" Chanell reflected. "Even if she does find a day care, it's still gonna be really crazy mad expensive."

These limitations exemplify a broader social service infrastructure organized around correcting poor people and people of color. Epitomizing what political scientist Andrew Polsky calls the "therapeutic state,"[3] the services to which CPS refers families are laser-focused on fixing their attitudes and choices. Helping children involves mitigating the risks posed by their parents, discussed in chapter 4. Direct aid has become virtually nonexistent in recent decades, with already stingy welfare benefits subject to time limits, work requirements, and other conditions. Racism underlies this aversion to unconditional assistance; fixated on preventing the "undeserving" (racialized as Black) poor from receiving aid, we focus on correcting marginalized people's mindsets and behaviors.[4]

Sabrina was the paragon of a deserving aid recipient to CPS, but this didn't last. A few months later, Ria told me that the cancer had spread and Sabrina had had emergency surgery; climbing the stairs to the attic wore her out. The hospital and Sabrina's daughter both called asking what CPS would do about housing, frustrating Ria: "CPS can't do anything!" Extremely sympathetic to Sabrina's plight previously, Ria now took a more judgmental tack, saying that Sabrina could have saved money while living in the attic rent-free.

Ria added that Sabrina knew what she was getting herself into and should "suck it up" and stay with her mother, whom she'd mentioned as a last resort, if she needed to leave.

The therapeutic nature of the service referrals available to CPS frames the agency's perspective on what families need. Ria, seeing no paths to housing assistance, believed that Sabrina had to "suck it up." Even as individual staff knew that families needed material assistance, their work routines centered around therapeutic service referrals.[5] Staff directed their attention where they felt they could make a difference. Recall Fred's assessment of Jazmine from chapter 4: He recognized housing and employment as stressors but, given the limited tools at his disposal, pathologized her adversity instead. Fred's manager opened Jazmine's case for ongoing CPS oversight "to ensure [she] complies with [the recovery program] and addresses her MH and SA [mental health and substance abuse]." Meanwhile, her housing and work situations didn't change. CPS offered services to investigated families, but these services focused on remedying personal deficiencies, rather than conditions of racialized poverty.

Help at a Cost

Parents and children alike may find therapeutic services, such as those to which CPS refers families, beneficial. But when these services come in a CPS package, they carry costs as well. Gina and her husband, a veteran with multiple traumatic brain injuries, were about to close on a house in the Northeast Corner when her husband died in a car crash, leaving Gina with their two young sons. After the accident, Gina, through her grief, spent her days navigating the various bureaucracies. Veterans Affairs withdrew the loan for the house, so, Gina said, they were homeless for a while, staying in a camper before ultimately getting a loan. Going through her husband's things was difficult, but she tried to unpack little by little. She loved playing with her sons in the backyard when she had the energy, but an autoimmune disorder often left her weak and dizzy; her hair started falling out. "Some days, I'm really, really tired," Gina said. She knew that the house was messy. But she reasoned, "I get to it when I get to it. I cannot wear myself out to the point where I cannot take care of them."

Almost two years after Gina's husband died, a CPS investigator came knocking. CPS had received a report about Gina's daily drinking and the conditions of the home; a caller who requested to remain anonymous to Gina had visited one morning to find old food strewn around the house and Gina drinking and slurring her speech.

Gina, a White mother in her forties, answered the door, wearing celestial-patterned pajamas, her dark hair pulled back into a loose ponytail. In the living room, cartoons played as her two- and four-year-old sons ran around amid piles of toys. Gina could barely get the words out fast enough as she assured Vance, the investigator, that the caller was a woman who had been harassing her. Vance didn't respond; he knew that her guess was wrong.

Vance spent nearly two hours with Gina. Driving back to the office, he reflected, "A year and a half is still fresh to have your partner pass away. It's really, how do you deal with it? If alcoholism runs in their family, she's probably very susceptible to that as a coping mechanism." Vance summarized his assessment: "She needs help for sure."

Investigators saw therapeutic and case management services as a form of help for families. During the visit, Vance had asked Gina whether she wanted any services, perhaps to get her four-year-old into preschool. "You could benefit from some help—my suggestion."

Gina insisted that no one could help. She'd tried to sign up for different programs; food stamps, or even a tank of oil at the start of winter, could ease her financial stress, but she had learned that she didn't qualify, even as things were tight on her fixed income. "I think I have to be under $2,130 a month for me and the boys. I make $2,788."

Later, Vance circled back, raising the possibility of depression. Tears welled in Gina's eyes, her tough exterior softening. "I don't want everything at me all the time. I just want my kids and me to be left alone."

Vance, concerned about Gina and her kids, didn't want to leave them alone. He described the case management referral he could make. "I don't have safety concerns," he told her. But he pointed out the dog feces he'd seen in the basement. "That's not good."

"I have no help from anyone," Gina replied, despondent.

"That's why I think you could benefit," Vance urged. He suggested she sign the form to learn more; she could cancel anytime. Gina relented and signed.

To CPS investigators, therapeutic services offered surveillance as well as help. I asked Vance afterward about his encouraging Gina to accept the referral. After repeating that the services could help her, Vance added, "Those kids need eyes—another set of eyes." Investigators often echoed Vance's language of "eyes in the home" as they described the appeal of service providers' supervision. In this way, service referrals do not just reflect CPS looking out for parents' wishes; CPS also understands referrals as a way to continue monitoring them after the agency leaves, framing this monitoring as beneficial for children.

Mothers recognized the surveillance inherent in these service referrals too. Imelda, the mother who came to New Haven after Hurricane Maria, hesitated when her investigator, Heather, suggested the case management referral. Heather told Imelda that the program could help her find a new apartment or research summer camps. "I really was hoping she'd be a little more receptive," Heather said later. "I thought if anybody could use [those] services, this was a family that could." Imelda and her housemates didn't work or receive cash benefits; Imelda shared a single bedroom with her four children, her girlfriend, and her girlfriend's son. She did want support around housing and employment. But as she explained to me, "I thought they were using that to keep an eye on me—that's why I was so insecure yesterday. I thought that if they want me to do this program to keep an eye on me, I am going to feel pestered."

Offering social services through CPS could thus discourage participation in these services, as mothers wanted to keep the agency far away. For instance, I asked Deborah, the mother who accidentally overdosed, whether CPS could do anything to help her family. "No, not really," she replied. "Honestly, it's so fear-based, it's like—just, please go away. Go help somebody else." Almost all mothers I spoke with hoped that their CPS cases would close immediately and wanted CPS to leave them alone. CPS might aspire to be a vehicle for social services, but its child maltreatment focus and its coercive power undermined this goal, as mothers were keen to distance themselves from anything associated with the agency.

Relatedly, the agency's policing role sometimes made mothers apprehensive about asking for assistance. After a report came in about the condition of her home, Katrina, a White mother, appreciated her investigator Cheryl's help. Cheryl had collected some donated clothes for Katrina's children and was trying to get Katrina some bus passes. "That's helpful because I do take the bus a lot," Katrina said. Still, she hesitated to ask for more. "A lot of people tell me, 'Oh, get beds, get this.' I don't want them in my life forever, so I'm not gonna be like, 'Well, I need this, this, this, and this.'" Her son needed a bed, but Katrina planned to make do. "If you sit there and ask for a lot of things, then they feel like, 'Oh, well, she needs us, so let's try to keep it open longer.'" Mothers knew that CPS was not just a resource bank. With the agency interpreting their needs as risks, as we saw in chapter 4, they took care not to present themselves as too needy.

In other cases, like Gina's, CPS's power encouraged participation in services, but under duress. Even if the services offered were technically voluntary,
the suggestion coming from CPS made the decision fraught for mothers who
hoped to placate the agency. Investigators leveraged their authority when
pitching voluntary services to families they especially hoped would accept.
Vance told Gina that he could not require the services but framed the referral
as a way to be free of CPS: "We'd be out of your hair." Gina felt "trapped," as
though she didn't have a say. She thought that the service Vance suggested
would bring someone in to tell her how to run her household. She didn't want
her sons to go to childcare or receive developmental screenings, which CPS
was encouraging. "Like, what do I do?" The offer felt like a mandate. To Gina,
the message was clear: "This is something you could do so that we will leave
you alone." She conceded, accepting services not enthusiastically but reluctantly and strategically.

Vance ended up referring Gina to a more intensive program, offering clinical and case management services twice a week for two hours each. (On his
second visit, he'd arrived to find her home "in disarray," according to his notes,
with piles of dog feces and old food all over the floor—"far worse" than what
I'd seen, he told me.) Initially, Gina bristled at Vance's referral, telling me before the program intake that she was "just trying to get this over with" and
rolling her eyes at the time commitment.

During the intake, the clinical social worker assigned to Gina listened sym-
pathetically as Gina conveyed her frustration with Vance criticizing what Gina
saw as a typical home environment with toddlers. The clinician repeatedly
sought to align herself with Gina, affirming Gina's comments about building
forts and playing in the dirt with her kids. Explaining the program, she told
Gina, "I will never step in your shoes and take over—you're Mom." She added
that she would only discuss certain things with CPS, such as the goals on Gina's treatment plan; personal or sensitive things would "stay in here."

A month into the program, Gina told me that she'd found it "very helpful,"
explaining, "She's an easy person to talk to, just like you are. If I can just sit and
I can just talk, and I can get up and do what I gotta do, I'm not under so much
pressure." Gina distinguished the program from CPS. "They don't just come
at you trying to drill you into a corner. . . . They're more understanding [with]
it, and they're more willing to listen." She hadn't known what to expect at first
but said that she was glad to have the program in her life.

CPS's pressure ultimately connected Gina to a service she came to appreciate, one that might improve conditions for her children by helping her manage

her stress and offering parenting support. As we see, CPS's paternalism—we think we know better what you need—doesn't necessarily foreclose benefits for children and families. At the same time, this approach reinforces mothers' subordinate and precarious position with respect to state authorities.[6] Gina wasn't in charge—a state agency empowered to take her children was.

Jazmine, too, saw CPS foisting services on her. Fred, her investigator, recommended a program that visited three times weekly, pairing case management with treatment for substance use and mental health. Jazmine appreciated that Fred listened to her preferences and tried to identify a program that would be a good match. Still, she felt that the mental health and substance use components would "be a waste of time"—she'd been smoking marijuana since she was twelve and didn't plan to stop—or could even make things worse. Jazmine saw Fred's offer of services as a "test": "Basically, if you don't do this, we'll come and take him, and we'll leave him in our custody until you know how to comply." Even if CPS deemed the services optional, she contended, they weren't. "I'm in CPS. I can't refuse." And Fred pitched the program as a way to get assistance for Gabriel—childcare and perhaps support for his developmental needs. Jazmine even held out hope for help with housing. So she grudgingly accepted the pieces she didn't want to access the pieces she did, reasoning, "If I have to sit here and suck up my pride to get him where I want him to be, [that's what] it is."

As Jazmine's case shows, the assistance parents might want from CPS comes with strings attached. In Connecticut, CPS *can* offer subsidized housing to some families through a supportive housing program, but only in cases with ongoing CPS oversight. Sabrina, deemed "low-risk" for maltreatment, wasn't eligible. Her investigator, Ria, lamented CPS's inability to help:

> This is one of those cases where I almost wish Mom had a mental health problem . . . that would make her neglectful where you could transfer the case [to ongoing services] and know they're going to connect her with services. Not that we want her to be neglectful, but that's the only way that we can transfer and help.

CPS tethers its limited material assistance to oversight for child maltreatment risks. Recall Katrina, too, worried that asking for too much from CPS might invite continued monitoring. Ria framed the supportive housing as a means of reducing family stress and addressing multiple issues simultaneously but also recognized assistance such as housing as a benefit to be doled out conditionally to induce cooperation with other requests. As Ria explained, for parents with mental health and substance use needs, "the housing is the carrot.... To be eligible for the [supportive housing] program, you also have to be compliant with services." CPS thus delivers support through a vehicle of supervision.

And even when parents *want* help from CPS, the agency's focus on child maltreatment makes accessing this help difficult, practically and emotionally. Take the case of Zanobia, a soft-spoken Black mother of two whose thirteen-year-old son, Rashid, had major behavioral and mental health needs. Rashid's absences from school triggered a CPS report. Joe, Zanobia's investigator, recognized Rashid's needs—he was hospitalized twice during the investigation—and Zanobia's challenges managing his behavior. After Rashid pointed a knife at her, she feared for her and her younger son's safety. Zanobia wanted ongoing support from CPS. But what could CPS offer absent maltreatment or the risk thereof? As Joe told me, "The problem is that there is no abuse or neglect." So he encouraged Zanobia to request voluntary services.

Joe had just closed Zanobia's case when a new report came in: Rashid, off his medication, had gone to the emergency room, where he mentioned his mother whipping him with an electrical cord. "She was doing that to protect herself," Joe concluded. "I'm not gonna step on her."

Joe happened to arrive for a follow-up visit right after Rashid, brandishing knives, was chasing Zanobia around the apartment. Zanobia told Joe that she was "done." Joe called 911 and pled with the hospital to admit Rashid, because Joe didn't think he could find a foster home on a Friday night. Zanobia wasn't ready for Rashid to come home. Seeing no other options, Joe started the removal paperwork, and Zanobia braced herself to place Rashid in foster care.

Eventually, the hospital recommended that Rashid transition to a two- to three-month residential program, obviating the need for foster care. Zanobia considered herself lucky that Rashid happened to have a doctor who knew of the program. Otherwise, she said, "I would have just gone ahead with the foster care option"—an option that would categorize her situation a certain way. She knew that she wasn't an abusive or neglectful parent, but routing the services through CPS carried an indelible mark. "That can have huge effects on the family and the parents in the future, because it doesn't go away," Zanobia explained. "Even when the child gets older, they'll still have that case."

Zanobia is the rare example of a parent willingly seeking CPS's ongoing intervention. Her case reveals the tensions inherent in CPS's service mission: Even the limited, primarily therapeutic assistance CPS offers is conditional on the agency identifying maltreatment concerns. And this assistance comes with baggage, saddling families with surveillance premised on their abusive or neglectful tendencies.

No Harm Done?

In chapter 2, we heard some reporting professionals and CPS staff assert that "no harm" comes from reporting. Mothers, meanwhile, identified profound harms attached to reports and investigations, even if CPS investigated and promptly closed out. Sometimes, mothers remarked that investigations had increased their awareness, so they kept a more watchful eye on children playing outside, for instance. But this education, when delivered through an investigation for child maltreatment, came at a cost.

At the most basic level, investigations involve appointments: multiple home visits and sometimes substance use or other evaluations as well. These activities take time, often scarce for parents juggling many responsibilities. Mothers rearranged their schedules and called out of work to meet their investigators. Zanobia, for instance, described investigations as "a hassle as a parent." On top of the "traumatizing" nature of the investigation, "you have to miss work. What do you tell your boss?" Working in retail, without paid time off, it wasn't always easy to accommodate CPS's meetings.

Investigations can be stressful for children, with a stranger entering their home to question them and their parents. Investigators try to talk to children alone; occasionally, they pull children out of class at school. If there are allegations of physical abuse, they may ask children to lift their clothing. A few mothers recognized these experiences taking a toll on their children. Rosie, reported after a domestic violence incident with her girlfriend, Amelia, didn't mind talking to CPS, but it bothered her that CPS had to speak with the children. "They have no idea what happened, and here comes a stranger asking them questions," she said. Rosie said that her seven-year-old had been asking questions since CPS visited: "Like, 'Mom, where's Amelia, and why isn't Amelia here? And why does the lady ask questions about her?'" Rosie added that she and Amelia tried to hide their arguments from the children. "So if someone's coming [to] ask them, 'How often does mommy and your stepparent fight?' and they're like, 'We don't know'—it puts them on edge."

April, the mother introduced at the start of the chapter, received a phone call about an hour into our first interview, the day after CPS came by. The school was calling to tell April that her son, Michael, had "had a bad day." April told me that CPS's visit "was heavy on him" and relayed what she'd just heard from the school. Apparently, Michael had some words with another student, landing him in the principal's office. Once Michael arrived at the principal's office, "he's sobbing because he's all turned up about the CPS situation." The principal had Michael speak with the social worker. "They said that the whole time, he's just crying. . . . [With] CPS, yeah, it's a lot. It's a lot." We ended the interview, and April left right then to pick Michael up early from school.

For mothers, child removal wasn't the only threat the investigation posed. For instance, as discussed in chapter 1, mothers took pride in their motherhood; this too became precarious when CPS arrived. The agency's very presence suggested someone doubting their mothering, no matter the "strengths-based" veneer of the investigation. "It just made me feel like I was a bad mother," said Maggie, in Providence, recalling her investigation. "I just felt embarrassed . . . like, I don't know, like a failure, that I'm not doing my job." Brooke, also in Providence, described her investigations, promptly closed, as "traumatizing," making her "feel like less of a parent." Paulina, a Providence mother recently investigated for the first time, felt her motherhood put on trial—"They're asking you how you're raising your own child"—leaving her hurt and apprehensive. "I was nervous as hell and I knew my room was clean, but it's just the fact that you have to defend your motherhood," Paulina said. Facing the judgment of investigators, mothers felt a heavy burden to convey their good mothering. These emotional and psychological costs reinforce mothers' marginal social positions. Coming from an entity focused on child maltreatment, CPS's intervention jeopardized mothers' deeply held identities as good mothers.

Additionally, investigations thwarted mothers' sense of autonomy, underscoring their powerlessness and precarity by bringing an outsider in to assess their parenting. Jazmine described the emotional ordeal of the investigation, beyond fears of family separation:

> Now I have CPS in my life, so now I have another person to sit here and monitor how I raise my child. . . . When I carried my child for nine months, when I fed the child, when I took him to the bath, took him to the park, did everything for him, and now you see me do one thing that you don't like and now it's, "Oh, you're a bad parent. No, that's child abuse."

The investigation brought more authorities into her life, poised to oversee her mothering. Investigations remind mothers that someone else has ultimate say—that even as they may have custody of their children, their parenting is perpetually provisional. In this way, too, investigations exacerbate investigated mothers' marginal social status.

Investigations also threatened mothers' sense of privacy. Chapter 3 detailed the extensive surveillance involved in CPS investigations, whereby CPS gathers substantial information about families' intimate lives. Mothers sometimes resented these intrusions. "I just don't want outsiders in my business," explained Nikki, introduced in chapter 4. "They go in people's past and—my son is sixteen. Do you know what my son say? He said, 'Ma, he gotta know that I'm on probation and all of this.' You don't need to know all that. . . . They just do too much." Her son's probation status was unrelated to the initial allegations around domestic violence, but CPS nevertheless wanted to know. By the time we met again a couple months later, CPS had closed out. Nikki hoped that they'd never return.

> *The case closed—what is it about it that makes you not want to go through it again?*
> Just having them in your life. Just having somebody else in your life that's not supposed to be here, you get what I'm saying? Asking all these questions and want to know all this stuff that they don't need to be knowing. No. I would never want to go through that again, and I would never advise nobody to go through that.

Administrative records would show CPS quickly out of Nikki's life. Nikki's two children remained with her, and CPS brought over backpacks and a debit card for bedding and clothes as the school year started. Still, she was loath to relive the experience of CPS digging into all aspects of her personal life.

The hazy bounds of CPS's surveillance could make mothers apprehensive as well, producing a lingering sense of unease. They weren't always sure that they could trust that CPS had fully closed out. Might the agency still be in their lives somehow, ready to strike at a moment's notice? Imelda, the mother we met in chapter 4 whose toddler got out of the house while Imelda's friend babysat, worried that CPS could return after the investigation closed, perhaps to check in with her friend, whom the court referred to a yearlong diversion program. "Maybe it scares me that they are not satisfied with the information they have," Imelda offered. "Maybe they'll want to verify how things are going." CPS wouldn't visit Imelda's family again unless another report came in; still, Imelda wasn't confident that they were completely gone. Similarly, Sherea, also introduced in chapter 4, learned from her experience growing up that "once they're in your life, they're in your life." She didn't think that she needed to worry, but she couldn't be sure. "It's just like—are they still in my life?" she wondered. "Do they ever just go? Oh, shit, I gotta—I can't really tell if they're really out there. They can say yeah, but it can also be a lie." Or information provided to CPS might make its way into the hands of other government agencies: CPS staff assured an undocumented mother that they would not share her documentation status, but this mother still worried that her CPS case could put her on the radar of immigration enforcement authorities. Such concerns are understandable among mothers who have repeatedly encountered untrustworthy institutions.[7]

Investigations create lasting records for families in CPS's database.[8] Mothers emphasized that they wanted nothing to do with CPS, even if cases were promptly closed, because they did not want to be "in the system" in any way. As Terri, a Providence mother, remarked, "As soon as they put your name in the computer, it stays there. It will never erase. . . . You could be the best mom ever, but as soon as you are in the system, you're screwed." Indeed, as described in chapter 4, previous CPS investigations figure heavily in the agency's assessments. Mothers recognized that closed cases now could come back to affect them later. With many employers running child abuse registry checks, a CPS record could also affect mothers' employment aspirations.[9] For instance, Gina had a childcare license for years and worried that her investigation would come up if she wanted to return to that work. Janelle, in Providence, said that she had a job lined up working with schools—"a nice job," paying $13 hourly, above the minimum wage she could get as a teacher's assistant.

> When I went to go get fingerprinted, [it said] my cases are closed, but they're still on my record. I lost that job. I lost that job. After I lost that job, CPS tells me, "Oh, if you want to appeal it, it takes 180 days." By that time, that job's gone.

In this way, CPS contact can undermine families' economic opportunities and well-being.

States also screen prospective foster and adoptive parents for CPS history. Certainly, they do not want to place foster children in danger. And in Connecticut, I saw CPS staff work with prospective caregivers to appeal records from years before. When describing the harms of investigations, though, mothers occasionally pointed to restricted foster parent opportunities. Yajaira recalled feeling "so pissed off" when a cousin reported her, "because she basically ruined my life doing that." Yajaira said that she had paperwork in to get custody of another cousin's children, but the report derailed her efforts, devastating her: "I hate it so much because I wanna become a foster mom. I wanna give those children that don't have the opportunity, I wanna give them the opportunity because I was them once."

Thus, even if closed promptly, the investigations launched when we treat family adversity as maltreatment are not innocuous, as they threaten mothers' sense of identity, privacy, and autonomy. These collateral consequences reverberate beyond investigated parents to shape the economic and caregiving resources available to family and community networks.

Distrust and Disengagement After the Report

The aforementioned harms mothers attribute to the investigation persist even absent callous CPS staff; they are inherent in the agency's very orientation around policing parenting. A few mothers decried their treatment by investigators, especially mothers whose cases continued beyond the investigation. (These perceptions were not just sour grapes; I saw the same investigators shift their approach with families they viewed as higher-risk.) For example, Gina, whose case CPS opened for ongoing oversight, said that Vance "refused to listen to anything, really, that I had to say. I didn't like that at all. He cut me off." Indeed, during the visit, Gina had been eager to talk, and Vance redirected the conversation to get what he needed. When she went on at length about her frustrations with the Veterans Affairs bureaucracy, Vance remained focused on his task, keeping his eyes on his paperwork as he requested her pediatrician's contact information. Afterward, I asked whether Gina felt that CPS was there to help her. "No, they're here to scrutinize me," she replied. "That's just how I felt, you know? He was looking for something. Just looking for something."

Important exceptions like Gina aside, mothers by and large felt positively about their investigators, particularly in investigations that ultimately closed. Ashley, also investigated by Vance, appreciated him referring her to a program she felt would help her son and called Vance "a really good contact." And even as they chafed at some of CPS's requests, mothers understood that investigators were just doing their jobs. Sherea, for instance, deemed her investigator "nosy" but clarified, "It's not, they're being nosy. It's their job. They have to. They're mandated to look into every detail of what's going on." Mothers described their investigators as "mak[ing] you feel at ease," "understanding," "open-minded," "considerate," "calm," "accommodating," "friendly," "kindhearted," "respectful," and "very professional."

Mothers attributed the investigation's injuries instead to the callers who triggered CPS's visit. As mothers recognize, it's almost always third-party professional and personal contacts that activate CPS, rather than CPS staff themselves. Katrina remarked that she usually got "a little angry" when CPS came.

Who are you angry at?
The person that called. It's never the workers, because the workers are just doing what they have to do. I just get mad when people call because my opinion is, instead of calling them right away, why don't you come talk to me first and find out why this happened or why this was like that?

CPS might just be doing its job, but as mothers saw it, callers' discretionary decisions had brought the agency to their doorsteps. Callers might have been trying to get help, but turning to CPS often conveyed something different to mothers, given the agency's maltreatment focus and its family separation authority. To mothers, reports signaled someone threatening their children, insulting their motherhood, and betraying their trust. Even when mothers ultimately found CPS investigations helpful or at least benign, the fact remained that someone had summoned a coercive authority making allegations of abuse or neglect, an act mothers took seriously. Despite appreciating Vance's assistance, for instance, Ashley felt "very upset" at the school for calling CPS, adding that meeting with school staff since the report had been difficult: "I don't even want to sit across from some of these people. . . . The person who made the report—in your head, that's not filtered, you're like, 'What a B word.'" Reports informed mothers about callers' (lack of) trustworthiness, inhibiting families' engagement with potential sources of social and institutional support.

Fallout with Professional Reporters

Many CPS reports come from systems aiming to partner with families to care for children. And, as detailed in chapter 2, reporting professionals almost always say that they call CPS to help families. But time and again, mothers recounted feeling hurt and resentful when schools, hospitals, and other service providers told CPS that mothers might be abusing or neglecting their children. These feelings are important in themselves, exacerbating a sense of exclusion. By fueling distrust and disengagement, they also distance families from systems tasked with assisting them in ways that can perpetuate marginality.

Mothers understood legal mandates to report but often believed that reporting professionals should have handled situations differently. For example,

Zanobia resented the school truancy officer's report. As she explained, school staff called her frequently yet told CPS that they could not reach her to find out why her son was not in school: "It could've been done a different way. I mean, I was kind of pissed off at that." Especially when reports came from support-oriented systems where families had repeated contact, such as schools and mental health care providers, mothers felt upset that callers turned so readily to CPS without contacting them first. Sandra, reported by her child-care center after her son's scooter injury, said that rather than immediately calling CPS, "I would have sat down with the child and his dad, and I would have asked for an explanation, how things happened. With a five-year-old child, you don't know if he's telling the truth or a lie. She should have communicated with us and had a meeting."

CPS reports had a chilling effect, prompting disengagement with the systems that filed reports. Mothers mentioned switching doctors or canceling social service programs after these providers called CPS; they said that they would think twice next time before going to the hospital or calling the police when experiencing domestic violence. These protective efforts echo what we saw in chapter 1: mothers carefully navigating interactions with service systems, aware of these systems' connections with CPS. After being reported themselves, what before might have been a hazy possibility coalesced into concrete evidence of untrustworthiness.

Mothers spoke poignantly about the intimate wounds reporting professionals inflicted. Desiree arrived in Providence addicted to heroin. She arranged for her mother to watch her two young daughters while she went to a detoxification program at a hospital. The hospital notified CPS. Seeking help, Desiree instead felt betrayed.

> I go to you to get better, and you called CPS on me. . . . You didn't find me on a park bench and a needle up my arm. You didn't find me in the street like I was before. I came to you because I'm sick of this life. I wanna be a better mom. . . . They completely blindsided me. . . . I went there with high hopes of getting my shit together, you know? I'm like, "Okay, I'm gonna come in here an intravenous drug user. I'm gonna leave here clean, sober, and a better mother." That's what I thought.

She turned to drugs that night to numb herself and never returned to that hospital. Even years later, upon meeting other mothers addicted to substances, Desiree said that she has not recommended, and would not recommend, that program.

Mothers didn't always cut off services from reporting systems entirely; these services often offered things they needed and wanted for their families. But even when participation continued, things weren't necessarily the same. Reports taught mothers about the consequences of disclosing vulnerabilities to helping systems, making them wary about continuing to do so. Upon hearing that the hospital reported her for testing positive for marijuana during her pregnancy, Sherea recalled, "I was like, 'Oh, [the prenatal clinic] snitched on me.' That was my first reaction." She felt that the prenatal clinic and delivery hospital should have notified her in advance of the need to report. I asked how this made her feel about these providers. "That I can't trust them," she replied. "I felt, with you guys not mentioning it to me, now you got me thinking that you set me up." Afterward, Sherea hesitated to share information with the midwife at the clinic.

> It was certain stuff that I didn't wanna say to her because I didn't know if she's gonna go and tell. Like, I thought when I first had him that I was going through postpartum [depression]. I don't tell them how I feel. I don't tell them any of that, because I don't need them to say, "Oh, she's going through postpartum. She's gonna hurt the baby."

So Sherea stayed quiet. Sharing her depression symptoms might have opened up a fruitful conversation, perhaps enabling her health care provider to offer additional support. But Sherea had learned that the clinic wasn't necessarily on her side—that staff might jump on any admission of vulnerability to shuttle her to a punitive state system.

For Gaby, a mother of two who had recently immigrated to New Haven from South America, the CPS report undermined rapport and engagement with the reporting party. Gaby's teenage daughter, Livia, met each week with a therapist, Alma; Gaby usually attended and participated as well. During one session, Gaby and Livia told Alma about an incident the prior night that culminated in Gaby physically disciplining Livia.

Gaby had grown close to Alma, entrusting Alma to help her family. Alma had seen how Gaby always tried to support her daughter, so Gaby never thought that Alma would call CPS. Nevertheless, Gaby found her openness rewarded with a CPS report. Alma hoped that CPS could assist and educate Gaby's family, and Gaby understood the reporting mandate, but Gaby nevertheless felt hurt and upset, her trust betrayed:

> [Alma] is not being helpful, she is just making my life more complicated, that's the way I see it. . . . I needed help from her, and she did the

opposite. . . . Instead of bringing peace, she messed everything up for us. . . . Thanks to her, you can't sleep, you are not calm, you can't eat. . . . The confidence we have placed in her by telling her our life, making her part of our life, we lost that confidence in her. . . . It really hurts, because there are people who tell me, "You shouldn't tell everything," but how can someone help me if I don't tell them everything?

Alma, interviewed a few weeks later, said that Livia had continued therapy but Gaby kept her distance:

> The first time, I asked Mom if she wanted to talk because I knew CPS had already gone out, and she declined. The second time, I noticed that Mom had gotten a haircut, and I said, "Oh, you got your hair cut." That was the extent of our conversation. [*Laughter*] She's like, "There's Livia. You can take her upstairs." I said, "Okay. So, do you have nothing—you know, you can come up if you wanna talk." She said, "No, I'm good."

Alma hoped that with time, she could repair their relationship. Still, Gaby found the experience immensely painful. "I can't believe I left everything for my children's future, for my children's well-being, and now I'm being judged, or they are trying to blame me for doing something against them," she reflected. "I live for them. I'm here, away from my family, from my country. I'm breaking this country's rules by being here for them." The report stung. By reporting, Alma, formerly a trusted ally, threatened the center of Gaby's world: her children.

Jazmine, too, continued meeting weekly with Cate, her housing case manager, after Cate's report, as this was a condition of her housing assistance. But, as in Gaby's case, the relationship shifted. Two months after the report, I sat in on one of their meetings. The interaction felt perfunctory, both of them just trying to get what they needed from the other. Jazmine dutifully answered Cate's questions—about things such as Jazmine's cash assistance and her work schedule—but didn't offer any information beyond what Cate asked. Separately, Jazmine told me:

> Honestly, it's just been like, it's not the same. She just comes in and she talks. Honestly, with me, it's just, because I can't trust you. You broke that trust that we were building. . . . Do you really think that when we come and meet it's gonna be oh, ha-ha-ha-hee-hee like it used to be? No, it's not. Just do what you gotta do and that's it. Go. Go on your way. That's it.

Cate had seen Jazmine nearly every week for two years, through her triumphs and struggles. Jazmine felt betrayed: "I told her my past, everything. She watched me change and grow into the person that I've become. It's like, that's where you crossed the line, because you know damn well I do not abuse my child." She'd opened up to Cate, only for Cate to turn her in as a suspected child abuser. So Jazmine opted to keep things superficial going forward.

Reports could also foster distrust beyond the specific reporting party. At the start of our interview, Selena, in Providence, told me, "Having friend is like—you turn around and they put the knife in your back." I asked her to tell me about a time she'd been burned like that. I hadn't yet mentioned CPS, but Selena told me about Milagros, who had provided early intervention services for her baby and knew "everything" about Selena's family. Milagros reported Selena to CPS, concerned about Selena's baby's feeding difficulties. "When I found out, I throw her out of my house. I told her that I don't want her program no more," Selena declared. Milagros's call also cultivated a broader sense of distrust. When I asked what she had learned from the experience, Selena described her wariness approaching others.

> When I got problem, I keep it to myself. I can't trust people. You never know, trusting people. You never know what they gonna do behind your back. . . . [Milagros] was judging me. She didn't even know me. For me, it's hard to trust people. I really got—I got problem, and I always stay quiet and not say to no one, because you never know what they're gonna do.
> *Tell me about some of those things that you feel like you can't tell people because you just don't know.*
> I don't know, like if I need something, or sometimes if I don't—like I haven't paid my rent yet. . . . Stuff like that I don't say to the social worker.

Though she described other experiences with untrustworthy others, stemming from childhood and family relationships, this betrayal was front-of-mind for her. With its report, the early intervention program showed Selena that it could not be trusted. As sociologist Judith Levine writes, specific experiences of untrustworthiness foster a sense of distrust for low-income mothers that ripples across numerous domains of social life.[10]

Reports can thus become turning points, crystallizing for mothers how systems operate in ways that inform their engagement going forward. "That was the breaking point of when I was learning that the system [is] not always here to help you all the time," said Leslie, a Providence mother who recalled the hospital alerting CPS about her housing instability. Two years after we met, things were especially rough for Desiree, the mother reported after trying to detox. Welfare had sanctioned her months prior, cutting off her cash assistance. She stole cat food and shampoo if she had to and was looking into escorting to bring in cash. Still, she shied away from requesting help, even from a care coordination program her doctor had offered.

> I'd rather lay in bed and cry all day long than call anybody, because I'm afraid it's just gonna work against me. I've been through so much that it's just hard for me to trust anybody no more. I don't trust nobody.
> *Not the doctors? Tell me about that.*
> Because that time that I went to [that] hospital . . .

Desiree recounted the same story she'd shared when we first met. In the years that followed, this experience continually surfaced as she weighed the costs and benefits of engaging with service providers.

In general, mothers found CPS reports particularly hurtful when they had closer relationships with reporting professionals, with more repeated and sustained contact.[11] Christina, introduced in chapter 1, explained that a report from her son's day care pained her much more than one from the police, "because the day care was more intimate," whereas "I don't know those cops." When mothers already had negative experiences with or expectations of the reporting party, often the case when reports came from police, CPS reports didn't inspire the same feelings of betrayal. Lizette, in the Northeast Corner, felt frustrated with the police and their disrespectful attitude when they came to talk about her son playing outside unsupervised. But Lizette wasn't surprised that this punitive entity called CPS. When relationships were acrimonious already, CPS reports just piled one more thing on.

Thus, negative ramifications emerged especially when support-oriented systems called CPS. These systems are precisely those tasked with assisting marginalized families and promoting social integration: schools, hospitals, mental health care providers, and social service providers. But referring families to state surveillance that threatens child removal instead strains families' engagement with these service systems, exacerbating family adversity, marginality, and social exclusion. A CPS report shattered Gaby's trust in her daughter's therapist, kept Sherea from sharing her depressive symptoms with medical providers, and made Desiree afraid to reach out for help she desperately needed.

Fallout with Personal Reporters

Mothers also felt deeply upset with social ties who called CPS. Nearly everyone I interviewed who believed that someone in their social network had reported them described the negative and often intense repercussions for that relationship afterward, even if the CPS case ultimately closed. To mothers, reporting revealed others' malicious or untrustworthy character, fueling and justifying distrust to erode social support.

When parents suspected that a relative had reported them, CPS reports exacerbated family conflicts. Nikki, the mother from chapter 4 investigated following allegations about her children's exposure to domestic violence, didn't say much when her CPS investigator, Joe, first arrived. Joe started asking about her relationship with her boyfriend, Cyrus, but Nikki seemed somewhat in shock still, taking in what was happening. She mused, "I'm trying to figure out who called y'all and for what." The caller had requested to remain anonymous to Nikki, but by the end of the visit, Nikki concluded that her mother had reported. (Sometimes, mothers were mistaken; in fact, the call came from someone else with whom Nikki's mother had shared concerns.)

Two days later, on a sweltering New England summer afternoon, I returned to Nikki's home myself. Nikki, nibbling at a bowl of pasta at the dining table, began our conversation by saying, "I just think like this—every family goes through stuff." From there, she grew more animated as she talked about how much her mother's (supposed) report upset her. She felt betrayed by her mother inviting the punitive state into private family affairs. Nikki—along with Cyrus, who popped in and out of the dining room as we spoke—asserted that her mother had reported so that she could claim the children on her taxes and control their social security benefits. Nikki saw the situation clearly: "You didn't do that because you care for me. You did that because, to be honest, you want money. What you're doing is gonna backfire. It's just making me not wanna deal with you."

Indeed, the day of the report, Nikki didn't answer her mother's call. Nikki's mother texted an inspirational religious image the day of our interview; Nikki ignored that too: "I read it and didn't even respond to her, 'cause I really don't have anything to say to you. Do you know what you could have done? You coulda had my kids ripped out of their home because you want money." Their relationship had long been strained; Nikki recalled the abuse she endured from her mother as a child. But they had taken steps toward rebuilding their relationship. Just a week or so earlier, Nikki had stayed with her mother for a few days for some "peace of mind." But now, she proclaimed, "I can't deal with my mom. It hurts, but I can't deal with her." She had just learned that she was pregnant and vowed not to allow her mother around the baby when it came.

About an hour and a half into our interview, Nikki's mother and stepfather arrived at the house. Nikki's daughter went with Cyrus to speak to them. I took the opportunity to talk with Nikki alone, but it was difficult to focus with the loud shouting at the door. The group converged on the dining room, circling Nikki where she sat. Amid the yelling, she repeatedly said that she didn't want to talk and asked her mother to leave.

"You need to tell the truth," Nikki's mother urged. "He beatin' on you."

"But you called, and it's a whole bunch of ruckus that you did, Ma," Nikki countered. Seeming overwhelmed, she got on her phone and just started scrolling until her mother and stepfather went back outside.

Two months later, Cyrus was locked up, and Nikki had moved to a new place with a friend. Things with her mother remained icy. Nikki said that she didn't say much when her mother called. Her mother had asked when Cyrus was coming home, but Nikki told her that she didn't know: "I'm not gonna tell her, for one, because I can't trust that, you know what I'm saying? She already did this, and she'll do it again."

Recall from chapter 4 that Nikki had limited social support before the report. Now, with her relationship with her mother even more strained, she found herself alone to navigate her pregnancy, save for a close friend. *Stressful* was the word she kept returning to. "I'm going through it by myself, so it gets really stressful at times," Nikki reflected. "I do not advise somebody to be pregnant by theyself. . . . It gets stressful. My God, it gets stressful."

Nikki said that she was careful now, because her mother could "call and lie about something else." Ultimately, that's what she took away from her run-in with CPS—that her misstep had been speaking freely with her mother.

Is there anything you wish you'd done differently in dealing with them?
What, with CPS? No, because I did everything I was supposed to do, hm-mm. I just know when I go through certain things, I just know not to tell my mother. Not even tell her or just to confide in because it'll get twisted around, so I know that now.

Even after the immediate shock of the report, even after her CPS investigation closed, her mother's betrayal loomed large, and Nikki wasn't going to let it happen again. CPS, Nikki emphasized, was "not somebody you want in your life at all," and she held her mother responsible for bringing the agency to her door.

CPS reports also come from romantic partners and ex-partners. Children typically benefit from their fathers' active involvement in their lives,[12] but fathers' CPS reports strain their relationships with mothers. Because mothers often act as "gatekeepers" to children, these conflicts can inhibit fathers' participation in child-rearing. For instance, Barbara, a Portuguese mother in

Providence, said that she had not talked to her young daughter's father in over two years, cutting off contact after he called CPS multiple times when their daughter was a baby:

> How are you gonna complain about not [getting] to be a father on Facebook and stuff, but when you have a chance to, you don't be a father. You rather try to get her tooken away from me. . . . That's why I don't even allow him [to see the child].

All three reports were unsubstantiated, but to Barbara, the calls exemplified the father's attitude toward her and their daughter. The father might have called CPS strategically, for personal gain. Or he might have genuinely felt concerned about his daughter. Perhaps it was a bit of each. But given CPS's role scrutinizing parenting, calling CPS undermined his relationship with Barbara and perhaps their daughter as well.

Likewise, Deandra, a Black mother in Providence, recalled her daughter's father making allegations about Deandra's mental health to CPS, which led to her infant daughter's removal. In her mind, the father, rather than CPS, had inflicted this pain. Two years later, her daughter back in her care, Deandra tried to be cordial with him, but she couldn't move past his invoking CPS: "To this day, for me to still let him see his daughter, it's big. . . . Even right now, I'm ready to cry because I'll never forget it." She still monitored what she shared with her daughter's father.

> *Tell me, are you doing anything differently now, since all this happened?*
> I watch what I say and do around her dad. I just try to keep him outta my business because any little thing—I just feel like, if he did it once, what makes me think he won't fucking call again on me?
> *Tell me more about things you wouldn't say.*
> I can't even express that I'm mad or overwhelmed with being a single mom too much to him, because he'll take it as I wanna jump off a frickin' cliff, or I'm gonna leave the baby in the house by herself, or something stupid.

Deandra felt that she had to bottle up her parenting stressors, keeping the father at a distance to protect herself against another report; she'd seen firsthand what could happen if she opened up to him. Multiple factors undermine trust in relationships between low-income mothers and nonresidential fathers.[13] Involving CPS constitutes an additional strain, as mothers like Barbara and Deandra interpret CPS reports as evidence of fathers' antagonism, justifying distancing themselves and their children.

Some mothers, initially furious, eventually rebuilt personal relationships frayed after reports. In many other cases, though, mothers described long-term consequences of CPS reports, with previously close relationships fracturing for good. As mothers told it, things just weren't the same after a report. Social ties reaching out to CPS (or even mothers believing that they have) thus strains the social relations critical for family well-being. Retreating after CPS reports is a rational, protective response, but one that also distances mothers and their families from potential sources of support.

In the investigation, CPS isn't just trying to determine whether abuse or neglect occurred and whether to continue oversight. As we saw in chapters 2 and 3, the idea of CPS *assisting* "at-risk" families justifies far-reaching investigations that delve deeply into private life. CPS does connect families with various programs during the investigation; mothers often appreciate this assistance and come to see CPS as a helping agency. Nevertheless, this chapter has illuminated limits and costs of routing assistance through CPS, organized around parents' maltreatment and empowered to separate families.

Specifically, the assistance CPS can offer is limited and conditional. Families face challenges related to financial resources, housing, employment, childcare, transportation, health care, and other basic needs. But CPS referrals are largely limited to therapeutic services focused on fixing family behavior and to case management services that can do little more than direct families to an inadequate social safety net. And as CPS and mothers alike understand, these services introduce additional surveillance. In some instances, mothers declined services investigators offered, perhaps wary of programs' connections to CPS. Other times, mothers reluctantly acquiesced, accepting to appease CPS rather than to access a service they themselves desired. Both responses reflect the counterproductive ramifications of using an agency with coercive power to link families to social services.

In this way, CPS's offer of "help" is help on professionals' terms: They know best, and their means of helping involves surveilling and correcting poor families' behavior. And CPS investigations come with profound costs to social inclusion, community well-being, and family engagement with support systems. Far from doing no harm, even closed investigations take a toll on mothers, amplifying their sense of precarity. The most respectful, compassionate investigators are still state agents entering the home, asking all manner of questions, taking notes to put in a state database, conveying their authority, and reinforcing parents' powerlessness. Subjugation of marginalized families—poor families and families of color—by state authorities is part and parcel of the interaction no matter how much investigators might want to help. Moreover, positive engagement with schools, health care providers, social services, and social networks is critical to child well-being, offering important resources. Yet, in its wake, CPS often leaves mothers wary of those that reported them, damaging trust in potentially supportive systems and social network ties to further isolate families in need. Notably, this is the case even when mothers' child removal fears do not materialize, as CPS reports and investigations necessarily involve accusations of subpar parenting.

To the extent that CPS can be integrative, connecting families to services they want, we might see this as laudable. Think of April, grateful that CPS got her son into summer camp and recommended a grief counselor. But must it be CPS in this role? Through CPS, help depends on accusations of maltreatment and comes with coercive threats. Certainly, the agency goaded Gina, the mother grieving her husband's unexpected death, into services she might not have accepted but came to appreciate. But this doesn't mean that the only possible path ran through CPS's insistence; we can imagine, for instance, another trusted person vouching for the service to encourage Gina to try it. Relying on CPS for assistance funnels support through an experience mothers find threatening, one that ultimately exacerbates marginality and social exclusion. For mothers whose investigations do not close, especially those whose children CPS removes, this marginalizing experience is especially pronounced, as we will see in chapter 6.

6

Devastation and Demobilization Beyond the Investigation

TWO AND A HALF YEARS before a convenience store in Minnesota called the police on Black father George Floyd, suspecting a counterfeit bill, a convenience store in Rhode Island called the police on Christina Rayford, a Black mother, after she argued with the checkout clerk. Christina, whom we met in chapter 1 shortly after her son, Anthony, was born, had continued working low-wage jobs—fast food, an auto parts shop—and trying to secure permanent housing in the years since we'd met. She was living in a family shelter and taking classes at the local community college, still striving toward her goal of launching a non-profit organization for youth. "I think I was called to help people," she often said. By this time, Anthony, still the center of her life, was two years old.

As Christina later recalled it, she ran into the convenience store with Anthony in tow to get change for bus fare. The cashier didn't want to change Christina's $20 bill and started making snide comments. "All youse government bitches . . . ," she sneered. Christina took offense. Racialized slights like that, no matter how common, hurt.

"Don't say stuff like that to people," Christina recalled responding. From there, the argument escalated. Christina said that the cashier came out from behind the counter and got in her face. Christina left the store, but not before the store made a "keep the peace" call to the police.

But the police didn't keep the peace—they disrupted it. When the police stopped her, Christina was already on her way to work, pushing Anthony's stroller across the street. Exasperated, Christina recalled saying, "Officer, if I would've destroyed the store or did something, I could see me being stopped, but I left the store, so can I please go?" If anyone needed police intervention, Christina thought, it was the cashier, "'cause she was in my space."

Yet the officers arrested Christina, citing disorderly conduct, resisting arrest, and obstruction. They didn't appreciate her challenging their authority; the officers acknowledged to CPS that they would have let her go had she not protested. The police account stated that Christina "went ballistic" and "started acting irrationally," swearing and spitting at, kicking, and hitting the officers, with one officer telling CPS that he had not seen someone so out of control in a long time. Christina, meanwhile, described how the two officers pushed her, crying, to the ground when trying to handcuff her. This didn't make it into the police's or CPS's report. Anthony, watching his mother's arrest, squirmed out of his stroller to intervene.

The police held Christina and took her to jail. Anthony waited at the police station until CPS arrived to pick him up. The CPS caseworker described Anthony as "cooperative and pleasant," "hyper" but "easily redirected." Christina didn't initially want to give her name or sign any forms but gave her brother's name when asked where her son could go. So CPS placed Anthony with Christina's brother—not informally, as a temporary caregiver while Christina was locked up, but formally, with the state taking legal custody. The doctor who examined Anthony upon his entry into state custody wrote that the toddler "show[ed] no concerns for neglect or injury." Nevertheless, the doctor authorized CPS to hold Anthony for seventy-two hours while the agency prepared to petition the court for custody,[1] recounting the altercation with police and citing a relative's comment that Christina was not taking medication for her mental health needs. CPS didn't speak to Christina before these legal filings.[2]

That's how fast it happened. CPS hadn't been in her life that morning, and Christina had little expectation that they would be. The situation didn't even snowball; it came like an avalanche.[3]

Although most CPS cases close after investigation—the primary focus of this book thus far—some, like Christina's, do not. In these cases, CPS keeps the case open for ongoing monitoring while children remain home, or it requests a court order to take custody and place children out of home. Here, precarity reaches its zenith as mothers confront their greatest fear. Each year, more than 250,000 U.S. children enter foster care, disproportionately Black and Native American children.[4] This forcible family separation leaves deep scars. Research documents the trauma of foster care placement for children.[5] For their mothers, too—losing their ability to raise their children and unsure whether or when their children will return—the experience generates immense pain and trauma.

This is not to imply that the state should stand by and leave parents to raise children alone in contexts of extreme adversity. Mothers I interviewed sometimes recalled their own harrowing experiences of child abuse and neglect and wished that the state had done more to keep them safe. Children in such situations deserve protection. But as this chapter shows, rather than incorporating marginalized families and cultivating supportive communities, the present approach to child protection leaves mothers feeling increasingly isolated, powerless, and cynical as they wind their way through CPS. From their ordeals with the agency, mothers come to see the state as an adversary, working against them given their marginal social position. Even at court, the venue meant to hear their case, officials (including their own attorneys) silence them. Though mothers may aspire to advocate for their rights and for systemic change, at every turn the system reminds them of its authority and mothers' tenuous position, suppressing mobilization for change. Mothers drawn deeply into the system get a clear message: someone else—an antagonistic government—is in charge of their motherhood.

"They Took My Whole Life Away"

From jail, Christina phoned her brother, who informed her that CPS had taken her son. Within a day of the arrest, CPS had already placed Anthony in a new day care. "They said I couldn't see him no more. I don't have custody. I don't have rights. Nothing."

That news broke her. She started crying and screaming. Another woman by the phone tried to calm her down, telling her that Anthony would be okay with her brother. But that wasn't the point. "The point was, I didn't deserve my son to be taken."

Christina was out of jail a couple days later. The criminal case closed; the charges were dropped. But CPS wasn't so easy to shed. Though the state took Anthony in an instant, it would be a long journey to return him home.

The legal filings in Christina's case cited neglect and lack of supervision, which she didn't understand, because she was with her son when the incident occurred. In court, Christina heard the police report, which noted that Anthony, observing the scene, began hitting and biting officers—evidence, in CPS's telling, of Christina's neglect.

But whose actions upset Anthony? Anthony saw his mom in danger—on the ground, being handcuffed. Christina wondered why the officers hadn't arrested her quietly, telling her to put her hands behind her back, to avoid traumatizing Anthony. "If you use force—my son seen that, and he got out of the carriage and he started sticking up for his mom." As one recent study found, witnessing paternal arrests affects children's physiological stress levels.[6] But while CPS is highly attuned to the trauma of children's exposure to violence within the home, trauma directly inflicted by state authorities—such as exposure to police violence—goes unacknowledged.

Back home from jail, Christina desperately missed her son. "I was a wreck. . . . I'm used to getting up at night, checking on my son." Her voice broke as she reflected on the pain of losing Anthony. She felt as though she was grieving him. With everything going on, all the stress, she failed her classes that fall semester. "I really feel like they took my whole life away. It hurt so bad."

CPS may not inflict physical violence, but mothers recognized the immense injury of family separation. Candis, in Providence, watched her children leave in the caseworker's car, fussing and banging on the window in tears. It pained her to see her children hurting like that. "I felt like somebody just stabbed me in the heart," Candis said. To Alex, the removal decision "felt like a death sentence." Desiree recalled the day CPS took her two young daughters:

I think I must've used so much drugs that night just to numb myself, because it was the worst feeling ever. It was the worst. You have no idea. *What was the feeling?*
Oh my goodness. Um, it's like if somebody took a knife and fucking punched your lungs over and over. I couldn't breathe. I couldn't. Everything I looked at, I just cried. I couldn't eat. I couldn't do anything. I couldn't sleep. I didn't sleep for three days, because all I kept thinking was, "Who's changing my daughter's diaper? She's scared of the dark. Who's she sleeping with?" Those are my babies. You know what they are, what they like, what they eat.

Desiree's daughters had been by her side through traumatic experiences, through crises, through extreme poverty. She'd kissed them as she left that morning but didn't get to say goodbye—and now, she didn't know where they were or who was taking care of them.

As Desiree's experience shows, the trauma of child removal can undermine CPS's goals of "rehabilitating" mothers, pulling mothers back into behaviors many were trying to avoid.[7] Bethany recounted the moment she learned that her newborn daughter wouldn't be coming home from the hospital with her, due to her substance use history: "I crumbled to the seat. I fell to the chair, and my first thought was, 'I wanna die.' My second thought was, 'I wanna get high.'

I wanna get high.'" Quantitative research finds that, compared with similar mothers, mothers who lose custody of children are more likely to overdose.[8] Latanya, a Black mother whose four children were removed, explained: "It's hard not to drink, because when you sit there, you're looking at your kids' pictures, you're thinking about stuff. And it's like, when I drink, I don't think about it no more." Latanya knew that this wasn't healthy, but "it works for me"—it was how she managed to cope.

As the initial shock subsided, mothers' pain and loss deepened as they spent more time away from their children. They worried about their children being abused in foster care; they longed for their breakfast and bath time routines; they lamented missing milestones in their children's lives. "It really hurt because my daughter started walking. My sister seen her take her first steps," recalled Deandra, whose daughter was removed at nine months. "That hurts because I'm her mom. . . . When she started teething and all that, my sister was there for all that." Even after her daughter returned home, Deandra grieved the time she'd lost. "Those moments can't be given back to me. . . . I can't relive her teething. I can't relive the things she used to do that would probably make my sister laugh, before she went to sleep."

Seeing little boys at her job, in the bakeshop of a supermarket, reminded Christina of the hole in her life. "Today, I almost cried, 'cause I seen this little boy," Christina shared, nine months after the removal. "The little boy was being like my son, like jumpy and stuff." Christina offered the boy's mother a cookie to give to him. "She's like, 'What do you say?' He's like, 'Thank you.' I was like, damn. I miss my son. I want my baby."

A year later, CPS returned Christina's son to her care. She proudly showed me around their new two-bedroom apartment. Not much adorned the place, except affirmations Christina had written on bright pink sticky notes, posted on the cabinet: "you will be succesful," "Today will be a good Day," "Christina you are Beauital," "god Loves you Everyday."[9]

Things were looking up. "Everything is just, I guess, fallin' in place," she beamed.

Still, Christina thought often about what she'd lost. "I can't even believe they took two years of my life," she sighed. "They took two years of my son's life that I can't get back."

Almost always, child removal is a one-sided affair. Once state agents decide that children are unsafe at home, parents don't have much say. Charlene Berry, for instance, had just a few days with her newborn daughter before CPS whisked the baby into foster care. Charlene, a White mother, was staying in Massachusetts, so Massachusetts CPS came to investigate after the hospital reported positive toxicology tests for Charlene and the baby, along with concerns about inconsistent prenatal care and inadequate supervision at the hospital.

Charlene planned to move back to northeastern Connecticut with the baby, so Connecticut CPS became involved as well. Even before meeting Charlene, staff expected to remove her baby given the report. The Connecticut intake manager phoned a manager in Massachusetts and then announced the verdict across the office: "It looks like she's gonna be ours, unfortunately." Overhearing this, an administrative assistant joked, "I'll start the OTC [order of temporary custody] paperwork."

The Massachusetts and Connecticut investigators converged on Charlene's hospital room, where she sat cross-legged on the bed next to her boyfriend rocking the newborn in her arms. Charlene, who had experienced substantial childhood trauma, spoke softly but earnestly. She seemed eager to please the investigators and readily acceded to their requests: signing releases of information, agreeing to a drug screen. Charlene told me that she felt "overwhelmed" with the two states coming at her—she was trying to be a "good mom," she said, but "they make you feel like you're not."

Sarah, the White investigator from Connecticut, and LeAnn, the Black investigator from Massachusetts, agreed that Connecticut would take the case. LeAnn told Sarah that if it were Massachusetts, "we would've taken the baby." She quickly added, as an afterthought, "We would've seen the house, but. . . ." Her implication was clear—they'd already made up their minds.[10] Sarah felt similarly, saying repeatedly as we left the hospital that Charlene didn't seem to recognize or care about the impact of her substance use during pregnancy.

But Connecticut had started trying something different in recent years: When considering removal, the agency sought to bring families to the table to discuss various options and perhaps avert removal. These meetings, led by trained facilitators at CPS and widely praised by staff for enabling a more collaborative process, occurred before nearly 80 percent of removals. A CPS report linked the strategy to "the diversion of children from out of home care and non-relative foster care."[11] Sarah told Charlene and her boyfriend that CPS held these meetings to see how families and their supports could work on the presenting issues themselves, instead of leaving it to the state.

But the state was there, of course, and the state had decision-making power.[12] Three days later, I met Charlene at the maternity ward to head over to the meeting.

"I'm ready but not ready." Charlene took a breath and then adjusted her shirt: "Trying to look a little more presentable." She'd brushed her long, strawberry blonde hair through.

"You look beautiful," the hospital social worker said encouragingly.

Charlene and her boyfriend, Marcus, dropped the baby off at the nursery, and the hospital social worker wove us across the hospital—on the elevator, through a maze of hallways—to the meeting room. "I'm trying not to have a heart attack," Charlene said.

When we arrived at the cramped, windowless meeting room, CPS staff were waiting: Sarah, Sarah's supervisor, the meeting facilitator, a staff member from the foster care unit, and a trainee. Name tents identified each person's role. Charlene grabbed a marker to write "Mom" on hers.

I attended a number of these meetings. Each began with introductions, followed by the facilitator describing the meeting's structure and goals. The hope, the facilitator explained, was to get everyone's input to make a decision together, but ultimately, CPS would have the final say if people disagreed.

Sarah rattled off the concerns, reading the report printout: taking medication not prescribed, leaving the baby unattended on the bed, minimal prenatal care. Charlene jumped in. "We're new parents," Charlene explained, "learning" and "trying to do the best we can." She added that hospital staff had given conflicting instructions regarding letting the baby sleep or waking her to feed. "It's stressful to figure out how to do it," Charlene said. She and Marcus vehemently emphasized that they'd never left the baby unattended.

Like an attorney cross-examining a witness, Sarah's supervisor posed short, direct questions. "You drank together? And used marijuana and Vicodin together?"

Charlene replied that she used Vicodin to relieve back pain after an injury, maybe half a five-milligram tablet after work. As Marcus explained, he was prescribed Vicodin for a long time, but the prescription lapsed when they moved across the country.

"So the two of you used Vicodin," Sarah's supervisor said.

"Yes and no." Charlene noted that she only took it when needed, exhausted after a full shift on concrete. During her pregnancy, she'd worked more than full-time at a retail job.

But, Sarah's supervisor countered, it wasn't prescribed and she was pregnant. "So you made a decision, and the child has withdrawal as a consequence of your behavior."

"Yes," Charlene acknowledged. "I feel like a piece of crap." To me, she seemed remorseful and anxious, trying to keep her calm.

Sarah's supervisor shook her head. "I'm not sure if you get it." In terms of the plan for the baby, she continued, it was "problematic" that the couple had used together during Charlene's pregnancy, adding that this "didn't show a level of responsibility and judgment."

Later, she asked about the gap in Charlene's prenatal care. Marcus rubbed Charlene's back as she explained that her uncle had died. Then, due to their move, there was an insurance issue, and Charlene's work schedule made appointments difficult. Sarah's supervisor said that this spoke to their "judgment and decision-making regarding the child."

"I agree," Charlene replied, starting to cry. Marcus said that they were trying to do what was best for their daughter.

"I passed my piss test today," Charlene added. "I'm trying to make the point that I'm trying. I really am."

The meeting facilitator asked about a home visiting program. The room fell silent, conveying that CPS staff didn't want to discuss in-home services with Charlene—they'd made their decision.

Charlene said that she was willing to do counseling or groups. "I want to make sure she has a better life than I did." I felt uneasy, knowing what was to come, as Charlene went on about the baby monitor she'd purchased—over $100 but "worth it" and a "good investment." She smiled slightly. Sarah and her supervisor didn't smile, their faces blank.

Speaking clearly and slowly, Sarah's supervisor described the options CPS was considering. She said that she "would lean to an OTC"—an order of temporary custody, requesting state custody of the baby—as she felt that Charlene didn't understand the significance of her actions.

Nothing Charlene or Marcus said that day satisfied CPS. They disputed the hospital's account of inadequate supervision, but to no effect. Charlene detailed the ways she was trying to prove herself a capable caregiver, but CPS wasn't convinced. It was what sociologist Harold Garfinkel would call a "degradation ceremony"[13]—a ritual requiring parents to enact their subordination while CPS shamed their poor judgment and irresponsibility.

All Charlene and Marcus could do was go along. Fighting it would make things worse; recall from chapters 3 and 4 how CPS wanted parents to acquiesce. In another case, the mother's own mother became distraught about the prospect of removal during the meeting. The investigator described the grandmother as "really hostile"; the facilitator told me that she was "cuckoo." CPS had considered placing the baby with her. But the investigator said, "She was becoming this person that we would never consider. I mean, there's a difference between having emotions and being upset, and just attacking."

Another day, I shadowed an investigator named Kerri called out to assist with a removal, which played out on the lawn of a low-rise public housing complex on an unseasonably warm February afternoon. Two police officers, summoned by CPS, stood by as Kerri and the family's caseworker spoke with the parents, the grandmother, and the mother's sister. Ruthie, a young White woman with hair dyed dark red in a loose ponytail, sat on the curb, moving her bare toes through the gravel. She kept repeating that she didn't want her three young children to go with strangers.

"I know you're upset," Kerri told her. "But what your kids need is for you to be calm."

Later, Ruthie raised her voice. "I have rights!" she exclaimed, adding that she hadn't signed anything. "This isn't okay with me. You guys are gonna scare the shit out of my children."

The police officer echoed Kerri: "By you escalating, it's gonna make it harder for them," he told her. He and Kerri might have wanted to make the children's transition as smooth as possible, but in doing so, they also dictated acceptable emotional expressions. In this most traumatic experience, parents couldn't express themselves freely.

The CPS caseworker told Ruthie sternly that the children were now in state custody. She and Kerri moved to gather the children and their things: teddy bears; a small Spiderman backpack; the baby's bottle, filled with warm milk.

"We're gonna go for a ride, okay?" the caseworker said. The oldest child, maybe four or five, looked apprehensive and started to cry. The caseworker distracted him by asking whether he wanted to listen to some music. Then she drove off, the kids in the back seat.

In Charlene's case, after Sarah's supervisor mentioned the custody order, Marcus's face reddened. "We're trying to do everything we can." Choking up, he could barely get the words out before stepping out of the room. Charlene joined him. Sarah's supervisor left the room too, to phone the manager.

When they returned, Marcus was crying. Tears streamed down Charlene's face. The supervisor delivered the news: placement of the baby in foster care.

Marcus protested, asking how they could prove they could care for the baby. Sarah's supervisor said that they would work through that in court, through their participation in services. CPS had made its decision. Marcus buried his face in his hands.

Charlene and Marcus signed the plan CPS wrote up. Then, the group began the long walk back to the maternity ward, where the parents would say goodbye to their newborn. Charlene held Marcus's hand. We all stood in the elevator in silence.

Back at the maternity ward, Sarah handed Charlene something to sign allowing the provision of routine medical care. "Of course," Charlene agreed, instantly cooperative. As Sarah left to photocopy the forms, Charlene collapsed into the arms of a family friend who had come with her. She'd be leaving that day, without her baby.

"They didn't give us a chance," Marcus remarked. Charlene agreed—CPS staff had come in with their minds made up. It felt as though she'd signed over the rights to her child. Despite efforts to engage parents, to incorporate their voices, CPS did what it wanted, and parents were largely powerless to say otherwise.[14]

From that point, court was just a formality. The next week, at the courthouse, Charlene's court-appointed attorney told Charlene that she could go to trial to contest the allegations or waive her right to trial, saying she wanted services.

Charlene paused. "With the positive screen, that probably. . . ." She trailed off.

The attorney agreed. In the courtroom, Charlene didn't state any case; her attorney reported that she would sustain the order, and the judge set the next court date.

"That's it?" Charlene said after we walked out a few minutes later.

That was it. At the courthouse, she'd met her new CPS caseworker, who rushed brusquely through a series of questions and didn't seem particularly interested in getting to know Charlene. "As soon as a child comes into care, the clock starts ticking," the caseworker instructed her. So now, the process to get her baby home began.

System Involvement as Political Learning

When Christina got out of lockup following her arrest outside the convenience store, she recalled calling her CPS caseworker, who said that her son could be home within three to six months. The caseworker noted that Christina acknowledged having "anger issues," and Christina told me that at first, she tried to see the positive in the situation. "I was like, 'All right, you know what? I'll use this time to go to school and get myself together, and I won't think about it as him being taken away from me.'"

But the pathway to get Anthony home became long and arduous, with CPS adding obstacles Christina hadn't anticipated. At her first court hearing, the judge ordered that Anthony be placed at CPS's discretion. "Okay. I'm thinking that's good. 'CPS, can I get my son back?' 'No, you can't get your son back. . . . You have to do stuff to get him back. . . . Classes, this, that, the third.'"

Mothers like Christina learn from these experiences. What scholars call "political socialization"—how people develop their views and opinions on government—might conjure images of students in civics classes or families conversing across the dinner table. But as social scientists have shown, people's everyday experiences interacting with the state—with public benefits programs, police, and schools, for instance—fundamentally shape what they know and think about government, inequality, and justice.[15] In particular, experiences of state social control are central to the political lives of people marginalized by race and/or class.[16] CPS, too, gives parents, especially mothers, firsthand lessons about government operations.

These experiences, especially after child removal, convey the adversarial position of state authorities and make clear that these authorities determine whether and when mothers can raise their children. Initial optimism turned to disillusionment, frustration, and cynicism as the months passed. Caseworkers, attorneys, and judges claimed to help families. But in mothers' experiences, these officials just told them what to do, often working *against* their interests; no one was on their side.

Christina started therapy but said that the next court hearing, and the one after that, was more of the same. She asked CPS staff whether Anthony could come home after a certain number of therapy sessions, but according to CPS records, the supervisor told Christina that her service providers would determine when she was "stable." CPS didn't want therapy to be just a box to check off; the agency wanted Christina to demonstrate progress—as CPS defined it—in her ability to parent her son. But, frustrated, Christina contended that she'd complied with what CPS had asked, yet Anthony still wasn't home.

Sitting outside, on a metal bench next to a small playground area, Christina looked out at the play structure and the hopscotch marked onto the asphalt, wistfully recalling how she used to sit there and watch Anthony play. She was anxious about her case, because it was coming up on a year, and she knew that the state could hold the timeline against her, even as court officials' summer vacations were delaying her next hearing. "I'm scared because they keep playing with me," she said.

Two days later, I accompanied Christina as she visited with Anthony at a local park. Her caseworker, Meghan, was there to supervise. When Meghan arrived with Anthony, Anthony bolted at full speed across the grassy field toward Christina and the playground. As Christina and Anthony chased one another jubilantly around the playground, Meghan, an upbeat, mid-thirties White woman, hung back, not staring directly at them but keeping an eye out.

Anthony's father, a young Black man with a bright, easygoing smile, arrived, too. The three of them seemed thrilled to be spending this time together. I saw Christina relax and simply let her guard down to play with Anthony. She held him up to do the monkey bars and clapped wildly when he made it across. Anthony's father pushed him on the swing, higher and higher. Anthony reveled in it, pumping his legs, grinning widely, and laughing. With a big smile on her face, Christina kissed Anthony on the head when the swing came to rest.

Meghan shared with me that she wasn't worried about Christina's case—Christina's parenting and conduct at the visits didn't concern her, and she even tried to give Christina extra time with Anthony. She deemed Anthony's father "appropriate" as well but added that "he just can't stay out of prison long enough to parent." Anthony was always excited to see Christina, Meghan noted; when Meghan picked him up at day care, Anthony ran to give her a big hug, exclaiming, "We're gonna go see Mommy!" I wondered why the visits had to be supervised. Meghan replied that she'd advocated for unsupervised visits, but the judge had decided otherwise, as Christina hadn't been showing up for her drug screens. Had Christina done the screens as requested, Meghan said, she would have had unsupervised visits.

CPS entered Christina's life following the convenience store incident and, once in, could add all manner of conditions—conditions that shifted over the course of the case. Many affluent White parents recreationally use marijuana, Christina's substance of choice, without CPS intervention. Moreover, Christina was working two jobs and had to drive a half hour to the courthouse to do the drug screens, but CPS didn't help alleviate this burden. Instead, anything less than perfect compliance became a reason to prolong the case and continue supervising her parenting.[17]

Like Christina, other mothers I met described how their cases dragged on. The first days without their children were devastating. The days became weeks, then months, then years. CPS kept coming up with new services they needed to complete. With its broad focus on child safety, the agency did not want to ignore concerns that arose over the course of the case. But as mothers saw it, CPS kept adding hurdles. They went to counseling; they did regular drug tests; they did anger management and domestic violence and substance use treatment. It felt as though as soon as mothers met one request, CPS added another. Their cases kept getting continued in court. "I'm tired of all this going back and forth to court. It feels like a hobby," said Latanya. In my observations, court was less a moment of the state issuing decisions—cases almost never went to trial—and more a check-in point to maintain the status quo. The parties would update the judge, who would set a new court date. Several months later, everyone would come back to court, lather, rinse, repeat. Meanwhile, the kids were growing up.

Criminal cases, where the state prosecutes individual defendants, place people against the state. On paper, child welfare cases are supposed to be different. Usually, parents and CPS have the same goal; both, in theory, want to reunify children with their parents or keep children at home. Colleen recognized these shared aims as she gushed about her caseworker from years ago. "Without her, I wouldn't be where I'm at right now—she did a lot to help me," Colleen said, recalling the nine months her two young children spent in foster care. "CPS, they do rip apart families, but my [caseworker], I still love her to this day. We still email. I send her pictures of all the kids. . . . She wanted me to get my kids back."

But Colleen's experience was the exception—and remember from chapter 1 that Colleen approached CPS herself about placing her children in foster care when she and her boyfriend were using drugs. Generally, mothers whose children CPS removed involuntarily saw caseworkers working at odds with them, rather than alongside them.[18] As we saw previously, CPS could align itself with parents in cases deemed lower-risk, such that mothers felt CPS wanted to help them. In cases that escalated to removal, meanwhile, mothers saw the agency taking a different tack. Latanya described her caseworker: "She's no help. She don't talk about the good things that I do. She talks about the negative when we get in front of the judge." Mothers described how caseworkers looked down on them. "The way she would talk to me and look at me, I felt like to her I was trash," Candis recalled. "It's an experience that I think I will never forget."[19]

One morning, at the Providence courthouse, I spotted Stacy, a White mother, sitting on a bench nearby. Stacy had been trying to get—and keep—her five children home in the two years I'd known her. When I asked how she was doing, she offered a terse reply: "Not good. They took my son." At one point, when Stacy stepped away, her caseworker Theresa, also White, approached a social services worker who had accompanied Stacy. Alluding to

Stacy's demeanor, Theresa said that she was "itching" to cancel Stacy's visit with her son that day. "If she keeps being nasty, it's not gonna be a good scene."

Later, Stacy told the social services worker and me that she wanted another caseworker. The social services worker responded pragmatically: "Unfortunately, she holds all the cards, so you don't wanna give her a reason to cancel the visit." Theresa had the power in this interaction, and everyone knew it.

Later, Theresa mentioned a parenting program Stacy would participate in now that her son was in foster care again. Stacy asked why she had to repeat these programs. Theresa went on about how Stacy was "still having the same problems" and "still making some poor parenting choices." Theresa told Stacy that Stacy could either do the work or argue with her. The message was clear: Stacy had little choice but to get on board. After listing all the things Stacy had to do differently, Theresa insisted, "I'm on your team, Stacy, I really am. Believe me, I did not wanna remove [your son]." Theresa said that she knew how hard it was for her son and for Stacy. "But still, you gotta pull it together."

Caseworkers might say that they sided with parents, but mothers saw everything else—caseworkers' actions, their words, even the looks they gave—saying otherwise. Theresa put everything on Stacy to "pull it together" and get her son home; Theresa's contribution to Stacy's "team" would be to supervise Stacy in the tasks Theresa assigned. Stacy had sole responsibility but little power.

CPS set the terms: what mothers had to do, when they could see their kids, and for how long. Such experiences taught mothers about state power and how they could work to counter it. When her case first opened, Christina said, she repeatedly called the caseworker and supervisor, "cussing them out" and telling them to give back her son. Then, she noticed that with this stance, CPS was delaying returning her son home. So she struck a different chord. "Now, I talk to [the supervisor] calmly, but it's just a psychological thing I'm doing, trying to get my kid." She enacted the same superficial acquiescence with her new therapist. "I'm making her think that my mind has changed," she said. "Because I want my son back, and I want him fast. . . . I know what they wanna hear." As in sociologist Paige Sweet's study of women receiving domestic violence services, Christina had learned to craft a narrative of self-transformation for institutional gatekeepers.[20]

Bianca, a Guatemalan mother, initially spoke openly with CPS, telling them that her job growing marijuana helped people feel better. She questioned the treatment CPS pushed, because she enjoyed using marijuana recreationally: "You're powerless of choice because you're on drugs? Like, I don't get it. Dude, if I light up one, it's 'cause I enjoy doing it, not 'cause I'm sick." But highlighting the benefits of marijuana to the family court judge didn't work out so well. Now, she understood, she had to "lie to them—they like that." Bianca told them "whatever they want to hear. You're an ignorant person. Yes, I am, I am ignorant. You're sick and you're powerless of your drug. Yes, I am. . . . Just agree." Bianca repeated these sentiments during the years I interviewed her. The acquiescence Bianca and Christina learned to perform didn't facilitate child well-being goals. Instead, akin to Charlene's degradation experience in the "considered removal" meeting, CPS staff continually impressed upon Bianca that there was something wrong with her, and she learned to nod along.

Because poverty puts mothers on CPS's radar and draws them into more intensive intervention, as discussed in chapters 2 and 4, mothers navigating ongoing CPS cases usually have limited material resources. Their poverty and marginality exacerbates their powerlessness as they deal with CPS. Mothers saw that the system worked differently for those with resources. Christina said that her attorney didn't know much about her case. She wished that she had the funds to hire a lawyer, "because if I get a paid lawyer and he sees what's going on, I bet you any amount of money I would get my kid back just like that." The inequalities Christina noticed taught her how the system worked:

> You notice people who have major support system, like . . . a paid lawyer, those are the people who get out and stuff like that, 'cause they have a great support system. Other people like me, very low income, not great support system, bad background, the system's made for people like me. . . . It's great for them to antagonize me, 'cause they're like, "Oh, she don't got nobody. She don't know the ins and outs. We could whip her right into shape, or we could do whatever we want, basically."

As Christina saw it, she didn't have money or power, so the system knew that it could have its way with her.

Bianca, too, mentioned her boyfriend's brother, who also had a CPS case. He and his girlfriend were addicted to heroin and sleeping in their car. But "he dress good. . . . They're very American." CPS never took their kids. I asked why Bianca felt that this case differed from her own. "She's American. She's White. She lives in [town] in a really fancy house. His parents were there for her," Bianca replied. To Bianca and Christina, the message was clear: the system favored affluent White parents over poor parents of color like themselves.[21]

Poverty also makes it difficult to meet CPS's requests. A few months after Anthony's removal, Christina had to miss a couple visits with him due to her work schedule. Low-wage work hours are often unpredictable; missing a shift may mean being let go. CPS case records documented her work conflicts. Even still, the caseworker wrote, "It appears that Mom is exhibiting signs that she does not want visits with her son." Christina eventually paid for a medical marijuana card, which she said helped get Anthony home: "It was $200 to get my kid back. Screw that." Additionally, without children at home, mothers lost important benefits, which kept them from completing their service plans. It was Kafkaesque: they couldn't get a two-bedroom apartment through the housing authority because they didn't have their kids, but they couldn't get their kids because they didn't have a two-bedroom apartment.[22]

CPS's requests can tax parents' limited resources, such that what looks like noncompliance is actually poverty. During the five years I talked with Barbara, she stayed with different family members and worked a series of fast food jobs. In the first few weeks after CPS removed her three young children, Barbara felt hopeful about CPS's intervention. She missed her kids but hoped that maybe it was for the best. "It needed to happen," she reasoned. "When I get them back, I'll be a happier mom and a better mom." She appreciated CPS connecting her with counseling services, which she found helpful.

Four months later, Barbara's perspective had shifted. She'd been doing nearly everything CPS had asked, but her kids still weren't home. CPS had asked her to do drug screens, but they weren't court-ordered, as Barbara said her caseworker had forgotten to mention it at court. So Barbara had to pay for the screens—$25 each week, more than she could afford—out of pocket. "I'm clean and stuff, so I'm getting negative screens, just I haven't been able to do them, 'cause of the money." Barbara said that this was the only item on her service plan with which she hadn't been fully compliant. She'd tried to tell her caseworker it was unfair that she had to pay for the screens, especially as her case came in for domestic violence, not substance use, but her caseworker was "just not hearing it." At first, Barbara had deemed her caseworker understanding and helpful, but now, she felt that she had no say in the matter—she was "just another case."

Mothers didn't feel that their voices were heard in court either. At court, the isolating, adversarial, and disciplinary nature of the system comes into sharp relief, reinforcing mothers' marginal positions. "When court comes, it's just like, I just sit there and listen to what has to be said," Barbara remarked. In theory, they had attorneys to advocate for them.[23] But mothers didn't find their attorneys particularly helpful. Barbara left messages for her attorney and didn't hear back; she'd told her attorney what was going on, but it didn't seem to make a difference: "I literally am stuck in a corner with nobody on my side."

Christina, too, said that after getting out of jail she called the legal aid office every day, asking about her assigned attorney so they could prepare her case. The secretary told Christina to stop calling, as she wouldn't meet her attorney until the court date. When that date finally came, her attorney approached her with the wrong case file; he didn't know anything about her case. At her most recent court date, a different man said that he'd just been appointed as her attorney and asked Christina for her information. "[Legal aid] doesn't service me," Christina concluded. At court, legal aid attorneys like Christina's didn't have a moment to themselves; they spent their mornings in and out of the courtroom, flitting back and forth to touch base with clients when waiting to be called into court. With multiple cases scheduled each day, and pressed for time due to their high workloads, legal aid attorneys chatted with parents for just a few minutes before and after going into court.

Yet attorneys' inattention due to time and resource constraints was not the only source of mothers' disempowerment. Sometimes, mothers doubted whether their attorneys—the people specifically designated to be on their side—stood with them. In both Rhode Island and Connecticut, legal aid attorneys and CPS caseworkers laughed and chatted informally at court.[24] Alex assessed her legal aid attorney: "Honestly, I wonder who she works for half the time." Alex recalled a snide remark her attorney had made: "She's like, 'Well, if you hadn't had that one dirty, maybe you'd have her back by now.' And that about flipped me out. That threw me for a loop." Alex drew a sharp intake of breath, like she was trying to hold back tears.

Desiree suggested that lawyers didn't care—it wasn't their children at stake. "At 4:00 they clock out. They go to a nice comfy home, to their nice comfy bed, with their kids, and I'm the last thing on their mind." She recalled how intimidating it was to see the "gang of lawyers"—"a pair for CPS, a pair for my kids"—across from her. She didn't get to speak in the courtroom; only CPS and the lawyers could. "I don't get to say what I really feel. Even if I tell my lawyer, she's like, 'Uh-uh-uh-uh-uh,' and that's it. To her it's just like, 'Oh, this woman is talking so much.'" Desiree whined to mimic her lawyer's annoyance. As Desiree's comments suggest, court literally silences mothers. Perhaps in the name of judicial efficiency, attorneys speak for parents in court; court officials discipline parents attempting to express themselves. In this respect, rather than offering a more nurturing environment, family court parallels the criminal court.[25]

Even the courtroom's physical setup exposes the adversarial relationships and powerlessness mothers identified. At the Providence family court, the judge sits up on a platform behind a large, imposing table, looking out onto two smaller tables. As Desiree's comments indicate, parents and parents' attorneys sit at one table. The CPS caseworker, CPS attorney, and children's attorney sit at the other. In mirroring criminal cases—where prosecution sits across from defense, two sides to battle it out—the layout conveys parents' interests as opposed to children's interests and CPS's interests, despite CPS's talk of shared reunification goals. Mothers saw it this way too; Christina recalled "the prosecutor, the people who was against me," recommending unsupervised visits to the judge. After I probed, she explained, "I call them prosecution, but I think it's CPS [and] their lawyer.... I'm calling them the prosecutors because they're CPS, they're the ones who are saying ... 'She did this and she did that.'"

Entering the courtroom for her first hearing, Christina felt relieved to see a Black judge. She thought that he would understand, perhaps having "had a struggle" himself. But the judge silenced her anyway. Christina described how she kept raising her hand to speak, but as she recounted it, attorneys and the judge advised her not to talk. "The judge is like, 'Put this on her record. We're advising her not to speak. She still wants to speak, so she can speak.'" Christina said that this "infuriated" her. She saw her silencing as an insult to her intelligence—as though her lawyer expected her to "mess up" and say something wrong—and as an injustice. "You should give me that right, you understand? You're already taking my rights away from me."

Still, Christina spoke, rebutting something the CPS attorney had said. As she recalled later, the judge admonished her for speaking up: "He's like, 'Ms. Rayford, you're being a little aggressive.' I said, 'I'm sorry, Your Honor. I don't mean to be aggressive, but I'm really just trying to get my son home.' It's really not aggression. It's aggressive, but it's more a passion." Such experiences taught mothers like Christina how the system viewed them—through racialized and gendered lenses framing advocacy as aggression to be squelched. "He's trying to teach me a lesson, like, 'Don't mess with me, 'cause I'm the judge.'" She felt that she didn't have a say. "It's killing me because it's like a major energy force pushing me down, I feel. The judge as being the powerful. It's like, who can override him besides the Supreme Court?" The judge, who saw her for a couple minutes every few months and didn't hear directly from her, had the power to determine whether Anthony could come home.

Rather than a neutral weighing of facts to mete out justice, court often became a display of discipline and control.[26] In Providence one January, I observed a hearing where a children's attorney mentioned the child's Adderall prescription going unfilled for two or three weeks, among other concerns. The mother, Angie, with light skin and dark hair, started explaining her challenges managing three kids and the recent snowstorm without a car. As she began getting worked up, the bailiff, a tall, older man with white hair, stood in front of her on the other side of the table, putting both hands on the table and blocking her view. The position struck me as intentionally threatening. "You have to be quiet," he commanded.

Angie, still seated, kept talking, undeterred. "You don't need to stand in front of me."

"I'm going to order you to be quiet right now," the judge instructed.

A little later, the bailiff told Angie to shut her phone off. She replied that it wasn't on. To this, the judge told her, "You need to bring yourself under control"—otherwise, she would be brought downstairs, where the criminal courts were. He struck a condescending tone: "What will your decision be today?"

The judge gave his order. "So the kids are getting taken today?" Angie asked. The judge told her she'd heard what he said. She protested that she would do all the programs and services. But it didn't matter. Angie rushed out of the courtroom, crying, as soon as the proceeding concluded.

All in all, mothers' experiences with CPS teach them how the state operates. Their emerging cynicism, their perceptions of injustice, and their acute recognition of their precarity in the face of governmental power may ultimately shape political engagement. I asked Melanie, a White mother whose children CPS had taken permanently, how she thought CPS had affected her life beyond her parenting:

> They've made me a fricking mess. Like, they make me not like anything to do with state affairs. Like anything that has to do with the state, I have animosity towards. Like, I don't like court-appointed lawyers. I don't like to go into the tax building. I don't like—see what I'm saying? I don't like the welfare building. Now I think everybody's against me. Do you know what I'm saying? Because that's what they were doing.

Court officials denied working against her, Melanie said, but she saw their friendly banter and heard that they had a "quota" of terminations to fill. "It's made me not trust people," she concluded.

I met Amy, a petite Puerto Rican mother with long, dark hair, in the grocery store parking lot on a balmy spring day. She was loading groceries into her minivan, her four young daughters hanging on the open doors. We had to reschedule several times due to her full-time work schedule, but she kept in touch, texting, "I'm really interested about your study esp cause there's no manual to this motherhood thing lol." When we finally met, she was eager to share her perspective while doing several large loads of laundry at the Laundromat down the street. Then, we continued the conversation in her parked minivan. She was trying her best to keep it together amid her financial challenges and the ensuing stress.

Nine months later, we met up again after Amy got off work. CPS had removed Amy's children two weeks prior. After an incident of domestic violence perpetrated by her girlfriend months before, she'd spoken with a domestic violence advocate at the hospital, whom Amy believed notified CPS. From that, as described in chapter 5, Amy learned not to open up about such things: "I feel like, great, everywhere I go for help, they're just going to snitch me out and put me in danger of losing my kids." Her children remained home after that initial report, but CPS received another call several months later, when Amy's older daughters shared with a relative their fears of witnessing domestic violence. Because her daughters had mentioned not feeling safe, CPS arranged for the older two to stay with their father, instructing him to obtain a restraining order against Amy, while taking Amy's two younger daughters into state custody.

Being home alone, without her daughters, was painful. "I feel like I'm mourning my kids," Amy shared. She'd recently had a panic attack that brought her to the hospital. As we wrapped up, I thanked Amy for talking with me. "It helps," she replied. "It helps because, honestly, I have nothing to do after work anymore except cry. I try to fall asleep by 7:00 'til the next day, because it's just easier than to deal."

When we first met, Amy had shared concerns about others judging her and calling CPS, like if her home was a mess. But she'd deemed CPS "a great service" because "children need advocates." So when CPS got involved, Amy hoped that they would treat her fairly. Amy acknowledged that she'd been stressed out and "very overwhelmed," so, like Christina and Barbara, she initially thought that the intervention could be a blessing in disguise, helping her get into counseling or other needed services. And she believed that CPS would see her as "a good mom" and a victim of domestic violence who had done everything they asked: "I always thought the law was on my side. I always thought that the law would prevail and that the law would find out the truth."

But with her daughters placed out of home and her caseworker unsympathetic, Amy became "angry," "upset," and "very disappointed" with CPS. She didn't understand why CPS had taken her kids so swiftly and didn't know what would happen. The experience gave her another perspective on the government. Amy told me that she wasn't using a legal aid attorney.

> Nope. I don't trust anything that has to do with the state. It sounds so messed up. I don't.
> *Is that new, or have you always felt that way?*
> Yeah, that's new.
> *Okay. Tell me more about that.*
> I love my country. I love my state. I love the fact that they provide such great services for people that are low-income. . . . When I went through [legal aid] for previous stuff, like my last divorce, I always had great experiences, always. Now I feel like . . . there's these strings being pulled that I can't see. I don't know what's going on.
> *How do you feel about the state now? Not just CPS but the government generally.*
> I feel like you could only win when the public eye is involved or when you're related to the state somehow, when you have a family member that works for the state. That's the only way now, when you're connected, for you to actually be treated well. That's how I feel now. I don't trust them at all.

CPS's intervention shifted Amy's orientation toward the state. To Amy, government was no longer a trusted source of support. Instead, she viewed the state with cynicism and wanted to keep her distance.

Christina, too, didn't know why Anthony couldn't come home or what more CPS wanted from her. It was frustrating. Echoing Amy, she said, "I feel like it's secretive, like there's things, there's missing pieces. I feel like they're out to get me." It seemed as though no one wanted to help her—even nonprofit organizations were just "in it for the money."

She had recently watched a documentary series on Kalief Browder, a teenager incarcerated for years without trial for allegedly stealing a backpack. Christina saw their experiences as linked, part of a larger narrative of racialized injustice. She recognized how the system had "beat him down to the ground" without evidence of his wrongdoing. One minor, questionable incident somehow spiraled into a traumatizing, years-long saga. Christina, too, tried to prove her innocence, but to no avail. "Sometimes I feel like [Kalief], closed in, no one can help me," she said. Whatever boxes she checked, she felt it didn't matter. So she'd learned "to remain humble," because "no matter what I say or do, I'm not in control." Still, Christina remained resolute. She would continue to stand up for what she knew was right. "I'm not letting [the judge] take my power away from me," she declared.

Anthony remained in CPS's custody for nearly two years in all. When the judge ordered Anthony home, Christina didn't think that anything about her situation had changed—maybe she'd secured a medical marijuana card, but that was all. She'd simply been assigned to a different judge who saw no reason Anthony couldn't come home. And she figured her caseworker had grown tired of dealing with her. By this time, her baby had outgrown his stroller. Now four and a half, he was getting ready for prekindergarten.

Stifled Advocacy

Like Christina, mothers weren't keen on lying down and accepting what the state told them. When they acquiesced, they often did so strategically. They also found ways of resisting CPS's demands. As political scientist James Scott contends, much resistance by oppressed people does not take the form of large-scale, formal movements but, rather, transpires in relatively mundane, individual machinations.[27] Mothers told me about visiting their children surreptitiously, outside CPS's prescribed visit schedule, or withholding information from CPS. Barbara continued communicating with her boyfriend, jailed after assaulting her, against CPS's instructions. Sometimes mothers could angle to modify their cases within the system. For instance, though Stacy didn't think that filing a complaint against her caseworker would make a difference—"Who's gonna believe me over the CPS lady?"—Desiree switched caseworkers after writing a letter expressing her dissatisfaction: "They changed it right away."

Nevertheless, when mothers sought to contest CPS's claims or express their opposition to CPS's decisions, they often found this advocacy stifled. As discussed above, mothers were literally silenced at court, the venue specifically designated to hear them make their case. This pressure on mothers to submit to the state's requests, no matter how much mothers oppose these requests, persists throughout the course of a CPS case but reaches its pinnacle when the state seeks to legally and permanently terminate parental rights.

Christina, Barbara, Amy, and others eventually saw their children come home, at long last. But for others, as years passed, the state pursued what has been called the "civil death penalty."[28] Once parental rights are terminated, parents have no legal connection with their children. Children's names can change; parents may never see or hear from them again. The 1997 Adoption and Safe Families Act requires CPS agencies to file to terminate parental rights (a prerequisite for adoption) when children have spent fifteen of the most recent twenty-two months in foster care. The federal government monitors states' compliance with this timeline, and CPS often draws criticism for the length of time children spend in care. When a case has been open for years but CPS remains dissatisfied with parents' progress, then, the agency turns to termination. This prospect is beyond devastating—a trauma in itself that can set parents back. Latanya recalled her reaction upon hearing that CPS was looking toward adoption: "I was like, 'Well, I'm not even gonna waste my time trying to get into another [drug treatment] program.'" She saw where CPS intended to take the case. "So I just didn't go back into the program."

Like the criminal courts, family courts cannot accommodate every case taken to trial. Given this limited capacity, prosecutors offer plea deals, and CPS offers termination deals. In Rhode Island, I saw how these deals were false choices, not driven by child well-being considerations but manufactured by the system to encourage parents to agree to termination. Sometimes, CPS pitted mothers' older children against their younger children, forcing tough decisions. Susan acquiesced to the adoption of an older child to have a chance of keeping her newborn. Bianca, too, agreed to a similar bargain, pressured by her attorney. ("That's why I don't want public defenders, but I guess I have no choice and should be grateful," she said.)

CPS also used promises of visitation after termination to entice parents to agree, presenting parents with an impossible choice. They could sign the papers and be guaranteed visits with their children, perhaps four a year. Or they could decline to sign and go to trial—but if they lost, they could get no visitation whatsoever. In this wrenching situation, mothers faced substantial pressure to sign over their rights, as they loved their children more than anything and wanted to maintain that connection.

Outside court one day, an attorney discussed the trial option with her client, India, telling her that signing the adoption papers was the only way to guarantee that India could see her young daughters. "The age they are, they won't know you fought," the attorney said, alluding to India's desire to show her children that she hadn't given up on them. "What's important is that you see them as they grow up." The attorney told India that it was India's decision but explained that even if India won the trial, her children wouldn't automatically come home; moreover, winning at trial would be extremely difficult.

Here, we see court officials drop the facade of acting in the best interests of the child. No one argued that India would endanger her daughters with quarterly visits. Post-adoption visitation would hinge not on what was best for India's children but on whether India surrendered her legal right to a trial, where, through her attorney, she could present evidence to contest the termination of her parental rights. (And the court could set visitation even after a mother lost at trial and supposedly relinquished her right to visits, further underscoring the extent to which the offers are threats intended to chill advocacy.)

When faced with the prospect of termination, mothers wanted to fight for their rights to their children. Eventually, though, under pressure, nearly all mothers I met in this position reluctantly acceded. Stacy, the mother I'd run into at court, had had a lifetime of adversity and faced numerous challenges in raising her children. Stacy herself had been adopted as a young child and endured abuse from both her biological and adoptive parents. In the decade before we met, Stacy's five children had been in and out of foster care as she battled a cocaine addiction and experienced violence in intimate relationships. Her life was unstable; she frequently ended up homeless or in jail. Once, playing a game on her phone, she exclaimed happily upon advancing to the next level. "I pretend I live on these paradises," she added.

When I first met Stacy, on the bus, only her six-year-old son was placed with her. She was in her late thirties but looked much older, with her pale skin weathered, her hair graying, and her voice gruff and often hoarse. By the next year, Stacy's oldest child, nearly eighteen, was living with an aunt whom Stacy agreed could be the teenager's legal guardian, and CPS planned to file to terminate her parental rights to three other children.

Like Latanya, Stacy found this news discouraging and counterproductive. "As soon as they said TPR [termination of parental rights], I started to give up," she said. "I said, 'Not until you said you were going to TPR on me did I even think about using.'" She wrestled with whether to consent to the adoptions and be guaranteed visits or to oppose them and risk no visitation whatsoever if she lost at trial. At first, she was defiant, declaring, "I don't care. I will fight all the way. If I don't see my kids, my kids know where I live. They will be back."

Several months later, I met Stacy at her friend's place, where she was staying. The first adoption hearing, for her eleven-year-old, would be later that week. Her friend encouraged her not to sign, to "fight for her child." Stacy weighed the risk. "I don't wanna lose and then not see him at all until he's old enough to run away." Still, she resolved to fight: "I already missed four years with my kid. If I'm gonna go out, I'm gonna go out with a fight, okay? Not signing no papers."

Stacy arrived at court wearing a black button-down shirt, gray slacks, and gray ballet-style flats. She'd lint-rolled her clothes and meant to straighten her hair but was running late that morning. As it turned out, we waited all morning to be called. Stacy showed me pictures of her kids from the prior day's visit—her twelve-year-old daughter was now taller than her. At 12:30, the bailiff told Stacy to come back after lunch, at 2:00.

Finally, after hours waiting, Stacy went into the courtroom. Stacy's attorney conveyed that Stacy was unwilling to agree to the adoption. The judge, eager to move the case to its conclusion given how long it had been open, asked whether everyone would agree to start the trial the following day. From the back row of the courtroom, I heard Stacy mutter to her attorney, "I don't have a choice."

I called Stacy the next day. She told me that things didn't go well at court and that she had to "give one kid up to get the rest." No witnesses were called; no evidence was presented. In mediation beforehand, CPS staff offered monthly visits with her eleven-year-old if she signed his adoption papers—more than their prior offer of quarterly visits. To Stacy, the message was clear: if she didn't "give up" her eleven-year-old, she would have no chance to get the others home. She signed. The mediator told Stacy that she would go through the stages of grief after signing. So Stacy was in the "crying phase." When we talked, she was shoveling snow, trying to get her mind off of things.

The next month, when we ran into each other at court, we again waited for Stacy's case to be called. As the hours passed, the area started emptying out, until only a few others lingered in the typically packed waiting area. Then, a crowd of people came through, impossible to miss. Everyone looked jubilant, an unusual sight for family court. Stacy's caseworker told Stacy that they were there for an adoption and that her case would be called as soon as they finished. Stacy watched the children dancing and skipping around, posing for pictures by the window, the two young girls sporting rainbow tutus and sparkly silver shoes. Her voice quiet and tentative, she wondered aloud if the parents came to the adoptions.

"No," replied the social services worker who'd accompanied her to court. "Just the adoptive parents."

In the months that followed, Stacy repeatedly tested positive for cocaine, reversing a pattern of negative screens. Her CPS caseworker wrote that Stacy "presented as depressed" and "expressed feeling very hopeless about her children returning home." Over the next year, each of her children's cases progressed to adoption. Her youngest had a new last name. Grudgingly, worn out, she'd signed all the adoption papers.

Beyond their individual cases, mothers knew that the system needed to change as well. Yet they were hesitant about getting involved to mobilize for reform.[29] This did not reflect any general indifference. Rather, with CPS and other authorities underscoring mothers' subordinate and stigmatized status at every turn, mothers expressed skepticism about the prospect for systemic change. Barbara, for instance, knew that CPS was overdue for reform but had no interest in working toward those changes. "'Cause they're at the top of the head right now." Barbara traced these perceptions to her experiences. When I mentioned that sometimes people talk about getting a group together to improve the system, Barbara responded that she'd tried to contact the CPS supervisor about her daughter's treatment in foster care. "She didn't even want to look into it." This experience shaped how Barbara thought about the potential for change: "They probably have so much power that you feel useless. There's nothing you can really do." I pressed once more, suggesting that there might be power in numbers. But Barbara countered, "There's also people that are advocating against us. 'Oh, you have a neglect against you. You have this against you.' You know what I'm saying? They'll probably bring that up and stuff. I feel like it would be useless, to be honest."

Desiree, too, didn't think that anyone would listen to her. "You can write a shitload of letters, but that'll just go in the trash. You know what I mean? Phone calls, that'll get put on hold." Like Barbara, Desiree cited her subordinate status as a reason for her skepticism:

> 'Cause I'm a no one. I'm a nobody. I'm just a junkie to them. I'm no one. Why would they listen to me? . . . I don't have any money to give them, so they can pass the law. . . . I'm just a minority in this little fucking city, talking out my ass. "She's just mad because she lost her children. She'll say whatever."

Desiree had not experienced a just or democratic system, where people could come together to decide what was right, but, rather, a system where money (and Whiteness) talked. As a low-income Dominican mother accused of neglect, she didn't see her voice carrying much weight.

And Desiree worried that CPS could retaliate. Mothers with CPS cases just wanted the agency out of their lives; once their cases closed, the sense of precarity persisted, and they hesitated to get involved in anything that might get them back on CPS's radar. Desiree had thought about suing CPS but feared that this could adversely affect her case; she knew that CPS could go to court and make false allegations about her drug use or anything else. As she had learned, recalling her lawyers silencing her in the courtroom, what CPS said went, and things could get worse for her if she spoke up. By repeatedly silencing and dismissing mothers, CPS and related authorities conveyed the system's power over them—a tactic effective in chilling mothers' potential mobilization and maintaining the status quo.

"I have great news!" I hadn't heard from Isabela Matos in several months, so I wasn't expecting her call. She sounded energized, far from the muted, listless demeanor I'd encountered in our prior conversations.

When we first met, two years before, CPS had had her four children for nearly a year already. Since then, the agency had filed to terminate her parental rights, so I thought she might tell me that somehow, improbably, her children were back in her care.

Instead, Isabela, a Dominican mother in her late twenties, was calling to invite me to a meeting the following week, saying that she and others were getting the community together to raise awareness about CPS. More than twenty people had come to the last meeting; they had run out of chairs. Isabela told me that the group was coming up with a chant, trying to get media coverage, and planning a rally at the courthouse.

After Isabela had her youngest daughter, Isabela's mother had urged her to seek treatment for her mental health needs at a psychiatric hospital. Her mother watched the children informally during Isabela's hospital stay but eventually called CPS. Isabela chalked it up to her mother needing state benefits to care for the children. Indeed, CPS's summary of the investigation noted that Isabela's mother was "running out of food" and that the baby, born with a disability, wasn't receiving services. Affluent families might manage such a situation through informal care, but in Isabela's case, CPS took custody of her children. Isabela felt helpless. But she participated in the therapy CPS recommended and took medication for her bipolar disorder even though it made her feel like "a zombie." She missed her outgoing, bubbly self. She used to love making big, fancy breakfasts for her kids, serving them orange juice in wine glasses. Now, heavily medicated and longing for her kids, Isabela barely recognized the sad, withdrawn person she'd become.

Unlike other mothers I'd met, Isabela wasn't giving in to pressure to sign away her rights; she intended to take her case to trial. And more than that, she wanted to agitate for change through the grassroots group she was convening. Isabela's notes listed a long-term goal of reunifying families while working to "build awareness—outreach plan—educate others—gain press outreach." "Return our kids to *their* home," read the flyers she'd made to spread the word. "Let's *Fight* for change in CPS . . . Join us—Every Voice Matters." She'd gone to public events to approach elected officials and brainstormed places to do outreach: bus stops, churches, the YMCA.

At the next meeting, in a community organizing space on a cool, drizzling evening, fifteen to twenty people gathered over pizza and chicken empanadas to share their experiences with the system and tips for navigating it. Isabela's main focus was planning a rally outside family court the following month, timed to coincide with her court hearing.

On the morning of the rally, I arrived to about a dozen people—some with kids, others without—gathered to hold signs and banners on the corner. "Bring the Matos Kids Home," read one, stenciled on a large banner. "Who Do You Call When 'CPS' Is Abusing Kids," read another. Isabela's mother handed out strips of masking tape for participants to cover their mouths, to represent their voices not being heard.

I went upstairs to court with Isabela. She'd straightened her hair and pulled it back into a low bun, put on lipstick, and painted her fingernails and toenails bright red. Inside, she approached her caseworker and the caseworker's supervisor a couple times, but they brushed her off, telling her to talk to her lawyer. "See how they always dodge me?" Isabela sighed.

A White legal aid attorney in a navy suit, around Isabela's age, strode over. She introduced herself as Isabela's new lawyer, Leah, and said that she'd tried to call Isabela. Was her phone disconnected?

Isabela gave a measured but assertive response: "It wasn't disconnected. It was just off for the day."

"Right," Leah said dismissively. She then gestured out the window to the rally below and told Isabela that what was going on outside wasn't good for her. By way of explanation, when I probed, Leah deemed the protest "combative" and "adversarial." Isabela countered that it was completely separate from her case.

"Your kids' names are on the banner!" Leah exclaimed, her frustration evident. Leah's message was clear: activism would be punished.

Leah then turned to Isabela's legal strategy, suggesting that they prioritize Isabela's contact with her kids, perhaps by advocating for an open adoption. But Isabela was clear: "I only want reunification."

Leah said that she would advocate for that if Isabela wanted but that Isabela should consider what she was willing to risk. Leah added that she wasn't optimistic about Isabela's chances at trial, pointing to Isabela's boyfriend's domestic violence and what this suggested about Isabela's "protective capacity." When Isabela disputed this, Leah, ever the attorney, shot right back, bringing in additional details from the case file.

"If I'm feeling attacked right now, I'm only imagining what CPS feels like," Leah said at one point. Echoing Stacy's caseworker, Leah told Isabela, "I'm on your side."

As Leah spoke, Isabela stared back, her eyes wide. She seemed to be holding back tears, trying to stay in control. When Leah stepped away, Isabela paced back and forth, upset. She didn't see Leah as on her side at all. "I'll represent myself if I have to."

Leah returned, asking whether we were ready to go into court. Isabela requested a few minutes to step outside.

"For a cigarette?" Leah asked.

Isabela responded that she didn't usually smoke but she needed one.

Leah softened. "Sure," she said—she'd tell the court that we would be ready shortly. I told Isabela I'd catch up with her outside.

I didn't see her at first when I went out back. I was about to turn around when I spotted her lying on her back on a concrete bench, knees bent, looking up at the bright blue sky. I asked whether she wanted to be alone.

"It's fine," she said. A few silent beats passed before her body started shaking. Isabela put her hands on her face and began audibly sobbing. After a couple minutes, she wiped her eyes and asked an older woman smoking nearby for a cigarette. A tall young man offered one, lighting it for her. "I hope things get better for you," he told her.

"We really should get back inside," Isabela said. She put out her half-smoked cigarette, placing it in her purse.

In court, the case was continued for a trial date the following month. I texted Isabela afterward about the community meetings. She wasn't sure about going—she didn't want the court to find out and hold it against her. The judge, she recalled, was "kinda pissed" and wanted her to have no part in what was going on outside.

As her case moved to and through trial over the next year, Isabela felt that she was fighting alone. Her attorney, Leah, brushed her off; Isabela didn't think that Leah was even working on her case. Once, she'd come upon Leah and her caseworker laughing together, their demeanor changing only when they saw Isabela approach. So she didn't think that she could trust Leah.

The group she'd started was still trying to get people together, but Isabela had stepped back. The judge had instructed her not to do any rallies or organizing, she said, so she had to "lay low." In Rhode Island, an advocacy organization had just settled a class action lawsuit with CPS and was seeking stakeholder input for the settlement. But Isabela planned to wait until her children came home to contact the advocacy group. She didn't want to jeopardize her case.

A year after the courthouse rally, Isabela was about to lose all her parental rights for good. She lay in her bed, with its upholstered silver headboard, and pulled the fluffy white comforter over her shoulders as she contemplated what she'd learned from her experience. Isabela thought about her caseworkers, "using children as a pawn," and felt disillusioned to know that "people in this world exist like that." She thought back to a time before CPS entered her life.

> If I were to see a bird and it looks like it's dying, I'd be like, "Oh, my God, that bird. I can save its life." Now, I'll look at a bird, and it's struggling, I'll be like, "Oh, well, tough luck for you, bird. It's a cruel life." This whole thing with CPS and shit like that is turning me into a person I don't like, a person that I am not, a cruel person like everybody else in this world.

This fired-up young woman hoped that she could "be a voice, someway, somehow," even after the termination became final. But the system had stifled and punished her efforts at advocacy, leaving Isabela not only devastated about her permanent separation from her children but also worn out from the fight and disenchanted about humanity, society, and prospects for change.

Although mothers drawn into CPS may start optimistic about CPS's involvement, hoping that the agency can help them, their experiences leave them increasingly disillusioned. Caseworkers and court officials assure mothers that they're on the same team, all while giving mothers ever more hoops to jump through. Mothers learn that if they don't comply, they risk losing everything. This precarious position leaves them feeling isolated, with little say in the matter, especially given their marginalized social positions. With the system wearing them down, they acquiesce to salvage what they can: their children's swifter return home, occasional visits post-adoption. When they don't, when mothers like Isabela exercise their rights to resist, CPS and court officials discipline them, underscoring the agency's power.

Overall, ongoing CPS cases and child removal push mothers—most already at the edge of society, facing multiple oppressions and stigmas—further to the margins. The forcible separation from their children traumatizes them, and their experiences navigating the system reinforce their tenuous hold on motherhood, their position in society, and the government's stance toward people like them. The loss and the lessons stay with mothers, potentially discouraging mobilization and civic engagement.

And because CPS intervention is concentrated among marginalized groups, it reifies, naturalizes, and exacerbates race and class hierarchies. Through CPS, poor women of color in particular are further marginalized, further destabilized. This, too, is how the state exerts power over marginalized people: not only through direct force (taking children) but also by subjecting them to a system that disciplines and disregards them. These are injustices as well. From their experiences, CPS-impacted mothers come to see their place in the polity, as subordinate others whose perspectives merit little consideration from the state. CPS intervention thus produces what sociologist Monica Bell calls legal estrangement—that is, "the process through which institutions perpetuate the idea that marginalized groups do not fully share in all the rights and freedoms that flow to other Americans."[30]

In the United States, CPS puts hundreds of thousands of mothers through this devastating and demobilizing experience every year. Each of these is a person who deserves to be treated with dignity, who ought to have a say. Their experiences also ripple outward, as these mothers are part of family and community networks. Many end up raising their children or grandchildren; the trauma of child removal as well as their understandings of justice and the state carry over as they bring up the next generation. Their experiences become part of collective knowledge in marginalized communities—the very collective knowledge that generates the CPS fears and caution detailed in chapter 1.

Certainly, mothers drawn deeply into the system are often experiencing substantial adversity; they cannot always meet their children's needs in their current circumstances. And when their cases moved to closure, mothers sometimes reflected on CPS's intervention with appreciation. Amy, who described losing her faith in the state, ultimately felt grateful for CPS two years later: "Because if it wasn't for this whole experience, no matter how traumatic it was at first to be without them, I'm like, who knows what would've happened?" Barbara, too, looking back at her experience, said that it refocused her: "God was trying to say to me, 'You need to get your life together.'"

But even these admirable outcomes come at extraordinarily high costs. CPS put Amy, Barbara, and others through years of trauma, grief, silencing, and dismissal, all of which communicated their subordinate status. Their children lost time with them. Other children had no guarantee of seeing their parents again.

We can—and must—do better. Precarity can make mobilization challenging; it can also create new opportunities for activism. "The term 'precarity' is often associated with a European social movement," sociologist Arne Kalleberg writes, in which workers "began to organize around the concept of precarity as they faced living and working without stability or a safety net."[31] Impacted parents, and impacted mothers in particular, are leading the way in organizing for systemic change. Around the country, parents are speaking out, galvanized by their experiences with CPS.[32] When the coronavirus pandemic hit, it was Rep. Gwen Moore, a Wisconsin congresswoman who had had a child placed in foster care herself, who introduced legislation suspending federal deadlines to terminate parental rights. Listening to impacted parents reveals the costs of our present child protection approach. It also offers us a way forward.

Conclusion

IN A TEN-STORY OFFICE building in Hartford, it feels like the phone never stops ringing. Every day, well over one hundred calls come in. Calls about children like Nikki's, seeing Nikki's boyfriend hit her. Children like Jennifer's preteen, not receiving the mental health treatment recommended by a clinician. Children like Imelda's toddler, who let herself out of the apartment one rainy morning. Callers describe the situations, and the staff answering the calls calmly take in the information, organizing what they hear to populate a database of "alleged perpetrators" and "alleged victims."

Each call creates a narrative of child abuse and neglect. And each call launches a formal process in which state agents scrutinize intimate family life. For low-income families, especially low-income Black families, this experience is not uncommon. For those facing the greatest adversity and instability, the CPS investigation is almost a rite of passage. Most investigations do not lead to formal sanctions: CPS does not find sufficient evidence to substantiate allegations of abuse or neglect and closes the case. And yet, as this book has shown, the investigation is a moment of acute uncertainty for Nikki, Jennifer, Imelda, and others. Someone—a family member, a teacher, a doctor, even a stranger—has judged their parenting subpar, jeopardizing their ability to raise their children. It falls to state authorities they've never met to decide what happens next. Parenting, and mothering in particular, becomes precarious.

Precarity is not the goal of a CPS investigation. Those who trigger and carry out investigations no doubt see themselves as helpers. After all, CPS operates under state and federal human services divisions, and its funding comes from the Social Security Act and state welfare allocations. It sends out social workers whose job is to refer families to therapeutic services. Indeed, except in the relatively few cases they were especially concerned about, the investigators I shadowed approached families with an eye to how they could help. In turn, many of the mothers I met appreciated the referrals and resources their investigators offered. Those whose cases promptly closed often gushed about the compassion, warmth, and respect their investigators conveyed. Even those who had children removed sometimes looked back with appreciation for CPS helping them turn their lives around.

But help and precarity can coexist. And, as I saw, a certain kind of help expands and intensifies precarity. The preceding chapters have traced the ramifications of invoking CPS to respond to family adversity writ large. No matter how friendly investigators are or how many service referrals they make, CPS at its core remains a coercive entity focused on individual wrongdoing. Helping families facing adversity, then, takes the form of surveillance and risk assessment; the assistance it offers is conditional and corrective. The CPS response comes with implicit threats: threats to child custody, of course, as well as threats to one's identity as a good mother, threats to privacy, and threats to one's sense of trust and security. As we see, motherhood for marginalized mothers is precarious not only because adversity—this confluence of poverty, trauma, racism, hardship, and exclusion—makes child-rearing challenging. It is also precarious because of how the United States tries to assuage this adversity: by passing it off to CPS for investigation.

A Social Policy of First Resort

The child welfare system is often considered the backstop—where families land after all other options have been exhausted.[1] Expanding our perspective to the full range of child protection interventions reveals CPS as a social policy of *first* resort as well. More privileged families might get the benefit of the doubt and direct intervention from someone who knows their family well—a concerned neighbor or guidance counselor who responds another way, offering a second or third or fourth chance before calling the hotline. But for marginalized families, CPS occupies a central role in our social welfare state. In the latter part of the twentieth century, child welfare system infrastructure expanded just as employers stripped protections from low-wage work. With welfare support gutted, what's left to catch parents? A vast child welfare apparatus offering the promise of help through therapeutic social services. By making the call, professionals who believe that families need rehabilitation can pass them off to an entity obligated to respond in some way. With this approach to reporting, CPS's reach expands to all manner of family challenges and families deemed challenging.

Even in states like Connecticut and Rhode Island, where poor families receive more welfare supports than elsewhere in the country, myriad problems of poverty and adversity end up at CPS's door. The agency epitomizes what sociologist Celeste Watkins-Hayes calls a catch-all bureaucracy: "As the 'first responders,' 'last resorts,' and perhaps many things in between for disadvantaged families, these institutions are confronted by the individual-, family-, and community-level challenges that arise as individuals navigate the bottom of our economic, political, and social system."[2] And CPS is a catch-all bureaucracy with a twist. In responding to the situations that come its way, it treats them as potential wrongdoing.

Certainly, some reports reflect professionals' misunderstandings or parents' accidents. And many involve judgments regarding what children need, about which reasonable people may disagree. But overall, I think that most of us would want something to change for the children in the considerable majority of situations reported to CPS.[3] Often, children are in difficult circumstances, even in investigations that close. From this baseline, there are, in theory, multiple ways to interpret the challenges children and families face. CPS is set up to approach adverse situations as child abuse or neglect, a framing that sees perpetrators, typically mothers, poised to harm children through their actions or inactions.

Once a CPS report comes in, the frame of child maltreatment structures everything that follows. When our tool is the CPS hammer, everything becomes a child maltreatment nail. CPS collects poverty problems but can really only deal with parenting problems. Its response initiates extensive surveillance of family life. It assesses families through a lens of future risk, subjecting the most marginalized families to ongoing state oversight. It directs families to therapeutic treatment to address their needs. And the stakes are high: CPS is a catch-all bureaucracy with enormous power over people. Even the kindest, most understanding investigator represents an agency fundamentally focused on parental failures and empowered to separate families. CPS's far-reaching investigative apparatus, then, sows fear and distrust, even before the agency comes knocking and after it closes out. When CPS removes children, the experience is especially traumatizing and marginalizing for mothers, who see CPS as an adversary rather than a partner in supporting child well-being.

With CPS's pervasiveness and power, it can feel like a monolithic behemoth. In reality, of course, it's *people* actively maintaining, extending, and even resisting the agency's reach. Rather than a puppet show orchestrated from above, CPS reporting, investigations, and ongoing casework involve a jumble of people making decisions about what they think children need. Sometimes CPS staff disagreed with policies they carried out—for instance, Joe didn't think that visiting families three times was necessary in all cases. As chapter 3 described, CPS investigators felt that many cases did not need their involvement specifically. And professionals are not robots. Some reporting professionals were eager to call, while others tried to hold off; some CPS supervisors had a reputation around the office for being harder on parents than others. Overall, reporting professionals and CPS staff struck me as people trying to get through their workdays while doing the best for children and families that they could.

Professionals do not act in a vacuum, though; they make decisions in a broader context of opportunities, resources, and risks. Their fears, for instance, led them to embrace CPS surveillance and assessment. Worried that something bad might happen, professionals hoped that turning over one more stone could help them prevent tragedy.[4] Beyond fear, they also felt hopeful about CPS, invoking a sense of altruism mixed with paternalism. Drawing on research presented in trainings and on their professional experience, they felt that they knew what was best for families and wanted to nudge families in that direction to protect children. Typically, this took the form of urging treatment— for Jazmine's and Sherea's marijuana use, for example, or for Jennifer's daughter's mental health needs. This potent combination of fear, altruism, and paternalism expands and intensifies CPS's reach, such that professionals actively perpetuate the practices that foster precarious motherhood.

In response, mothers do not just passively follow along but, instead, find their own ways through the system. The women I interviewed mostly believed that acquiescing to CPS would serve them better. In other instances, the fear of CPS we saw in chapters 1 and 3 prompted defensiveness and resistance to investigators' requests. Some were quieter; others asked questions or cracked jokes. Surely, they kept some things to themselves when deciding what to disclose to reporting professionals, CPS staff, and even me. But they weren't necessarily putting on a front, constantly watching their words; the mothers I met often told me that they wanted to be open and honest with professionals.[5] When Jazmine began substance use treatment, for instance, she told the clinician that she had no intention of giving up marijuana; she knew that it helped her cope and it wasn't endangering her son, as she made sure to smoke when someone else was watching him. Mothers tried to make CPS's involvement work for them, recognizing that perhaps CPS could pay for a summer camp or get them a childcare slot. Recall from chapter 5 how Jazmine agreed to the services CPS recommended because the program promised some help finding housing. "At the end of the day, it's not really for me. It's for him," she said. Even when CPS removed children, the mothers in chapter 6 balanced their grief with optimism, hoping that they would ultimately be better off.

In the end, in most cases, CPS investigations are a revolving door, depositing families right back where they were. Reports and investigations simply "redistribute the poor," in the words of sociologist Armando Lara-Millán, transferring marginalized families across state institutions to give the impression that something has been done.[6] For closed cases, CPS essentially operates as a glorified referral service—albeit, of course, one accompanied by the threat of child removal. For the most part, CPS cannot transform the conditions under which parents are raising children. But in processing so many parents with an eye to the risk they pose, this widespread "catch and release" leaves its mark. The steady drumbeat of investigations produces a lingering uncertainty, a precarious motherhood, in marginalized communities.

Governing Poverty, Governing Parenting

Seeing CPS for what it is—a way station through which all manner of family adversities pass—reveals a central way the United States approaches problems of poverty: as problems of parenting, more specifically problems of mothering, and even more specifically problems of Black mothering. As we see, families are not just economic units, of interest to the state as potential workers or dependents. Through CPS, the state hones in on intimate family relations, threatening these relations as a means of managing marginality. This endeavor draws in multiple arms of government, nongovernmental organizations, and even lay community members. Together, they—we—end up governing poverty by governing parenting.

Likewise, attending to CPS makes clear how central state intervention is to family inequality, parenting, and motherhood. Traditionally, sociology of the family focuses on the state insofar as it affects families' economic conditions, for example, by intervening in the market and structuring the welfare state. For instance, scholars analyze paid family leave and other public policies at the work/family intersection. Amid mass incarceration, family scholarship has increasingly examined how punitive state systems affect parenting. Recent research details how marginalized mothers pursue "defensive," "hypervigilant," and "inventive" mothering as they navigate surveilling systems, including CPS.[7] The state's child protection apparatus—permeating family life for marginalized families, even those not under formal CPS supervision—both reflects and drives contemporary family inequality. For marginalized mothers, CPS shapes how they understand their maternal autonomy and how they procure resources for their families. With affluent White families largely shielded from CPS intervention, CPS layers onto existing inequalities to further divide families' experiences.

This widespread, uneven CPS intervention reflects broader ideas about race, gender, and class. Precarious motherhood in the United States is nothing new; it is foundational to the nation, with forcible separation of Black and Native American families dating back centuries. Scholars such as Dorothy Roberts conceptualize the child welfare system as a political tool that people or groups use to exercise power over others. The figure of the child, innocent and vulnerable, serves as a powerful imaginary, a mythical ideal that can inspire moral urgency and galvanize action. Our innate sympathy for children, when accompanied by particular interpretations of children's caregivers, gives states broad license to intervene. Stereotypes of "bad," neglectful Black mothers, deviating from normative, White femininity, make it all too easy to interpret manifestations of poverty and racism as child maltreatment.[8] As we see in other contexts, such as schools and courts, racism in CPS today does not primarily take the form of explicit discrimination or animus.[9] But as chapters 2 and 4 demonstrated, it does not need to. Racism (especially as it intersects with ideas about poverty and gender) structures families' conditions and how professionals interpret these conditions—as problematic or risky, for instance, stemming from maternal shortcomings—which feeds a sprawling system embracing supervision and correction as a means of help.[10] This racialized and gendered response sets a template that can also be applied to fathers, White mothers, and others facing adversity.[11]

In turn, CPS and the systems sending families to it also construct race, gender, and class. In identifying and responding to suspected child maltreatment, these systems establish the bounds of appropriate parenting, especially appropriate mothering, as we saw in chapters 2 and 4. The public must then make sense of a system disproportionately populated by low-income families of color. These patterns perpetuate stereotypes of poor mothers and Black mothers as irresponsible, bound to endanger their children unless state institutions intervene. As chapter 4 described, funneling families to CPS frames mothers as potential risks to their children. And for mothers themselves, CPS experiences convey their social standing—recall Christina's remark in chapter 6 that the system was "made" for low-income people like her, whom CPS could "whip . . . right into shape." Dispatching CPS to so many low-income mothers and mothers of color reinforces their subordinate status. Moreover, the precarious motherhood fostered by CPS reduces (though certainly does not extinguish) the capacity of marginalized mothers to organize and fight against the conditions of poverty, racism, and sexism they face.

CPS's rhetoric of help and partnership isn't just empty talk. We saw in chapters 3 and 5 how investigators tried to connect families with available resources; in most cases, investigators did not rush to vilify mothers' parenting. But as the preceding chapters have shown, it's precisely by embracing holistic, proactive, family well-being goals that CPS and adjacent professionals generate a precarious motherhood. This process illuminates the broader commingling of care and coercion ubiquitous in contemporary efforts to manage poverty, apparent in everything from policing and courts to substance use treatment and health care. CPS underscores how care expands possibilities for coercion. Almost all reporting professionals interviewed hoped that their reports would help families, and the idea of preventing child maltreatment justified CPS's expansive inquiries and risk assessments. Coercion, in turn, undermines efforts at care. CPS reports, or even the possibility of such reports, deter those who need help from seeking it and strain relationships with the very institutions that are supposed to assist. Embracing coercion alongside care is seductive—the "all-purpose agency" reporting professionals imagined in chapter 2—but ultimately reinforces marginality.

Where to Go from Here

When I first met Christina—the mother whose son CPS removed after the convenience store altercation—the twenty-one-year-old shared vivid memories of the abuse she'd experienced as a child. To introduce me to her life, she recited, from memory, a rap she'd written:

> . . . Mommy came running with a spoon on fire
> Burned me on my arm and made me lie to
> Doctors, teachers, friends, and more
> If I said the truth, I had a whuppin' in store . . .

Years later, these memories remained painful. Christina said that she looked at her scars every day. CPS had visited after she broke down one day at school but left her at home, only to get a beating after the caseworker left. At the time,

Christina wished that CPS had intervened more aggressively. "I always wanted to get taken out," she said.

Six years later, reading a draft of these chapters, Christina was struck by the story of Sandra from chapter 3, the mother overwhelmed by her son's difficult behavior who said that she sometimes put him in the bedroom and cried. "That kid was me," Christina reflected. "Sandra was my mom who didn't know how to handle the situation." As she'd grown up, Christina said, she'd looked back and recognized what her own mom, raising five kids, must have been going through. Christina didn't condone abuse, she emphasized. "But at that time, my mom didn't have the necessary tools to handle me," she said.

It might seem natural to respond to the violence Christina experienced by blaming her mother and taking Christina away. But addressing harm (or suspected harm) to children doesn't need to take this form. By taking a closer look at how mothers experience CPS, the research presented in this book points us toward better ways to meet the needs of everyone involved.

Shrinking CPS's Net

As I've argued, CPS investigations make motherhood precarious—fostering anxiety and breeding distrust—for a wide swath of mothers, predominantly those marginalized by race and/or class. Scholars and practitioners have long recognized the mismatch between what families need and what CPS does.[12] One way of responding to this mismatch is *expanding* what CPS can provide— repaving CPS as a pathway toward assistance. In this view, when CPS focuses on identifying abuse or neglect, we miss opportunities to intervene early and provide services to prevent future maltreatment. Agencies around the country have embraced "differential response" policies that divert some reports away from a traditional, forensic investigation. Connecticut and Rhode Island investigators, for example, can refer families on this alternative track to community-based service providers. A trainer in Connecticut explained that the referral aims to provide assistance "so ideally [the family doesn't] come back to our attention." New York City's CPS commissioner from 2017 to 2021, David Hansell, touted the agency's differential response program by saying, "Often times, families reported to the New York State child abuse hotline are simply in need of a helping hand—whether that's food, clothing, or extra support—and specially trained child protective staff help connect those families to the resources they need."[13] Intervening in relatively minor incidents, the thinking goes, allows CPS to address families' needs and prevent more severe harm from occurring.

This same vision of prevention underlies the landmark Family First Prevention Services Act, passed with bipartisan support by Congress in 2018. At first glance, Family First turns federal support for child welfare on its head. Previously, states could only recoup the costs of foster care from the federal government. Under Family First, federal funds are no longer contingent on child removal; now, they can support programs for substance use, mental health, and parenting while children remain home, if CPS deems these services necessary to avert foster care placement. This represents a major shift for CPS, one that, like differential response, strengthens its (therapeutic) service provision capacity.

However, leaning into CPS's helping role does not negate its coercive power. As this book has shown, support delivered through CPS remains inextricably tethered to surveillance; the promise of care is inseparable from the threat of removal. Connecticut mother Alex explained, "They're not trying to help me. They're trying to make sure that I'm not gonna harm anyone else." CPS may offer social services. But as Alex indicated, at its core, the agency is organized around stopping mothers like her from harming their children. Whatever services may come through CPS cannot shake that association. As I saw in Connecticut, differential response often gives families essentially the same thing in different wrapping paper.[14] And although parents may prefer "preventive services" to child removal, we saw in chapter 5 how they do not necessarily see these services as unequivocal supports, given the connection to CPS.

Moreover, strengthening CPS's service provision role is poised to expand its purview, widening the net it casts.[15] Recall chapter 4: When CPS is a gatekeeper for social services, an agency oriented around child abuse and neglect ends up collecting families with social service needs, justified by the "risk" these needs purportedly pose. What does it mean to route our social welfare state through an agency with coercive authority? Rhode Island, for instance, delivered some behavioral health services for children through CPS contracts; some services were only available to families with open CPS cases. Laura, in Providence, told me that due to her daughter's health issues, "they opened a CPS case so that one of the adjoining companies can get paid for the services. . . . They're like, 'It's open, but it's not for you. It's for the payment.'" Often, CPS is the gateway to assistance—in rural areas with few social services as well as urban areas that prioritize CPS-involved families for essential benefits such as housing vouchers and subsidized childcare.[16]

Think, too, of Sabrina from chapter 5, desperately trying to leave the rodent-infested attic. Reading Sabrina's story, we might want CPS to offer ongoing housing support to meet her family's needs. We might want Ria, her investigator, to help Sabrina get into another apartment, one less hazardous for the family. But should CPS be the one delivering this support? In the New York City commissioner's words, should "connect[ing] . . . families to the resources they need" fall to "specially trained child protective staff"? Sabrina needed safe housing—but not necessarily from an agency focused on child abuse and neglect. Any rental assistance Ria could offer would be conditional on CPS oversight. (Indeed, Connecticut did offer supportive housing for some families with open CPS cases; recall Ria calling housing "the carrot" to encourage compliance with therapeutic services.) And boosting Ria's ability to help families like Sabrina's, deemed lower-risk for maltreatment, would attract even more referrals from professionals interested in connecting families with assistance. Already, the reporting professionals I interviewed hoped that CPS could help families with housing. Ironically, the more "low-risk" cases CPS receives, the more it tries to respond to these cases by offering assistance. But this only widens the net further, inviting more low-risk cases.[17]

Likewise, running Family First–funded services through CPS may increase the scope and perhaps the intensity of CPS intervention. In New York City, at the forefront of the move toward "preventive services," a homeless services provider told me that at every case conference meeting, "Call CPS, get them into preventive [services]" was a frequent refrain to solve problems they encountered with families. Staff didn't believe that children were in danger but turned to CPS to connect families with social services and monitoring, as in chapter 2.[18] Family First and other efforts to amplify CPS's service provision role may thus expand CPS's reach.

As my research shows, we need not give CPS more "helping" tools to promote child well-being; routing social services through CPS can be counterproductive. But CPS could instead do the opposite: actively work to *reduce* its involvement with families. As most CPS investigations close within weeks, it stands to reason that we could safely narrow the system's "front door." Child welfare reform tends to focus on ongoing services and foster care, with reporting and screening often afterthoughts.[19] From a performance management perspective, perhaps this makes sense; reports are inputs to the system, and agencies want to focus on what they can control.

Yet CPS could conceptualize the front door as part of its responsibility as well. Agencies do not just passively receive reports; as chapter 2 detailed, their messaging—through trainings and comments to press, for instance—fuels widespread reporting. Presently, mandatory reporter trainings and public awareness billboards urge people to call everything in, no matter how slight their suspicions; reporting professionals I interviewed often referenced this guidance. CPS could instead follow the lead of grassroots efforts that are educating mandatory reporters about what CPS investigations entail and alternatives they might consider.[20]

Even once reports come in, CPS's hands are not tied, as hotline staff screen reports to assess whether allegations meet statutory criteria for investigation. Given broad definitions of "child neglect," agencies could advocate for statutory changes to clarify what falls outside their purview.[21] CPS might also reallocate staffing resources so that those answering the phones could direct callers to meet families' needs themselves, by providing referrals and guidance, for instance. As chapter 2 described, hotline operations are not incentivized to spend more time with callers. What they see are caller wait times; the costs— in terms of investigators' time and families' apprehension—can feel distant. Shifting resources to the front end, giving hotline staff the time and training to problem-solve with callers in real time, could help callers respond to families in ways that do not trigger CPS investigations.[22]

Importantly, narrowing the front door requires taking political risks, as Rhode Island's example shows. When I started fieldwork there, Rhode Island had an "information/referral" category (called "I/R") for incoming hotline calls. Hotline screeners who provided information or a referral to callers could mark "I/R" to resolve the case; it would not be sent to investigators. After several children died in 2016 and 2017, media, advocacy, and legislative attention zeroed in on I/R as the problem. CPS had received calls about these families before the children died, but many of the calls were designated I/R. Reviewing I/R cases, the state's Child Advocate concluded that CPS's overuse of I/R "left young children at risk, with no follow up or 'eyes-on' the child to ensure their safety or well-being." The Child Advocate recommended repealing I/R and investigating all reports of children under six, based on her finding that one-quarter of I/R cases sampled were improperly classified. She listed examples of I/R reports that merited a CPS response: inadequate housing and parental substance use; concerns related to cleanliness, along with a mother's live-in partner's history of substance use and incarceration; lack of electricity; "deplorable living conditions"; and a child missing school.[23] These adverse conditions echo those I saw reported and investigated in my fieldwork.

Taking these situations on their face, how should we respond? My research suggests limitations and costs of an approach oriented around investigating parental wrongdoing. But political considerations often hold the day. In 2017 and 2018, Rhode Island legislative committees held a series of hearings in which legislators boosted the narrative of I/R as problematic, and the Child Advocate assured them that I/R was her "most immediate concern." The agency moved to eliminate it, placing cases that would previously have been designated I/R on a "family assessment" track (akin to what I saw in Connecticut) beginning in 2018. Rhode Island's experience shows how scaling back CPS investigations can meet substantial resistance in the face of tragic events.

So reforming CPS will require courageous leaders as well as a public supportive of protecting children beyond CPS. During her time on the bench in New Orleans, Judge Ernestine Gray oversaw enormous foster care reductions, simply deciding not to remove children unless she deemed it absolutely necessary. Foster care caseloads fell from two hundred—already well below state and national rates—to just twenty children,[24] "levels unmatched anywhere in the country," *The Washington Post* reported. "You have to have courage," Gray told the *Post* reporter.[25] Joette Katz, Connecticut's CPS commissioner from 2011 to 2019, was called "the gutsiest leader in child welfare" for resisting the all-too-familiar rush to separate more families in the aftermath of high-profile child fatalities.[26] In an essay entitled "Fixing Child Welfare Means Not Letting Tragedies Become Catastrophes," Katz wrote that she "was determined not to allow [CPS] to be driven by the crisis-and-response cycle that causes so much damage nationwide. . . . We needed more courage and less fear."[27] As she described, she reversed practice recommendations of showing up at families' homes unannounced, advising staff to call families in advance unless this would put children in danger. Analysts found no evidence that Judge Gray's and Commissioner Katz's approaches jeopardized child safety.[28] Yet such shifts are easily undone, requiring sustained commitment in the face of tragic incidents. During my fieldwork, for instance, a review of infant fatalities found that most visits in these cases were prescheduled, leading some to push back on the recommendations against unannounced visits.

Any child's death is awful, and when the gross negligence of a state agency has contributed, it's essential to hold it accountable. We should do everything in our power to protect children from fatal or near-fatal abuse and neglect. But it's a false choice between reducing CPS intervention and keeping children safe. More CPS intervention isn't necessarily safer. Flooding the system with cases spreads staff time and resources thin. And as Judge Gray put it, "Foster care is put up as this thing that is going to save kids, but kids die in foster care, kids get sick in foster care."[29]

Moreover, walking back reports and investigations doesn't mean leaving children in danger. We saw this during the initial months of the COVID-19 pandemic. CPS reports across the country plummeted due to families' reduced contact with reporting professionals such as school personnel; many worried about increases in severe maltreatment absent CPS involvement. But such concerns did not pan out. Nationally, child maltreatment fatalities between October 2019 and September 2020 were no greater than in previous years, actually declining from the prior year.[30] Emergency room visits for child abuse and neglect dropped, and hospitalizations for abuse and neglect were similar to pre-pandemic rates.[31] After schools reopened, there was no "rebound effect" suggesting serious, unreported abuse or neglect. Legal scholar Anna Arons, analyzing data from New York City, concluded that "with less surveillance and fewer separations, children stayed just as safe."[32] Meanwhile, as a subway train conductor and mother of two told *The Marshall Project* in the early months of the pandemic, "Poor people are usually constantly inspected by all these agencies. . . . Now there is kind of a peacefulness."[33] The pandemic experience shows us that it's possible to scale back CPS without compromising child safety. Of course, the start of the pandemic also saw profound shifts along many dimensions, including increased governmental support and attention to families' needs—responses that offer lessons in how we can support children and families beyond CPS.

Rethinking Child Protection

When I started planning this research, I hoped to learn how CPS could better serve children and families. Over time, I came to see CPS as just one agency in a broader landscape of systems and supports. Improving child protection is not so much about tweaking CPS practice, I learned, but, rather, about changing other structures outside the agency singularly tasked with "child protection." Many people and groups, both within and beyond CPS, are thinking about what this could look like and taking steps to realize their ideas.

Beginning to unwind CPS and the precarious motherhood it generates does not mean ignoring family adversity. As I have shown, however, when we try to prevent child maltreatment by focusing on individual families, we inevitably see the task as identifying and monitoring "risky" parents. This framing portrays marginalized parents themselves as potentially threatening, which justifies a vast surveillance system and points us toward reforms such as training investigators to make more "unbiased" decisions and devising more highly predictive risk assessments.

Broadening our focus beyond individual families leads us somewhere different. Considering who or what is harming children in society as a whole implicates a wide array of others, including but not limited to the police, schools, and juvenile justice facilities that criminalize children; the corporations that spew toxins and exploit parents' labor; the landlords who neglect their properties; and the politicians who make all of this possible. This perspective leads us to ask what about society must change—rather than what about individual parents must change—to keep children safe and healthy.

Those who want to reform the system stand alongside those working to abolish it in urging a societal perspective on child protection. CPS agrees that protecting children can't be its responsibility alone. Following highly publicized child fatalities, Trista Piccola, Rhode Island's CPS commissioner from 2017 to 2019, emphasized that it isn't CPS that keeps children safe: "Communities keep children safe."[34] (I heard this sentiment repeatedly from CPS administrators in both Rhode Island and Connecticut.) In a piece entitled "Toward the Abolition of the Foster System," attorney and activist Erin Miles Cloud writes, "We must envision a world where families are safe not because we have threatened, punished, or policed them, but because we have built up community, prioritized equitable distribution of material resources, and regarded families and neighbors as the first response to trauma."[35]

This may seem overly idealistic, but shifting resources to local community organizations has been effective in reducing violence.[36] Research is clear that antipoverty policies such as minimum wage increases, the Earned Income Tax Credit, and childcare subsidies reduce child maltreatment risk and CPS intervention.[37] Although child safety is often pitted against parents' rights, children do best when their parents have what they need. To the extent that children in affluent White areas experience less harm, it's not because their parents care more about them but, rather, because their parents have the family and community resources to raise their children in the ways they want. Clearly, increasing support for labor rights, the cash assistance safety net, housing, food, childcare, health care, transportation, and other material needs is essential, as is investing equitably in libraries, parks, and other public spaces. All of this—improving the conditions under which families and communities raise children—is child protection work.[38]

Other approaches in this vein seek to provide services and information in community with parents. Justifying their intervention, reporting professionals and CPS staff reiterated that it takes a village to raise a child. But in practice, with social life highly segregated by race and class, professionals are often intervening on behalf of a village of systems and strangers—a largely White professional class of pediatricians, schools, mental health clinicians, and social workers. If these professionals were actually embedded in community with families, if they went to the same churches and block parties and grocery stores, perhaps they could activate support in different ways.[39] A consortium of Native American tribes in California offers another model. As former tribal court judge William Thorne writes, "They didn't just offer 'services' to families 'at risk.' Instead, they offered events, services, and engagement to the entire community and then took special efforts to make sure the at-risk families were a part of, not separate from, the community."[40] In this approach, services are widely available, and community members work to integrate families with additional needs into the fold.

Relatedly, if the professional class takes as given that parents want the best for their kids, then the task becomes how to provide guidance in ways that resonate, delivered by people parents can trust, rather than lectures from on high.[41] For instance, the success of community health workers and *promotores de salud* suggests investing in trusted messengers from child welfare–impacted communities.[42] Advocates and impacted parents at Rise in New York City call for building "networks of peer support and community care" that would promote safety and well-being by building relationships, providing information, and connecting families to resources.[43] This kind of peer support and information-sharing has proven effective in supporting parents and their families.[44]

When people have concerns about children and families they cannot address themselves, or when caregivers want help, they need somewhere to turn. CPS provides information and service referrals, but there's no reason CPS has to be the one doing this. Some envision, instead, creating and investing in a response outside the CPS infrastructure, such as a family support hotline designed by parents and parent advocates.[45] Police diversion programs offer a potential model. For example, when people are experiencing mental health crises, the Crisis Assistance Helping Out on the Streets program in Eugene, Oregon, deploys clinicians and medical providers instead of armed police officers.[46] Seattle's Let Everyone Advance with Dignity program redirects disorder complaints to provide harm-reduction outreach and services, rather than sending police.[47] Regarding child welfare, another entity might offer service referrals and guidance without the power to remove children, without framing family adversity as a problem of abusive or negligent parents.[48]

My research affirms these various approaches. The mothers I met wanted adequate support for their parenting, rather than the monitored services on offer from CPS. As Bianca put it, "I want to be able to take care of my kids, without other people on top of me or telling me what to do or how to behave." Mothers were eager to learn more about how they could best set their children up for success. They did not necessarily eschew professional advice; they embraced it when provided in nonjudgmental ways by people whom mothers trusted had their best interests at heart.

And those I interviewed wanted professionals in community with them, who could look for collaborative solutions first. Before sending out CPS, Desiree advised, "get to know me first. Shit. Ask me out to coffee or something and ask me, 'Hey, is there anything I can do to help you?'" If her daughter mentioned something concerning, Desiree said, "don't automatically call the authorities. Come to me as a woman, as a mother, and say, 'Hey, your daughter told me this, that, and the third. Is there something I can do to help?'" As it stood, mothers told me, professionals just phoned CPS and left mothers to deal with the repercussions themselves. Jazmine suggested:

> If the parent of the child has to take time out of their day, then the person who called should have to take time out of their day. Everybody who's involved with the child has to take time out of their day because they're trying to do what's best for the child.

Ashley envisioned her son's school meeting to brainstorm solutions with her before calling CPS. Instead of the school conveying that "I'm a horrible parent, that I hurt my kid," Ashley recommended "starting [with], 'Hey, we know stuff goes on with him. He has a hard time. This is something he brought up. . . . We have ways to help. We have steps we can take.' Whatever. It might have felt a little bit different."

Mothers like Desiree, Jazmine, and Ashley wanted the professionals in their lives to offer support rather than rush to report.[49] Providers such as pediatricians and school counselors might be in a better position than agents of family separation to make service referrals that parents embrace. Many professionals do try to provide proactive outreach and assistance, but time and resource constraints make this challenging. Devising protocols to do so, as well as ensuring that professionals have some "slack" in their workloads and adequate

training to accommodate emergent situations, could make an important difference in families' experiences with state authorities.

Indeed, people draw on an ethic of care and mutual responsibility all the
time to respond to harm without invoking CPS. Desiree herself once saw a
mother slap her young son, hard, from across the street. Other passers-by
wanted to alert the police. Instead, Desiree approached the mother, who
started crying, overwhelmed by her stress. "I literally took an hour out of my
day and sat there with the mom and the kids, just to give the mom a few minutes just to recollect of what she just did." Desiree felt compelled to do something because the mother was about to get behind the wheel. "All it takes [is]
for her to turn around and scream at him or hit him, or her to swerve, and that's
it. She's gone, those kids are gone, and that's that. I could have done something
to prevent that." So, Desiree said, "I told her a little bit of my experience, and
I gave her my number." Desiree told me she was still in touch with this mother.
"She calls here and there when she's angry, and she's like, 'I just don't know
what to do. I'm driving myself crazy.' I'm just like, 'Breathe. Take a second. Is
there anybody else in the house that can watch the kids while you go to take a
walk?'" They had met for lunch a couple weeks prior, and Desiree had helped
her restart her cash assistance at the welfare office. It may feel easier to pass off
children in concerning situations for someone else to handle, but Desiree
shows us a model of preventing harm that centers around community support—
a practice that all of us would do well to emulate.

Harm and violence may never be fully preventable, and it's important to
reckon with this reality. There may be cases—hopefully very few, with robust
social supports—where children cannot safely be with their parents or caregivers. My research does not suggest sitting back and doing nothing; recall
Christina's rap about her childhood trauma. But the crux of it is who gets to
decide what happens, to whom the response is accountable. Technically,
elected officials appoint CPS commissioners, and CPS staff work for the state.
But these staff—especially higher-level administrators who set policy—
typically do not represent, in any real sense, those most impacted by their decisions. Chapter 6 showed how mothers found CPS intervention profoundly
demobilizing; they saw no meaningful mechanism to raise grievances and
enact change. Often, efforts to bring families and communities to the table,
such as the much-heralded meetings Connecticut holds when considering
child removal, still give CPS the final say.

Ultimately, those in child-serving systems must trust Black parents, Native
parents, poor parents, and other marginalized parents. As a part of this trust,

the (predominantly White) professional class must step back, and I include myself in that. It's relatively straightforward to encourage "expanding the social safety net"; it makes people more uneasy to talk about shifting power.[50] Most agree that we should expand treatment services. Indeed, especially in rural areas, increasing access to services is essential. But in my fieldwork, access wasn't the primary issue. Rather, service providers struggled to get parents to do the things they believed parents ought to do. Here, CPS, with its coercive power, applied pressure. As this book has shown, such a model undermines positive relationships between families and service providers. Another approach could focus on developing treatment programs in partnership with parents to create services they want to access. This would mean following the leadership of people directly impacted. It would mean humility from professionals who recognize that they may not know what families need or want. It would mean professionals who ally with families to get families what they need from the state, rather than using the power of the state to pressure families into a certain mold. This may make child welfare professionals uncomfortable, with their ideas about what families should do. But we should start from the place that parents want to do what's best for their children and see to it that they have what they need.

The foremost question, then, is not so much what specifically must change but, instead, who gets to decide. Who sets the agenda? Who gets to say whether a certain approach is effective? Everyone—including those without CPS experience—has a role to play; mothers I met emphasized the importance of outsiders agitating for change alongside them. Academics like me can contribute to the conversation. But we are not the experts.

Jazmine shared her vision of child protection: "The first thing would be the housing, because you can't do anything without housing." The second thing "would be day care or schooling," she added. "Just getting the parent on their feet to be able to take care of the kid. Once the parent is taken care of, the kid can be taken care of." Heeding Jazmine's call, we can shift our response to family adversity away from an approach that engenders precarity. We can promote child well-being by ensuring that all of us—children and their families and communities—have what we need to thrive.

METHODOLOGICAL APPENDIX

THIS APPENDIX DESCRIBES how I came to learn what I learned about CPS. I share these reflections to help readers understand how I generated my data and analyses. I also hope that these details are useful to other researchers considering something similar.

As scholars have debated the relative merits of ethnography versus interviewing, I think of Kathryn Edin recounting how a mentor, Howard Becker, didn't think about the two methods as separate. Instead, he espoused something broader called "fieldwork," encompassing observations, interviews, and document review. That's how I view what I did: as fieldwork. I don't consider my research to be ethnography in any strict sense; I didn't immerse myself particularly deeply in others' lives. But I got to tag along to various encounters and talk with people about them afterward. And likewise, speaking with people about their experiences offered a window into their lives for a couple hours, not only from what I heard but also from what I saw.

My personal relationship to CPS—more specifically, my lack of personal experience—undoubtedly informs this research. I came to this topic through my interest in children and families. My undergraduate coursework introduced me to child welfare and foster care, and I wrote several term papers on these issues. After graduating, I worked on impact litigation on behalf of children in foster care. From this work, I knew that child welfare was a critically important system for marginalized children and families. But growing up in affluent, predominantly White suburbs, CPS hadn't even been a thought in my mind. My parents never raised it as a concern, and I did not know of any friends or classmates placed in foster care. CPS was absent from my upbringing and also from the sociological scholarship I later encountered. Although my graduate school professors had extensively studied urban poverty and inequality, they hadn't paid much attention to the child welfare system. I found this omission, and my own extreme insulation from the agency, striking. It made me want to learn more.

Interviewing Mothers in Rhode Island

I moved to Providence in summer 2014. That fall, I walked around the south side, chatting with people I encountered, visiting community organizations, and volunteering at a food pantry. When I told people I hoped to speak with parents about social services, especially CPS, they were immediately skeptical, both about my safety ("You will get killed," I heard) and about the likelihood people would speak openly about CPS with me. Those I met explained that people didn't want to talk about CPS and that people wouldn't trust me, as I didn't fit in. "Like it or not, you are in that category," one person said, referring to the panoply of professionals circling families in the area.

Keeping these warnings in mind, I thought I'd see what I could learn and began recruiting interviewees in January 2015. I put up flyers on the south side and approached people where I could find them: in line at the welfare office, at bus stops, at the Laundromat, at the food pantry. "Parent Perspectives Wanted," read the flyers, advertising a study aiming "to learn what parents think about different agencies and services." I didn't really have to screen for poverty; Providence is a poor and segregated city. But, as a check, I asked whether parents received or were eligible for SNAP before arranging interviews. I only turned one prospective participant away for income reasons.

I conducted audio-recorded interviews wherever participants wanted— usually their homes but sometimes the local McDonald's or Dunkin Donuts for those with unstable housing situations. Initial interviews typically lasted around two hours. Participants received $20 cash; this motivated at least some of them, who indicated as much to me. Participants also said that they appreciated the opportunity to share their perspectives on social services, in hopes that things would change. My being a student at the time and looking young likely facilitated recruitment as well. At the time, I was in my late twenties, but participants often took me for a college student a decade younger and seemed to want to help me out. For instance, Tonya spoke at length about her discomfort discussing her background and parenting with service providers. I told her that I was curious what made her want to talk to me. "Well, I know you're in school, and I had to do that as well," Tonya said. "So I know what it feels like. But I mean, honestly, if you was anybody else, I probably would've told you no."

The first set of participants tended to be those out and about—going to the welfare office, taking the bus, living at homeless shelters—during a snowy winter. They likely faced more challenges than low-income parents in the city more broadly. I invited participants to refer me to others and, over time, expanded my recruitment to places such as grocery stores, pediatric primary care waiting areas, and WIC clinics. Still, mothers who might have found it more difficult to sit for a two-hour interview, such as those working several jobs, are likely under-represented (though not absent) among interviewees.

After the initial data collection period in January 2015, I continued recruiting here and there over the next several months while beginning to analyze the data collected thus far, writing memos and doing multiple rounds of coding. I then took a year away from data collection to continue analysis and begin writing, which helped me see areas where additional data collection would be useful.[1] The few fathers I interviewed (and one adoptive mother) had less to say about CPS, so I decided to focus on biological mothers. In spring 2016, I started reaching out to mothers I'd interviewed the year before for follow-up interviews, prioritizing those with children at home with them. Instability marked many participants' lives, so I had to be persistent. They moved, they changed phone numbers, they forgot about meeting times we'd set, or things came up. I hoped to learn more about the experiences of those transitioning into parenthood, with no firsthand experience with CPS as parents, so I also specifically sought out first-time new or expectant mothers, while accepting other eligible mothers into the study as well.

Ultimately, I interviewed eighty-three Rhode Island mothers, fifty-four at least twice, for a total of 175 interviews over more than four years. Where possible, I incorporated ethnographic "hangouts," meeting twenty-one mothers more informally or accompanying them as they ran errands or went to appointments. The interviewees include mothers who identified as Latina, Black, and White in roughly equal proportion. The vast majority reported incomes below (usually well below) the federal poverty line, but their situations varied.[2] Some had been out of work for years; others worked in jobs such as childcare and food services. Some were living in shelters or staying with friends; others stably rented their own apartments. Some were cycling between jail, treatment facilities, and shelters; others had no such experiences. Some had never encountered CPS; for others, the agency was a mainstay in their lives.

Although this book focuses on CPS, I spent a lot of time with participants discussing other things. I knew that CPS was a sensitive topic, one where building rapport beforehand might facilitate parents speaking more candidly. I did not only want to recruit parents who felt they had something to say about the agency, and I was interested in how it might come up organically in interviews. I began by asking participants to "tell me the story of your life" and then probed their experiences with welfare, health care providers, schools, police, and social services. About two-thirds of participants raised CPS themselves in the course of these conversations. Otherwise, I mentioned it toward the end of the interview, simply saying, "Tell me about CPS," and seeing where participants wanted to take the conversation.

As an Asian American Ph.D. student who grew up upper middle class in affluent, White areas, my own identity and background differed from that of participants. Often, we were about the same age but had led very different lives. My approach in the fieldwork was to sit back and learn from participants—they truly were the experts, teaching me. I didn't have to feign ignorance; as a newcomer to Providence without children, I was genuinely asking what things were like for parents around town. None of the parents I interviewed identified as Asian—Providence doesn't have a substantial Asian population—but participants across race/ethnicity imagined points of affinity given my racial identity. Some White mothers felt comfortable disparaging Black people and especially immigrants with me; others, meanwhile, invoked our shared identities as people of color subject to racial/ethnic stereotypes.

My social class, embodied in my comportment, speech, and dress, aligned me with the bevy of social workers, therapists, case managers, and other professionals who came around. Some participants remarked that others around them—partners, relatives—wondered whether I was a social worker. I ran into Angela, whom I later interviewed, at the bus stop after she saw me outside interviewing another participant. After I told her about the study, not mentioning CPS, Angela said that she'd wondered about me: "I was like, 'Is she CPS or something?'" Indeed, I arrived with a folder and forms for participants to sign. CPS and other social service professionals dress informally and try to engage parents in conversation about family life, as I did. Describing a visiting social worker, Vera said offhand, "They ask me questions, just like you."

As the data presented in this book show, many mothers shared deeply personal experiences. Yet they weren't always fully forthcoming with me—perhaps an extension of the risk aversion described in chapter 1 or just hesitance to share their personal lives with someone new. Several kept things surface-level; they were perfectly friendly, but I had the sense that they were keeping me at a distance and being careful with their words. Sometimes, based on the life circumstances mothers described, I sensed more CPS involvement than they let on, a skepticism sometimes warranted when I later reviewed their CPS records. I interviewed two mothers who, in addition to a minor child, had adult daughters they referred to the study. In both cases, the adult daughters described much more extensive CPS involvement as children than their mothers had shared, telling me about siblings removed at a young age whom their mothers had not mentioned to me. One, Colleen, said, "She don't like to talk about the other ones, because they got taken away. Like, it still frickin' eats at her, you know? So she don't bring it up. I know she didn't bring it up with you." Such seeming contradictions are analytic insights in themselves.

Like all adults in Rhode Island, I was legally mandated to report suspected child abuse or neglect. I did not want to have to call CPS, so I did not delve too deeply into mothers' parenting practices. But consistent with the findings from chapter 1, I think that mothers knew what lines not to cross with me. Occasionally, they told me in later interviews that we'd previously met during a time when they were actively using drugs. I did not press beyond what participants felt comfortable sharing and respected the boundaries they set.[3] With Jesenia, I probed a bit to see what might draw her out. Then she replied, "I don't wanna talk about this topic no more. I don't like them [CPS]." So we moved on. It was an immense privilege to be invited in to hear what moms felt ready to share. Thus, though the interviews yielded rich data, I remain open to the possibility that more remained concealed, consciously or unconsciously, from me.

Repeated contacts—returning to meet with participants again months or years later—seemed to help. In later contacts, participants often overestimated how long we'd known one another and revealed things they hadn't shared the first time. When we first met, Carol recounted her oldest son's placement with a legal guardian at birth, several CPS investigations, and another son's out-of-home placement for behavioral and truancy concerns. Six months later, she shared that her four younger children had been in foster care for the past few years as well. "I was gonna tell you before, but I was kind of scared," Carol said. "Because I didn't know what would happen with you. I'm just so petrified." These shifts constituted important data, as participants worked through the versions of themselves they wanted to present to me. I didn't call them on inconsistencies, instead just providing another opportunity to talk in case they wanted to share more. In follow-up interviews, I shared more of my specific interest in CPS, talked about emerging research findings, and sought mothers' advice about the next stage of my research. I went to court with a few participants and sat in on CPS meetings. In the second round of data collection, I asked participants whether, to enhance presentations of the research, they would allow me to take and share a photograph and/or play snippets of audio from the interview. I also asked whether they would allow me access to their CPS records to supplement my understanding of their cases. They agreed to these options far more enthusiastically than I'd expected (81 percent agreed to photos; 86 percent, to audio; and 92 percent, to CPS records access).

Observing mothers' meetings with professionals such as home visitors and CPS workers helped me see differences in our approaches. Service providers see their role as guiding parents; even informal conversations become teaching opportunities. When Vanessa's visiting nurse arrived, Vanessa excitedly showed off her ultrasound pictures, explaining that the baby was moving a lot as Vanessa had coffee that morning. Still friendly, the nurse immediately shifted to questioning her: "Now, how are you with caffeine normally? Like, how much are you taking?" She pressed Vanessa for details about her coffee habits, outlining how caffeine affected the baby. "So you wanna be careful with that." Meanwhile, I was clearly not an expert on child-rearing or child development, so mothers often gave me advice and taught me what they knew about parenting.

Social service providers also have high workloads, so I observed them asking direct questions to try to corral mothers' stories and move on. In contrast, I sat with and listened to mothers as long as they wanted. Other small things distinguished me from service providers. I didn't have my own car, so I rode the bus a lot, which confused some mothers at first. Sometimes, they gave me rides. Desiree once told me that I "wouldn't make it" as a social worker. "You would be so distraught. . . . To get that kind of job, you have to be cold." Mothers repeatedly told me they liked the idea that their participation could help others, a dynamic different from interactions with other professionals. Helen said that it was important to tell the "big-suited people" what things were like. Stacy mentioned feeling comfortable being open with her substance use counselor. When I asked whether she felt similarly about others, she replied, "Like you. I know you would never go and say anything. 'Cause you're trying to build something. You just want input because you never been through it. You're looking at it from an outside point of view." These kinds of reflections suggest that over time, an outsider like me, willing to learn and enter with humility, could create opportunities for connection.

Mothers told me that they appreciated being able to reflect on their journeys on their own terms. Maggie said that she wanted to get back into counseling: "I need someone to talk to. That's honestly why I was happy to come out here." I reminded her that I wasn't a counselor but, instead, hoped to listen and learn from her. "But just listening helps, believe it or not, because I don't have a lot of people to talk to," Maggie replied. Still, I felt uneasy about the prospect of the interview as a therapeutic encounter. Inviting mothers to share their life stories often elicited detailed narratives laden with traumatic experiences: severe child maltreatment, sexual assault, violence, and more. These life histories provided context to understand mothers' perspectives on CPS, and I didn't press mothers, who seemed to appreciate sharing their stories. I occasionally encouraged mothers to connect with mental health services, providing phone numbers. But because mothers' adverse experiences weren't central to my research questions about CPS perceptions and experiences—essentially none of this material made it into this book—it sometimes felt as though I was just collecting traumas. I don't think that I was prepared for the level of adversity I heard about, and I'm not sure that I would take the same life history approach again.[4]

Providence is a relatively small city. I couldn't keep the research fully bounded from the rest of my life. My partner worked at the local children's hospital, so he returned home shaken and unable to talk about the horrific injuries he saw inflicted on "Baby Tobi," the severely abused infant from chapter 3 who died from the abuse. I often ran into participants at places like family court or McDonald's or found out later that two mothers I'd met separately knew one another. Throughout the research period, I volunteered as a court-appointed advocate (called a "CASA") for three siblings in foster care. This involved regular court appearances, CPS meetings, and close collaboration with children's attorneys. As chapter 6 noted, CASAs sit alongside CPS representatives, not parents, at court. Going to court with participants meant juggling these multiple roles. Once, when I was accompanying Isabela to court, the attorney I worked with came up to me, looking perplexed. After I said that I was there with a friend for a project, he replied, "Okay, I got worried. I didn't think our case was on." Though I presume Isabela heard this, she didn't mention it to me. Other times, the person calling cases identified me as a CASA in front of participants. When I arrived at the family court rally against CPS described in chapter 6, Isabela's mother handed me a sign to hold and masking tape to put over my mouth in protest, like the other attendees. People were live-streaming the event and taking photos for press. I saw this activity as separate from my CASA work but wasn't sure whether my colleagues would feel the same. At the time, I was also trying to negotiate research access to CPS in Rhode Island. (I held the sign and put on the tape, though ended up leaving the rally shortly thereafter to follow Isabela up to court.) These different roles tugged at me—a feeling I would have to get comfortable navigating in my research with CPS.

Getting Access to a Child Welfare Agency

I initially felt ambivalent about conducting research with a child welfare agency, as I was committed to centering mothers' perspectives and experiences. By early 2017, I had conducted a lot of interviews in Providence—enough, I thought, for a dissertation. However, my advisor at the time, Devah Pager, strongly urged me to think more ambitiously given the research funding I had from a national fellowship. I explored fielding a large-scale survey to build on the qualitative findings about mothers' CPS fears, described in chapter 1. In weighing different options, I was inspired by scholars such as Nicole Gonzalez Van Cleve who study power and inequality by shifting the focus. "Plenty of ethnographic accounts turn the lens on marginalized populations," Gonzalez Van Cleve writes, but we must also "turn the lens on those in power as they do the marginalizing."[5] I also recognized limitations of my Rhode Island data. Sometimes, substantial time had passed since the CPS investigations mothers described. What narratives might they have shared during the investigation, with its outcome uncertain? How might their accounts compare with those of other stakeholders? Connecting with mothers currently under investigation would require going through a child welfare agency.

I hoped to observe investigations to understand CPS's broad reach and the many contacts that do *not* trigger child removal. I had other dissertation ideas, so I wasn't willing to compromise and study other aspects of the system. For instance, my years of CASA volunteer work had given me a close working relationship with the head children's attorney at the family court, who offered to help facilitate court-watching research. Observing court would have been an easier "sell" to gatekeepers but would have taken me away from my core interest in the front end of the system.

I first approached the Rhode Island Department of Children, Youth, and Families in mid-2017. Child welfare agencies are hierarchical, so I knew that I needed to approach higher-level officials first to get them on board.[6] My efforts to access Rhode Island interviewees' CPS records had put me in contact with administrators. Starting with those contacts and a professional connection, I had a series of meetings with administrators that summer and fall—a period of crisis for the agency as administrators and staff navigated the fallout from recent child fatalities and overhauled their investigative response protocol.

The director of the intake division was enthusiastic about the project; she said that she wanted staff and families to have input and that such feedback could improve practice. "I want this to happen," she assured me. But, in a high-profile position under considerable media scrutiny, she was also extremely busy. Corresponding and meeting with me was understandably not her top priority. She also raised concerns about my interviewing parents during an open investigation, as parents might make disclosures that could muddy the investigative process and I could be called to testify. Additionally, she felt

uncomfortable about embedding research into a moment of crisis, high un-
predictability, and information-gathering. Could I contact families after investigations closed, families different than those whose cases I shadowed? she
wondered. "I wish I could say, 'Just go and do it,' but this is complex."

In January 2018, I met with several top administrators. One, whom I had never
met before, immediately shut down conversation about the project, even when
the intake director tried to jump in to explain. This administrator stated emphatically that the agency was not in a position to have a research project underway.
She noted that staff had a tremendous amount of work, the agency was redesign-
ing the front-end response, and there were confidentiality issues. "This is problematic," she concluded. I tried to shift the conversation to brainstorm ideas for
how we might understand investigative experiences, suggesting that it could help
with their redesign implementation. She replied that they had their own internal
mechanisms for doing so. When I mentioned my interest in the perspectives of
frontline staff, whose contact information was publicly available online, she said
in no uncertain terms that I was not to contact any investigators or caseworkers
myself. She then stood to announce that she was concluding the meeting and
would escort me out. (She called me within the hour to apologize for being
"curt" and said that the timing simply wasn't right for them.)

Simultaneously, in spring and summer 2017, I was exploring research possibilities with administrators in Massachusetts, with whom I'd connected
through professional contacts. One high-level administrator told me that all
of the agency's policies had recently been rewritten—a "huge undertaking"
following highly publicized child fatalities. She said that my questions about
staff and parent experiences of investigations were important to the agency
but that "we can't get distracted by other good projects." She encouraged me
to send a proposal that she could discuss with the commissioner. I did so that
week. I didn't hear back, though nor did I follow up, as I figured I'd see how
things shook out with Rhode Island.

I also reached out to a contact at the Connecticut Department of Children
and Families (DCF) in summer 2017. As I began graduate school, I was interested in the spatial concentration of CPS contact and hoped to work with an
agency to geocode its investigation data. In fall 2013, I connected with someone willing to share my research proposal with New England child welfare directors. Connecticut and Vermont responded expressing interest, and I went
with Connecticut. After more than a year getting approvals in place, I spent long
days in a cubicle in Hartford geocoding the data and preparing a de-identified
data set. The time at DCF's central office helped me get to know staff in the

research and evaluation division, who remained supportive of my research and facilitated my presenting the findings to the commissioner and her senior administrative team in December 2016. Following that meeting, two regional directors reached out, interested in my preparing presentations tailored to their areas for staff and community partners, which I did in spring 2017.

That August, I emailed one of those regional directors to gauge interest in a potential research partnership. A few weeks later, I met with him and one of his field office directors, in the Northeast Corner. It was an enormous stroke of good fortune to have this administrator in this role. He saw himself as a data person, having previously headed the agency's research and evaluation division. He loved analyzing data and embodied the agency's commitment to data-driven strategy. I think he hoped that my research could more directly assist the office with systems evaluation and quality assurance efforts. In that first meeting, he told me that what piqued his interest was the possibility of illuminating the needs of rural areas that received less attention than their urban counterparts. As he explained, children in his region were in extremely challenging situations—with high rates of substance use, suicides, and sexual abuse—yet received little community or external support.

A couple weeks later, I met with the office's intake manager. As we met, staff popped in and out of her office to give her updates or ask questions. "This is what it's like," she said. Upon skimming my proposal, her first words were, "This is a heavy lift." But, she said, it seemed highly interesting and valuable. From there, beginning in October 2017, I shadowed informally to learn more about work in the office while securing permissions for the study. I traveled to the office whenever I could, about once a week, to attend investigative visits, meetings, and other office activities.

The project went before the full university Institutional Review Board (IRB) for discussion in October 2017. The IRB kicked it back, with lots of questions. I tried to explain the project to the IRB coordinator but didn't feel that I was getting through. An advisor, Jocelyn Viterna, then went with me to the IRB office, across campus, to meet with the coordinator and her supervisor. We described in more detail why I proposed the research procedures I did—such as obtaining written consent from parents after observing their visit with CPS—and how these procedures were in human subjects' best interests. In November, the full board again reviewed my protocol, this time approving it.

DCF's IRB required approval from other IRBs before its process could begin. I started by completing an agency "impact assessment" in November. My protocol was first discussed at the board's January 2018 meeting. The board had concerns and questions and invited me to attend its February meeting to address questions in person. In the January meeting, I heard afterward, the research and evaluation director emphasized that DCF was responsible for getting feedback from clients and that this was an important way to do so. But one member worried that my presence at the start of the investigation could hinder the agency's legal case moving forward, the same concern raised in Rhode Island. During the January meeting, I learned, the IRB cold-called the intake manager in the Northeast Corner. This manager was often in meetings and resolving emerging crises, but miraculously, they caught her at her desk and she spoke with the IRB for half an hour, telling them about my engagement skills and explaining why she did not share the concerns raised. In debriefing the January meeting with administrators, it was clear that my having spent time in-office—nearly four months at this point—made a difference. "I wouldn't consider this request if it came from outside," the regional director commented.

To address concerns about the research impacting crisis situations, I was willing to exclude "critical incidents" (fatalities and other severe injuries) from the study. The intake manager suggested affirming that anyone along the chain of command could exclude a case from the study for any reason, such as based on the mother's current psychiatric condition. I was amenable to this, though it didn't end up occurring.

The IRB coordinator had suggested I invite regional staff to the February meeting, so the regional director attended as well. We stepped out during the board's initial discussion, more than half an hour. When the IRB coordinator came to get us, she shook her head with a look indicating that things weren't looking great for the project. "Tough crowd," she said to us under her breath. It was an animated—and difficult—meeting. For nearly an hour, I tried to answer members' questions as best I could. The regional director noted that concerns about compromising DCF's investigation were present in many other contacts DCF facilitated, such as referrals to local social services. As in Rhode Island, the IRB was skeptical that the Certificate of Confidentiality I had obtained from the National Institutes of Health would protect me from having to share data with a court issuing a subpoena.[7] I'd hoped to use the meeting to brainstorm potential solutions with the IRB, but we didn't quite get there.

As we left, the regional director also surmised that things weren't looking promising. I emailed the IRB coordinator that night trying to salvage the project, asking whether the IRB might approve a project that interviewed mothers after investigations closed or, barring that, one that removed the interviews with mothers entirely. The regional director replied right away, copying the

IRB. He reflected that the discussion had focused on "concerns about the interests of the agency beyond worries about protections for the clients." He wrote that, in his role, the agency's interest was his primary consideration but that such issues might not be relevant to human subjects concerns.

The next morning, the IRB coordinator emailed me, approving the study with conditions that did not substantially change the research protocol: "The IRB regards this research as a very ambitious project that would provide extremely useful feedback to the agency. . . . Kelley, we are familiar with your previous geo-spatial research project and with your attention to details in the work that you complete." I made the requested modifications and officially started fieldwork in the Northeast Corner the following week.

I also wanted to include a more urban office site in the study. In December 2017, I'd visited the Hartford office to pitch the project to its office director and intake managers. The office director said that she was open to the project but did not want it to be an additional burden on staff, whom she said typically were not interested in research given their workloads. They didn't want to foreclose any interested investigators from participating, but it didn't seem as though they would facilitate my efforts either. The next month, they said that they would email intake supervisors to see whether any of their staff were interested in participating. I responded, suggesting the possibility of informal shadowing so staff could meet me; I didn't hear back, though nor did I follow up.

As I was planning to move from Providence to New York City that summer, New Haven became appealing given commuter trains between the two cities. The year before, in February 2017, my partner was traveling to New Haven to interview for a fellowship. I had been analyzing DCF's administrative data and was always interested in opportunities to see casework in practice to better understand the data. DCF's research and evaluation office put me in touch with New Haven administrators, who welcomed me for a day of informal shadowing. The intake manager, with whom I'd been emailing, had been running around dealing with various situations all day, but she greeted me excitedly when I finally met her at the end of the day. When I reached out a year later—in March 2018, the Northeast Corner research already underway—she remembered me and readily arranged for us to meet with the field office director. To my surprise and relief, they approached the meeting presuming that the research would be happening there and we just had to work out the details. In that first meeting, we hammered out a plan to get started. I introduced the project to New Haven intake supervisors in early April and returned at the end of the month to begin.

I'm often asked how I got access to a child welfare agency, whose activities are typically closed to the public and which have rarely allowed journalists or researchers to observe. I take several lessons from my experience. First, by the time I made the request, I had gotten to know key administrators over the course of months, in some cases years. I prepared detailed presentations responsive to their interests, work I never published in academic journals. This incubation period was essential and made them feel comfortable that I would not overburden staff or muckrake.

Second, it's not lost on me that this fieldwork happened because important people took time to help me. The regional director overseeing the Northeast Corner office was part of the commissioner's senior administrative team, a "cabinet" of sorts. I believe that his attending the IRB meeting—a forty-five-minute drive from his office—made a difference, and likewise with the Northeast Corner intake manager taking an impromptu phone call and even a dissertation advisor going across campus to meet with IRB staff. With different people in these roles, the project might have fallen through. Relatedly, as sociologists we often focus on factors other than chance, but here I was simply in the right place at the right time. I did the bulk of my Connecticut fieldwork in early/mid-2018. That fall, the state elected a new governor. He installed a new DCF commissioner, who restructured the agency; when I returned for follow-up fieldwork, I constantly saw memos about strategic planning and organizational transitions. Staff told me that I likely would not have been able to get access a year later, with the agency turned inside out to reconfigure itself. Likewise, when the pandemic hit the following year, 2020, investigators rapidly shifted to remote work, which would have made coordinating the fieldwork extremely difficult, if not impossible.

Finally, my experience underscores how organizations willing to participate in research are not a random sample. Child welfare advocates in Rhode Island and Massachusetts told me not to take it personally if agencies there declined to work with me: they were "guarded," I was just "too risky," and they "may not want to invite in additional oversight." These states were reeling from highly publicized child fatalities and substantially shifting case practice in response. During this time, Rhode Island administrators were attending state legislative hearings where legislators excoriated the agency for its failings. While preparing to implement a new intake response system, the statewide intake director—in a senior administrative role—told me that she spent her mornings personally reviewing stacks of reports that had come in the previous night, to see whether she needed to flag any for a response.

Like all child welfare agencies, Connecticut DCF draws its share of criticism, and tragic incidents aren't unknown. But it struck me as, overall, a very well-run agency in comparison. From my vantage point, things seemed to run smoothly; there were standard protocols for everything, and people generally followed them. For instance, staff had to commence, then complete, investigations within a certain timeframe, and managers regularly reviewed their units' performance on these measures. The agency was interested in the project because of its commitment to learning from research and from stakeholders. Child welfare agencies are constantly pilloried in the press and scrutinized by advocates and legislators. But DCF seemed strangely unbothered by this possibility. The regional director told me he suspected that the agency was intervening well; he saw the project as focusing on structural issues, things beyond individual staff members' control. Indeed, I observed investigative practice in line with best practice guidelines, and I sought to analyze individual staff actions in their broader context. DCF never asked me not to name the site, and I saw no compelling reason to mask it.[8]

So Connecticut DCF is not representative or generalizable in any sense— we cannot expect this of a single case.[9] It's a case that shows us how CPS operates in a relatively well-functioning organization. This is critically important. But we should also consider what we miss when some of our most important organizations, perhaps the most tumultuous, are closed off to researchers. Going forward, I hope that researchers can develop the relationships with such agencies needed to learn more about everyday practice there.

Studying Investigations in Connecticut

I was less interested in a traditional "organizational ethnography" of CPS because I saw my object of study as the investigation—involving players outside CPS—rather than intra-organizational processes. I designed the study around a relatively small number of cases and sought to understand them from multiple perspectives. For selected reports, I observed at least one of CPS's visits with the family, typically the first visit. I briefly interviewed the investigator shortly thereafter and sought to interview the professionals who filed these reports as well as the mothers under investigation.

I spent two to three months at each office, full-time (weekday business hours). Each office had twenty to twenty-five staff members who exclusively conducted investigations, a group that was almost all White in the Northeast Corner and racially and ethnically diverse in New Haven. I sat in a cubicle alongside investigators; as chapter 3 described, things are constantly coming up in investigative work, so this allowed me to "be there" when things happened and when investigators conversed informally. Often, we did similar work. I arrived in the morning to write up field notes from the previous day and make phone calls to set up interviews; they did the same, typing their case notes and calling people connected to their cases to get information or arrange a meeting. I shadowed investigators on dozens of other family visits beyond the focal cases and tried to observe different settings: the hotline call center, conferences with external partners such as service providers and hospitals, supervisory and managerial consultations on cases, supervisor meetings to assign incoming cases, peer-to-peer professional development sessions, case review meetings, forensic interviews at child advocacy centers, and formal meetings to discuss child removal. I attended weeks of in-person and online trainings. And I joined in on all-staff office meetings as well as celebrations like birthday potlucks and holiday brunches.

Because of my focus on mothers, eligible study reports alleged a biological mother perpetrating abuse or neglect, though reports might have included other alleged perpetrators as well. Thus, I excluded reports in which the only alleged perpetrators were fathers, stepparents, aunts or uncles, grandparents, foster or adoptive parents, school staff, and so on. The study was restricted to mothers who spoke English or Spanish.[10] I also excluded a small number of cases the agency deemed "critical incidents"—involving fatalities or serious injuries—and those designated internally confidential, typically because a case participant was connected to a staff member. Initially, I wanted to capture mothers' first experiences with the agency as parents, to understand what they learned. With children's high levels of cumulative exposure to CPS, many families, especially Black families, have this "first encounter." But because most incoming reports involve families with CPS history, staff encouraged me to include these cases to get a clearer picture of their clientele. I implemented this change partway through the study, as soon as I received approval from both IRBs. Both offices were unusually slow when I was there, so the study could accommodate this expansion.[11] Still, I prioritized cases with less CPS history.

The study ultimately included thirty-seven cases, eleven from the Northeast Corner and twenty-six from New Haven, assigned to twenty-five different investigators.[12] Almost all cases were reported by professionals (thirty-three of thirty-seven), and physical neglect was by far the most common type of alleged maltreatment (alleged in thirty-one of thirty-seven cases), consistent with state and national data. In seven cases, mothers had prior CPS history as parents, but none had children previously removed. Table 1 lists the

TABLE 1. Connecticut Focal Cases

Mother	CPS Investigator	CPS Reporter	Other Household Members	Mother's Race/Ethnicity	Summary of Initial Maltreatment Allegation(s)	Allegations Substantiated?	Case Kept Open After Investigation?
			Northeast Corner				
Alex[F]	Pat	Hospital	Husband and newborn	White	Substance use during pregnancy	X	X[RD]
Ana	Shawn	School	Boyfriend, two children (7 and 2), boyfriend's grandparents	Puerto Rican	Child with unexplained bruise		
Ashley	Vance	School	Husband and 7-year-old child	White	Child hit on the head; parents not partnering with school to manage child's behavior		
Charlene[F]	Sarah (CT)/LeAnn (MA)	Hospital	Boyfriend and newborn	White	Substance use during pregnancy; hospital concerned about parents' care for newborn	X	X[RD]
Danielle	Mallory	Emergency medical technician	Boyfriend and three children (14, 11, 6)	Latina	Child not in car seat during car accident		
Deborah	Sarah	Hospital	Adult son and two minor children (12 and 9)	White	Mother hospitalized following overdose		
Gina[F]	Vance	Relative	Two children (3 and 2) and brother	White	Mother drinking around children; poor housing conditions	X	X[RA]
Lizette	Lauren	Police	Two children (8 and 3)	Latina	Child outside unsupervised		
Louise[F]	Tammi	Police	Boyfriend and two children (14-year-old twins)	White and Black	Children exposed to domestic violence	X	X[RA]
Marlena	Alison	Emergency medical technician	Husband and three children (4 and 2-year-old twins)	Middle Eastern	Poor housing conditions		
Stefani[F]	Teresa	Hospital	Newborn, mother, four siblings	Puerto Rican	Limited capacity to care for newborn		

New Haven

Alicia	**Bonnie**	Police	Boyfriend and 3-year-old child	White	Marijuana use around child	X
April[F]	**Heather**	School	Husband, 10-year-old child, mother, brother, niece	Black	Child permitted to smoke marijuana	
Gaby	**Ria**	Mental health professional (Alma)	Boyfriend and two children (15 and 8)	South American	Child hit with belt on legs	
Graciela	**Dan**	School (Amaryllis)	Three children (11, 8, toddler), mother, stepfather	Dominican	Lack of response to school's request to pick up sick child	
Imelda	**Heather**	Police	Girlfriend, four children (13, 10, 8, 3), friend's three children, friend's sister	Puerto Rican	Child outside unsupervised	
Jazmine[F]	**Fred**	Housing case manager (Cate)	2-year-old child	Black and Puerto Rican	Child hit on hand	
Jennifer	**Natasha**	Mental health professional (Marla)	Adult daughter and 12-year-old child	Puerto Rican	Child's mental health needs unmet	
Joyce	**Sheila**	Children's father	Homeless, staying with different relatives, previously with boyfriend and three children (6, 3, infant)	Latina	Mother abandoned children, leaving them without food assistance benefits	
Katharine	**Heather**	Social service provider	2-year-old child	Latina	Children left with babysitters while mother was drinking heavily; mother previously threatened father with a knife in front of child	

Continued on next page

TABLE 1. (*continued*)

Mother	CPS Investigator	CPS Reporter	Other Household Members	Mother's Race/Ethnicity	Summary of Initial Maltreatment Allegation(s)	Allegations Substantiated?	Case Kept Open After Investigation?
				New Haven			
Katrina	Cheryl	Hospital	Two children (8 and 5), father	White	Inadequate supervision while child was touched inappropriately by neighbor		
Leidy	Sheila	School	Husband, two children (8 and 4), brother-in-law	Central American	Child swatted with hairbrush, leaving bruise		
Lourdes	Ria	Relative	Homeless, staying with different relatives	Puerto Rican	Parents left 4-year-old with relatives and without support		
Makayla[F]	Heather	Police (Justine)	Two children (2 and infant), sister, father	Black	Child outside unsupervised		
Monica	Patrice	Mental health professional	Boyfriend and 8-year-old child	Latina	Child agitated as parents argued		
Nataly	Fred	Childcare provider	Two children (4 and 1), brother, sister-in-law, brother's two children	Puerto Rican	Mother's mental health needs unmet		
Nikki[F]	Joe	Mental health professional	Boyfriend and two children (16 and 11)	Black	Children exposed to domestic violence		
Norma	Ria	Hospital	Husband and three children (16, 12, newborn)	Puerto Rican	Marijuana use during pregnancy; mother going to methadone clinic		

Roberta	**Bridget**	Social service provider	Husband, 2-year-old child, husband's 6-year-old child	Black	Mother's mental health needs unmet		
Rosie	**Bridget**	Police	Girlfriend and three children (7, 4, infant)	Puerto Rican	Baby exposed to domestic violence	X	
Sabrina	**Ria**	Hospital	Three children (14, 13, 11)	Black	Unstable housing and poor housing conditions		
Sandra	**Dawn**	Childcare/mental health professional (Polly)	Husband and two children (5 and 1)	Dominican	Child riding scooter unsupervised; concerns about child's exposure to domestic violence and pornography		
Shaniece	**Marya**	Domestic violence advocate	One-year-old child, two friends, friend's child	Jamaican	Child exposed to physical fighting		
Sherea[F]	**Gail**	Hospital	Newborn, friend, friend's child	Black	Marijuana use during pregnancy	X	X
Tameka[F]	**Heather**	Hospital	5-year-old child, mother, stepfather	Black	Child's lack of medical care; mother's hospitalization following suicide attempt		
Tatiana	**Chanell**	Child's father	Three children (10, 8, infant)	Black	Infant left with unknown babysitter, no crib, no electricity		
Zanobia[F]	**Joe**	Hospital	Two children (13 and 6)	Black and Latina	Child hit with extension cord		X

Note: Bold indicates participants who were interviewed. All names are pseudonyms. Race/ethnicity is as identified to me and/or CPS. CPS = Child Protective Services, as shorthand for the Connecticut Department of Children and Families. [F] = completed follow-up interview and/or observation. [RD] = CPS removed child(ren) during the investigation period. [RA] = CPS removed child(ren) sometime after the investigation concluded, as of February 2020; mothers whose case records I did not access (those not interviewed, plus Jennifer) may have had children removed after the investigation concluded as well.

thirty-seven cases with some basic details. After investigating, CPS closed thirty of these cases. Maltreatment allegations against the mother were substantiated in six cases, a case-level substantiation rate (16 percent) comparable to the 17 percent child-level substantiation rate nationwide.[13]

I briefly interviewed each of the investigators assigned to these cases, along with twenty-one of the professionals who reported the cases and seventeen additional reporting professionals, recruited by contacting other local organizations.[14] Finally, I interviewed twenty-seven of the mothers (eight of eleven in the Northeast Corner and nineteen of twenty-six in New Haven), all but one of whom granted me access to their case records. Twelve mothers participated in follow-up interviews and/or additional observations. Most mothers interviewed had no more than a high school education, though two had bachelor's degrees. The monthly median household income among mothers interviewed was $1,790; approximately half were not formally employed when I interviewed them, and several reported no current income. I interviewed four New Haven mothers (Gaby, Imelda, Leidy, and Sandra) with assistance from a certified Spanish interpreter.[15]

My case flow typically went as follows: In each office, a "screener" received and printed incoming reports. I worked with the screener to identify cases eligible for the study and then approached the assigned investigators to remind them of the project and invite them to participate. If they were amenable, I asked them to let me know when they planned to conduct a visit, so I could tag along. Because of confidentiality protections, I could not contact CPS reporters myself. Investigators usually called those who filed reports to ask additional questions, so in cases reported by professionals, I asked investigators to tell the reporters about the study in these calls (giving them a brief script) and request reporters' permission to share contact information with me. I then reached out to reporters.

Investigative work is impossible to plan. I spent a lot of time with investigators attempting visits that didn't pan out. Sometimes they called families in advance to set up a meeting time; other times they visited unannounced. Investigators might have another visit nearby fall through and then swing by in case someone was home. I couldn't be in two places at once. Because investigators had to meet with children during visits, investigators often tried to visit after school hours so school-age children would be home. This meant that I usually couldn't attempt more than one visit per day. I just attempted as many as I could and hoped that things would align on at least some of them.

At the start of the visit, I introduced myself as a student researcher not working for the agency and asked whether it would be all right for me to sit in on the visit.[16] I jotted notes and tried to be as unobtrusive as possible. At the end of the visit, I met with mothers to explain the project, get written consent to include the visit observation in the study, and invite them to participate in an individual interview. To reduce any pressure to participate they might feel with the investigator present, I spoke with mothers alone, while investigators waited in the car or interviewed other household members. I emphasized that participation was optional, would not affect mothers' cases, and would not be disclosed to investigators. If mothers agreed to include their cases in the study, I developed my jottings into extensive field notes shortly thereafter.

When people learn I observed CPS investigations, they sometimes say something like, "Wow, you must have seen some really awful things." But I didn't, at least not in the way one might think. I focused on run-of-the-mill, mundane CPS cases; the vast majority involved children CPS deemed safe at home. I heard about, and saw indications of, poverty, domestic violence, substance use, and other challenges, but not any more intensely than in the Rhode Island interviews. My approach was to listen and learn, but at times, the observations were emotionally wrenching, especially in the (relatively few) cases that moved toward removal. After a particularly rough removal meeting, I must have looked shaken; a supervisor asked whether I was okay. I tried to compartmentalize but often felt helpless just sitting there taking notes while such momentous things were happening.

I usually interviewed investigators in the car as we drove back to the office, keeping these interviews relatively brief. Interviews focused on their perspective on the case and what we'd just observed. Investigators provided written consent for observations and audio-recorded interviews. As cases progressed, I tried to check in with investigators informally, especially when the investigation concluded. I spoke with all participants up front about the possibility that, because I was interviewing multiple parties, people involved in their case might be able to identify them in research products. But I did not directly disclose any information shared with me by one party to any other. I assured participants that I would not share any details about them or their cases that would identify them to the general public.[17]

I met with reporting professionals at their workplaces for thirty- to forty-five-minute audio-recorded interviews; each received a $5 gift card. These interviews were straightforward to schedule and conduct; professionals seemed to treat them like other meetings in their workdays. I asked about general topics, such as recommendations for CPS, but much of the interview traced their observations, decision-making, and expectations regarding a specific case: the focal case for case-specific reporting professionals and the most recent case reported for others.

I interviewed almost all mothers at their homes, usually for about an hour but sometimes for up to four hours. I audio-recorded these interviews and gave mothers $20 cash in appreciation of their time. I asked mothers to recount their expectations, perceptions, feelings, and experiences related to CPS and its recent visit. At the end of the interview, I asked mothers whether they would allow me access to their CPS case records.[18] When mothers had relevant case activities, such as meetings or court hearings, I sometimes asked to tag along. As nearly all of these interviews occurred while CPS's investigation was open, in several cases I reached out for follow-up interviews in the year or so following the report. Mothers provided written consent for all interviews and observations.

Throughout the fieldwork, I felt insecure about whether the project would yield new information for staff. They already knew or had a sense of what I was seeing, so I struggled to articulate how the project could benefit them. Agency staff expected much more deductive research, with supervisors asking about specific hypotheses I expected to confirm. I suggested that my research could give others who didn't understand CPS a sense of what investigators dealt with, but that aim might have been too vague and far-off. "At the end we will have research!" chirped the New Haven intake manager when we pitched the project to supervisors. But she immediately recognized and articulated how supervisors saw the research as yet another thing on their plates. The agency had many different review processes already. I emphasized that this was not an evaluation or quality assurance effort.[19] The project's time-limited nature helped, in contrast to another, longer-term external research effort in which staff were engaged.

Staff had mixed reactions to the project. Supervisors mostly tolerated it, neither aiding nor impeding my approaching investigators. Different investigators were more or less amenable to the project and more or less friendly with me. I felt like an outsider with moms, and I also felt like an outsider with CPS. I tried not to take it personally; they just had jobs to do. One investigator, Dan, told me early on that he probably knew which investigators I'd been out with, naming a few who had indeed warmed to me and the research. "But good luck getting [other investigator]." Indeed, this investigator had verbally expressed openness to the study when I approached her about cases but never let me know when she planned to visit. I tried to be persistent—investigators had a lot going on, so found the reminders helpful—but also to respect when investigators were trying to decline without outright rejecting me. Ultimately, across both offices, I shadowed thirty different investigators. I had approval to conduct individual in-depth interviews with investigators (and, incidentally, also attorneys) that would cover more of their background and approach to investigations more generally, rather than their perceptions of a specific case. However, I didn't end up conducting these interviews, as I didn't want to overburden investigators and thought I would prioritize the focal case visits.

It would be naive to think that my presence had no effect on CPS's investigative process. Even if silent, I found it difficult to recede completely into the background during visits. It's possible that because I was there, investigators asked more questions at the first visit, so it didn't seem as though they were shirking their responsibilities. This possibility became apparent to me when a case requiring immediate response came in late one Friday afternoon. We couldn't find the investigator up next on the rotation, and some surmised he'd left for the weekend. I approached his supervisor about contacting him. To my surprise—I found supervisors generally ambivalent about the project—she said that she would like me to go out with him. "I trust you more than him," she said, adding that sometimes investigators "rush through it" and she didn't want that to happen. When I called the investigator, who had expressed interest in the project previously, he said, "I can't use you on this one. . . . I can use you on the next one." So perhaps investigators did more thorough initial assessments with me.

But they had to get all the information anyway—as chapter 3 detailed, they were held accountable for it—and I do not think that my presence affected investigations more than others where investigators bring trainees, interns, or medical students along. Investigators saw me in that light and treated me as someone they wanted to teach and engage. After visits, they almost always asked what I thought, which I found difficult to navigate as I did not want to sway their assessments. I tried to reply vaguely, highlight facts if needed, and turn it back to them. For instance, in Nikki's case (discussed primarily in chapter 4), the investigator, Joe, asked what I thought and where the case ranked on the "interesting factor." I said that I didn't think I'd seen anyone not sign the safety plan, which prompted Joe to talk about his experience with parents signing safety plans.

I was also constantly attuned to how my responses to investigators and mothers might affect families' CPS cases by giving credence to either party's perspective. To build rapport, I was taught to affirm—not endorse but affirm—participants' experiences and perspectives, for instance, by nodding, responding with an empathetic sound, or repeating the last part of participants' responses to encourage them to say more. I found this approach helpful in the Rhode Island interviews, but in Connecticut I saw how it might have unintended consequences. For instance, after interviewing Nikki and her boyfriend, I wrote in my field notes:

> Both of them frequently referenced moments from the visit as if to support their points, since I'd been there too—like, remember when he said this or I said this. . . . It was a tricky balance in this interview, though. I wanted to convey that I was on their side and affirm what they were saying—but I also didn't want to be giving my blessing to their point of view, to make them even more confident that their interpretation was the truth and DCF was entirely in the wrong, because I felt that could have negative ramifications for their DCF case.

Likewise, I worried that even just nodding—or not pushing back—when investigators shared their assessment of the family might be read as an endorsement. I was there, and if I didn't contest, investigators might feel more confident that another "professional" saw things similarly. In response, I tried not to be too expressive with my facial or verbal reactions and focused on probing details: what made you think that, what gave you that impression. But I wondered about how this response hindered rapport.

In some instances, I directly supported CPS's work. For instance, I accompanied a newer investigator on a case that resulted in her first removal, after hours. (This case was ineligible to include as a focal case, as the mother spoke neither English nor Spanish.) The investigator was stressed and unsure of herself. I was another pair of hands: helping the child get her things and staying with the child in the car while the investigator interviewed other household members. Afterward, I reassured her that she had done a great job. But I did not help in these ways in focal cases, where I might interview the mother as well.

In order to interview mothers *during* the investigation—the raison d'être of the project—I had to meet them through CPS. As Matthew Desmond has noted, doing relational fieldwork with "an interconnected web of people . . . bound in relationships of antagonism" comes with particular challenges.[20] Especially early on, mothers likely associated me with CPS. After all, I arrived alongside investigators, and mothers knew that the agency was helping me identify cases for the research. Indeed, to get building and computer access, I was officially an "intern" in the agency's system. Nevertheless, I sought to convey that my project was separate from CPS. I reminded investigators before visits not to introduce me to parents as their colleague or coworker as they did for trainees and other interns. The formality of consent forms, which listed university rather than CPS contacts and described confidentiality protections, also seemed to help mothers understand my work as distinct. Centering mothers' experiences—connecting with them where they were—sometimes meant distancing myself from CPS. When mothers came to the office for meetings, for instance, I met them outside and went through security with them, even though I could buzz in and skip the security check; I averted my gaze when we saw other staff around the office with whom I had a friendly relationship. Such experiences gnawed at me: In my efforts to communicate that I wasn't a CPS investigator, was I underplaying my access to CPS? Technically, I did not work for CPS, but I spent almost all day with CPS investigators.

Trying to maintain rapport and distance simultaneously, with all parties, was stressful. In one family team meeting, Gina met with staff in CPS's ongoing services division. The conversation turned to Gina's home conditions at the start of the investigation, which no one in the room except me and Gina had observed, as her investigator had moved to another office. As I wrote in my field notes:

> [The manager] said when she read about the conditions at the beginning, it wasn't just toys. [Manager] seemed frustrated, almost at a loss for words, like she was tired of continually contesting this. She leaned forward and turned to look at me expectantly, saying that I was there. She seemed to want me to back up her account of the conditions of the home. It was a tricky ethical moment . . . to maintain alignment with both Gina and the DCF staff. I was in the middle of writing notes as this happened so it kind of caught me off-guard. I shook my head apologetically and said something like, "I can't—." [Manager] and Gina both nodded, quickly jumped in, and repeated something like, "You can't."

This moment of feeling torn epitomized what the relational fieldwork felt like.

Though I had a friendly relationship with many investigators, we weren't particularly close personally, and I didn't socialize with them outside of work. This was a requirement in my IRB protocol (an agency representative had raised questions about boundaries between me and staff), but I also needed time away to decompress. Upon reflection, I think my not being buddy-buddy with investigators helped mothers see my role as different from that of CPS.

There were likely things they didn't feel comfortable sharing with me, and as in Rhode Island, some were more talkative than others. Still, it surprised me how willingly some mothers let their guard down with someone they'd met through CPS and how building rapport felt similar to the Rhode Island interviews. Mothers seemed to appreciate the chance to process and reflect with a willing listener, usually shortly after CPS's visit. In contrast to investigators, trying to get the information they needed so they could move on to their next task, I could sit and listen to whatever parents wanted to talk about.[21] Again, I leaned on my role as a student. Deborah, for instance, called our interview "necessary," saying, "How do we expect things to change if we don't have students? . . . Nothing will ever be looked at differently, if we don't give our side of things to the independent person taking the information." She added, "Who listens to the moms that's a middle ground? Nobody. You are that middle ground. You are that person who is just there to get people's perspectives, perceptions, and data."

Maintaining some distance—including symbolic distance—from CPS in my interactions with mothers involved trade-offs with respect to the data. In Rhode Island, with mothers' phone numbers changing or disconnected, I sometimes mailed cards and/or stopped by to invite them to a follow-up interview. In Connecticut, I decided early on never to visit mothers unannounced or mail anything unsolicited; due to my association with CPS, I did not want to "pop up" on them. Perhaps I was overly cautious, but I likewise opted not to do longer-term follow-up given the concerns participants shared regarding whether CPS would ever fully be out of their lives. When I first interviewed April, the school called partway through our interview to request that she pick up her son, who had become distressed after CPS's visit the day before. April invited me to come along, telling me to follow her in my car. Her investigator had not mentioned my research to the school, which reported April's case, so going to the school was not only a potentially illuminating observation in itself but also an opportunity to invite the reporter to the study. I began following April but then pulled over and called her, saying that upon further reflection, perhaps her son shouldn't see me at school, because CPS was making him anxious and he had seen me the previous day with the investigator. Although zealously pursuing as much as possible might have yielded more data—no one reacted negatively to my outreach—I am comfortable with my approach favoring less intrusion.

I found the fieldwork extremely draining, especially as an introvert. I was constantly asking people for things and observing sometimes heavy emotional moments. In the Northeast Corner, I drove over an hour each way to the office; in New Haven, I sublet a studio apartment and returned to Providence or New York on weekends. At the end of each day, I just wanted to lie down in the dark alone, but I had to write field notes and prepare for the next day. On weekends, I didn't hang out informally with mothers but, rather, decompressed, wrote field notes, and moved to New York. An advisor had suggested that because it had taken so long to get access, perhaps I might spend a little longer in the field to get more cases. No one at the agency asked me to leave at a certain point. But I had planned to travel to a conference in mid-August 2018, and having that end date for the full-time fieldwork in mind helped keep me going. Though I truly respect and admire immersive, multi-year ethnographic fieldwork, I don't regret the limits I set for my well-being.

Finding the Story

When I started data collection, I was firm in my interest in what was happening at the front end of the system, but I knew that my specific research focus might evolve. My dissertation prospectus drew on labeling theory, asking how the state responded to family needs with a process oriented around detecting abuse and neglect: what happens when self-identified "good mothers" encounter a system that defines them otherwise. Research questions focused on how mothers responded to these labels—I suggested that rather than internalize labels, mothers might resist them—and how professionals reconciled these labels with the structural barriers mothers faced.

During my first month of informal shadowing in the Northeast Corner, I wrote a memo with initial thoughts, including my surprise that staff rarely spoke about "abuse, neglect, motherhood, bad parenthood, parents harming children, etc. The frame is very much *child safety*." Because of this, the labeling process didn't seem particularly salient to investigators (although in hindsight, this would have been interesting in itself to probe). I was also starting to see how reports—highly discretionary and typically involving families facing adversity—opened the door for the state to inquire about all aspects of home and family. As I began the formal data collection, I continued to write analytic memos and code initial data using an inductive, open coding approach. Things started to "click" and come into focus as I interviewed reporting professionals. Two points struck me. First, they didn't think that children needed to be removed. Second, an advisor, Mario Small, had suggested asking counterfactual questions. So I asked, "Would you have reported this case if you weren't legally mandated?" Reporting professionals typically said yes, absolutely, even as they didn't see children in imminent danger. What, then, were they hoping the agency could do? This line of inquiry helped me see different puzzle pieces fit together: callers' aspirations to support, oversee, and educate families bringing lots of "low-level" cases in and then all of these cases getting the full surveillance treatment and putting families through an ordeal that threatened family separation. I could then see these processes reflected in large-scale data showing copious reports but relatively few with maltreatment allegations confirmed—a sort of surveillance without substantiation. I reanalyzed and recoded my data with this in mind, writing an article based on this analysis.

To bring the Rhode Island and Connecticut data together in the book, I returned once more to the data, reading through all the information to identify what, descriptively, the data contained. I organized these descriptive findings—ordering them temporally, based on families' trajectories through CPS—and then recoded the data based on these topics, which became the initial outline for the book's empirical chapters.

About a year after my full-time fieldwork concluded, I presented findings to investigative staff at both offices. I wrote a three-page brief outlining different perspectives on the investigation and prepared handouts with examples from that office, including praise for the agency from reporting professionals and mothers. As noted above, I wasn't revealing anything groundbreaking to them; they knew they made parents apprehensive. But they seemed to appreciate hearing the findings from me as an outsider. One supervisor who hadn't been particularly receptive to the project noted upon seeing the positive things mothers had said about their experiences (described in chapter 5) that I'd been out with fifteen different New Haven investigators. She mused with admiration, "We have such great workers—*such* great workers."

When sharing initial findings with the agency, I was apprehensive about introducing the surveillance angle I used in the academic write-ups, even as the brief and presentations I prepared for them said essentially the same thing. I worried they would feel defensive or even betrayed as I pointed out limitations of their work. But I've been impressed (and relieved) with how they engaged the research. They see these issues up close every day; they recognize the trauma they can inflict in the name of trying to help. A senior administrator summarized the approach of the new commissioner, sworn in several months after my full-time fieldwork ended, as wanting CPS to be the *last* call people make, rather than the first call. I heard this sentiment reiterated at multiple points, and I hope that my research can inform efforts to move toward that goal.

ACKNOWLEDGMENTS

I AM IMMENSELY GRATEFUL TO the research participants in Connecticut and Rhode Island who made this book possible by inviting me in and teaching me about their lives and their work. They continually inspired me with their commitment to children amid numerous challenges and constraints.

The mothers I met truly kept me motivated to write this book. In particular, the Rhode Island mothers I spent the most time with over the years encouraged me and believed in me as much as anyone. Every time we talked, I'd sheepishly tell them that I was still working on the project. I'm proud that I can say I'm finally done, and I hope that they see how profoundly they've shaped me and this work.

At the Connecticut Department of Children and Families, I thank current and former staff Betty Dasher, Jennifer Davis, Allon Kalisher, Rhonda Moore, Fred North, David Silva, Susan Smith, and Lynette Warner, who had no obligation to help an unknown graduate student but enthusiastically welcomed me in and facilitated my access nonetheless. All analyses, interpretations, and conclusions are my own and do not necessarily reflect the agency's views.

I conducted this research in graduate school, where I was fortunate to learn from some of the best around. First, I'm grateful for the opportunity I had to learn from the incomparable Devah Pager. Devah consistently pushed me to think big and to stay focused on my core interests in poverty, inequality, and social policy. She generously engaged with my ideas, no matter how messy, and her detailed, insightful, and timely feedback always left me invigorated to move forward. Quite simply, the Connecticut fieldwork wouldn't have happened without Devah's encouragement. I hope that this book would have made her proud.

Jocelyn Viterna, Bruce Western, and William Julius Wilson guided my dissertation project to the finish line after Devah's passing in 2018; all have been important supports since my first year of graduate school. Jocelyn has been a steadfast mentor, offering critical guidance and advice at every stage. When I doubted myself, Jocelyn's belief in the promise of my research kept me going.

Her sociological acumen and her remarkable ability to cut to the core of any idea immensely improved my work. Bruce is a model of thoughtful, rigorous, human-centered, and justice-oriented scholarship. His comments and questions always somehow managed to give me greater clarity on my research—and issues of justice and inequality more broadly—while unsettling things I thought I understood. And it has been such a privilege to learn from Bill, who always advised me to pursue research about which I was passionate, emphasized the importance of good descriptive work, and encouraged me to think beyond academic audiences to the public impact my research could have. These reminders along with his comments on my work buoyed me and kept me focused on what mattered to me.

I'm indebted to a number of people for generously reading and commenting on the full manuscript, though errors, of course, remain my own. My very first readers, going through the book with me as I drafted each chapter, were impacted mothers whose reflections on the work were invaluable. My sincere thanks go to Keyna Franklin, Shamara Kelly, "Christina," and "Desiree," for believing in this project and sharing your expertise with me. Kathryn Edin and Bruce Western were the best first academic readers I could have asked for: sharp, generative, and attentive to not only the work's implications for sociological theory but its implications for public policy and social justice. Every book writer should have someone like Frank Edwards in their corner, who sees through the mess to identify and elevate what you are trying to do. Jeff Chang, Teyora Graves-Ferrell, Ron Richter, Tim Ross, and, especially, Nora McCarthy offered great feedback to help the book speak to policy and practice audiences. Comments from anonymous reviewers of the book proposal and the full manuscript also clarified and strengthened the work.

My writing groups provided an encouraging, supportive community that kept me making progress on the book from beginning to end. They also read and commented on the book proposal and multiple chapters. My gratitude goes to Jennifer Bouek, Christina Cross, Hope Harvey, Anna Rhodes, and Casey Stockstill and also to Bailey Brown, Brittany Fox-Williams, Kathleen Griesbach, Dialika Sall, and Anthony Ureña.

Edwin Amenta, Joanne Golann, Ann Hironaka, Matty Lichtenstein, Mical Raz, Alex Roehrkasse, and Cathy Sirois gave me helpful feedback on individual chapter drafts. I also appreciated the opportunity to talk with audiences at the Institute for Research on Poverty and the New York University Ethnography Workgroup about the findings presented in chapter 4. Anna Arons and Michelle Bezark provided informative consultation on some of the specifics of child welfare practice and history. "Isabela" reviewed the section I drafted on her advocacy (noting just one, nonsubstantive correction, which I accepted). David Lobenstine provided incisive feedback on the book project as a whole and detailed comments on three chapters; David's comments, cutting to the heart of the material, made the work clearer and helped me get unstuck. At the book proposal stage, Laura Portwood-Stacer offered helpful guidance and resources.

I wrote much of this book while at the School of History and Sociology at Georgia Tech, where I could not have asked for more supportive and generous colleagues. In particular, thank you to Eric Schatzberg, Hanchao Lu, Dan Amsterdam, Kate Pride Brown, Allen Hyde, Mary McDonald, Todd Michney, Willie Pearson, Jennifer Singh, Johnny Smith, Germán Vergara, and Bill Winders. Robert Hampson and Brittany Skanes expertly administered everything to facilitate my work. I loved navigating the tenure track at Tech with Lindsey Bullinger, who set a great example for me and always gave spot-on advice.

I thank my colleagues in the sociology department at the University of California, Irvine, especially David John Frank and Maryann Zovak-Wieder, who welcomed me into the department and made sure I had what I needed to finish the book. Many Irvine colleagues also talked with me about the book project during a pivotal point in the writing and revision process.

I couldn't have written this book without a wonderful community of colleagues, mentors, and friends. In addition to those named above: Julie Wilson has been my child welfare guru for a decade now. Always making time to talk and broker introductions, Julie energized me every time we met and kept me grounded in policy and practice. During graduate school, Mario Small, Sasha Killewald, and Matt Desmond taught me about the research process and academic life; they, along with Jim Quane, gave helpful feedback on my work as well. Pam Metz is an absolute gem, consistently going above and beyond to build community and advocate for students. For me and others lucky enough to cross her path, she made so much possible. Jessica Matteson deftly managed everything behind the scenes for sociology graduate students. Stefanie DeLuca and Kathryn Edin welcomed me onto their fieldwork team for two summers—what a privilege to learn qualitative data collection and analysis from two of the best role models I could imagine, alongside the "How Parents House Kids" team. Chris Wimer and Rachel Wright offered professional advice and opportunities at key junctures. Al Camarillo, my undergraduate advisor, introduced me to research and to publicly engaged scholarship. It was Al who first encouraged me to interview parents—and I haven't looked back. Blythe

George and Siobhan Greatorex-Voith have helped me get through graduate school and beyond. I'm grateful to have Hope Harvey on this journey with me as well. Thanks also go to many others for professional and often personal support along the way, including Laura Adler, Asad Asad, Victoria Asbury, Monica Bell, Emily Bosk, Kristina Brant, Brianna Castro, Matthew Clair, Jennifer Darrah-Okike, Sarah Faude, Cayce Hughes, Jeremy Levine, Miguel Quintana Navarrete, Eva Rosen, Jasmin Sandelson, Jared Schachner, Lisa Schelbe, Andreja Siliunas, Mo Torres, Van Tran, Alix Winter, Tom Wooten, Youngmin Yi, Lilly Yu, Sherry Zhang, and Fangsheng Zhu. I thank Dorothy Roberts, Alan Dettlaff, Tracy Serdjenian, Richard Wexler, the "SOC-CWS" crew, and the broader child welfare/family policing advocacy communities; because of you all, I never felt as though I was working alone. Thank you for challenging me, commiserating with me, and doing work that inspires me.

At Princeton University Press, I thank Meagan Levinson for championing this project from the start and providing sharp feedback. Meagan, along with Erik Beranek, Ali Parrington, and others at the press, as well as Elisabeth A. Graves, also skillfully brought the book to fruition.

Funding—and in some cases a vibrant interdisciplinary community—from several sources made the data collection, analysis, and writing possible. I am grateful for support from the Multidisciplinary Program in Inequality and Social Policy, the Doris Duke Fellowship for the Promotion of Child Well-Being (especially Deb Daro and Lee Ann Huang), the Julius B. Richmond Fellowship at the Harvard Center on the Developing Child (especially Lisa Haidar and Tien Ung), the National Science Foundation Graduate Research Fellowship, and the Ivan Allen College of Liberal Arts Small Grant for Research.

Some examples and themes in the book previously appeared in the *American Sociological Review* (vol. 85, no. 4, pp. 610–38), *Family Integrity and Justice Quarterly* (vol. 2, pp. 70–79), and *Social Forces* (vol. 97, no. 4, pp. 1785–1810). I thank the editors and anonymous reviewers of those articles for their constructive feedback.

Finally, my family and my partner, Josh, have supported me every step of this journey, as we all crisscrossed around the country. It doesn't matter where we are; I'll always be home with you. To my mother in particular, who was always in my heart as I wrote a book on motherhood, thank you.

NOTES

Introduction

1. For consistency, I substitute "CPS" for research participants' references to the Connecticut Department of Children and Families and the Rhode Island Department of Children, Youth, and Families.

2. Kim et al. 2017.

3. U.S. Department of Health and Human Services (HHS) 2021a.

4. Collins and Mayer 2010; Edin and Shaefer 2015.

5. Online Etymology Dictionary 2022.

6. HHS 2021a.

7. Petruccelli, Davis, and Berman 2019.

8. Stephens 2019; Western 2015.

9. *Prince v. Commonwealth of Massachusetts* 1944:321.

10. Carson 2020; HHS 2020a.

11. Fong 2019b.

12. Putnam-Hornstein et al. 2021. Nationally representative data indicate that more than half of children experiencing CPS investigations (57 percent) live in households below the federal poverty line (Dolan et al. 2011b)—three times higher than the overall child poverty rate.

13. Yi, Edwards, and Wildeman 2020.

14. Roberts 2002, 2022; see also Vasquez-Tokos and Yamin 2021.

15. Author's calculations from Dolan et al. 2011b; HHS 2020b (comparable data on all maltreatment investigations are unavailable).

16. Social work scholars have vigorously debated whether the overrepresentation of poor children and children of color in CPS reflects differences in children's conditions or a biased reporting and intervention process (Dettlaff et al. 2021; Jonson-Reid, Drake, and Kohl 2009). On balance, both mechanisms play a role—and all explanations identify systemic racism and classism as root causes of unequal CPS intervention.

17. Berger and Waldfogel 2011.

18. Our conceptions of maltreatment also encompass families deviating from norms or expectations. Queer families, families in which parents have disabilities, and families that don't do what authorities say may also find themselves under scrutiny. Even well-off families delaying vaccines or supporting transgender children know that others may accuse them of maltreatment (Meadow 2018; Reich 2016).

19. Edwards 2016; Soss, Fording, and Schram 2011; Woodward 2021. CPS's poverty governance role hearkens back to late-nineteenth-century Societies for the Prevention of Cruelty to Children, the smaller-scale, nongovernmental precursor to CPS. Seeking to correct predominantly poor, Catholic immigrants' parenting, these organizations constructed "cruelty" as behavior outside the middle-class White, Anglo-Saxon, Protestant norm, such as drinking alcohol and raising children beyond the nuclear family structure (Gordon 1985).

20. Of course, the United States has always destabilized marginalized families. For centuries, enslavers separated families at will, and missionaries and federal agents sent Native American children to residential institutions.

21. Smeeding and Thévenot 2016.

22. This brief historical overview draws on Briggs (2020), Gordon (1985), Myers (2006), Nelson (1984), Pearson (2011), Raz (2020), and Rymph (2017). I do not provide a detailed history of U.S. child welfare, so I refer interested readers to these resources for more information.

23. U.S. Government Printing Office 1909:10. Formal state responses such as this are relatively recent developments in the United States, as raising children was historically understood as the province of parents, at least for White families. This meant that parents were not entitled to government assistance to care for children; parents without sufficient resources had to rely on social networks, turn to charity, or give children up to indenture or orphanages. But the state also refrained from interfering with (White) parenting, privileging parents' rights to privacy and autonomy. This shifted in the mid-nineteenth century, when conceptions of children as miniature adults and economic assets gave way to notions of childhood as a distinct stage of vulnerability and development (Pearson 2011; Zelizer 1985). New understandings of children as innocent, sacred, and deserving of protection raised questions about society's responsibilities to ensure they received adequate care.

24. With Black families largely cut out of New Deal public assistance and social insurance programs, White reformers turned to foster care in response to Black children's poverty (Simmons 2022). The U.S. government also forcibly separated Native children from their parents, operating "boarding schools" through the mid-twentieth century that explicitly sought to destroy children's "Indianness" and assimilate them into White society. Before the 1978 Indian Child Welfare Act provided tribes some sovereignty over child removal proceedings, as many as 25 to 35 percent of Native children were removed, nearly all to non-Native homes or institutions (Rocha Beardall and Edwards 2021). Thus, White advocates' commitment to supporting parents to care for children at home only extended so far.

25. This has been called the "rediscovery" of child abuse, as the issue initially garnered attention in the late nineteenth century. Following a highly publicized 1874 case, elite reformers in cities such as New York and Boston created charitable organizations to respond to what they deemed "cruelty" to children, but the influence and activity of these organizations waned by the early twentieth century.

26. CAPTA's advocates intentionally framed child maltreatment as a medical and psychological issue that affected all Americans regardless of class and thus did not require increased economic support for families. Mondale understood how economic resources facilitated childrearing but took a different strategic tack, emphasizing in CAPTA hearings that child abuse "is not a poverty problem; it is a national problem" (Raz 2020:12).

27. Waldfogel 1998.

28. Recall, for instance, Daniel Patrick Moynihan's infamous 1965 report, which proclaimed, "At the heart of the deterioration of the fabric of Negro society is the deterioration of the Negro family" (1965:5).

29. Other assistance, such as the Earned Income Tax Credit, does not reach the nation's poorest families (Edin and Shaefer 2015). For six months in 2021, families with children received unconditional cash transfers via an expanded Child Tax Credit; the credit slashed child poverty, but Congress did not extend it due to opposition from Republican senators (and one Democrat, Joe Manchin).

30. Social Security Act of 1935, Title IV, Section 401.

31. Center on Budget and Policy Priorities 2022.

32. Bell and Rice 2018; Congressional Research Service 2023; Office of Family Assistance, Administration for Children and Families 2019.

33. Children's Bureau 2023.

34. HHS 2021a.

35. Although CPS investigators are commonly called social workers, they do not necessarily have social work degrees. In a nationally representative survey, 14 percent of CPS investigators held a master's degree in social work, and another 22 percent held a bachelor's degree in social work (Dolan et al. 2011a).

36. Some agencies, including Connecticut's, operate "differential response" systems that do not make substantiation decisions on every report.

37. In most places, including Connecticut and Rhode Island, the family receives a new case-worker at the end of the investigation; in others, this caseworker is the same person who conducted the investigation.

38. As Anna Arons (2022a) explains, family courts' orientation around "rehabilitating" families positions judges as investigators and counselors, not just legal arbiters.

39. Bourdieu 1998:81.

40. Cooper 2014; Griesbach 2020; Kalleberg 2009; Pugh 2015.

41. Bourdieu 1998:82–84.

42. This insecurity can take many forms. Reflecting on Black mothers losing children to traumas such as infant mortality and neighborhood and police violence, Dána-Ain Davis writes that "because so many of our children are taken away from us, many Black mothers live with uncertainty—never quite sure if our children will return home. . . . Black mothers are vulnerable as a result of being stalked by the terror of losing, or the threat of losing, children" (2016:10–11).

43. Both scholars also discuss investigations but focus primarily on later-stage system contacts; all parents interviewed by Reich (2005) and nearly all interviewed by Lee (2016) had children removed.

44. HHS 2021a.

45. HHS 2006a, 2020a. This trend will likely continue given recent policy shifts, such as the 2018 Family First Prevention Services Act.

46. Office of Children and Family Services 2023. Annual New York City foster care entries fell from 13,000 in 1997 to 3,500 in 2019.

47. Rates in Figure 2 reflect unique children subject to CPS investigations and/or foster care placement. For 1996–2004, only duplicated investigation rates are available (i.e., a child

investigated twice would be double-counted). Unique investigation rates range from 83.8 to 86.0 percent of duplicated investigation rates during 2005–9; therefore, I estimate unique investigation rates for 1996–2004 by multiplying the duplicated investigation rate by 84.7 percent, the 2005–9 average. Roehrkasse (2021) estimates foster care rates for 1996–99, reporting 95 percent confidence intervals (e.g., the 1996 interval is 7.27–7.48).

48. HHS 2006b, 2021a.

49. HHS 2021a.

50. This trend is not limited to the United States; we see similar patterns elsewhere (Bilson and Martin 2017; Trocmé et al. 2014).

51. As Sarah Brayne writes, "Lower levels of criminal justice involvement may be as consequential for institutional involvement as more serious contact" (2014:379) such as incarceration. See also Weaver and Lerman 2010.

52. Goffman 2009; Herring 2019; Prowse, Weaver, and Meares 2020; Shedd 2015; Stuart 2016.

53. Social work scholars have typically treated investigations as an indicator of potential maltreatment or just an entry point to deeper system involvement. Yet investigations are a key point of contact between families and the state in themselves, in which parents, children, and state agents negotiate power (Reich 2005).

54. Children's Bureau 2023.

55. Connecticut Department of Children and Families 2023.

56. Likewise, if a stranger on the street punched a child walking with a parent, CPS would reject the report—it isn't in the agency's purview, though it could be referred to police.

57. Thus, CPS ends up holding individual parents responsible for social structural injustices such as poverty and racism (Lee 2016; Merritt 2020; Reich 2005; Roberts 2002, 2022; Woodward 2021).

58. Rise 2021, 2022; Roberts 2022.

59. We see the fusion of support and punishment across numerous institutions tasked with managing problems of poverty (Bach 2022; Chiarello 2015; Flores 2016; Gustafson 2011; Haney 2010; Headworth 2021; McKim 2017; Rios 2011; Shedd 2015; Stuart 2016). As this research shows, embracing care alongside coercion is fraught in ways that can perpetuate marginality.

60. Soss et al. 2011.

61. State caseworkers initially assessed eligibility for welfare by visiting applicants' homes to determine "suitability"; this idea of judging whether mothers "deserve" assistance continues to shape the politics of welfare provision today.

62. Conceptions of "poverty governance," in focusing implicitly or explicitly on labor market regulation (Bonnet 2019; Haney 2004; Piven and Cloward 1971; Soss et al. 2011; Wacquant 2010), envision social policy regulating families as a means of controlling labor. That is, states take an interest in family relations because families organize and divide work. For instance, in encouraging married, two-parent families, welfare policy invokes goals of reducing dependency (on welfare) and promoting responsibility (in the form of paid work). CPS shows how family structure and work aren't the only aspects of family life drawing governmental attention. As Susila Gurusami and Rahim Kurwa (2021) demonstrate, domestic space itself is a critical site of state policing and poverty governance.

63. Federal data show that nationwide, CPS agencies accepted 3.3 reports per 100 children in federal fiscal year 2018 (each report may pertain to multiple children). However, national rates

are an undercount, as some states, including Connecticut, do not include reports sent to alternative responses when providing data to the federal government. Including alternative response cases, I calculate 3.7 reports per 100 children in Connecticut. The most recent data from Rhode Island show 3.6 reports per 100 children (HHS 2020b, 2021a). Compared with the United States overall, the two states also have slightly higher proportions of children substantiated by CPS as maltreated, as a share of the child population.

64. Williams 2020.

65. For instance, Jennifer Reich (2005) shows how fathers working to reunify with children must navigate CPS's expectations around masculinity and fatherhood.

Chapter 1

1. "Christina" was called "Lisa" in prior work (Fong 2019a), but she decided that she preferred a different pseudonym.

2. HHS 2021b.

3. The specter of CPS is a recurring theme in contemporary scholarship analyzing in-depth fieldwork with marginalized mothers even as this research does not focus specifically on CPS, suggesting that my findings are not anomalous (Bell 2016; Elliott and Bowen 2018; Elliott and Reid 2019; Fernández-Kelly 2015; Gurusami 2019; Lareau 2011; Paik 2021; Randles 2021).

4. Roberts 2002.

5. This echoes prior research (Edin and Kefalas 2005).

6. Collins 1987; Edin and Lein 1997; Elliott and Aseltine 2013; Verduzco-Baker 2017.

7. Collins and Mayer 2010; Edin and Lein 1997; Edin and Shaefer 2015.

8. Randles 2021.

9. Desmond 2015:3.

10. Annette Lareau notes that "the idea that authorities would 'come and take my kids away'" never came up in her fieldwork with middle-class parents, whose demeanor regarding CPS was breezy and joking. Meanwhile, CPS concerns "repeatedly appeared among working-class and poor parents" (2011:231).

11. Collins 1994.

12. Others said that they didn't know or couldn't guess, sometimes adding comments like "It could be any [amount]" and "It's probably common."

13. Collins 2000.

14. Elliott and Reid 2019.

15. Although I interviewed low-income mothers, perceptions of CPS vulnerability may also extend to middle- and upper-class Black mothers, who may have social networks with CPS experience and recognize that their class status cannot protect them from racism.

16. Bell 2016, 2017; Roberts 2008.

17. JBS International 2011.

18. Prowse et al. 2020.

19. Fong 2022.

20. Declining to mention these strategies does not imply their absence, as a few mothers were reluctant to discuss CPS in the interview.

21. Goffman 2009; Rodríguez and Hagan 2004; Stuart 2016.

22. Fernández-Kelly 2015.

23. Waters and Sykes 2009:85.

24. Domínguez and Watkins 2003; Edin and Lein 1997; Thompson 2015.

25. Fingerman 2009; Granovetter 1973.

26. Collins 1987; Stack 1974.

27. Domínguez and Watkins 2003; Levine 2013.

28. Alex, a White mother in recovery in Connecticut, said that she'd looked into going to Canada or out of state to have her baby. She ultimately gave birth in Connecticut, though not enthusiastically: "When my water broke, I really didn't have a choice." When Alex had a second baby a year later, after using medical marijuana during her pregnancy, she chose a different hospital. I asked how she ended up there: "Someone told me that they really didn't care about THC."

29. Goffman 2009:355.

30. Elliott and Aseltine 2013; Verduzco-Baker 2017.

31. For marginalized mothers, moreover, efforts to provide for their children often go hand in hand with efforts to protect their motherhood (Elliott and Bowen 2018; Randles 2021).

Chapter 2

1. Connecticut Department of Children and Families 2021.

2. Child Welfare Information Gateway 2019a.

3. Palmer 2022; see also Palmer et al. 2022.

4. Gray 2011.

5. Finkelhor et al. 2019; Gershoff and Grogan-Kaylor 2016.

6. Petruccelli et al. 2019.

7. Moreover, allegations of mothers sexually abusing their children are extremely rare.

8. HHS 2021a; Kim et al. 2017.

9. Gilbert et al. 2009.

10. HHS 2021a.

11. See also Roberts, Zaugg, and Martinez 2022.

12. Maynard-Moody and Musheno 2000, 2003; Oberweis and Musheno 1999. Celeste Watkins-Hayes (2009), too, finds that many welfare caseworkers adopt a "social work" professional identity even as their job requirements have shifted to focus on determining client eligibility.

13. When children are severely harmed, reporting professionals would likely see removal as necessary, though such instances are a small minority.

14. Lipsky 2010[1980]:xii.

15. Lipsky (2010[1980]:132) briefly mentions that street-level bureaucrats can refer clients to other agencies; more recently, Armando Lara-Millán (2021) and Josh Seim (2020) document how people are "redistributed" or "shuffled" across medical and criminal legal agencies.

16. This framing suffuses scholarship on mandated reporting as well. Conceptualizing unreported maltreatment despite legal mandates as the problem or puzzle, research has focused accordingly on understanding why mandated reporters do *not* always report maltreatment, with little attention to why mandated reporters *do* decide to call in the situations they report.

17. See, e.g., Wexler 2019.

18. Connecticut General Statutes, Chapter 319a, Section 17a-101a.

19. Child Welfare Information Gateway 2019b.

20. Burian 2018.

21. Kovner 2018.

22. Roberts 2002:6.

23. HHS 2015; Kim et al. 2017.

24. HHS 2021a; Putnam-Hornstein and Needell 2011.

25. Feagin and Bennefield 2014; Kohli, Pizarro, and Nevárez 2017.

26. Research using experimentally manipulated vignettes yields mixed results (Ards et al. 2012; Laskey et al. 2012; Rojas et al. 2017; Stokes and Schmidt 2011). Fundamentally, though, this counterfactual causal model is a flawed approach to detecting racial discrimination, as the focus on manipulating subjects' racial statuses at a key decision-making moment "misrepresents what race is and how it produces effects in the world" (Kohler-Hausmann 2019:1169).

27. As in Emma's comments, reporting professionals' and CPS staff's concerns about bias often framed the problem as one of privileged children not receiving sufficient protection from the state. In this perspective, to address racial disproportionality, professionals should view White families the same way they view families of color: with a dose of skepticism.

28. Starck et al. 2020.

29. Connecticut State Department of Education 2020. As some of this chapter's examples indicate, though, professionals of color also report to CPS and, in my study, expressed ideas about reporting similar to the ideas of White reporting professionals I interviewed.

30. Roberts 2002.

31. Child Trends 2015.

32. Thomas and Dettlaff 2011.

33. Collins 2000:75.

34. Edwards 2019:65.

35. Roberts et al. 2022.

36. Connecticut State Department of Education 2020.

37. Bridges 2017.

38. Reporting organizations may also fear the power privileged parents can wield if they feel they are reported unjustly.

39. Ray 2019:35.

40. Brant 2021.

41. Even among mothers who alerted CPS themselves, we can imagine alternatives—housing and substance use treatment Colleen could access free from concerns about punishment or a world without child removal fears for Vanessa—where these same situations might not have become CPS reports.

42. Ho and Fassett 2021.

Chapter 3

1. HHS 2021a.

2. Nevertheless, unlike police investigations, CPS investigations have largely "escaped meaningful scrutiny" from courts interpreting constitutional protections, such as the Fourth Amendment protection from unreasonable home searches (Ismail 2022:63).

3. Ball and Webster 2003; Lyon 2003.

4. Seim 2020.

5. In the first half of 2018, New Haven CPS staff filed for custody in about twenty cases not already monitored by CPS's ongoing services division—fewer than one per investigator, on average. CPS removed children during the investigation in only two of the thirty-seven focal cases in the research study—Alex's and Charlene's, discussed in chapter 6—comparable to national rates (HHS 2021a).

6. Even Annie, the trainer who encouraged mandated reporters to follow their reporting instincts in chapter 2, recognized how expansive reporting had become. Checking her email during the break of another training, for CPS staff, she mentioned a new message about a change to the failure to report policy. "Hope it doesn't say, 'Report everything,'" an attendee replied. Annie laughed. "That's what we have already, right?"

7. HHS 2021a. Connecticut hotline workers complete a questionnaire to inform decisions about screening and CPS response time, but these tools do not replace individual discretion, especially in states like Connecticut where they only loosely guide decision-making (Bosk 2020).

8. Child Welfare Information Gateway 2017; DePanfilis 2018.

9. Tchelidze and Galvin 2018.

10. This information-sharing goes both ways. For example, after a mother's boyfriend agreed that CPS could contact his probation officer, an investigator named Kerri called to ask a couple questions, such as whether the probation officer felt that the boyfriend was okay around a four-year-old. Kerri then spontaneously shared that the family was staying at a certain motel right off the highway. (She noted later that the boyfriend had asked her not to tell probation he was at the motel, as he wanted to share this information himself.) Again without prompting, Kerri shared the room number, too—"in case you need it."

11. Such practices mirror welfare fraud investigators' surreptitious Facebook searches (Headworth 2019).

12. Fears of increased visibility to state systems of social control—as we see, perhaps well-founded fears—may ultimately depress political participation (Lerman and Weaver 2014).

13. Tchelidze and Galvin 2018.

14. Thus, I refer to family assessments and investigations collectively as "investigations," unless otherwise specified. Though the paperwork differs slightly and family assessment cases in Connecticut are eligible for an additional service referral, family assessments look much like investigations in practice, consistent with other research (Waldfogel 2008).

15. Kohl, Jonson-Reid, and Drake 2009.

16. Indeed, highly publicized fatalities and near fatalities profoundly shape child welfare policy and practice (Chenot 2011; Gainsborough 2010; Jagannathan and Camasso 2017).

17. Rhode Island Office of the Child Advocate 2017b:18; see also Bogdan and Mooney 2017a.

18. Rhode Island Office of the Child Advocate 2017a.

19. An investigator, Joe, became quite animated as he vented his frustrations with his manager's instructions. He pushed back: "'Cause if that baby dies, it's on me." I suggested he could document that the directive came from the manager. Joe shrugged. "The commissioner does not give a shit. She doesn't. She's fired people for less, you know?"

20. Considerable research documents the stress and burnout experienced by frontline CPS workers, contributing to high turnover (e.g., Schelbe, Radey, and Panisch 2017). Jennifer Reich (2005) also details the risks and stressors CPS workers attribute to their jobs.

21. Tchelidze and Galvin 2018.

22. As policy states, "If the parents refuse entry into the home and there is reasonable cause to suspect that the child is at imminent risk of harm, the [investigator] shall contact the police and request assistance." CPS offices had close relationships with local police departments, working collaboratively with police on some cases.

23. Reich 2005.

24. Ismail 2022. Moreover, even in Connecticut, I frequently observed investigators provide the brochure *after* gaining entry and interviewing the parent.

25. In Deborah's case, for instance, Sarah, the investigator, repeatedly pressed Deborah to get a drug test, even telling her, according to Sarah's notes, that CPS "make[s] decisions based upon available information" and "[Sarah] will not go away until mother provides a drug screen." Deborah did not get a drug test by the end of the investigation; perhaps reflecting Deborah's privilege as a White woman, the case still closed.

26. Kohler-Hausmann 2013.

27. CPS investigations epitomize the surveillance of domestic space that marginalized families experience more broadly, such as in subsidized housing (Gurusami and Kurwa 2021; Hughes 2020).

28. Khiara Bridges (2017) likewise details poor mothers' nonexistent rights to privacy in public assistance.

29. Lyon 2003.

Chapter 4

1. Rose 2000:332. More broadly, CPS's focus on risk reflects a contemporary "risk society" organized around reducing and managing risks as a means of controlling danger and assigning blame (Beck 1992; Douglas 1992; Ericson and Haggerty 1997).

2. Parton 1998.

3. DePanfilis 2018:64.

4. Here, I refer to questionnaires completed by caseworkers, rather than predictive analytics drawing on "big data" (Eubanks 2018).

5. Connecticut is a "loose state" (Bosk 2020), adopting formal decision-making instruments largely ceremonially.

6. Reporting professionals, deciding whether to report, also took a holistic approach. For instance, a primary care pediatric social worker explained that to assess whether mothers' marijuana use impacted children, "you need to look at everything else," such as domestic violence, children's school attendance, and children's health. "There is not a list of ten things . . . [to] call CPS on," she added.

7. Kelly Hannah-Moffat (2005) notes the penal system's blurring of risk and need, as authorities strategically align risks with needs to envision a "transformative risk subject," governable through hybrid management of these risks and needs.

8. Like risk assessments used to determine pretrial release of criminal defendants, CPS's formal risk instruments do not explicitly include race. Yet, in transforming "extreme structural racial inequalities . . . into risk classifications" (Hirschman and Bosk 2020:360), they naturalize racially unequal outcomes. "Risk factors" are not always distributed unequally by race, gender, or class; for instance, CPS is highly attuned to child age when assessing risk, taking heightened precautions with younger children and especially infants.

9. This bias also affects research on risk factors themselves, because child maltreatment, the outcome of interest, is often operationalized using CPS investigations or substantiations.

10. Brayne 2017:997.

11. Berger and Waldfogel 2011; Thompson 2015.

12. Crenshaw 1991:1245.

13. Still, investigators did not necessarily ignore home conditions in evaluating risk. One case involved a mother, Zanobia, struggling to manage her son's psychiatric needs and behavioral outbursts. Boxes and piles of clothes filled her kitchen. "It is unkempt," the investigator summarized afterward. "Do we have a problem with the house? Not really. I don't care. My main problem is that this is an indicator of what's going on," he added, alluding to Zanobia's mental health.

14. Henry et al. 2020; Hepburn, Louis, and Desmond 2020; Mundra and Sharma 2015.

15. Likely due to reporting processes described in chapter 2, I did not observe CPS investigating a well-off family following domestic violence. One case involved a multiracial (Black and White) mother, Louise, who owned a home with her common-law husband, a White ironworker bringing in about $2,400 monthly. When a protective order required Louise's husband to leave the home, he stayed with his parents for months while CPS monitored the case.

16. Research on the effects of marijuana use during pregnancy is inconclusive (Ryan, Ammerman, and O'Connor 2018). Nevertheless, the hospital social worker who reported Sherea agreed with the hospital policy of reporting when third-trimester toxicology screens came up positive, to "err on the side of caution." And she added, "If you don't have the ability to stop [using], or if you just choose to not stop . . . somebody has to look, like, what's your problem?"

17. Desmond 2012; Levine 2013.

18. In interviews, for example, mothers recalled acrimonious arguments they'd had over things such as using a household member's food stamps. For low-income mothers, the necessity of these resources for survival meant that arguments escalated, with one person kicking another out of the household or calling CPS—acts that made relationships difficult to repair.

19. As Jennifer Reich (2005) finds, the idea that mothers occupy a singular role in children's lives also grants mothers some privileges; after child removal, fathers struggle to get CPS and courts to see them as candidates for reunification.

20. Connections to women with significant needs can add obstacles to fathers' cases as well, as I observed in at least one case. But the gendered organization of caregiving means that CPS's focus on risk in relationships primarily affects mothers and their partnerships. Jennifer Reich (2005) describes how CPS pressures mothers who have lost custody of children to abstain from intimate relationships to focus on self-improvement.

21. During the investigation, when Gina shared her frustrations with the interpersonal conflicts she felt had initiated the report, her investigator, Vance, told her to take her attention away

from Nathan and that drama to "focus on here." Nathan was not her children's biological father, Vance noted. "I want you to focus on the kids," he emphasized.

22. Hays 1996.

23. Collins 1987; Gurusami 2019.

24. Gurusami 2019; Sweet 2021.

25. Chatters, Taylor, and Jayakody 1994; Collins 1994.

26. In deciding whether to substantiate allegations, CPS, following statutory definitions of maltreatment, also weighs "impact"—whether parents' actions (or lack thereof) have affected children.

27. These responses may stand at odds with mothers' positive parenting identities, such that what seems to CPS like mothers minimizing concerns may instead reflect mothers asserting their good motherhood (Sykes 2011).

28. The police officer, too, attributed his decision to arrest and charge Erica to the lack of insight he perceived, saying that Erica "shrugged like it was no big deal. That was the problem. . . . Your lack of concern just shows your overall attitude towards the situation and shows your credibility or lack of credibility as someone who is responsible in taking care of a child."

29. Heather drew on other factors in her assessment, too: "She's got her kids in day care, you know, five days a week. She's working, even if it's only part-time. She's got all these items for the kids. She just didn't give me the impression that she was somebody that just lost her kid." Makayla had limited financial means, like nearly all the parents Heather visited, but her self-presentation and stability reassured Heather.

30. Reich 2005; see also Lee 2016.

31. Notably, Jennifer's work in human services, with an annual salary of $65,000, likely granted her more resources, knowledge, and power in the investigation than many other CPS-investigated parents.

32. Louise, for example, told her investigator, Tammi, that after the domestic violence incident that precipitated her CPS call, "that's it"—she was done with her husband. Right away, I saw Tammi write in her notes that she "could tell" Louise was not done. When I met Louise the next day, she told me through tears, "I want him here [with me]." In the following months, Louise repeatedly took steps to be with her husband.

33. In Connecticut, during my fieldwork, the racial composition of children with investigations opened for ongoing CPS oversight (36.8 percent White, 33.5 percent Hispanic/Latino, 20.5 percent Black) roughly matched the racial composition of children reported to CPS (36.4 percent White, 32.7 percent Hispanic/Latino, 20.6 percent Black) (author's calculations from Connecticut Department of Children and Families 2019:42). So the risk assessments described here may not substantially increase racial disproportionality, but at the very least they maintain it.

34. Investigators' class and race often differ from those of the people they investigate. Although I did not see markedly different approaches to investigating based on investigators' racial/ethnic identities, our interviews did not focus on their personal background or professional identities. Prior research finds that street-level bureaucrats' racial identities shape how they approach their work (Watkins-Hayes 2009).

35. Eubanks 2018.

Chapter 5

1. Thus, seeing CPS as unilaterally helpful or harmful is an oversimplification. Leslie Paik (2021) and Paige Sweet (2021) capture these shades of gray in adjacent contexts, showing how marginalized women find the systems in their lives simultaneously affirming and stifling.

2. This aligns with Drake and Jonson-Reid (2007), citing research finding that 70 percent of investigated clients surveyed in Washington State felt that their CPS caseworker was there to help them.

3. Polsky 1991. See also McKim 2017; Sweet 2021.

4. Gilens 1999.

5. This institutionalizes a "discourse of desire" (Haney 2010:14), focused on regulating marginalized women's psyches.

6. Affluent parents seeking therapy can evaluate providers and choose the one they feel will best support them. CPS-referred parents don't necessarily have this luxury; rather than selecting a therapist, they are typically assigned one.

7. Levine 2013; Paik 2021.

8. States have different policies on the retention of records; Connecticut expunges unsubstantiated investigations after five years if no additional reports come in.

9. States vary in which cases they place on these registries and for how long (Henry and Lens 2021).

10. Levine 2013.

11. On the other hand, long-standing relationships occasionally led mothers to see reporting professionals' intentions as supportive. Sabrina, for instance, felt that the hospital reported her housing conditions "sincerely out of concern." Sabrina's time as a cancer patient had shown her how her doctor genuinely cared for her well-being: "She has always made me feel like . . . I'm not just another patient."

12. Wilson and Prior 2011.

13. Edin and Kefalas 2005.

Chapter 6

1. Rhode Island (but not Connecticut) is one of several states where doctors have this authority.

2. Later, CPS portrayed Christina's invocation of racism among the police as evidence of her lack of insight: "Mother minimized the incident and feels the [City] Police are racist and arrested her just because she is black," the caseworker wrote.

3. Other removals are more protracted. For instance, Gina's investigator kept her case open for ongoing CPS oversight, citing Gina's unaddressed mental health needs and substance use. CPS visited regularly, finding the home in various states of disarray and, at least once, Gina intoxicated while caring for her toddler sons. CPS had devised "safety plans," whereby the boys stayed informally with a relative for a couple days, and other agreements directing Gina's behavior. Gina felt anxious, at the mercy of CPS, and worried that CPS could forcibly remove them at any time. "I can't go anywhere. I can't do anything," she said, describing the uncertainty. "They're all saying that they're trying not to remove my kids from the home. However, the way

that I am seeing it is, they're always trying to remove my kids from the home. Without good reason." After seventeen months of this, CPS took Gina's children into foster care, citing "the ongoing pattern of neglect . . . and the deplorable nature of the home again."

4. HHS 2020a.

5. Folman 1998.

6. Muentner et al. 2021.

7. Kenny, Barrington, and Green 2015.

8. Thumath et al. 2021.

9. Spelling is reproduced from Christina's writing.

10. Later, LeAnn told me she thought that Charlene needed substance use and parenting support services. I asked whether the baby would be unsafe at home with these services in place. LeAnn's response highlighted the impulse to remove and the paternalism inherent in these decisions: "I don't know if the mother could actually really focus on that. . . . She needs to really stabilize herself to really be able to focus on this child."

11. Connecticut Department of Children and Families 2019:23. These "considered removal" meetings are a form of family group conferencing, a model introduced by the Maori in New Zealand and widely used in U.S. child welfare today.

12. I observed these meetings in just one office. Sometimes, it seemed that the agency convened the meeting as a threat—intending not necessarily to remove but to impart the seriousness of the situation to parents. In other cases, such as Charlene's, CPS anticipated removing the children barring revelatory new information and sought parents' input regarding relatives or others who might care for the children.

13. Garfinkel 1956; see also Gonzalez Van Cleve 2016.

14. David Tobis notes that including parent advocates in such meetings often makes a difference, allowing "a genuine exploration of alternatives" (2013:182) to removal.

15. Lerman and Weaver 2014; Michener 2018; Shedd 2015.

16. Soss and Weaver 2017.

17. See Reich 2005 and Lee 2016 on how reunification hinges on parents' compliance.

18. Of the twenty-eight Rhode Island participants who recounted CPS removing at least one child, two unequivocally described CPS and their CPS caseworkers as allied with them; two others had little to say on the topic. Eight articulated mixed experiences (e.g., different perspectives on different caseworkers). But even recognizing "good" caseworkers didn't imply that mothers saw the system on their side. As Barbara put it, "She's a good worker, but she still works for the state, and she still has control of my kids and can take them away [permanently] as easy as 1, 2, 3."

19. Darcey Merritt (2020), drawing on interviews with New York City mothers receiving services contracted by CPS, likewise describes how mothers feel judged and shamed in their interactions with CPS.

20. Sweet 2021.

21. Bianca told me that she didn't know much English when CPS removed her children five years prior, but she didn't receive an interpreter. Parents like Bianca face considerable challenges in their child welfare cases due to the system's limited linguistic competencies (Earner 2007) and court officials' stereotypes of "Spanish speakers" as deficient (López-Espino 2021).

22. As Leslie Paik (2021) illustrates, poor parents navigating multiple institutional entanglements are "trapped in a maze," with different systems often imposing conflicting demands.

23. Rhode Island and Connecticut provide indigent parents with legal representation; in several other states, parents in child protection cases do not have this right to counsel (Sankaran 2017).

24. Legal aid attorneys and caseworkers see one another at court often. With these repeat encounters, legal aid attorneys not only may enjoy socializing with caseworkers but may see getting along with caseworkers as advantageous for their defense, as Gonzalez Van Cleve (2016) suggests in the criminal court context.

25. Clair 2020. Nevertheless, the notion of family court as collaborative and rehabilitative grants parents fewer constitutional protections than in criminal court and pressures them not to assert the rights they do have (Arons 2022a).

26. These dynamics echo those in other courts that intervene coercively with predominantly marginalized people, such as criminal and child support courts (Battle 2019; Clair 2020; Gonzalez Van Cleve 2016).

27. Scott 1985.

28. *Drury v. Lang* 1989.

29. This initial hesitance can be overcome; Tobis (2013) and Rise (2022) chronicle successful mobilization by impacted parents in New York City.

30. Russell Sage Foundation 2023.

31. Kalleberg 2009:15.

32. JMacForFamilies 2023; Tobis 2013.

Conclusion

1. "When other systems designed to help poor families have failed, often all that remains is foster care," writes Catherine Rymph (2017:5).

2. Watkins-Hayes 2009:190.

3. We would likely say the same about many privileged children as well. Affluent youth report high levels of substance use, anxiety, and depression, attributed to family and community dynamics (Luthar and Latendresse 2005), yet rarely come to CPS's attention.

4. This concern extended beyond fears of legal liability. At a training, Annie, the trainer from chapters 2 and 3, recounted in detail a domestic violence case she'd investigated. Several months after Annie closed the case, the husband shot and killed his wife and then himself. Years later, it haunted her. "I think about that case every August, because it happened in August," Annie said, shaken. As the report was a "family assessment" rather than a full investigation, the trainers used Annie's case to convey the importance of taking these supposedly lower-risk reports seriously.

5. As Paige Sweet (2021:16) writes, women often engage with social service bureaucracies both authentically *and* strategically—it isn't an either/or distinction.

6. Lara-Millán 2021.

7. Elliott and Bowen 2018; Gurusami 2019; Randles 2021.

8. Roberts 2002.

9. Gonzalez Van Cleve 2016; Lewis and Diamond 2015.

10. Victor Ray writes, "In isolation, individual prejudice and racial animus may matter little [for the persistence of racial inequality], but when these are put into practices in connection to

organizational processes"—such as those funneling families to and through CPS—"they help shape the larger racial order" (2019:27).

11. See Bridges 2020 for a related discussion of how criminalizing (primarily Black) women during the crack cocaine epidemic created a precedent to criminalize (many White) women during the opioid epidemic.

12. Waldfogel 1998.

13. Dalton 2020.

14. Jane Waldfogel summarizes a national study on differential response: "In many jurisdictions, the same workers carried out both assessments and investigations, and some reported that many of their activities were similar regardless of the track" (2008:238). As chapter 3 described, Connecticut cases tracked as lower-risk received a substantively similar response, from the same staff.

15. Cohen 1985.

16. Bouek in press; New York City Housing Authority 2022.

17. A former CPS administrator in Connecticut, Allon Kalisher, highlighted this vicious cycle in "higher-risk" cases as well, writing to me: "There are families in need of a lot more help than is readily available to them, and the design relies too much on CPS as the entity to coordinate solutions for the most challenging situations. That design incentivizes CPS to figure out better ways to support families, reinforcing and motivating partners to lean on CPS."

18. Moreover, families become eligible for Family First services when CPS deems children at imminent risk of removal and establishes these services as necessary to prevent family separation. What happens, then, when parents decide that they no longer want to participate in services or when they cannot manage all the appointments? Despite its goals of family preservation, Family First may end up pushing families more deeply into the system.

19. For instance, when Rhode Island CPS identified key challenges in 2015, all focused on placements and permanency; none addressed intake. Connecticut CPS, transitioning to a new commissioner in 2019, identified seven key outcomes for its operations division, such as prioritizing kinship care, reducing congregate care, and ensuring timely permanency. Here, too, the agency included nothing on intake.

20. JMacForFamilies 2023.

21. Redleaf 2022.

22. Of course, this invites the "net-widening" possibility of prospective callers using the CPS hotline as a general referral hotline. As discussed in the following section, shifting to a general support hotline separate from CPS could address these concerns.

23. Rhode Island Office of the Child Advocate 2017a:14.

24. Carter, Church, and Sankaran 2022.

25. Webster 2019.

26. Wexler 2018.

27. Katz 2019:30–31.

28. Carter et al. 2022; Wexler 2018.

29. Webster 2019.

30. HHS 2022.

31. Sege and Stephens 2022.

32. Arons 2022b:5.

33. Hager 2020.

34. Bogdan and Mooney 2017b.

35. Cloud 2019.

36. Sharkey, Torrats-Espinosa, and Takyar 2017.

37. Berger et al. 2017; Cancian, Yang, and Slack 2013; Raissian and Bullinger 2017; Yang et al. 2019.

38. It is also reproductive justice work, which includes as a central tenet "the right to parent children in safe and healthy environments" (Ross and Solinger 2017:9).

39. I thank Casey Stockstill for raising this point.

40. Thorne 2020.

41. I sat in on meetings where Rhode Island and Connecticut administrators discussed strategies to educate parents about safe infant sleep practices, identified as an urgent public health concern. Meanwhile, I was interviewing mothers who felt badgered by safe sleep advice. Roxanne resented home visitors: "They always start with, 'You know, the baby can't sleep with you.'" Paulina recalled her CPS investigator telling her that co-sleeping was "illegal. . . . I could get in trouble." This provoked a defensive response: "I feel like you shouldn't tell me what I can and can't do in my home. . . . I'm not a heavy sleeper anyway. I definitely don't move a lot." Vanessa said that her visiting nurse told her how she and the baby were "supposed to" sleep. Vanessa didn't tell the visiting nurse about not following this guidance, because she expected admonishment: "If I was to tell her that she actually does sleep with me on the bed . . . she'd just be like, 'Oh, you know, she's not supposed to,' and blah blah blah." Although it may aim to be affirming, much of the parenting information marginalized mothers get feels accusatory, as though they're doing something wrong. As chapter 1 described, criticism of their parenting stings.

42. WestRasmus et al. 2012.

43. Rise 2021:5.

44. National Center on Substance Abuse and Child Welfare 2018; Rise 2021.

45. Rise 2020.

46. Beck, Reuland, and Pope 2020.

47. Stuart and Beckett 2021.

48. Wald 2022.

49. Harvey, Gupta-Kagan, and Church 2021; JMacForFamilies 2023.

50. From the U.S. perspective, Scandinavia's robust welfare state and the orientation of child welfare systems around "family support" may seem like a panacea. Yet these supports alone are insufficient; in contexts of racism, nativism, and marginalization, groups vulnerable to child removal recount fears—and reactions to those fears—akin to what I heard in the United States (Handulle 2021).

Methodological Appendix

1. This time away also resulted from nearly a year waiting for the Institutional Review Board to approve follow-up interviews covering the same topics as the initial interviews.

2. For demographic information on Rhode Island participants, see Fong 2019a.

3. Following Cayce Hughes, who reflected on how interviewing poor mothers "unwittingly recreat[es] precisely the dynamic of coercive information solicitation that mothers lamented

in the welfare context" (2018:116), I sought to respect participants' privacy, creating openings for discussion but not pressing them to disclose more than they wanted.

4. In part for this reason, I did not do life history interviews in Connecticut and thus did not discuss participants' childhood experiences unless participants raised them.

5. Gonzalez Van Cleve 2016:xv.

6. Sarah Brayne (2020) similarly wrote about gaining access to the Los Angeles Police Department from the top down.

7. They may be correct (Khan 2019).

8. Naming the sites allows me to provide important context, though it means that I share only limited information about individual investigators, who were part of a relatively small group in these two offices during the study period. See Jerolmack and Murphy (2019), advocating for ethnographers not to mask their sites by default.

9. Small 2009.

10. The initial research proposal limited the study to English-speaking families, but DCF felt strongly that Spanish-speaking families should be included.

11. Periods around my fieldwork in each office were busy; I told staff I must be good luck. When I reminded an investigator, Joe, about this the following year, he remarked that the summer I observed was "the greatest summer of [his] life." This made data collection more challenging, as I had fewer case shadowing opportunities, though had investigators been more overburdened, it might have been more difficult for them to accommodate the research.

12. For more details on the characteristics of cases included in the study compared with eligible cases, see Fong 2020. In two cases observed, mothers declined to participate, and in one more, I learned during the visit that the case was ineligible.

13. HHS 2021a.

14. Four of these additional professionals reported a case selected for but ultimately not part of the study, due to my inability to observe a visit or a mother declining to include her case in the research.

15. I understand Spanish and generally listened to mothers' responses without interpreter assistance, but I wanted an interpreter present to ensure that mothers clearly understood study procedures and interview questions. These interviews were translated into English during transcription.

16. I requested this oral consent from all parents I visited, even those not part of the focal cases. I did not solicit written consent up front; CPS typically asks parents to sign a stack of paperwork during the visit, so asking for a signature right away could have affected parents' inclination to sign CPS's documents, in a sort of "signature fatigue." Moreover, parents are often eager to hear about the allegations when CPS arrives and so might not be able to give the consent process their full attention.

17. As such, this book adjusts a few minor details, such as parents' exact workplaces.

18. In both states, negotiating access to these records—even as mothers are entitled to this information and had signed releases allowing me access—was an ordeal. The process in each state involved about two years of pestering agency administrators and going back and forth with lawyers. In the end, Rhode Island allowed me access to the records on the computer system rather than providing me with participants' files, so I spent two weeks full-time in a cubicle taking notes.

19. Still, especially at the start, investigators sometimes made lighthearted comments about my evaluating them. When going over audio-recording during the consent process, Heather quipped—jokingly but also as though she was actually wondering—"[Manager]'s not gonna hear it, right?"

20. Desmond 2014:569.

21. Investigators often became frustrated when parents went on at length about tangentially related topics, sometimes rolling their eyes if they were on the phone or apologizing to me afterward. Even when CPS asks open-ended questions, it has a different goal. As training documents explained, "What makes it an interview versus a conversation is that the purpose of it and direction is to develop the case plan [and] assess for safety, permanency and well-being."

REFERENCES

Ards, Sheila D., Samuel L. Myers, Patricia Ray, Hyeon-Eui Kim, Kevin Monroe, and Irma Arteaga. 2012. "Racialized Perceptions and Child Neglect." *Children and Youth Services Review* 34(8):1480–91.

Arons, Anna. 2022a. "The Empty Promise of the Fourth Amendment in the Family Regulation System." Available at SSRN (https://ssrn.com/abstract=4192039).

Arons, Anna. 2022b. "An Unintended Abolition: Family Regulation During the COVID-19 Crisis." *Columbia Journal of Race and Law* 12(1):1–28.

Bach, Wendy A. 2022. *Prosecuting Poverty, Criminalizing Care.* Cambridge, UK: Cambridge University Press.

Ball, Kirstie, and Frank Webster, eds. 2003. *The Intensification of Surveillance: Crime, Terrorism and Warfare in the Information Age.* London: Pluto Press.

Battle, Brittany Pearl. 2019. "'They Look at You Like You're Nothing': Stigma and Shame in the Child Support System." *Symbolic Interaction* 42(4):640–68.

Beck, Jackson, Melissa Reuland, and Leah Pope. 2020. "Case Study: CAHOOTS." Vera Institute of Justice. Retrieved January 30, 2023 (https://www.vera.org/behavioral-health-crisis -alternatives/cahoots).

Beck, Ulrich. 1992. *Risk Society: Towards a New Modernity.* London: Sage.

Bell, Alison, and Douglas Rice. 2018. "Congress Prioritizes Housing Programs in 2018 Funding Bill, Rejects Trump Administration Proposals." Center on Budget and Policy Priorities. Retrieved January 30, 2023 (https://www.cbpp.org/research/housing/congress-prioritizes -housing-programs-in-2018-funding-bill-rejects-trump).

Bell, Monica C. 2016. "Situational Trust: How Disadvantaged Mothers Reconceive Legal Cynicism." *Law and Society Review* 50(2):314–47.

Bell, Monica C. 2017. "Police Reform and the Dismantling of Legal Estrangement." *The Yale Law Journal* 126(7):2054–2150.

Berger, Lawrence M., Sarah A. Font, Kristen S. Slack, and Jane Waldfogel. 2017. "Income and Child Maltreatment in Unmarried Families: Evidence from the Earned Income Tax Credit." *Review of Economics of the Household* 15(4):1345–72.

Berger, Lawrence M., and Jane Waldfogel. 2011. "Economic Determinants and Consequences of Child Maltreatment." OECD Social, Employment and Migration Working Papers, No. 111. Paris: OECD Publishing.

Bilson, Andy, and Katie E. C. Martin. 2017. "Referrals and Child Protection in England." *British Journal of Social Work* 47:793–811.

Bogdan, Jennifer, and Tom Mooney. 2017a. "'Baby Tobi' Dies After Months on Life Support." *Providence Journal*, November 30.

Bogdan, Jennifer, and Tom Mooney. 2017b. "Children at Risk: DCYF Boosts Frontline Staffing, but Budget Woes Persist." *Providence Journal*, December 30.

Bonnet, François. 2019. *The Upper Limit: How Low-Wage Work Defines Punishment and Welfare.* Oakland: University of California Press.

Bosk, Emily A. 2020. "Iron Cage or Paper Cage? The Interplay of Worker Characteristics and Organizational Policy in Shaping Unequal Responses to a Standardized Decision-Making Tool." *Social Problems* 67(4):654–76.

Bouek, Jennifer. In press. "The Waitlist as Redistributive Policy: Access and Burdens in the Subsidized Childcare System." *RSF: The Russell Sage Foundation Journal of the Social Sciences.*

Bourdieu, Pierre. 1998. *Acts of Resistance: Against the New Myths of Our Time.* New York: Polity Press.

Brant, Kristina. 2021. "In the Epicenter: Surveilling, Supporting, and Punishing Families amid the Rural Opioid Crisis and Beyond." Ph.D. dissertation, Department of Sociology, Harvard University.

Brayne, Sarah. 2014. "Surveillance and System Avoidance: Criminal Justice Contact and Institutional Attachment." *American Sociological Review* 79(3): 367–91.

Brayne, Sarah. 2017. "Big Data Surveillance: The Case of Policing." *American Sociological Review* 82(5):977–1008.

Brayne, Sarah. 2020. *Predict and Surveil: Data, Discretion, and the Future of Policing.* New York: Oxford University Press.

Bridges, Khiara M. 2017. *The Poverty of Privacy Rights.* Stanford, CA: Stanford University Press.

Bridges, Khiara M. 2020. "Race, Pregnancy, and the Opioid Epidemic: White Privilege and the Criminalization of Opioid Use During Pregnancy." *Harvard Law Review* 133(3):770–851.

Briggs, Laura. 2020. *Taking Children: A History of American Terror.* Oakland: University of California Press.

Burian, Heather. 2018. "Montville Administrators, Sub Linked to 'Fight Club' Case in Court." *NBC Connecticut*, September 25.

Cancian, Maria, Mi-Youn Yang, and Kristen Shook Slack. 2013. "The Effect of Additional Child Support Income on the Risk of Child Maltreatment." *Social Service Review* 87(3):417–37.

Carson, E. Ann. 2020. *Prisoners in 2019.* Washington, DC: Bureau of Justice Statistics.

Carter, Melissa, Christopher Church, and Vivek Sankaran. 2022. "A Quiet Revolution: How Judicial Discipline Essentially Eliminated Foster Care and Nearly Went Unnoticed." *Columbia Journal of Race and Law* 12(1):496–516.

Center on Budget and Policy Priorities. 2022. "Policy Basics: Temporary Assistance for Needy Families." Retrieved January 30, 2023 (https://www.cbpp.org/research/family-income-support/temporary-assistance-for-needy-families).

Chatters, Linda M., Robert Joseph Taylor, and Rukmalie Jayakody. 1994. "Fictive Kinship Relations in Black Extended Families." *Journal of Comparative Family Studies* 25(3):297–312.

Chenot, David. 2011. "The Vicious Cycle: Recurrent Interactions Among the Media, Politicians, the Public, and Child Welfare Services Organizations." *Journal of Public Child Welfare* 5(2–3):167–84.

Chiarello, Elizabeth. 2015. "The War on Drugs Comes to the Pharmacy Counter: Frontline Work in the Shadow of Discrepant Institutional Logics." *Law and Social Inquiry* 40(1):86–122.

Child Trends. 2015. "Attitudes Toward Spanking." Retrieved January 30, 2023 (https://www .childtrends.org/wp-content/uploads/2015/01/indicator_1420212520.5577.html).

Child Welfare Information Gateway. 2017. *Making and Screening Reports of Child Abuse and Neglect*. Washington, DC: U.S. Department of Health and Human Services.

Child Welfare Information Gateway. 2019a. *Definitions of Child Abuse and Neglect*. Washington, DC: U.S. Department of Health and Human Services.

Child Welfare Information Gateway. 2019b. *Immunity for Reporters of Child Abuse and Neglect*. Washington, DC: U.S. Department of Health and Human Services.

Children's Bureau. 2023. *CB Fact Sheet*. Retrieved January 30, 2023 (https://www.acf.hhs.gov/cb /comms-fact-sheet/childrens-bureau).

Clair, Matthew. 2020. *Privilege and Punishment: How Race and Class Matter in Criminal Court*. Princeton, NJ: Princeton University Press.

Cloud, Erin Miles. 2019. "Toward the Abolition of the Foster System." *S&F Online* 15(3) (https://sfonline.barnard.edu/toward-the-abolition-of-the-foster-system/).

Cohen, Stanley. 1985. *Visions of Social Control: Crime, Punishment, and Classification*. Cambridge, UK: Polity Press.

Collins, Jane L., and Victoria Mayer. 2010. *Both Hands Tied: Welfare Reform and the Race to the Bottom of the Low-Wage Labor Market*. Chicago: University of Chicago Press.

Collins, Patricia Hill. 1987. "The Meaning of Motherhood in Black Culture and Black Mother-Daughter Relationships." *Sage* 4(2):3–10.

Collins, Patricia Hill. 1994. "Shifting the Center: Race, Class, and Feminist Theorizing About Motherhood." Pp. 45–65 in *Mothering: Ideology, Experience, and Agency*, edited by E. N. Glenn, G. Chang, and L. R. Forcey. New York: Routledge.

Collins, Patricia Hill. 2000. *Black Feminist Thought: Knowledge, Consciousness and the Politics of Empowerment*, 2nd ed. New York: Routledge.

Congressional Research Service. 2023. "Child Welfare: Purposes, Federal Programs, and Funding." Retrieved January 30, 2023 (https://sgp.fas.org/crs/misc/IF10590.pdf).

Connecticut Department of Children and Families. 2019. *Child and Family Services Plan, 2020–2024*. Hartford, CT: Author.

Connecticut Department of Children and Families. 2021. "Operational Definitions of Child Abuse and Neglect." Retrieved January 30, 2023 (https://portal.ct.gov/-/media/DCF /Policy/Chapters/22-3-rev-2-1-2021.pdf).

Connecticut Department of Children and Families. 2023. "Mission of DCF." Retrieved January 30, 2023 (https://portal.ct.gov/DCF/1-DCF/Mission-Statement).

Connecticut General Statutes, Chapter 319a, Section 17a-101a.

Connecticut State Department of Education. 2020. "Educator Race/Ethnicity Trend Report." *EdSight*. Retrieved May 10, 2022 (http://edsight.ct.gov/).

Cooper, Marianne. 2014. *Cut Adrift: Families in Insecure Times*. Berkeley: University of California Press.

Crenshaw, Kimberle. 1991. "Mapping the Margins: Intersectionality, Identity Politics, and Violence Against Women of Color." *Stanford Law Review* 43(6):1241–99.

Dalton, Kristin F. 2020. "City Expanding CARES Program, Focusing on Family Support, Resources." *SILive*, October 23.

Davis, Dána-Ain. 2016. "'The Bone Collectors' Comments for Sorrow as Artifact: Black Radical Mothering in Times of Terror." *Transforming Anthropology* 24(1):8–16.

DePanfilis, Diane. 2018. *Child Protective Services: A Guide for Caseworkers*. Washington, DC: U.S. Department of Health and Human Services.

Desmond, Matthew. 2012. "Disposable Ties and the Urban Poor." *American Journal of Sociology* 117(5):1295–1335.

Desmond, Matthew. 2014. "Relational Ethnography." *Theory and Society* 43(5):547–79.

Desmond, Matthew. 2015. "Severe Deprivation in America: An Introduction." *RSF: The Russell Sage Foundation Journal of the Social Sciences* 1(1):1–11.

Dettlaff, Alan J., Reiko Boyd, Darcey Merritt, Jason Anthony Plummer, and James D. Simon. 2021. "Racial Bias, Poverty, and the Notion of Evidence." *Child Welfare* 99(3):61–89.

Dolan, Melissa, Keith Smith, Cecilia Casanueva, and Heather Ringeisen. 2011a. *NSCAW II Baseline Report: Caseworker Characteristics, Child Welfare Services, and Experiences of Children Placed in Out-of-Home Care*. Washington, DC: U.S. Department of Health and Human Services.

Dolan, Melissa, Keith Smith, Cecilia Casanueva, and Heather Ringeisen. 2011b. *NSCAW II Baseline Report: Introduction to NSCAW II*. Washington, DC: U.S. Department of Health and Human Services.

Domínguez, Silvia, and Celeste Watkins. 2003. "Creating Networks for Survival and Mobility: Social Capital Among African-American and Latin-American Low-Income Mothers." *Social Problems* 50(1):111–35.

Douglas, Mary. 1992. *Risk and Blame: Essays in Cultural Theory*. New York: Routledge.

Drake, Brett, and Melissa Jonson-Reid. 2007. "A Response to Melton Based on the Best Available Data." *Child Abuse and Neglect* 31(4):343–60.

Drury v. Lang, 776 P.2d 843 (1989).

Earner, Ilze. 2007. "Immigrant Families and Public Child Welfare: Barriers to Services and Approaches for Change." *Child Welfare* 86(4):63–91.

Edin, Kathryn, and Maria Kefalas. 2005. *Promises I Can Keep: Why Poor Women Put Motherhood Before Marriage*. Berkeley: University of California Press.

Edin, Kathryn, and Laura Lein. 1997. *Making Ends Meet: How Single Mothers Survive Welfare and Low-Wage Work*. New York: Russell Sage Foundation.

Edin, Kathryn, and H. Luke Shaefer. 2015. *$2.00 a Day: Living on Almost Nothing in America*. Boston: Houghton Mifflin Harcourt.

Edwards, Frank. 2016. "Saving Children, Controlling Families: Punishment, Redistribution, and Child Protection." *American Sociological Review* 81(3):575–95.

Edwards, Frank. 2019. "Family Surveillance: Police and the Reporting of Child Abuse and Neglect." *RSF: The Russell Sage Foundation Journal of the Social Sciences* 5(1):50–70.

Elliott, Sinikka, and Elyshia Aseltine. 2013. "Raising Teenagers in Hostile Environments: How Race, Class, and Gender Matter for Mothers' Protective Carework." *Journal of Family Issues* 34(6):719–44.

Elliott, Sinikka, and Sarah Bowen. 2018. "Defending Motherhood: Morality, Responsibility, and Double Binds in Feeding Children." *Journal of Marriage and Family* 80(2):499–520.

Elliott, Sinikka, and Megan Reid. 2019. "Low-Income Black Mothers Parenting Adolescents in the Mass Incarceration Era: The Long Reach of Criminalization." *American Sociological Review* 84(2):197–219.

Ericson, Richard V., and Kevin D. Haggerty. 1997. *Policing the Risk Society*. New York: Oxford University Press.

Eubanks, Virginia. 2018. *Automating Inequality: How High-Tech Tools Profile, Police, and Punish the Poor*. New York: St. Martin's Press.

Feagin, Joe, and Zinobia Bennefield. 2014. "Systemic Racism and U.S. Health Care." *Social Science and Medicine* 103:7–14.

Fernández-Kelly, Patricia. 2015. *The Hero's Fight: African Americans in West Baltimore and the Shadow of the State*. Princeton, NJ: Princeton University Press.

Fingerman, Karen L. 2009. "Consequential Strangers and Peripheral Ties: The Importance of Unimportant Relationships." *Journal of Family Theory and Review* 1(2):69–86.

Finkelhor, David, Heather Turner, Brittany Kaye Wormuth, Jennifer Vanderminden, and Sherry Hamby. 2019. "Corporal Punishment: Current Rates from a National Survey." *Journal of Child and Family Studies* 28:1991–97.

Flores, Jerry. 2016. *Caught Up: Girls, Surveillance, and Wraparound Incarceration*. Oakland: University of California Press.

Folman, Rosalind D. 1998. "'I Was Tooken': How Children Experience Removal from Their Parents Preliminary to Placement into Foster Care." *Adoption Quarterly* 2(2):7–35.

Fong, Kelley. 2019a. "Concealment and Constraint: Child Protective Services Fears and Poor Mothers' Institutional Engagement." *Social Forces* 97(4):1785–810.

Fong, Kelley. 2019b. "Neighborhood Inequality in the Prevalence of Reported and Substantiated Child Maltreatment." *Child Abuse and Neglect* 90:13–21.

Fong, Kelley. 2020. "Getting Eyes in the Home: Child Protective Services Investigations and State Surveillance of Family Life." *American Sociological Review* 85(4):610–38.

Fong, Kelley. 2022. "I Know How It Feels: Empathy and Reluctance to Mobilize Legal Authorities." *Social Problems*, Advance article (doi: 10.1093/socpro/spab079).

Gainsborough, Juliet. 2010. *Scandalous Politics: Child Welfare Policy in the States*. Washington, DC: Georgetown University Press.

Garfinkel, Harold. 1956. "Conditions of Successful Degradation Ceremonies." *American Journal of Sociology* 61(5):420–24.

Gershoff, Elizabeth T., and Andrew Grogan-Kaylor. 2016. "Spanking and Child Outcomes: Old Controversies and New Meta-analyses." *Journal of Family Psychology* 30(4):453–69.

Gilbert, Ruth, Cathy Spatz Widom, Kevin Browne, David Fergusson, Elspeth Webb, and Staffan Janson. 2009. "Burden and Consequences of Child Maltreatment in High-Income Countries." *The Lancet* 373(9657):68–81.

Gilens, Martin. 1999. *Why Americans Hate Welfare: Race, Media, and the Politics of Antipoverty Policy*. Chicago: University of Chicago Press.

Goffman, Alice. 2009. "On the Run: Wanted Men in a Philadelphia Ghetto." *American Sociological Review* 74(3):339–57.

Gonzalez Van Cleve, Nicole. 2016. *Crook County: Racism and Injustice in America's Largest Criminal Court*. Stanford, CA: Stanford University Press.

Gordon, Linda. 1985. "Child Abuse, Gender, and the Myth of Family Independence: A Historical Critique." *Child Welfare* 64(3):213–24.

Granovetter, Mark S. 1973. "The Strength of Weak Ties." *American Journal of Sociology* 78(6):1360–80.

Gray, Peter. 2011. "The Decline of Play and the Rise of Psychopathology in Children and Adolescents." *American Journal of Play* 3(4):443–63.

Griesbach, Kathleen. 2020. "Positional Uncertainty: Contingent Workers Seeking a Place in Unstable Times." Ph.D. dissertation, Department of Sociology, Columbia University.

Gurusami, Susila. 2019. "Motherwork Under the State: The Maternal Labor of Formerly Incarcerated Black Women." *Social Problems* 66(1):128–43.

Gurusami, Susila, and Rahim Kurwa. 2021. "From Broken Windows to Broken Homes: Homebreaking as Racialized and Gendered Poverty Governance." *Feminist Formations* 33(1):1–32.

Gustafson, Kaaryn S. 2011. *Cheating Welfare: Public Assistance and the Criminalization of Poverty.* New York: NYU Press.

Hager, Eli. 2020. "Is Child Abuse Really Rising During the Pandemic?" *The Marshall Project*, June 15.

Handulle, Ayan. 2021. "Beyond Fear of Child Welfare Services: An Ethnographic Study Among Norwegian-Somali Parents." Ph.D. dissertation, Department of Social Studies, University of Stavanger.

Haney, Lynne. 2004. "Introduction: Gender, Welfare, and States of Punishment." *Social Politics: International Studies in Gender, State and Society* 11(3):333–62.

Haney, Lynne. 2010. *Offending Women: Power, Punishment, and the Regulation of Desire.* Berkeley: University of California Press.

Hannah-Moffat, Kelly. 2005. "Criminogenic Needs and the Transformative Risk Subject: Hybridizations of Risk/Need in Penality." *Punishment and Society* 7(1):29–51.

Harvey, Brianna, Josh Gupta-Kagan, and Christopher Church. 2021. "Reimagining Schools' Role Outside the Family Regulation System." *Columbia Journal of Race and Law* 11(3):575–610.

Hays, Sharon. 1996. *The Cultural Contradictions of Motherhood.* New Haven, CT: Yale University Press.

Headworth, Spencer. 2019. "Getting to Know You: Welfare Fraud Investigation and the Appropriation of Social Ties." *American Sociological Review* 84(1):171–96.

Headworth, Spencer. 2021. *Policing Welfare: Punitive Adversarialism in Public Assistance.* Chicago: University of Chicago Press.

Henry, Colleen, and Vicki Lens. 2021. "Marginalizing Mothers: Child Maltreatment Registries, Statutory Schemes, and Reduced Opportunities for Employment." *CUNY Law Review* 24(1):1–34.

Henry, Meghan, Rian Watt, Anna Mahathey, Jillian Oullette, and Aubrey Sitler. 2020. *The 2019 Annual Homeless Assessment Report to Congress.* Washington, DC: U.S. Department of Housing and Urban Development.

Hepburn, Peter, Renee Louis, and Matthew Desmond. 2020. "Racial and Gender Disparities Among Evicted Americans." *Sociological Science* 7:649–62.

Herring, Chris. 2019. "Complaint-Oriented Policing: Regulating Homelessness in Public Space." *American Sociological Review* 84(5):769–800.

Hirschman, Daniel, and Emily Adlin Bosk. 2020. "Standardizing Biases: Selection Devices and the Quantification of Race." *Sociology of Race and Ethnicity* 6(3):348–64.

Ho, Sally, and Camille Fassett. 2021. "Pandemic Masks Ongoing Child Abuse Crisis as Cases Plummet." *AP*, March 29.

Hughes, Cayce C. 2018. "Not Out in the Field: Studying Privacy and Disclosure as an Invisible (Trans) Man." Pp. 111–25 in *Other, Please Specify: Queer Methods in Sociology*, edited by D. R. Compton, T. Meadow, and K. Schilt. Oakland: University of California Press.

Hughes, Cayce C. 2020. "A House but Not a Home: How Surveillance in Subsidized Housing Exacerbates Poverty and Reinforces Marginalization." *Social Forces* 100(1):293–315.

Ismail, Tarek Z. 2022. "Family Policing and the Fourth Amendment." Available at SSRN (https://ssrn.com/abstract=4219985).

Jagannathan, Radha, and Michael J. Camasso. 2017. "Social Outrage and Organizational Behavior: A National Study of Child Protective Service Decisions." *Children and Youth Services Review* 77:153–63.

JBS International. 2011. *Federal Child and Family Services Reviews Aggregate Report.* Washington, DC: U.S. Department of Health and Human Services.

Jerolmack, Colin, and Alexandra K. Murphy. 2019. "The Ethical Dilemmas and Social Scientific Trade-Offs of Masking in Ethnography." *Sociological Methods and Research* 48(4):801–27.

JMacForFamilies. 2023. "Mandated Supporting." Retrieved January 30, 2023 (https://jmacforfamilies.org/mandated-supporting).

Jonson-Reid, Melissa, Brett Drake, and Patricia L. Kohl. 2009. "Is the Overrepresentation of the Poor in Child Welfare Caseloads Due to Bias or Need?" *Children and Youth Services Review* 31:422–47.

Kalleberg, Arne L. 2009. "Precarious Work, Insecure Workers: Employment Relations in Transition." *American Sociological Review* 74(1):1–22.

Katz, Joette. 2019. "Fixing Child Welfare Means Not Letting Tragedies Become Catastrophes." Pp. 29–38 in *Collaboration, Innovation, and Best Practices: Lessons and Advice from Leaders in Child Welfare*, edited by C. James-Brown and J. Springwater. Washington, DC: Child Welfare League of America.

Kenny, Kathleen S., Clare Barrington, and Sherri L. Green. 2015. "'I Felt for a Long Time Like Everything Beautiful in Me Had Been Taken Out': Women's Suffering, Remembering, and Survival Following the Loss of Child Custody." *International Journal of Drug Policy* 26(11):1158–66.

Khan, Shamus. 2019. "The Subpoena of Ethnographic Data." *Sociological Forum* 34(1):253–63.

Kim, Hyunil, Christopher Wildeman, Melissa Jonson-Reid, and Brett Drake. 2017. "Lifetime Prevalence of Investigating Child Maltreatment Among U.S. Children." *American Journal of Public Health* 107(2):274–80.

Kohl, Patricia L., Melissa Jonson-Reid, and Brett Drake. 2009. "Time to Leave Substantiation Behind: Findings from a National Probability Study." *Child Maltreatment* 14(1):17–26.

Kohler-Hausmann, Issa. 2013. "Misdemeanor Justice: Control Without Conviction." *American Journal of Sociology* 119(2):351–93.

Kohler-Hausmann, Issa. 2019. "Eddie Murphy and the Dangers of Counterfactual Causal Thinking About Racial Discrimination." *Northwestern University Law Review* 113(5):1163–1228.

Kohli, Rita, Marcos Pizarro, and Arturo Nevárez. 2017. "The 'New Racism' of K–12 Schools: Centering Critical Research on Racism." *Review of Research in Education* 41(1):182–202.

Kovner, Josh. 2018. "Calls from Schools to DCF Child-Abuse Hotline Have Risen Sharply This Fall." *Hartford Courant*, December 13.

Lara-Millán, Armando. 2021. *Redistributing the Poor: Jails, Hospitals, and the Crisis of Law and Fiscal Austerity*. New York: Oxford University Press.

Lareau, Annette. 2011. *Unequal Childhoods: Class, Race, and Family Life*, 2nd ed. Berkeley: University of California Press.

Laskey, Antoinette L., Timothy E. Stump, Susan M. Perkins, Gregory D. Zimet, Steven J. Sherman, and Stephen M. Downs. 2012. "Influence of Race and Socioeconomic Status on the Diagnosis of Child Abuse: A Randomized Study." *The Journal of Pediatrics* 160(6):1003–8.e1.

Lee, Tina. 2016. *Catching a Case: Inequality and Fear in New York City's Child Welfare System*. New Brunswick, NJ: Rutgers University Press.

Lerman, Amy, and Vesla Weaver. 2014. *Arresting Citizenship: The Democratic Consequences of American Crime Control*. Chicago: University of Chicago Press.

Levine, Judith A. 2013. *Ain't No Trust: How Bosses, Boyfriends, and Bureaucrats Fail Low-Income Mothers and Why It Matters*. Berkeley: University of California Press.

Lewis, Amanda, and John Diamond. 2015. *Despite the Best Intentions: Why Racial Inequality Thrives in Good Schools*. New York: Oxford University Press.

Lipsky, Michael. 2010[1980]. *Street-Level Bureaucracy: Dilemmas of the Individual in Public Service*. New York: Russell Sage Foundation.

López-Espino, Jessica. 2021. "Raciolinguistic Ideologies of *Spanish Speakers* in a California Child Welfare Court." Pp. 205–23 in *Metalinguistic Communities: Case Studies of Agency, Ideology, and Symbolic Uses of Language*, edited by N. Avineri and J. Harasta. Cham, Switzerland: Palgrave Macmillan.

Luthar, Suniya S., and Shawn J. Latendresse. 2005. "Children of the Affluent: Challenges to Well-Being." *Current Directions on Psychological Science* 14(1):49–53.

Lyon, David, ed. 2003. *Surveillance as Social Sorting: Privacy, Risk, and Digital Discrimination*. New York: Routledge.

Maynard-Moody, Steven, and Michael Musheno. 2000. "State Agent or Citizen Agent: Two Narratives of Discretion." *Journal of Public Administration Research and Theory* 10(2): 329–58.

Maynard-Moody, Steven, and Michael Musheno. 2003. *Cops, Teachers, Counselors: Stories from the Front Lines of Public Service*. Ann Arbor: University of Michigan Press.

McKim, Allison. 2017. *Addicted to Rehab: Race, Gender, and Drugs in the Era of Mass Incarceration*. New Brunswick, NJ: Rutgers University Press.

Meadow, Tey. 2018. *Trans Kids: Being Gendered in the Twenty-First Century*. Oakland: University of California Press.

Merritt, Darcey H. 2020. "How Do Families Experience and Interact with CPS?" *The ANNALS of the American Academy of Political and Social Science* 692:203–26.

Michener, Jamila. 2018. *Fragmented Democracy: Medicaid, Federalism, and Unequal Politics*. Cambridge, UK: Cambridge University Press.

Moynihan, Daniel Patrick. 1965. *The Negro Family: The Case for National Action*. Washington, DC: U.S. Department of Labor.

Muentner, Luke, Amita Kapoor, Lindsey Weymouth, and Julie Poehlmann-Tynan. 2021. "Getting Under the Skin: Physiological Stress and Witnessing Paternal Arrest in Young Children with Incarcerated Fathers." *Developmental Psychobiology* 63(5):1568–82.

Mundra, Kusum, and Amarendra Sharma. 2015. "Housing Adequacy Gap for Minorities and Immigrants in the U.S.: Evidence from the 2009 American Housing Survey." *Journal of Housing Research* 24(1):55–72.

Myers, John E. B. 2006. *Child Protection in America: Past, Present, and Future*. New York: Oxford University Press.

National Center on Substance Abuse and Child Welfare. 2018. *The Use of Peers and Recovery Specialists in Child Welfare Settings*. Washington, DC: U.S. Department of Health and Human Services.

Nelson, Barbara. 1984. *Making an Issue of Child Abuse: Political Agenda Setting for Social Problems*. Chicago: University of Chicago Press.

New York City Housing Authority. 2022. "Priority Codes for Public Housing." Retrieved January 30, 2023 (https://www1.nyc.gov/assets/nycha/downloads/pdf/nycha-priority-codes-revised-5-9-2022.pdf).

Oberweis, Trish, and Michael Musheno. 1999. "Policing Identities: Cop Decision Making and the Constitution of Citizens." *Law and Social Inquiry* 24:897–923.

Office of Children and Family Services. 2023. "Child Welfare Data Aggregate MAPS." Retrieved January 30, 2023 (https://ocfs.ny.gov/reports/maps/aggregate.php).

Office of Family Assistance, Administration for Children and Families. 2019. "TANF and MOE Spending and Transfers by Activity, FY 2018: United States." Retrieved January 30, 2023 (https://www.acf.hhs.gov/sites/default/files/documents/ofa/fy2018_tanf_moe_national_data_pie_chart_b508.pdf).

Online Etymology Dictionary. 2022. "Precarious." Retrieved January 30, 2023 (https://www.etymonline.com/word/precarious#etymonline_v_19364).

Paik, Leslie. 2021. *Trapped in a Maze: How Social Control Institutions Drive Family Poverty and Inequality*. Oakland: University of California Press.

Palmer, Lindsey. 2022. "What Is Neglect? A Content Analysis of a Population Based Sample of Child Maltreatment Investigations." Children's Data Network Brownbag Presentation.

Palmer, Lindsey, Sarah Font, Andrea Lane Eastman, Lillie Guo, and Emily Putnam-Hornstein. 2022. "What Does Child Protective Services Investigate as Neglect? A Population-Based Study." *Child Maltreatment*, OnlineFirst (doi: 10.1177/10775595221114144).

Parton, Nigel. 1998. "Risk, Advanced Liberalism and Child Welfare: The Need to Rediscover Uncertainty and Ambiguity." *British Journal of Social Work* 28(1):5–27.

Pearson, Susan J. 2011. *The Rights of the Defenseless: Protecting Animals and Children in Gilded Age America*. Chicago: University of Chicago Press.

Petruccelli, Kaitlyn, Joshua Davis, and Tara Berman. 2019. "Adverse Childhood Experiences and Associated Health Outcomes: A Systematic Review and Meta-analysis." *Child Abuse and Neglect* 97:104127.

Piven, Frances Fox, and Richard A. Cloward. 1971. *Regulating the Poor: The Functions of Public Welfare*. New York: Vintage Books.

Polsky, Andrew J. 1991. *The Rise of the Therapeutic State*. Princeton, NJ: Princeton University Press.

Prince v. Commonwealth of Massachusetts, 321 U.S. 158 (1944).

Prowse, Gwen, Vesla M. Weaver, and Tracey L. Meares. 2020. "The State from Below: Distorted Responsiveness in Policed Communities." *Urban Affairs Review* 56(5):1423–71.

Pugh, Allison J. 2015. *The Tumbleweed Society: Working and Caring in an Age of Insecurity*. New York: Oxford University Press.

Putnam-Hornstein, Emily, Eunhye Ahn, John Prindle, Joseph Magruder, Daniel Webster, and Christopher Wildeman. 2021. "Cumulative Rates of Child Protection Involvement and Terminations of Parental Rights in a California Birth Cohort, 1999–2017." *American Journal of Public Health*:e1–7.

Putnam-Hornstein, Emily, and Barbara Needell. 2011. "Predictors of Child Protective Service Contact Between Birth and Age Five: An Examination of California's 2002 Birth Cohort." *Children and Youth Services Review* 33(8):1337–44.

Raissian, Kerri M., and Lindsey Rose Bullinger. 2017. "Money Matters: Does the Minimum Wage Affect Child Maltreatment Rates?" *Children and Youth Services Review* 72:60–70.

Randles, Jennifer. 2021. "'Willing to Do Anything for My Kids': Inventive Mothering, Diapers, and the Inequalities of Carework." *American Sociological Review* 86(1):35–59.

Ray, Victor. 2019. "A Theory of Racialized Organizations." *American Sociological Review* 84(1):26–53.

Raz, Mical. 2020. *Abusive Policies: How the American Child Welfare System Lost Its Way*. Chapel Hill: University of North Carolina Press.

Redleaf, Diane. 2022. "The Challenge of Changing America's Amorphous, Limitless Neglect Laws." *The Imprint*. Retrieved January 30, 2023 (https://imprintnews.org/opinion/challenge -changing-americas-amorphous-limitless-neglect-laws/65055).

Reich, Jennifer A. 2005. *Fixing Families: Parents, Power, and the Child Welfare System*. New York: Taylor and Francis Group.

Reich, Jennifer A. 2016. *Calling the Shots: Why Parents Reject Vaccines*. New York: NYU Press.

Rhode Island Office of the Child Advocate. 2017a. *A Review of Four Child Fatalities and Two Near Fatalities*. Cranston, RI: Author.

Rhode Island Office of the Child Advocate. 2017b. *A Review of Two Child Fatalities and Four Near Fatalities*. Cranston, RI: Author.

Rios, Victor M. 2011. *Punished: Policing the Lives of Black and Latino Boys*. New York: NYU Press.

Rise. 2020. "Parents to City Council: Fund Communities, Not ACS." Retrieved January 30, 2023 (https://www.risemagazine.org/2020/11/fund-communities-not-acs/).

Rise. 2021. *Someone to Turn To: A Vision for Creating Networks of Parent Peer Care*. New York: Author.

Rise. 2022. "Centering Parent Leadership in the Movement to Abolish Family Policing." *Columbia Journal of Race and Law* 12(1):436–58.

Roberts, Dorothy. 2002. *Shattered Bonds: The Color of Child Welfare*. New York: Basic Books.

Roberts, Dorothy. 2008. "The Racial Geography of Child Welfare: Toward a New Research Paradigm." *Child Welfare* 87(2):125–50.

Roberts, Dorothy. 2022. *Torn Apart: How the Child Welfare System Destroys Black Families—and How Abolition Can Build a Safer World*. New York: Basic Books.

Roberts, Sarah C. M., Claudia Zaugg, and Noelle Martinez. 2022. "Health Care Provider Decision-Making Around Prenatal Substance Use Reporting." *Drug and Alcohol Dependence* 237:109514.

Rocha Beardall, Theresa, and Frank Edwards. 2021. "Abolition, Settler Colonialism, and the Persistent Threat of Indian Child Welfare." *Columbia Journal of Race and Law* 11(3):533–73.

Rodríguez, Nestor, and Jacqueline Maria Hagan. 2004. "Fractured Families and Communities: Effects of Immigration Reform in Texas, Mexico, and El Salvador." *Latino Studies* 2(3):328–51.

Roehrkasse, Alexander F. 2021. "Long-Term Trends and Ethnoracial Inequality in U.S. Foster Care: A Research Note." *Demography* 58(5):2009–17.

Rojas, Mary, Ingrid Walker-Descartes, and Danielle Laraque-Arena. 2017. "An Experimental Study of Implicit Racial Bias in Recognition of Child Abuse." *American Journal of Health Behavior* 41(3):358–67.

Rose, Nikolas. 2000. "Government and Control." *British Journal of Criminology* 40:321–39.

Ross, Loretta J., and Rickie Solinger. 2017. *Reproductive Justice: An Introduction.* Oakland: University of California Press.

Russell Sage Foundation. 2023. "Monica Bell." Retrieved January 30, 2023 (https://www.russellsage.org/visiting-scholars/monica-bell).

Ryan, Sheryl A., Seth D. Ammerman, and Mary E. O'Connor. 2018. "Marijuana Use During Pregnancy and Breastfeeding: Implications for Neonatal and Childhood Outcomes." *Pediatrics* 142(3):e20181889.

Rymph, Catherine E. 2017. *Raising Government Children: A History of Foster Care and the American Welfare State.* Chapel Hill: University of North Carolina Press.

Sankaran, Vivek S. 2017. "Moving Beyond *Lassiter*: The Need for a Federal Statutory Right to Counsel for Parents in Child Welfare Cases." *Journal of Legislation* 44(1):1–21.

Schelbe, Lisa, Melissa Radey, and Lisa S. Panisch. 2017. "Satisfactions and Stressors Experienced by Recently-Hired Frontline Child Welfare Workers." *Children and Youth Services Review* 78:56–63.

Scott, James. 1985. *Weapons of the Weak: Everyday Forms of Peasant Resistance.* New Haven, CT: Yale University Press.

Sege, Robert, and Allison Stephens. 2022. "Child Physical Abuse Did Not Increase During the Pandemic." *JAMA Pediatrics* 176(4):338–40.

Seim, Josh. 2020. *Bandage, Sort, and Hustle: Ambulance Crews on the Front Lines of Urban Suffering.* Oakland: University of California Press.

Sharkey, Patrick, Gerard Torrats-Espinosa, and Delaram Takyar. 2017. "Community and the Crime Decline: The Causal Effect of Local Nonprofits on Violent Crime." *American Sociological Review* 82(6):1214–40.

Shedd, Carla. 2015. *Unequal City: Race, Schools, and Perceptions of Injustice.* New York: Russell Sage Foundation.

Simmons, Michaela. 2022. "The Racialization of Family Preservation: White Uplift in New York City Foster Care, 1930–1963." Paper presented at the American Sociological Association annual meeting, Los Angeles, August 8.

Small, Mario Luis. 2009. "How Many Cases Do I Need? On Science and the Logic of Case Selection in Field-Based Research." *Ethnography* 10(1):5–38.

Smeeding, Timothy, and Céline Thévenot. 2016. "Addressing Child Poverty: How Does the United States Compare with Other Nations?" *Academic Pediatrics* 16(3S):S67–S75.

Social Security Act of 1935, Title IV, Section 401.

Soss, Joe, Richard C. Fording, and Sanford F. Schram. 2011. *Disciplining the Poor: Neoliberal Paternalism and the Persistent Power of Race*. Chicago: University of Chicago Press.

Soss, Joe, and Vesla Weaver. 2017. "Police Are Our Government: Politics, Political Science, and the Policing of Race-Class Subjugated Communities." *Annual Review of Political Science* 20:565–91.

Stack, Carol. 1974. *All Our Kin: Strategies for Survival in a Black Community*. New York: Harper and Row.

Starck, Jordan G., Travis Riddle, Stacey Sinclair, and Natasha Warikoo. 2020. "Teachers Are People Too: Examining the Racial Bias of Teachers Compared to Other American Adults." *Educational Researcher* 49(4):273–84.

Stephens, Tricia N. 2019. "Recognizing Complex Trauma in Child Welfare–Affected Mothers of Colour." *Child and Family Social Work* 24:42–49.

Stokes, Jacqueline, and Glen Schmidt. 2011. "Race, Poverty and Child Protection Decision Making." *British Journal of Social Work* 41(6):1105–21.

Stuart, Forrest. 2016. *Down, Out, and Under Arrest: Policing and Everyday Life in Skid Row*. Chicago: University of Chicago Press.

Stuart, Forrest, and Katherine Beckett. 2021. "Addressing Urban Disorder Without Police: How Seattle's LEAD Program Responds to Behavioral-Health-Related Disruptions, Resolves Business Complaints, and Reconfigures the Field of Public Safety." *Law and Policy* 43(4):390–414.

Sweet, Paige L. 2021. *The Politics of Surviving: How Women Navigate Domestic Violence and Its Aftermath*. Oakland: University of California Press.

Sykes, Jennifer. 2011. "Negotiating Stigma: Understanding Mothers' Responses to Accusations of Child Neglect." *Children and Youth Services Review* 33(3):448–56.

Tchelidze, Ekaterine, and Claire Galvin. 2018. "DCF: Social Work a Difficult, but Rewarding, Profession." *The Chronicle*, April 18.

Thomas, Krista A., and Alan J. Dettlaff. 2011. "African American Families and the Role of Physical Discipline: Witnessing the Past in the Present." *Journal of Human Behavior in the Social Environment* 21(8):963–77.

Thompson, Ross A. 2015. "Social Support and Child Protection: Lessons Learned and Learning." *Child Abuse and Neglect* 41:19–29.

Thorne, William. 2020. "After Years of Doing It Wrong as a Judge I Know We Can Do Better!" *Children's Bureau Express* 21(6) (https://cbexpress.acf.hhs.gov/article/2020/august-september/after-years-of-doing-it-wrong-as-a-judge-l-know-we-can-do-better/6138c003 1b92c150517620efe54bcb3e).

Thumath, Meaghan, David Humphreys, Jane Barlow, Putu Duff, Melissa Braschel, Brittany Bingham, Sophie Pierre, and Kate Shannon. 2021. "Overdose Among Mothers: The Association Between Child Removal and Unintentional Drug Overdose in a Longitudinal Cohort of Marginalised Women in Canada." *International Journal of Drug Policy* 91:102977.

Tobis, David. 2013. *From Pariahs to Partners: How Parents and Their Allies Changed New York City's Child Welfare System*. New York: Oxford University Press.

Trocmé, Nico, Alicia Kyte, Vandna Sinha, and Barbara Fallon. 2014. "Urgent Protection Versus Chronic Need: Clarifying the Dual Mandate of Child Welfare Services Across Canada." *Social Sciences* 3:483–98.

U.S. Department of Health and Human Services. 2006a. *The AFCARS Report, Final Estimates for FY 1998 Through FY 2002 (12)*. Washington, DC: Author.

U.S. Department of Health and Human Services. 2006b. *Child Maltreatment 2004*. Washington, DC: Author.

U.S. Department of Health and Human Services. 2015. *The AFCARS Report, No. 22*. Washington, DC: Author.

U.S. Department of Health and Human Services. 2020a. *The AFCARS Report, No. 27*. Washington, DC: Author.

U.S. Department of Health and Human Services. 2020b. *Child Maltreatment 2018*. Washington, DC: Author.

U.S. Department of Health and Human Services. 2021a. *Child Maltreatment 2019*. Washington, DC: Author.

U.S. Department of Health and Human Services. 2021b. *The Maternal, Infant, and Early Childhood Home Visiting Program*. Washington, DC: Author.

U.S. Department of Health and Human Services. 2022. *Child Maltreatment 2020*. Washington, DC: Author.

U.S. Government Printing Office. 1909. *Proceedings of the Conference of the Care of Dependent Children*. Washington, DC: Author.

Vasquez-Tokos, Jessica, and Priscilla Yamin. 2021. "The Racialization of Privacy: Racial Formation as a Family Affair." *Theory and Society* 50:717–40.

Verduzco-Baker, Lynn. 2017. "'I Don't Want Them to Be a Statistic': Mothering Practices of Low-Income Mothers." *Journal of Family Issues* 38(7):1010–38.

Wacquant, Loïc. 2010. "Crafting the Neoliberal State: Workfare, Prisonfare, and Social Insecurity." *Sociological Forum* 25(2):197–220.

Wald, Michael S. 2022. "Beyond CPS: Building a System to Protect the Safety and Basic Development of Children Experiencing Problematic Parenting." Pp. 697–728 in *Handbook of Child Maltreatment*, edited by R. D. Krugman and J. E. Korbin. Cham, Switzerland: Springer.

Waldfogel, Jane. 1998. *The Future of Child Protection: How to Break the Cycle of Abuse and Neglect*. Cambridge, MA: Harvard University Press.

Waldfogel, Jane. 2008. "The Future of Child Protection Revisited." Pp. 235–41 in *Child Welfare Research: Advances for Practice and Policy*, edited by D. Lindsey and A. Shlonsky. New York: Oxford University Press.

Waters, Mary, and Jennifer Sykes. 2009. "Spare the Rod, Spoil the Child? First and Second Generation West Indian Childrearing Practices." Pp. 72–97 in *Across Generations: Immigrant Families in America*, edited by N. Foner. New York: NYU Press.

Watkins-Hayes, Celeste. 2009. *The New Welfare Bureaucrats: Entanglements of Race, Class, and Policy Reform*. Chicago: University of Chicago Press.

Weaver, Vesla M., and Amy E. Lerman. 2010. "Political Consequences of the Carceral State." *American Political Science Review* 104(4):817–33.

Webster, Richard A. 2019. "One Judge's Tough Approach to Foster Care: It's Only for the Really Extreme Cases." *The Washington Post*, November 25.

Western, Bruce. 2015. "Lifetimes of Violence in a Sample of Released Prisoners." *RSF: The Russell Sage Foundation Journal of the Social Sciences* 1(2):14–30.

WestRasmus, Emma K., Fernando Pineda-Reyes, Montelle Tamez, and John M. Westfall. 2012. "'Promotores de Salud' and Community Health Workers: An Annotated Bibliography." *Family and Community Health* 35(2):172–82.

Wexler, Richard. 2018. "Connecticut Losing the Gutsiest Leader in Child Welfare." *Hartford Courant*, December 6.

Wexler, Richard. 2019. "I Took a 'Mandated Reporter' Training Course on Child Abuse." *Youth Today*, February 10.

Williams, Sarah Catherine. 2020. "State-Level Data for Understanding Child Welfare in the United States." Retrieved June 29, 2021 (https://www.childtrends.org/publications/state-level-data-for-understanding-child-welfare-in-the-united-states).

Wilson, Katherine R., and Margot R. Prior. 2011. "Father Involvement and Child Well-Being." *Journal of Paediatrics and Child Health* 47:405–7.

Woodward, Kerry C. 2021. "Race, Gender, and Poverty Governance: The Case of the U.S. Child Welfare System." *Social Politics* 28(2):428–50.

Yang, Mi-Youn, Kathryn Maguire-Jack, Kathryn Showalter, Youn Kyoung Kim, and Kristen Shook Slack. 2019. "Child Care Subsidy and Child Maltreatment." *Child and Family Social Work* 24(4):547–54.

Yi, Youngmin, Frank Edwards, and Christopher Wildeman. 2020. "Cumulative Prevalence of Confirmed Maltreatment and Foster Care Placement for US Children by Race/Ethnicity, 2011–2016." *American Journal of Public Health* 110(5):704–9.

Zelizer, Viviana A. 1985. *Pricing the Priceless Child: The Changing Social Value of Children*. Princeton, NJ: Princeton University Press.

INDEX

Adoption and Safe Families Act (1997), 184
adversity: consequences of CPS responding
to, 4, 105, 110, 119, 131, 140, 150, 156, 164,
194–95, 206–7; effects of childhood, 4, 28,
51; investigations triggered by, 3, 6–7, 16,
21, 30, 45, 48–51, 60, 64–65, 76; mothers'
concealment of, 41, 45; parenting in the
context of, 6, 20, 28, 30, 41, 45–46, 48–49,
51, 74, 185, 192; society's response to, 16,
22, 48, 69, 195; types of, 6, 19, 30, 49–51.
See also poverty; precarity
African Americans: CPS investigations of,
2, 51, 64–65, 69–70, 194; discipline
practiced by, 38–39, 68; in foster care, 5,
163; kin relationships and social support
among, 40, 123; policing of, 14, 34;
poverty and other adversity faced by, 69,
113–14; stereotypes of, 32–33, 69–70, 130,
199, 247n28; and welfare, 7–8, 139,
246n24. *See also* race and racism
alcohol. *See* substance use
allegations leading to investigations:
content of, 6–7, 16, 41, 48–51, 93;
contesting of, 171; substantiation of, 11,
108, 111, 124, 127–28, 232, 255n26. *See also*
screening of allegations
Arons, Anna, 206, 247n38
attorneys, 164, 171, 176–80, 182, 184, 189–91,
258n23, 258n24

Becker, Howard, 213
Bell, Monica, 192
Bourdieu, Pierre, 12–13

boyfriends, 26, 30, 73, 74, 80, 84, 87, 94,
101–2, 107, 111, 113, 116, 119, 120–23, 157–58,
167–68, 174, 176, 183, 190, 194, 236, 252n10
Brayne, Sarah, 111–12, 248n51, 261n6
Bridges, Khiara, 72, 253n28
Browder, Kalief, 182

care and coercion, in welfare and CPS
efforts, 21, 56, 79, 105, 142, 160, 195, 200
case histories. *See* prior contact
Certificate of Confidentiality, 223
child abuse. *See* child maltreatment
Child Abuse Prevention and Treatment Act
(CAPTA; 1974), 8, 246n26
childcare: challenges for investigators, 98;
mothers' reactions to reports from, 152,
156; providers' reports or perceptions of
reporting, 33, 53, 66, 72, 82; subsidies for
or assistance with, 8, 27, 139, 144, 203, 207
child maltreatment: definition and social
construction of, 2, 6, 8, 30, 47–52, 67–70,
75, 128, 204, 245n18, 246n19; extreme
cases of, 3, 6, 8, 35, 91, 94–97, 205, 225,
252n16; factors associated with, 5, 6, 49,
67, 112, 118, 207
child neglect. *See* child maltreatment
Child Protective Services (CPS): assistance
offered by, 15–16, 21–22, 135–46, 160–61;
attitudes toward, 1–2, 4, 14–16, 20–22,
24–25, 29–31, 33–46, 56, 80–82, 98–99,
133–35, 138, 142–44, 148–51, 158, 164,
174–83, 187–93, 214, 249n10, 257n18; case
flow, 10; expansion of services offered by,

Child Protective Services (CPS) (*continued*)
201–3; framing intrinsic to the approach
of, 4, 16, 21, 35–36, 89, 118–22, 128–29, 131,
147, 160–61, 195–96, 198, 202, 206–7, 239;
harms associated with, 2, 4, 14–15, 132–35,
140–61; limitations of, 22, 136–40, 160,
198; offices of, 18–19, 226–27; origin of, 8;
police compared to, 14, 16–17, 34–35, 37,
46, 104–5; police's relationship with,
58–59, 62–64, 69, 71, 253n22; power of, 1,
6, 15, 21, 56–60, 79, 81, 88, 98–102, 105,
143–44, 164, 175–83, 187–88, 191, 196;
precursor to, 246n19; prior contact with,
110–12; recommendations for, 200–211;
reduction of involvement of, 203–6,
208–9; rehabilitation as goal of, 54–56,
165; research access to, 219–26; society's
use of, for addressing child welfare issues,
3, 7–9, 16, 21, 22, 47–48, 51, 57, 60–64, 76,
105, 110, 161, 195–98; as source of precarity,
3–4, 15–17, 22, 25, 30–31, 33, 37, 43, 45–46,
110, 131, 134–35, 144, 160–61, 164, 192,
194–95, 197, 200, 201; terminology
associated with, 9; training of staff for,
3, 15, 61–62, 66, 78, 91–93, 97, 100, 109,
110. *See also* child welfare system;
investigations
children: questioning during investigations,
87, 99, 103–4, 146; stress or trauma
experienced by, 4–5, 8, 28, 50, 51, 146–47,
163, 165, 200. *See also* discipline and
supervision of children; foster care;
removal of children from families
Children's Bureau, 9
child welfare system: critiques of, 130;
expenditures on, 9; political lessons
learned from involvement in, 171–92;
research access to, 219–26; scale of, 2;
structure and organization of, 9. *See also*
Child Protective Services
civil death penalty, 183
classism, 21, 48, 52, 65, 67–68, 72, 130, 245n16
Clinton, Bill, 8
Cloud, Erin Miles, 207

coercion. *See* care and coercion, in welfare
efforts
Collins, Patricia Hill, 29, 69–70
Connecticut: author's research in, 3, 17–20,
226–39; caseloads in, 96; child removal
in, 167–71, 257n11, 257n12; child welfare
laws and practices in, 11, 48, 62, 63, 66, 85,
90, 92, 93, 99, 109–10, 119, 134, 135, 203,
253n5, 256n8; Department of Children
and Families (DCF), 9, 15, 18, 135, 221–26;
differential response policy in, 11, 92,
201–2, 259n14; legal representation
provided in, 258n23; New Haven, 1, 7, 11,
18–19, 27, 36, 47, 63, 66, 71, 73, 74, 82, 102,
107, 111, 133, 136, 142, 153, 224, 226–27, 232,
239, 240, 252n5; Northeast Corner, 18–19,
55, 58, 77, 98, 126, 140, 156, 222, 224–27,
232, 239; parents' rights in, 99; policy
context of, 19; poverty and welfare in,
27, 196; prevalence of CPS involvement
in, 5, 19; screening tools in, 252n7
co-sleeping, 93–94, 95, 101, 260n41
court. *See* family court
COVID-19 pandemic, 193, 206
CPS. *See* Child Protective Services
Crenshaw, Kimberlé, 112

day care. *See* childcare
Desmond, Matthew, 28, 236
differential response policy, 11, 92, 201–2,
259n14
discipline and supervision of children,
conflicts between mothers and others
over, 1, 6, 11, 32, 38–39, 47, 50, 61, 65,
67–68, 77, 88, 153
doctors. *See* health care providers;
professionals
domestic violence: children's traumatiza-
tion from, 50, 51; in families, 6, 28, 30, 41,
49, 55, 61, 110, 119, 124, 158, 190; investigations of, 49, 61, 63, 93, 111, 113–14, 119, 120,
124, 146, 181; police policies regarding, 71
drinking. *See* substance use
drugs. *See* substance use

Earned Income Tax Credit, 207, 247n29

Edin, Kathryn, 213

education personnel: CPS reports from or perceptions of reporting among, 33, 50, 54–56, 59, 63, 64, 67–69, 71–73, 76, 77, 84, 104, 132, 134, 200; mothers' reactions to reports from, 146–47, 151–53, 209; racial identity of, 66. *See also* professionals

Edwards, Frank, 71

Facebook, 90

family assessments, 19, 92, 205, 252n14

family court, 12, 121, 136, 171–74, 176–80, 184, 186, 189–91, 219

Family First Prevention Services Act (2018), 202–3, 245n45, 259n18

fathers of children: calls to CPS from, 73–74, 85, 120–21, 158–59; in mothers' CPS encounters, 24, 28, 89, 116–17, 119–23, 139, 168–71, 173, 181

Fernández-Kelly, Patricia, 38

foster care: African Americans and Native Americans in, 5, 163; effect of CPS involvement on opportunities to provide, 149–50; funding of, 9; numbers of children in, 5, 8, 13, 14, 19, 163, 205; placement of children in, 9, 11, 12, 13, 170, 205–6; voluntary placement in, 74–75. *See also* removal of children from families; termination of parental rights

Fourth Amendment, 251n2

Garfinkel, Harold, 169

gender: CPS investigations and, 5, 20, 46, 119–23; resource access and distribution related to, 110, 112; societal expectations related to, 32, 70, 179, 199

girlfriends, 124–25, 142, 146, 176, 181

Goffman, Alice, 44

Gonzalez Van Cleve, Nicole, 220

Gray, Ernestine, 205–6

Hansell, David, 201

Hays, Sharon, 120

health care providers: CPS reports from or perceptions of reporting among, 50, 53–57, 60, 62–63, 65–66, 71, 79–83, 86, 95, 104, 115–16, 127–28, 137, 155, 167–69, 181, 253n6; mothers' experiences with, 29, 31–32, 42–45, 145; mothers' reactions to reports from, 152–53, 156. *See also* mental health services/service providers; professionals

homelessness and homeless shelters, 19, 30, 38–39, 43, 74, 113, 121, 140. *See also* housing

home visiting services, 24–25, 218

hotlines. *See* screening of allegations

housing: challenges related to, 1, 27, 30, 49, 54–55, 74, 107, 112–14, 116–17, 121, 125, 136–37, 140, 142, 162; costs of, 27, 107, 121; CPS resources or lack thereof to provide, 138–39, 142, 144–45, 198, 203; as factor in CPS cases, 49, 112–14, 116–17, 136–37, 155, 177; vouchers for, 9, 55, 114, 203; waiting lists for, 43, 55. *See also* homelessness and homeless shelters

Hughes, Cayce, 260n3

immigration enforcement, 149

Indian Child Welfare Act (1978), 246n24

inequities. *See* systemic racism and other socioeconomic inequities

information-gathering, 78, 90–95, 98, 105–6, 148. *See also* surveillance

insight, in CPS risk assessment, 123–29, 256n2

Institutional Review Boards (IRBs), 222–25, 227, 237

investigations, 77–106; conduct of, 11, 87–90, 93; contexts leading to, 5–7, 21, 47–76; decision-making considerations in, 108–30; family assessments vs., 19, 92, 252n14; formal risk instrument used in, 109–10, 113, 252n7, 254n8; harms associated with, 146–50; information-gathering for, 78, 87–96, 98, 105–6, 148; mothers as subject of, 5, 20, 119–23;

investigations (*continued*)
mothers' participation in, 98–104, 129; numbers of, 2, 13–14, 31; open cases as result of, 11–12, 108, 117, 119, 140, 232; parents' rights in, 98–100, 103–5; racial disproportionality and racism in, 2, 5, 8, 51, 64–73, 130–31, 254n8; resolved with no finding of maltreatment, 4, 13–14, 17, 51, 78, 82, 83, 93, 105, 117, 194, 232; role of prior contact and case history in, 90, 110–12, 149; study of, 226–39. *See also* allegations leading to investigations; removal of children from families; screening of allegations

investigators: background of, 247n35; experiences of, 1–3, 15, 77–78, 83, 86–90, 94, 96–98, 100–104, 107–8, 113–17, 121–23, 125–28, 133, 137, 141, 145; liability concerns of, 94–97; research with, 226–27, 232–37; risks and dangers of the job for, 97; stress experienced by, 96–98; supervision of, 94–95, 251n2; training of, 3, 15, 78, 91–93, 97, 100, 109; work loads of, 96–98

Kalleberg, Arne, 193
Katz, Joette, 205
Kempe, Henry, 8
Kohler-Hausmann, Issa, 104

labeling theory, 239
Lara-Millán, Armando, 198
Lareau, Annette, 249n10
Latinx population: CPS investigations of, 64, 69; poverty and other adversity faced by, 69, 113. *See also* race and racism
Lee, Tina, 13
Levine, Judith, 155
liability concerns: of CPS, 79, 94–97; of reporting professionals, 62–64
Lipsky, Michael, 56–57
Lyon, David, 106

mandated reporters. *See* professionals
mandated reporting laws, 8, 9, 11, 53, 63–64

marginality. *See* adversity; precarity
material resources, 5–6, 27–28, 66–67, 112–14, 138, 176, 207. *See also* poverty; resources
medical providers. *See* health care providers
mental health concerns: about children, 47, 52–53, 129, 145; about parents, 6, 19, 27, 28, 30, 49–50, 136, 163, 188; investigations of, 44, 83–84, 104, 188
mental health services/service providers: in CPS cases, 103–4, 129, 133–34, 136–41, 143–45, 172–74, 177; CPS reports from or perceptions of CPS reporting among, 47, 50–53, 55, 57, 60, 62, 65, 71–73, 82, 84–85; mothers' reactions to reports from, 153–54. *See also* professionals
Mondale, Walter, 8
Moore, Gwen, 193
motherhood: mothers' commitment to, 24, 26, 28, 32, 81, 82, 121–22, 136, 154, 165–66; poverty and, 26–28, 198; precarity of, 3–4, 13–17, 20–21, 29–33, 110, 147–48, 164, 195; societal ideals and expectations concerning, 2, 32–33, 35, 120, 199. *See also* mothers
mothers: advocacy of, 183–91; assessment of, by CPS and others, 21, 25, 31–32, 35–36, 38–39, 41–44, 65, 81, 107–30, 181, 194, 199, 248n61; confidence and doubts of, 25, 30–32, 45–46, 81, 147, 167; fear of child removal, 1–2, 4, 15–16, 24–25, 30, 34–36, 42, 77, 81–82, 87, 98–102, 104–5, 124, 133, 135, 148, 163, 249n10, 256n3; gendered expectations experienced by, 32, 119–23, 254n20; interviews with, 214–19, 232, 234, 236, 238, 260n3; participation of, in investigations, 98–104, 129; prior contact with CPS, 110–12, 149–50; privileges accorded, 254n19; reactions and fears concerning calls to CPS, 21, 25, 39–41, 151–60, 209; rights of, in child welfare cases, 98–100,

103–5, 164, 170, 179, 183–85, 188, 258n25; stereotypes of Black, 32–33, 69–70, 199; stress experienced by, 2, 3, 27, 50, 77, 80, 83, 107–8, 110, 113, 115–16, 121, 122, 137, 144, 158, 210; as subject of CPS investigations, 5, 119–23; trauma experienced by, 22, 33, 87, 163. *See also* boyfriends; fathers of children; girlfriends; motherhood; removal of children from families

Moynihan, Daniel Patrick, 247n28

Native Americans: CPS investigations of, 64; in foster care, 5, 163, 199; government responses to poverty of, 246n20, 246n24; resources offered by communities of, 208. *See also* race and racism

Nixon, Richard, 8

Pager, Devah, 220

parens patriae doctrine, 5

parents. *See* fathers of children; mothers

paternalism, 16, 56, 69, 144, 197, 257n10

Piccola, Trista, 207

police/policing: brutality of, 32–33, 163–64; consequences of, 14; CPS compared to, 14, 16–17, 34–35, 37, 46, 104–5; CPS reports from or perceptions of reporting among, 57, 58–59, 62–65, 69–71, 119, 125–26, 162–65; CPS's reliance on, 99, 113, 170, 253n22; diversion programs, 208–9; mothers' reactions to reports from, 156; mothers reported to, 162–63; risk assessment in, 111–12. *See also* professionals

Polsky, Andrew, 139

poverty: child welfare system and, 176–77; government responses to and governance of, 7, 16, 27, 49, 108–9, 198–200, 207, 246n23; motherhood and, 26–28, 51; perceptions of child maltreatment and, 5, 6, 49, 55, 66–69, 109, 112–13, 207; traumas associated with, 28; U.S. rates of, 7. *See also* adversity; material resources

precarity: CPS as source of, 3–4, 15–17, 22, 25, 30–31, 33, 37, 43, 45–46, 110, 131, 134–35, 144, 160–61, 164, 192, 194–95, 197, 200, 201; employment-related, 12–13; of motherhood, 13–17, 20–21, 29–33, 110, 147–48, 164, 195; as opportunity for activism, 193. *See also* adversity

prevention, as stated goal of CPS, 15, 51, 92–94, 105, 108–9, 129–30

prior contact, of parents with CPS, 90, 110–12, 149–50

professionals: biases and discretionary practices of, 65–73; interviews with, 233–34; limited resources of, 57–60; mandated reporter training of, 61–62, 66, 204; mothers' reactions to calls to CPS by, 151–56; mothers' wariness concerning, 41–45; non-CPS referrals provided by, 209–10. *See also* childcare; education personnel; health care providers; mental health services/service providers; police/policing

race and racism: CPS reports/investigations and, 2, 5, 8, 36, 51, 64–73, 88, 199, 245n16; foster care and, 163; of investigators and their clients, 255n34; in judgments of parenting, 32–33; professional discussions of, 65–66; in research sites, 19–20, 215–16, 226; welfare and, 7–8, 139, 246n24. *See also* African Americans; Latinx population; Native Americans; systemic racism and other socioeconomic inequities

Ray, Victor, 72, 258n10

referrals to social services: alternatives to CPS provision of, 201, 204, 208–9; mothers' lack of follow-up on, 52–53, 56; professionals' capacity for making, 57, 73, 82, 86, 134; resulting from investigations, 11, 15, 75, 83, 93, 108, 118, 133–43, 160–61; surveillance resulting from, 141–42, 160

Reich, Jennifer, 13, 99, 129, 249n65, 254n19

removal of children from families:
advocacy against, 183–91; in child welfare
case flow, 11–12; frequency of, 252n5;
housing linked to, 177; mothers' fear of/
CPS threat of, 1–2, 4, 15–16, 24–25, 30,
34–36, 42, 54, 75, 77, 81–82, 87, 98–102,
104–5, 124, 133, 135, 148, 163, 249n10,
256n3; Native Americans, 246n20,
246n24; outcomes of, 12; political
lessons learned through, 171–92;
professionals' disinterest in, 54–56;
stories of, 83–84, 162–91; substance use
linked to, 83–84, 165–71, 175–76; and
termination of parental rights, 12, 183–91,
193; trauma resulting from, 22, 163–92.
See also foster care
reporting professionals. *See* professionals
reports to CPS, 2, 11, 52–76, 79–80, 82, 163,
203, 254n16; mothers' perceptions of,
151–60
research methodology, 17–20; 213–40;
access to child welfare agencies, 219–26;
author's background, 213, 216, 219;
ethnography and interviewing, 213, 226;
interviews, 214–19, 232–35, 238, 260n3;
overview of, 17–20
resources: inequities in access to/
distribution of, 5–6, 27, 51, 65, 72–73,
75, 112–13, 118, 207–8; investigators'
assessment of, 109, 112–19; material,
5–6, 27–28, 66–67, 112–14, 138, 176, 207;
reliance on CPS for provision of, 56–60,
70, 73; social, 25, 28, 39–42, 80, 114–19,
122–23
Rhode Island: author's research in, 3, 17–20,
214–19; caseloads in, 96; child welfare
laws and practices in, 84, 93, 202, 204–5;
CPS-related death in, 95–97; Department of Children, Youth, and Families,
220–21; differential response policy in,
201; interviews with mothers in, 17–18,
214–19; legal representation provided in,
258n23; policy context of, 19; termination
of parental rights in, 184

rights, of parents in child welfare cases,
98–100, 103–5, 164, 170, 179, 183–85, 188,
193, 258n25
Rise in New York City, 208
risk: CPS reports as indicators of, 92;
factors influencing judgments about, 90,
108–130; frequency of visits based on
designations of, 88; gender of parents as
factor in, 119–23; high vs. low, 88, 92–94,
110, 123, 127, 130
Roberts, Dorothy, 5, 25, 64, 67, 198–99;
Shattered Bonds, Torn Apart, 13
Rose, Nikolas, 108–9

safety, as stated goal of CPS, 91–92, 97,
108–9, 129–30, 239
safety plans, 91, 95, 113, 118, 120, 235, 256n3
Scandinavia, 260n50
schools. *See* education personnel
Scott, James, 183
screening of allegations, 11, 48, 62, 85, 98,
110–11, 204, 252n7. *See also* allegations
leading to investigations
service plans, 11–12, 177
shelters. *See* homelessness and homeless
shelters
Small, Mario, 239
SNAP. *See* Supplemental Nutrition
Assistance Program
social relations: mothers' concerns about
CPS involvement initiated by, 39–41,
156–60; reports by, of suspected child
maltreatment, 73–75; as sources of
support, 25, 39–40, 80, 114–19, 122–23
Social Security Act (1935), 7; Title IV, 9
Societies for the Prevention of Cruelty to
Children, 246n19
Special Supplemental Nutrition Program
for Women, Infants, and Children
(WIC), 74, 120, 215
street-level bureaucracy, 56–57, 70, 79,
255n34
stress: children's experience of, 165;
investigators' experience of, 96–98;

parents' experience of, 2, 3, 27, 50, 77, 80, 83, 107–8, 110, 113, 115–16, 121, 122, 137, 144, 158, 210. *See also* trauma

structural racism. *See* systemic racism and other socioeconomic inequities

substance use: child removal linked to, 165–71, 175–76; investigations of, 80–84, 89–90, 102, 118, 140–41, 152–53, 167; parents', 2, 6, 26, 28, 30, 42, 49–50, 72, 74–75, 89–90, 107, 115–18, 144, 165–69, 173, 175–76, 186, 197; testing and evaluations, 43, 71, 81, 83, 100, 102, 116–18, 146, 167, 169, 173–74, 177, 186–87

suicide, 47, 52–53, 65, 86, 135

Supplemental Nutrition Assistance Program (SNAP), 19, 74, 114, 115, 120, 214

surveillance: depth and breadth of, 78, 87, 90, 105; of families by the state, 4, 16, 78–79, 86–96, 105, 134, 148; justifications of, 91–96, 105; mothers' resistance to, 142, 147–49; records of, 90, 134, 148–49; referrals as source of, 141–42, 160. *See also* information-gathering

Sweet, Paige, 175, 258n5

systemic racism and other socioeconomic inequities: in child welfare system, 176–77, 179, 182, 187, 192, 195–96, 198–200, 245n16; individuals blamed for shortcomings attributable to, 2, 69; investigations and suspicions resulting from, 48, 64–73, 130–31, 254n8, 255n33; in labor market, 27; resource access and distribution

determined by, 5–6, 27, 51, 65, 72–73, 75, 112–13, 118, 139, 207–8; society's failure to address, 7–9, 16, 22, 27–28, 110, 198–99, 207, 260n50

teachers. *See* education personnel; professionals

termination of parental rights, 12, 183–91, 193

therapy and therapeutic services. *See* mental health services/service providers

Thorne, William, 208

trauma: experienced by children, 4–5, 8, 28, 50, 51, 107–8, 146, 163, 165, 200; experienced by mothers, 22, 33, 87, 111, 163; of foster care, 163; from poverty, 28. *See also* stress

undocumented mothers, 149

U.S. Supreme Court, 5

Viterna, Jocelyn, 222

War on Poverty, 7

Watkins-Hayes, Celeste, 196

welfare: CPS reports by people seeking benefits from, 74, 120–21; historical provision of, 7, 8–9; inadequate support from, 7, 27, 41, 43, 139, 155, 195; policy goals of, 7, 9, 248n62; race and, 7–8, 139, 246n24, 247n28; surveillance in, 16

WIC. *See* Special Supplemental Nutrition Program for Women, Infants, and Children

A NOTE ON THE TYPE

This book has been composed in Arno, an Old-style serif typeface in the classic Venetian tradition, designed by Robert Slimbach at Adobe.